Dignity and Discipline

DIGNITY & DISCIPLINE

Reviving Full Ordination for Buddhist Nuns

Edited by
Thea Mohr and
Jampa Tsedroen

WISDOM PUBLICATIONS • BOSTON

Wisdom Publications
199 Elm Street
Somerville MA 02144 USA
www.wisdompubs.org

Library of Congress Cataloging-in-Publication Data

Dignity & discipline : reviving full ordination for Buddhist nuns / edited by Thea Mohr and Jampa Tsedroen.
p. cm.
Articles originally presented at the International Congress held July 18–20, 2007 in Hamburg, Germany.
Includes bibliographical references.
ISBN 0-86171-588-8 (pbk. : alk. paper)
1. Ordination of women—Buddhism—Congresses. 2. Buddhist women—Congresses. 3. Women in Buddhism—Congresses. I. Mohr, Thea. II. Jampa Tsedroen, Bhikṣuṇī. III. International Congress on Buddhist Women's Role in the Saṅgha Bhikṣuṇī Vinaya and Ordination Lineages. IV. Title: Dignity and discipline.
BQ6150.D54 2009
294.3'657082—dc22
2009027244

14 13 12 11 10
5 4 3 2 1

Cover design by Dede Cummings. Interior design by Gopa&Ted2.
Set in Diacritical Garamond Pro 11.25/14.9.

Wisdom Publications' books are printed on acid-free paper and meet the guidelines for permanence and durability of the Production Guidelines for Book Longevity of the Council on Library Resources.

Printed in the United States of America.

This book was produced with environmental mindfulness. We have elected to print this title on 30 percent PCW recycled paper. As a result, we have saved the following resources: 18 trees, 6 million BTUs of energy, 1,678 pounds of greenhouse gases, 8,084 gallons of water, and 491 pounds of solid waste. For more information, please visit our website, www.wisdompubs.org. This paper is also FSC certified. For more information, please visit www.fscus.org.

Contents

Preface — ix
THEA MOHR AND JAMPA TSEDROEN

Abbreviations — xiii

Female Ordination in Buddhism:
Looking into a Crystal Ball, Making a Future — 1
JANET GYATSO

The Vinaya Between History and Modernity:
Some General Reflections — 23
JENS-UWE HARTMANN

Sects and Sectarianism
The Origin of the Three Existing Vinaya Lineages:
Theravāda, Dharmaguptaka, and Mūlasarvāstivāda — 29
BHIKKHU SUJATO

Some Remarks on the Status of Nuns and Laywomen
in Early Buddhism — 39
GISELA KREY

Women's Renunciation in Early Buddhism:
The Four Assemblies and the Foundation of the Order of Nuns 65
ANĀLAYO

The Revival of Bhikkhunī Ordination
in the Theravāda Tradition 99
BHIKKHU BODHI

The Eight Garudhammas 143
UTE HÜSKEN

A Need to Take a Fresh Look at Popular
Interpretations of the Tripiṭaka:
Theravāda Context in Thailand 149
DHAMMANANDA BHIKKHUNĪ

A Lamp of Vinaya Statements:
A Concise Summary of Bhikṣuṇī Ordination 161
TASHI TSERING

A Tibetan Precedent for Multi-Tradition Ordination 183
THUBTEN CHODRON

A "Flawless" Ordination:
Some Narratives of Nuns' Ordinations in the
Mūlasarvāstivāda Vinaya 195
DAMCHÖ DIANA FINNEGAN

Buddhist Women's Role in the Saṅgha 207
LOBSANG DECHEN

Preserving Endangered Ordination Traditions in the Sakya School 211
DAVID JACKSON

Presuppositions for a Valid Ordination with Respect
to the Restoration of the Bhikṣuṇī Ordination in the
Mūlasarvāstivāda Tradition 217
PETRA KIEFFER-PÜLZ

Creating Nuns Out of Thin Air:
Problems and Possible Solutions concerning the Ordination of Nuns according to the Tibetan Monastic Code 227
SHAYNE CLARKE

Bhikṣuṇī Ordination:
Lineages and Procedures as Instruments of Power 239
JAN-ULRICH SOBISCH

Human Rights and the Status of Women in Buddhism 253
HIS HOLINESS THE FOURTEENTH DALAI LAMA

Gender Equity and Human Rights 281
KARMA LEKSHE TSOMO

Appendix 291

Glossary 305

Bibliography 309

About the Contributors 325

Preface

As far back as 1987, His Holiness the Dalai Lama had asked for an examination of the current Tibetan Buddhist practice of not ordaining nuns, or bhikṣuṇīs, a practice at odds with the times of the historical Buddha over twenty-four hundred years ago. An extensive study was initiated by the Tibetan Department of Religion and Culture (India), and during a visit to Zurich on June 28, 2005, the Dalai Lama stated:

> There has been much discussion surrounding bhikṣuṇī ordination, but no decision has been reached. We need to bring this to a conclusion. However, we Tibetans can't decide this alone; it needs to be decided in collaboration with Buddhists worldwide. Were the Buddha to come to the twenty-first century and see the situation in the world now, he might well modify the rules.

The International Congress on Women's Role in the Sangha held in Hamburg in 2007 that gave rise to the contributions in this book was intended to fulfill His Holiness's request for the revival of the precepts of fully ordained nuns (Skt., *bhikṣuṇī*; Pāli, *bhikkhunī*) in Tibetan Buddhism. The scholars presented their papers to an audience of about 150 experts along with representatives of various Buddhist organizations, a broad range of academics, and members of the interested public. The conference concluded with a statement by the Dalai Lama, where he laid out the necessary steps for reestablishing full ordination of bhikṣuṇīs within the Tibetan tradition of Buddhism. At the same time, by including Buddhists of all traditions, the Hamburg conference aimed to create a worldwide consensus on the need for reestablishing bhikṣuṇī ordination in all Vinaya schools of Buddhism where it does not presently exist.

The assembled scholars included prominent Buddhist nuns and monks in the field of monastic discipline and history. The papers presented evidence relevant to the current debate on the status of ordained women, drawing on research both on classic Buddhist texts and on contemporary traditions in China, Korea, Taiwan, Tibet, Vietnam, and South Asia.

The specific topics addressed were:

- The status of women in Buddhism
- The controversy over full ordination for women in Buddhism
- The requirements and procedures for the full ordination of women and proposals for its restoration
- The implications of full ordination for women in Buddhist societies
- The potential for restructuring Buddhism in line with gender equity

Although full ordination is described in detail in the texts of all extant Buddhist traditions and the ordination is available for Buddhist women in China, Korea, Taiwan, and Vietnam, opportunities for full ordination are not available to women in the Tibetan and Theravāda traditions, which includes Buddhists in Mongolia, the Himalayan countries, and South and Southeast Asia.

One reason the issue of full ordination for women has become a major concern in the contemporary international Buddhist diaspora is that gender discrimination is in direct conflict with the ethic of social and spiritual equality maintained in Buddhist theory. In other words, there is nothing intrinsic to the Buddhist worldview that relies on the subjugation of women, and in fact the inequality between the sexes that exists in some Buddhist contexts is in marked tension with the Buddha's ultimate understanding of reality and of the universal potential for enlightenment shared by all beings. Thus, reinstating full ordination for women will bring the Buddhist tradition more in line with its core ideals.

At this congress scholars approached the topic from textual, philosophical, sociological, and feminist perspectives. One objective was to discuss the opportunities Buddhism theoretically offers women for spiritual and social advancement and how this theoretical equality contrasts with women's actual opportunities for education, training, and religious and social advancement in Asian societies mainly influenced by Buddhism. Another objective was to assess the current prospects for reintroducing full ordination for women in those Buddhist traditions where it is not currently available.

The congress focused on analysis of the legal status of ordained Buddhist women and the formulas or rites used to ordain them. It looked at the historical background on the issue, reviewed the key issues surrounding restoration of the lineage, and analyzed and refuted the objections by opponents of bhikṣuṇī ordination. The discussions also sought to highlight the role a vibrant bhikṣuṇī saṅgha can play in preserving Buddhist cultural institutions. The ultimate goal was to elicit a clear statement from H. H. the Dalai Lama on how the bhikṣuṇī lineage can be reestablished in the Tibetan tradition.

Preparations for the conference began in December 2005 when the Foundation for Buddhist Studies in Hamburg agreed to support the efforts to organize the conference. We are deeply thankful for the unceasing, wholehearted support that Gabriele Küstermann and the other board members—Christiane Meyer-Rogge-Turner, Professor Emeritus Lambert Schmithausen, and Dr. Wolfgang Trescher—gave to us. Without their advice and recommendations—and foremost their confidence in the importance of such a conference—it would not have been possible. We also thank all the sponsors, especially the Tara Foundation, for their generous gifts.

With the munificent support of the University of Hamburg, we were able to achieve an atmosphere of serene scholarliness. All the members of the Committee of Western Bhikṣuṇīs helped us tremendously to contact the esteemed scholars worldwide, among them Ven. Prof. Karma Lekshe Tsomo, who has for decades organized the Sakyadhita conferences of Buddhist women in traditionally Buddhist countries. We are deeply indebted to all the scholars who contributed so valuably to the success of the conference with their presentations. Unfortunately not all the papers could be included in this book, but our deep appreciation goes out to all of the presenters. We are grateful for the interest of Wisdom Publications before the start of the actual conference, and for the cooperation of MacDuff Stewart, for whose highly efficient work we are deeply thankful. Our special thanks go to David Kittelstrom, who actually first offered to publish the proceedings with Wisdom Publications and—after some detours—helped to bring the project to a successful end. Finally we want to thank the Department of Religion and Culture (DRC) of the Tibetan Government in Exile and the chair of the Tibetan Nuns Project, Kazur Rinchen Khandro. In particular we thank Ven. Prof. Samdhong Rinpoche, Prime Minister of the Tibetan Government in Exile and chair of the DRC Bhikkunī Ordination Committee, who always inspired us during the period of preparation as well as during the conference. Above all, His Holiness the Dalai Lama's desire for real progress in fully ordaining women practicing Tibetan Buddhism was a constant source of inspiration for all involved. Without it, the remarkable contribution the Hamburg conference made toward this goal would not have come about, and so we are deeply grateful.

It is our sincere wish that the historic publication of these articles will help to maintain and enhance the complete practice of Buddhadharma in modern times. We truly hope that this work will grant Buddhist women all over the world support and inspiration for the achievement of their spiritual goals, happiness, and liberation from suffering.

Thea Mohr
Jampa Tsedroen

Abbreviations

AN	*Aṅguttara-nikāya*
Ap	*Apadāna*
Bv	*Buddhavaṃsa*
CPS	*Catuṣpariṣatsūtra* (Waldschmidt 1957)
Cv	*Cullavagga*
D	Dergé edition of the Tibetan canon. See Situ Chos kyi 'byung gnas 1976–79.
DĀ	*Dīrgha-āgama*
Dhp-a	*Dhammapada-aṭṭhakathā*
Dīp	*Dīpavaṃsa*
Divy	*Divyāvadāna*
DN	*Dīgha-nikāya*
EĀ	*Ekottarika-āgama*
IATS	International Association of Tibetan Studies
Jā	*Jātaka*
Kangyur	*Bka' 'gyur* Tibetan Tripiṭaka, canonical scriptures
MĀ	*Madhyama-āgama*
Mā-L	Mahāsāṅghika-Lokottaravādin
MN	*Majjhima-nikāya*
Mp	*Manorathapūraṇī*
MSV	Mūlasarvāstivāda Vinaya
Mv	*Mahāvagga*

NP	*Naiḥsargikapātayantikadharma*
Pāc	*Pācittiyadharma*
Pāy	*Pāyattikadharma*
PED	*The Pali Text Society's Pali-English Dictionary.* Chipstead, 1921–25.
Ps	*Papañcasūdanī*
PTS	Pali Text Society
Q	Peking edition of the Tibetan canon. See Suzuki 1961
S	*The Tog [Stog] Palace Manuscript of the Tibetan Kanjur.* 109 vols. Leh, Ladakh: C. Namgyal Tarusergar, 1975–80.
SĀ	*Saṃyukta-āgama* (T 99)
SĀ[2]	(other) *Saṃyukta-āgama* (T 100)
SBV	*Saṅghabhedavastu* (Gnoli 1977)
SHT	*Sanskrithandschriften aus den Turfanfunden* (series)
Skt.	Sanskrit
SN	*Saṃyutta-nikāya*
Sp	*Samantapāsādikā*
Spk	*Sāratthappakāsinī*
SV	*Saṅghāvaśeṣadharma*
SWTF	*Sanskrit-Wörterbuch der buddhistischen Texte aus den Turfan-Funden* (Waldschmidt and Bechert, 1973–present)
T	Taishō edition (CBETA)
Tengyur	Tibetan *bstan 'gyur*, or canonical treatises
Th	*Theragāthā*
Th-a	*Theragāthā-aṭṭhakathā*
Thī	*Therīgāthā*
Thī-a	*Therīgāthā-aṭṭhakathā*
Tib.	Tibetan
Ud	*Udāna*
Vin	Vinaya
Vin-a	*Vinaya-aṭṭhakathā*
VRI	Vipassana Research Institute

Dignity and Discipline

Female Ordination in Buddhism:

LOOKING INTO A CRYSTAL BALL, MAKING A FUTURE

Janet Gyatso[1]

MANY OF THE ISSUES surrounding bhikṣuṇī ordination in Tibetan Buddhism are shared by other parts of the Buddhist world. And while some regard the bhikṣuṇī ordination movement to be largely driven by Western Buddhist converts, efforts to revive the female order have actually been initiated by various progressive Asian monks and nuns over the last century. New bhikṣuṇī groups at various sites—Korea, Sri Lanka, and Thailand would be three examples—are now at varying stages of maturity.[2] In dealing with the bhikṣuṇī issue, all of these groups are participating in an ineluctable movement across Buddhism, one that is ultimately to be connected to larger shifts in our contemporary global civil society. I am convinced that to look at the Tibetan case in such translocal terms will be pertinent even to quite local and particular features of the problem there. Indeed, it was a striking moment at the Hamburg conference when Bhikṣuṇī Dr. Myongsong Sunim of Korea baldly challenged the representatives of

1. I would like to acknowledge the influence of my conversations with Charles Hallisey upon this article, particularly in its orientation toward "making a future." Thanks to him too, as well as to Steven Collins, for comments on an earlier draft.

2. For information on the astounding success of the Korean bhikṣuṇī movement, see papers by Myongsong Sunim, Inyoung Chung, and Hyangsoon Yi presented at the Hamburg conference. For stories of early bhikkhunī ordination attempts in twentieth-century Thai Buddhism, see Kabilsingh 1991, especially chapter 5. Regarding nuns in Sri Lanka, see de Silva 2004 and Weeraratne 1998, available at http://www.buddhanet.net/nunorder.html. Regarding the ordination issue in Burma see Kawanami 2007.

both Tibetan and Theravāda Buddhism to catch up with the rest of the Buddhist world in its recognition and support of bhikṣuṇīs. I think she is right on target to look at the Tibetan question in precisely that global perspective.

To look at the bhikṣuṇī question from a global perspective shifts the focus in the conversation on bhikṣuṇī ordination to the needs and benefit of human society as a whole, and the role of Buddhism therein. While some of what follows will also touch upon the subjective needs and desires of individual women and other actors in the Buddhist world—and indeed such questions remain of utmost concern—I would like to attempt in this introduction to construe the largest horizon of the female ordination question in terms of our global society. I submit that to do so will allow us to see dimensions of the question that a personal, subjective, or even exclusively "Buddhist" perspective alone will not yield.

What I would like to explore in the context of the bhikṣuṇī question is the potential of Buddhist leadership and influence beyond Buddhism's own boundaries. How might a question within Buddhist communities in fact bear upon something outside of them? In asking such a question we are considering the possibility that developments in Buddhism have the potential to advance discussions about problems that are not exclusively Buddhist but concern the rest of the world as well. If that prospect is one that Buddhists would welcome, then what must come along with it is the recognition that not only does Buddhism have something to teach the world, it must also be the case that Buddhism has things to learn from the world around it. In trying to envision the best future for Buddhism, we are beginning to imagine a way that Buddhists rely not only on their past traditions but are also open to new insights and the contributions of other thinkers and leaders in the world as well.

To be sure, in referring to an "ineluctable movement" in Buddhism I am going out on a limb in predicting what will happen. My assumption is that, as has come to pass in other parts of the Buddhist world where initially there was strong resistance, we will see some Tibetan Buddhists conferring bhikṣuṇī ordination before long, although it is far from clear how many Tibetan women will seek it, and how many obstacles the innovation will face in the process. As for the claim that Buddhists who are working to foster bhikṣuṇī ordination are participating in a feministic world movement, that has its own complexities, to be touched upon in following chapters. And while the effort to determine the precedents and legality of the new ordination tradition for Tibetans is an extremely important part of recognizing what the growing bhikṣuṇī saṅgha holds for all of us, I am not going to address those questions myself, except briefly and in principle.

What I would like to do instead is to reflect on some of the larger moral and political issues related to the prospect of having a fully accessible bhikṣuṇī ordination in place throughout the Buddhist world and a fully developed bhikṣuṇī saṅgha in operation. While this might betray a certain impatience, and perhaps seem like a cavalier dismissal of the obstacles that still stand in the way, I think it is critical for us also to start to create the future toward which we are moving. I think it is important to envision how the Buddhist world—and indeed the world as a whole—will be different when we have a visible and powerful presence of esteemed women taking on the ancient Buddhist role of the fully ordained monastic, a role that stands for exceptional dignity, discipline, and wisdom.

My comments that follow are organized around three main themes: the challenges in forging a new bhikṣuṇī ordination; the question of status and prestige; and finally the promise that female monastics hold for the future of Buddhist moral leadership in our world. While in many respects the upshot of such a welcome development will be to create a new, genderless egalitarianism in Buddhism—one that has rarely been seen in Buddhist history, I might add—there is also a vision of this future that appreciates the gender-specific gains of having a fully ordained female saṅgha in place. There are some dimensions of this prospect that might trade on sex/gender difference, not for all times and places, to be sure, but specifically in the twenty-first-century situation in which we all, Buddhists and non-Buddhists alike, find ourselves. I will speculate briefly on what some of those female-specific virtues of the bhikṣuṇī saṅgha might be at the close of the essay.

Building a New Ordination Platform

There can be no question that the earliest Buddhist communities supported the full ordination of women, even were we to take as historical—which most modern scholars do not—the Buddha's role in the unflattering story of the first admission of women to the monastic order, with its attendant "eight heavy rules," a set of precepts that directly address monk-nun relationships and interaction.[3] That story aside for the moment, we see full provisions for the ordination of bhikṣuṇīs in all of the versions of the Vinaya as well as a flourishing of the bhikṣuṇī order in many parts of the world. While the reasons for the bhikṣuṇī order's eventual decline and ultimate disappearance in many places are complex and historically specific,[4] it is clear that the disappearance did not occur because of a lack of legal procedures to ordain women. Rather, we must look to cultural, social, economic, and political reasons for this unfortunate outcome.

Many scholars today believe that we can characterize the problem generally as a confluence of competition between the male and female orders for economic support and prestige, with androcentric cultural biases operating alongside patriarchal social structures. Epigraphical and literary evidence, as studied by Gregory Schopen, Nancy Barnes, and many others, suggests that such competition was already in full swing by the early centuries B.C.E.[5] We can also easily trace a corresponding prevalence of androcentrism and misogyny in practices and literature in Pāli, Sanskrit, Chinese, and Tibetan sources, as has been demonstrated by scholars like Diana Paul and Liz Wilson.[6]

If it is true that social and cultural issues determined the poor fortunes of the bhikṣuṇī order in Buddhist history, then it is likely that any revitalization of the bhikṣuṇī order today will also hinge on social and cultural forces. While a convincing legal argument based on historical precedents and analysis of the Vinayas will be key in this process, such arguments will ultimately be of service in building consensus and acceptance in Buddhist communities. That consensus trumps legality is already becoming clear in the case of Sri Lanka. There, against all odds, full ordination of bhikkhunīs has already begun to take place. There, despite the hesitancy of many con-

3. A recent and important scholarly rejection of the historicity of the Buddha's role in this story is von Hinüber 2007. See also Hirakawa 1998, cited by Kawanami 2007.

4. Evidence of the activities of bhikṣuṇīs in South Asia may be found in Gunawardhana 1979 and 1990, Schopen 1997 and 2004: 329ff., and Skilling 1994 and 1993/94.

5. See especially Schopen 1997 and 2004: 329ff. See also Barnes 2000.

6. Paul 1985 and Wilson 1996.

servative male saṅgha leaders, the real fate of the new female order is being decided by the lay community.

I was personally struck in this regard by the assertions of several Sri Lankan bhikkhunīs whom I met in Maharagama, outside of Colombo, in January 2005. These bhikkhunīs told me that Sri Lankan lay donors are increasingly skeptical of the corruption and worldliness of the male saṅgha, a situation that has allowed alternate kinds of Buddhist clerics to begin to flourish. One upshot is that the laity are coming to regard the new bhikkhunīs as especially devout, earnest, and pure adherents of Vinaya law. While we lack the ethnographic research to confirm this claim, it is interesting even as a sign of how some newly ordained women view what is at stake. One indication they report of changing sentiments is that the laity are increasingly asking female monastics rather than males to perform meritorious ceremonies (Sinhala *pinkama*; Skt. *puṇyakarma*) such as rites for the dead; they are also starting to trust nuns to better adhere to the ideals of a "field of merit" (Sinhala *puṇyakṣetraya*; Skt. *puṇyakṣetra*).

This is a canny observation on the part of these bhikkhunīs, and may well turn out to be a self-fulfilling prophecy. We should never lose sight of the fact that the flourishing of Buddhist monastic communities depends on the support of the laity; that dependence is built into the foundation of Buddhist monasticism from the start. Indeed the very Vinaya story to which I already referred, and which narrates the subordination of the female order to the male order, appears to be in large part about assuaging the prejudices of the lay community. It was primarily as a sop to the expectations of the laypeople that the Buddha is said to have placed nuns under the authority of monks, and to have worked to prevent the layfolks' wrong impression that men and women might not be sufficiently separated to ensure their purity.[7] On similar grounds, the question of whether the new bhikṣuṇī orders thrive will be determined by a process involving both consensus and political will. It will depend on whether a critical mass of the Buddhist community decides to support them, whether bhikṣuṇīs are deemed to be valuable to Buddhism.

7. See the account in *Cullavagga* X. Rules are made repeatedly after laypeople observe the behavior of monks and nuns together: "People looked down upon, criticized, and spread it about" (e.g., *Cullavagga* X.6.1, translated in Horner 1952: V.360). The Buddha also compares the Buddhist order to that of other sects and is unwilling to grant more leniency in male-female relations than is allowed by other sects (e.g., *Cullavagga* X.2.3).

Modification based on changing historical and cultural circumstances has always been possible in Buddhist monasticism. There can be no question that Vinaya rules and procedures have evolved over time, and new additions and subtractions were made on the basis of social pressures as well as inner debates and changing needs in the various saṅghas as they spread across Asia. Were that not the case, then all of the versions of Vinaya rules and vows would be identical, and they are not.[8] What's more, there is ample evidence that the Vinaya rules have been bent in any number of ways and in any number of circumstances historically. There is ample evidence of ad hoc monastic rulebooks cropping up throughout the Buddhist world and eclipsing the Vinaya in terms of what people actually use and follow.[9] More specifically, and relevant to the effort to collect precedents in Tibetan Buddhism, we have evidence of a handful of cases of bhikṣuṇī ordinations in Tibet from the eleventh to at least the sixteenth centuries—including, among others, the first Rdo rje Phag mo, Chos kyi sgron ma, studied by Hildegard Diemberger; the early yoginī 'Ong jo; and the perhaps sixteenth-century Lca mo Dkon mchog mtsho mo, both studied by Dan Martin.[10] And while there are few details of how the Tibetans who conferred those bhikṣuṇī ordination rituals modified the procedure, we know that they must have done so. There is no reason to think there were enough bhikṣuṇīs present at the time to have participated in these ceremonies, as is required under the "dual-ordination" system of bhikṣuṇī ordination.[11] But it is clear that such a modification in

8. For information on variations in Vinaya rules, see Pachow 1955 and Rosen 1959. Regarding variations in bhikṣuṇī rules, see Kabilsingh 1984 and Tsomo 1996. For a detailed study of debates and changes in the rules for bhikkhunīs in the Pāli Vinaya, see Juo-Hsüeh 2000.

9. For some examples of such alternate rules see Cabezón 1997, Foulk 1995, and Yifa 2002.

10. Diemberger 2007: 183 and Martin 2005: 67 and 72–73. Diemberger also refers to statements in the biography of Shākya Mchog ldan (1432–1507) that he had given full ordination to his mother and a female disciple (Diemberger 2007: 133). See also note 12 below.

11. The stipulation the women require a "dual ordination", i.e., the officiation by both male and female fully ordained monastics during the ritual, is the second of the eight heavy rules: cf. Roth 1970: xxxii. For a fragment of the ordination ritual for the Mūlasarvāstivādin Vinaya, see Bendall 1903. A longer fragment of the bhikṣuṇī ordination ceremony probably from the Sarvāstivāda Vinaya is in Ridding and La Vallée Poussin 1920: 123–43; reference to the "dual ordination system" is to be found on pp. 133–35. A very useful survey of the Mūlasarvāstivāda Vinaya in its Tibetan version is Panglung 1981. Another useful source that gathers together the relevant texts in Tibetan from the Mūlasarvāstivāda Vinaya as well as many commentaries by Tibetan scholars is Thub bstan byang chub 2000. The number of monks and nuns required for

order to ordain bhikṣuṇīs was the subject of considerable debate in Tibet for centuries.[12]

But we need hardly turn to the murky case of female ordination in Tibet for examples where Vinaya rules have been bent in practice. Bhikṣus in Tibet regularly handle silver, eat dinner, spend time alone with women in rooms, and sow seeds of dissent in the saṅgha. They regularly do those things without censure or punishment.

Establishing a Tibetan Bhikṣuṇī Order

Beyond the question of legality and precedent, then, the more germane question has to do with desire, consensus, and will: whether monastics in the position to grant ordination are willing to take the steps to establish a new bhikṣuṇī order, whether sufficient numbers of the already existing saṅgha will accept those bhikṣuṇīs, and whether there are lay communities who will support them. If sufficient numbers from these various sectors in Tibetan Buddhist communities are amenable and willing to take the steps to make it happen, a new bhikṣuṇī order in Tibetan Buddhism will be created.

There is of course no clear answer as to whether such consensus exists, nor what exactly a "sufficient number" would be. To begin with, there is no one single group, nor one single sentiment, in the Tibetan Buddhist community today. Rather there is a multiplicity of views and agendas regarding female ordination, which might be mapped onto class, educational, sectarian, regional, age, and even gender differences, as well as mere difference of opinion. This multiplicity is complicated further by the heterogeneity of the very category of "Tibetan Buddhism" today, since those who participate in it include not only a variety of Himalayan and South Asian people who are not Tibetan, either culturally or linguistically, but also a range of converts from the West, East Asia, and other parts of the world, with various levels of membership in and interaction with Tibetan Buddhist

---

the dual ordination is ten monks and twelve nuns (Thub bstan byang chub 2000: 37). Kong sprul Blo gros mtha yas, in his *Shes bya kun khyab mdzod*, states that in a remote region six nuns will do: Kongtrul Lodro Taye 1998: 97.

12. A summary of these debates is to be found in Tsering and Russell 2002: 158ff. and 169–70. For details, see Thub bstan byang chub 2000.

communities. But even were we to try to catalog the different ideas regarding the issue in Tibetan Buddhism, we would be mistaken to take any of those positions as fixed or definite. As with any highly contested question, opinions and desires change as people understand a situation more fully, become more educated, and are influenced by leaders and teachers. It is too soon, for example, to assess the impact of the current Dalai Lama, who has been making considerable efforts to convince the Tibetan saṅgha of the desirability of initiating a new bhikṣuṇī ordination.

There are also shifting attitudes in many corners of the Tibetan Buddhist world toward feminist concerns, with far more institutions for the education of nuns today, both inside Tibet—including both the Tibetan Autonomous Region and other regions of China—and in exile, than could ever have been imagined even thirty years ago. An intense debate is in progress, and it is premature for anyone, even the actors themselves, to say with finality "what Tibetan Buddhists want." What we can do best is to consider the issues in their specificity, with cognizance of the variety of forces that bear upon them and their shifting directions. All of us—that is, anyone who is interested in the topic at all, from the Dalai Lama, the Tibetan laity, and members of the Tibetan saṅgha, to modern academics, Western Buddhists, other Asian Buddhists, and a broad swath of educated readers across the globe who are not Buddhist at all—are in fact implicated in the process and have impact upon it. Not all of us have the same amount of impact, to be sure, but the fact that no one can describe a "state of affairs" or "what Tibetans want," but rather can merely witness and to some degree participate in a process of negotiation and evolution, reminds us that we all have a modicum of responsibility in what we say.[13] That means we need to be as educated as possible about the various factors at play. What is most important in that is for all of us to summon our most ethical selves, to summon a vision of a future that is for the most good of all, a vision that takes into account as best as possible the various constituencies and their needs.

13. Abeysekara 2002 provides a good theoretical model for the complex and shifting debates and contestations through which communities define identities and differences, a process he calls "contingent conjunctures"; see, e.g., pp. 3–4 and 236–38.

Full Ordination and Feminism

One of the key issues about which many of the women involved are trying to decide "what they want" concerns the feminist question of whether full ordination is desirable after all. We do know massively from the historical record that one principal way that Buddhist women responded to the decline in the female monastic order was by forming alternate orders—the *dasasilmātās* of Sri Lanka, the Thai *maechis*, the Tibetan *anis*, and so on, some more or less modeled on lesser levels of ordination in the Vinaya such as the *upāsikā*, others free of any structure of committed vows at all.

What has been documented by ethnographers repeatedly is that the diminished, vow-less status actually has advantages. In the case of the socially minded maechis of Thailand, their reduced number of restrictions allows them to tend to prostitutes and other people in compromised environments where fully ordained women would not be allowed to enter. In other cases, maechis are taking advantage of new opportunities to gain higher education and academic degrees. In Tibetan communities too, anis now have advanced educational opportunities apart from the question of their eligibility for bhikṣuṇī ordination. Such advantages of operating outside the strictures of monastic jurisprudence have moved many female ascetics to resist the movement toward full ordination. If this is true, then the question becomes one of why other women desire full ordination.[14]

It would certainly be correct to respond that the bhikṣuṇī movement is aligned with modern feminism, and that it is motivated at least in part by a desire to achieve equality and to break down gender stereotypes found in Buddhism, such as that women are softer and less disciplined than men.[15] And while much of the current impetus to create a bhikṣuṇī order in Tibetan Buddhism is coming from Western converts to Tibetan Buddhism, such a feministic impulse is shared by a variety of Tibetan monks, nuns, and male and female lay leaders, just as it is opposed by many others. In other parts

14. See Brown 2001, Bartholomeuz 1994, Barnes 1996, and Sasson 2007. Steven Collins and Justin McDaniel, in "Buddhist Nuns (*Maechi*) and the Teaching of Pāli in Thailand," unpublished manuscript, also make a related point, reporting interviews in which a prominent Pāli scholar maechi—Maechi Bunchuai—says she neither wants nor needs bhikkhunī ordination.

15. See Gyatso 2003.

of Buddhist Asia, too, many of the first efforts toward revitalizing bhikṣuṇī orders began in the early to mid-twentieth century among small groups of women and the male saṅgha members who supported them, facing significant opposition by others in the same communities.[16] In analyzing those various positions, it is not always clear exactly what is "feminist" about them, and even more so, what is "Western" in their inspiration and what is not. Moreover, it is possible that the women who have forged alternate renunciate communities, and are resisting the bhikṣuṇī option, are themselves informed by feminist sensibilities, if of a different variety.

One example of the variety of opinions even within the Tibetan Buddhist community, both about bhikṣuṇī ordination and its connection with an imputed "feminism," was evident at a charged event that occurred during the conference at Hamburg.[17] At an open evening discussion session attended by most of the participants in the conference, several young Tibetan and Himalayan anis under the umbrella of the Tibetan Nuns' Project in Dharamsala read statements that they did not feel ready for bhikṣuṇī ordination at this time. The reasons for that sentiment were not fully explained, but what a few of the anis did say is that they do not wish to be associated with feminist agendas. Several added further that the questions at stake in the ordination debates should not be about issues of gender or sexual equality.

The reaction to these statements, especially on the part of the many Western nuns in the audience, was one of shock and dismay. At the same time, other Tibetan and Himalayan anis from the same group read statements that they very well might want to take bhikṣuṇī ordination if that becomes a possibility for them, while simultaneously disavowing this desire as feminist in principle. And so let us note first that even the group of anis present at the conference at Hamburg were far from unanimous on the issue of bhikṣuṇī ordination. But before turning to the prospects for those Buddhist women who do want ordination, it is necessary to dwell a moment longer on this question of the connection between the bhikṣuṇī movement, feminism, and its purported Western or secular nature.[18]

16. See note 2 above.

17. It took place on the evening of Thursday, July 19, 2007.

18. Kawanami assumes without examination that feminism is a secular movement. I will save

While not wanting ordination is fully understandable, as already discussed, we need to exercise caution before identifying this as a sign of an incommensurability between Western and Asian values. Another very different kind of factor that might be over-determining the anis' reticence toward what they think of as feminism would be their expectation that forces in Tibetan society—particularly the very male monastics under whose direction these Tibetan-tradition anis from Dharamsala and other parts of South Asia now live—are themselves ill-disposed toward (and indeed perhaps threatened by) the specter of feminism. Some women might reasonably want to avoid arousing the ire of their male mentors as a strategic move to remain in their favor, even while some might also try to argue for bhikṣuṇī ordination on other grounds.[19]

It is essential to note, too, that the very occasion on which these anis were given the microphone to speak—an occasion that they very much desired, as evidenced by their deep disappointment when it appeared they might not get the chance to read the statements they had prepared—was made possible precisely because of the feminist commitments of the organizers of that evening session, and indeed the entire conference.[20] These commitments include a conviction that it is important to encourage women to speak for themselves, in their own words. Even the anis who said they did not want to align themselves with feminism were benefiting from its gains during that session.

The Dalai Lama gave a powerful speech on the final day of the Hamburg conference in which he argued at length about the value of feminism in our world and for Buddhism. He admitted that women have not had equal opportunities in Buddhism. He also maintained that there are certain social virtues that women tend to develop better than men because of

---

my own thoughts on the question of secularism and feminism for a future paper. For a study of the diversity of positions of women regarding the issue of ordination in Buddhism, see Cheng 2007.

19. Cf. a similar speculation on the reasons why many Burmese nuns are disavowing feminist bids for ordination: Kawanami 2007: 238–39.

20. I was one of the organizers of the evening session who, along with Michael Zimmermann, Petra Kieffer-Pülz, and others, made special provisions to ask the anis to speak, since they were otherwise not on the program of the conference. We did so in response to a complaint that they expressed to me en masse that same afternoon.

women's greater ties to childbearing; these virtues, he said, can form a particularly strong basis for developing the high Buddhist value of compassion. He called on women to develop their potential as Buddhist leaders in the twenty-first century, when more than ever people of the world need to learn how to live together.

The Dalai Lama was acting as a world leader, a moral authority to whom people listen, on that day. Equally so, he was also acting as a leader of his own Tibetan Buddhist community. It would be mistaken and simplistic to contend that his speech was entirely motivated by his desire to please his Western supporters. He faces considerable opposition to his progressive vision about the future of bhikṣuṇī ordination from conservative leaders in his own order. He was doing exactly what he needed to do that day, to begin to educate his followers on the value of the aspirations of feminism. Or perhaps more precisely, what the Dalai Lama was trying to do was to define a kind of feminism in his own terms.

It is too soon to know how effective he will be in changing the minds of his most conservative saṅgha leaders, helping them to see both the legitimacy of forging a new bhikṣuṇī order and its value for the male saṅgha as well. But it is far too Orientalist and nearsighted to continue to insist that feminism is merely a Western concern in which traditional women around the world do not also have a stake. Exactly how the goals and means of feminism are construed, of course, remains very much an open question. In fact, we have every reason to expect to learn a new and inspirational variety of feminism from Tibetan women, be they anis, fully ordained bhikṣuṇīs, or simply lay female leaders.

It is also too soon to assess how much anis and other women in the Tibetan Buddhist community will be encouraged by the Dalai Lama's support, and will take the opportunity that he is offering to consider more closely the value of feminist perspectives and insights. It is exactly the intervention of influential leaders and opinion-makers such as himself and the other powerful people in his entourage on this occasion, such as Samdhong Rinpoche and Rinchen Khandro, that will help create the necessary will to foster a new bhikṣuṇī order. The same leadership also needs to educate the Tibetan Buddhist community about the past: how Vinaya ritual has indeed been altered under certain conditions, how in fact women have been ordained in Tibet under exceptional conditions. It is exactly such leadership and education that can forge the cultural conditions for Tibetans to begin to recognize a new bhikṣuṇī order, and make room for them in the traditionally revered place that fully ordained clerics occupy in their world.

In any event there is much more to the bhikṣuṇī movement than feminism, regardless of our definition of the term. There is also an appreciation on the part of modern Buddhist women—indeed, including some of the Tibetan and Himalayan anis who spoke at Hamburg—for the power of the traditional life, as well as for the training and position of fully ordained, fully celibate Buddhist monastic figures. Some women simply want to partake of those dynamics themselves. While that desire need not be feminist in nature at all but rather located in the age-old dynamics of the role of Buddhist monasticism, there are steps that need to be taken in order to make its realization possible.

Status and Prestige

In addition to fostering the communal will to craft and sanction an ordination ritual for a new lineage of bhikṣuṇīs in Tibetan Buddhism, there is another critical task if Buddhist bhikṣuṇīs are to flourish. It is crucial to develop an intentional stance on the famous eight heavy rules, the provisions that institute patriarchy in Buddhist monasticism and upon which the Buddha supposedly insisted before granting women permission to take ordination. An explicit position on the status of these eight provisions today needs to be articulated publicly. Leaders of the Buddhist saṅgha—male and female alike—need to address and acknowledge them clearly, and specify how they are to be handled in the twenty-first century. The contingencies of our current world context require the formation of such an intentional position.

Some in the current Buddhist saṅgha, in Asia as well as the West, would like to disavow the eight heavy rules altogether. Recall, they require the unconditional deference by all nuns to all monks, regardless of merit or seniority; they call for the supervision of nuns' living arrangements and ritual procedures by monks; and they prohibit nuns from reviling or admonishing monks, while explicitly permitting monks to admonish nuns.[21] The eight heavy rules provision is a key part in the defining story of women's original acceptance into the Buddhist monastic order.

While this enshrinement of patriarchy in the rules of bhikṣuṇīs is unfortunate and damaging, it poses a recalcitrant problem. We cannot easily write it out of the Vinaya. Not only is the story included in all versions of the Vinaya, but all of the eight provisions save one have been incorporated into the *prātimokṣa* governing the nuns' rules of behavior and punishments for their infractions.[22] They are intricately woven into monastic ritual and tradition; simply to wipe them out would entail so many changes that it might be difficult to claim that the new female order was indeed the same as the bhikṣuṇī tradition known from historical Buddhism. A similar question has long been debated in other religions, and especially in Christianity: is there a way to accommodate and reinterpret elements of one's tradition that are patriarchal and/or androcentric, if not misogynist, or is it necessary to change the tradition radically, or even abandon it entirely?[23] This complex debate is likely to develop among Buddhists too, unfolding gradually with different ramifications in different contexts. But it would be unfortunate to allow it to derail the quest by Buddhist women to reestablish the order in its traditional form. I would suggest that it be treated with restraint for now.

That is not to say that the eight heavy rules can be left in place without comment. They are a liability, not only to the success of the bhikṣuṇī movement but also to Buddhism as a whole. They damage the reputation of Buddhism as a religion of egalitarianism and equanimity. The eight heavy rules imply that in Buddhism, renunciant women are lower in status than men and also not deemed capable of managing their own affairs. Both fly in the face of the broad-based call for sex and gender equality that has been percolating throughout the world for the last century at least.

The eight heavy rules need to be addressed both because of their detrimental impact on the aura of the new bhikṣuṇīs and for the harm they do

21. See note 22 below.

22. Hüsken 2000. Compare Roth 1970: xxix–xxxii.

23. One classic example of the debate from the seventies and eighties may be found in Ruether 1979 and a response in Christ 1987: 105–16. See also Ruether 1985, and for some of these issues in Judaism see Plaskow 2005.

to the reputation of Buddhism among civilized nations everywhere. To do this would not mean that the Buddhist leadership is acquiescing to popular trends and public opinion. Rather, it is essential to realize that image, respect, and prestige underlie the very nature of Buddhist monasticism from the start. The Buddhist saṅgha was designed precisely as an exemplar of the optimum religious lifestyle. Its survival depends on the generosity of the lay, whose support fluctuates in exact proportion to their conviction that the monastic community is maintaining its purity and the highest standards of behavior and wisdom. Indeed, the eight heavy rules themselves are cast in the story as necessary precisely in order to assuage the concerns of the Buddhist lay community.[24]

The same is true now, except that lay expectations have shifted. There are different sets of concerns in the global lay community. We need to have a public pronouncement stating that in the Buddhist saṅgha of the twenty-first century, despite the technical inclusion of the eight heavy rules in the Vinaya texts, bhikṣus and bhikṣuṇīs will be considered to have equal status and prestige, and be subject to the same rules of seniority; there shall be in practice no difference based on sex or gender alone. Buddhist leaders need to affirm that the eight heavy rules had their time and place but their conditions no longer remain. They need to do this to retain the respect and support of the lay Buddhist world.

But just as much, to work for gender equality is simply on the side of what is right. There can be no question that Buddhist doctrine, throughout its history, agrees. The patriarchy and misogyny that we do find in Buddhist sources is to be attributed to historical and social circumstances rather than reasoned or ethical principle. There is never a principled argument for gender inequality in Buddhist literature.

The Buddhist saṅgha needs to lead its own communities in fostering the best path, the best values—indeed, as it has always endeavored to do. The best path and the best values in the world favor gender equality and the elimination of patriarchy and misogyny. What is more, it is critical to the success of the bhikṣuṇī saṅgha that they have no shadows, no grounds to disparage their prestige and status; hence the necessity to confront and deal with the eight heavy rules.

24. See note 7 above.

One way to counteract the shadow cast by the eight heavy rules would be for the male saṅgha to deliberately and overtly show their respect for bhikṣuṇīs. Monks should go out of their way to display their respect for nuns at every opportunity, to put them on a high chair and to treat them as equals. Along these lines, it was extraordinary to hear the Dalai Lama proclaim in Hamburg that feminism is wonderful and important, celebrating the strong talents that women have for modeling Buddhist values. Hearing such an intentional statement of support from a figure like the Dalai Lama helps women to hold their heads high in the Buddhist world. Such support will help redress and reverse the prejudice that women have endured over the centuries in Buddhism. In particular, displays of such esteem toward bhikṣuṇīs by monks could be cast explicitly as a deliberate attempt on the part of the Buddhist saṅgha to show that it regards the eight heavy rules only as an archaic relic from a previous period in Buddhist history.

It is crucial to repeat again that prestige and status are essential to the success of the Buddhist saṅgha. It would be a grave mistake to conflate concerns about prestige and reputation with the kinds of problems of ego that Buddhism always warns us against. Regard and respect is at the bottom of the entire system of the Buddhist saṅgha; it is essential for the support of the laity, and that support is essential for the saṅgha to survive. It is a mistaken sense of the ascetic path to think that the bhikṣuṇī saṅgha can operate without proper facilities and resources. Without such support the bhikṣuṇī saṅgha will experience a second decline.

Those contemporary Buddhist women who have argued that the eight heavy rules should not be contested but rather regarded as providing a good opportunity for women to work on their egos are pursuing a mistaken strategy.[25] Although it is certainly true that the situation is a good chance to

25. As when Bhikṣuṇī Thubten Chodron states, "As nuns, having more precepts only makes us more aware and scrupulous in our actions" (Chodron 2001: 32). This essay in general is an admirable and generous attempt to provide a way for women to think about the situation of female subordination in the Buddhist saṅgha and is in many ways strategic and wise. The same can be said of the rest of the book, written by Bhikṣuṇī Wu Yin. But while it is to be praised for taking on some of the delicate issues of women's subordination to men in the saṅgha, attributing the eight heavy rules to the cultural context of India at the time of the Buddha, and especially for advising bhikṣuṇīs to be confident and take leadership roles, it is also largely apologetic for the eight heavy rules, characterizing them as needed because of women's specific biology and greater emotional character as compared to men, and seems

work on one's ego—most situations are!—we should hardly welcome the disparagement of an order whose entire purpose is to provide models of dignity and discipline. That would defeat the very purpose of everything we were doing at the conference at Hamburg.

The Promise of a Future with a Strong Bhikṣuṇī Order

The perception that full ordination confers status and prestige is at the heart of why Buddhist women today are seeking it. But this does not imply that they desire fame or fortune. Rather it is a prescient perception on the part of these women that full ordination allows a role for women in Buddhism that holds a special kind of promise for the future. I have already suggested one reason for this, albeit so far largely presented in negative terms: given the increasingly egalitarian sentiments in many parts of the world today, for the Buddhist saṅgha to maintain a bias against women's ordination or status would mean to grossly undercut the credibility of Buddhism altogether in the modern world. This motivation alone is a decisive reason why the bhikṣuṇī order should be restored and supported at the highest level. Without it there is little chance for Buddhism to take up the role that it is poised to assume in the modern world. Without addressing the patriarchy, androcentrism, and misogyny that have cropped up in sectors of the Buddhist world, it is unlikely that Buddhism can maintain widespread respect in the international community today.

But more is at stake than the concern that without gender equality, Buddhism will be deemed too retrograde to assume leadership on the world stage. More important yet are the positive grounds for fostering a strong bhikṣuṇī saṅgha. There is the very exciting prospect of women taking a leadership role in ways that they have only rarely done in the past, even in China, where indeed the bhikṣuṇī order has been maintained since its first establishment there.[26]

---

to understand women's subordination to men in the saṅgha as beneficial to the Dharma; see especially pp. 81–89.

26. For materials in English on outstanding Chinese bhikṣuṇīs of the past, see Pao-ch'ang 1994, Grant 2003, and Grant 1996. See also Faure 2003: *passim*.

Envisioning the Future

The moment is ripe for envisioning what the new order of fully ordained women might become. For one, we cannot overestimate the importance of the perception we already see signs of in Sri Lanka: an appreciation that the women who are pioneering the full ordination movement are uncommonly dedicated and determined individuals choosing to live as celibate monastics according to the full Vinaya regulations. Women will be choosing this lifestyle carefully and with understanding of what it entails. The very fact that it is such an intentional effort on their part will exactly bestow on them the patina of moral fortitude that the Buddhist monastic order was designed to confer on its members in the first place. And given the current concerns in many parts of the Asian world about the corruption of the modern saṅgha, the exceptional personal resolve written on the body of the Buddhist nun will place her in a special light.

Pure Buddhist monastics—male and female alike—can have an exceptional role to play in the coming years in our global society. This opportunity is in no small part due to the special perception today of Buddhism among world religions. Buddhism is perceived—in the media, in advertising, in literature, in people's imagination, in people's fantasy, in many parts of the world today and cutting across class and race lines—as the religion of peace. To be sure, invoking such an image of Buddhism is to participate in a romantic conception. The actual historical record—including the last hundred years, with particularly troubling examples from Japan, Thailand, and Sri Lanka—shows both Buddhist monastics and laypeople sometimes engaging in warfare and violence, sometimes in the name of Buddhism itself. The same can be said of all world religions. But Buddhist leaders can make a virtue of the widespread belief in Buddhism's commitment to peace and self-discipline and use it as a model for what Buddhist monastics and leaders can in fact be. While there is room for hypocrisy in every religion, there is also a way to capitalize on the promise of a positive image. By cultivating such models of excellence realistically, honestly, and deliberately, without falling prey to romanticism, and with full cognizance of the complexity of the record and the real difficulty in achieving such an ideal, Buddhist leaders stand to carve out a space for themselves to serve as exceptional exemplars of a moral life, exemplars who can have particular salience in our contemporary situation.

In short, Buddhist monastics have an opportunity to make their ideal image a reality, and thereby to make a real impact in our world today. Buddhism is often seen today as one of the few alternatives to an increasingly violent world caught up in power struggles, sectarian violence, and competition for scarce resources. Buddhism is seen in many parts of the world as the religion that can help us live happily with less. Buddhism is seen to have the resources to teach us how to conserve energy, to treat others with compassion, to avoid jealousy and ego, to reduce stress, to mediate difference. Buddhist monastics have the opportunity to present themselves as potent symbols of what it takes to achieve equilibrium and insight. Buddhist monastics represent the possibility of a life that can do those things. They have the chance to represent self-discipline in arguably the most self-indulgent global society that humanity has ever known. We might even say that Buddhist monastics represent the alter ego of militarism and violence; quasi-militarists in their own right, the monastic's shaved head, minimalist clothing, and simple lifestyle can be intentionally configured to represent self-control, peace, and, especially, wisdom.[27]

The Buddhist monastic in female form will make a startling impression on the world stage. People will be able to read in her demeanor an exceptional resolve and an exceptional accomplishment. And while in general we can say she is poised to model exactly the same virtues as male monastics can, it might also be worthwhile to ask whether there is something peculiar to the bhikṣuṇī order's special history—not to mention another slew of stereotypes, this time relating to gender—that might similarly be turned around and intentionally cultivated to model special Buddhist virtues of value for our current global society.

If in fact the Buddhist order is meant to erase sexuality, it is yet to be determined how it relates to gender. It is yet to be understood whether the Buddhist monastic has a gender at all and, if so, of what that consists.[28]

27. It must be noted of course that Buddhist monastics have also actually cultivated martial arts and have used them for violent and nefarious purposes; Buddhist monastic groups have also risen in armed rebellion or served as quasi-militias.

28. One essay that has tried to consider the gender of the Tibetan monastic with much intelligence and interesting ethnographic detail is Makley 2005. Faure 2003 provides a

It has further yet to be contemplated whether female Buddhist monastics have had, or will have, a different gender footprint than male monastics. Certainly, the answer to such a question will vary over time and place; we should not expect any gender conception to be the same in all circumstances, and definitely not to be tied essentially to the sex of its representatives. What I think we can say with confidence about the bhikṣuṇī *qua* woman—that is, in this particular historical moment—is that she will represent a victory over patriarchy and misogyny. We can also expect that her spareness and lack of coyness or adornment of any kind will surprise even feminists. Perhaps her uncommon dignity will signify exceptional strength of character. Perhaps her lack of adornment will signal new heights in the pacification of ego.

If we can still attribute to woman special proclivities that stem from her close connection to maternity—as the Dalai Lama himself argued, and as has long been an integral part of Buddhist images of the female—perhaps we can suggest that the bhikṣuṇī order of the twenty-first century might strive to excel at modeling a new kind of enlightened community. Perhaps the new female order might work to separate the rhetoric of homelessness from the reality of monastic living communities. Perhaps members of the female order will realize that since they are a relatively new phenomenon, they have a chance to invent, and expressly to valorize, a model of community living that would specifically embody Buddhist virtues. Perhaps what the female order might contribute is a new self-consciousness of what has always been true, namely that communal life is one of the great opportunities for the Buddhist saṅgha to position itself as a model for the ethical life. Perhaps it could be a disciplined community that still understands itself as a circle of humans with human needs. Perhaps it could become a disciplined community that excels at empathy. Perhaps also the bhikṣuṇī order might strive to excel at peacemaking in the world, and at modeling the respectability and wisdom of compromise. And perhaps, having struggled through such a dilemma themselves, the new bhikṣuṇīs will lead the way in teaching

---

wide-ranging look at issues relating to the female gender and, to some extent, the relation of gender to monasticism in Buddhism. Charles F. Keyes (1984) has a detailed investigation of a variety of female gender associations in Thai Buddhism, including some that are pertinent to Buddhist ordination. For a detailed study of gender and renunciation in South Asia outside of Buddhism, see Khandelwal 2004.

us how to discern when to accept difficult circumstances and when to act against the grain to change them. Perhaps the new bhikṣuṇī of the twenty-first century will teach the world how to eschew absolutes. And perhaps the new bhikṣuṇīs can also model for us how to be good listeners, with dignity.

I here offer my own hope that the leaders of Tibetan Buddhism, and indeed all the leaders of Buddhism, will have the fortitude to set the new orders of bhikṣuṇīs onto their paths with generosity, foresight, and care. This is a special moment in Buddhist history.

The Vinaya Between History and Modernity:
SOME GENERAL REFLECTIONS

Jens-Uwe Hartmann

FOR MANY YEARS I have been following the endeavor to reestablish the bhikṣuṇī ordination, mostly by reading about it, but also through some participant observation, especially in connection with a research project on modern forms of Buddhism in Nepal during the 1980s.[1] At present I am engaged in research on the recently discovered Buddhist Sanskrit texts from Afghanistan, and there are a number of fragments of Vinaya texts among them, but regrettably they do not contribute anything new as far as the subject of this conference is concerned. Therefore I am unable to present new facts from old texts; what I will do instead is summarize three of the more general thoughts I have had observing the attempts to reintroduce the ordination of nuns.

These thoughts start from the question whether scholarship—and especially our kind of academic scholarship—is in a position to help in solving in a narrower sense the legal and in a wider sense the religious problems connected with such a phenomenon as the reinstitution of an order of nuns in forms of Buddhism from which it has disappeared or the establishment of a nuns' order where it was never introduced. Apparently there are certain objections to the reinstitution of the nuns' order within the relevant traditions, and these objections are centered on legal and historical questions. I am not a specialist in Buddhist law and therefore feel unable to address the

1. Bechert and Hartmann 1988.

legal intricacies; however, sometimes I wonder if the legal problems serve only as a pretext and hide a more general and not very rational reluctance to introduce major changes in those traditions. If this impression is correct, scholarly research will not be able to provide an efficient antidote, since scholarship by definition employs rationality in its argumentation and argues against rational objections, not against emotions. In a way, I am even asking if a conference such as ours has any hope at all of providing results that will move things forward in the desired direction. I am by no means arguing against holding such a conference; rather I am asking how much the process of taking a final decision will be informed by, and profit from, the kind of knowledge generated on such occasions by scholarly research. Striving for a decision is, as in politics, more a quest for majorities than for insights. On the other hand, insights will not hurt, and sometimes they may even help in winning the necessary majorities.

A second, and to my mind very important, problem is the question of perspective within the field of religion. There are various perspectives from which it is possible to view, analyze, and understand any given religious phenomenon. Religious texts are such phenomena, and a compilation of rules and regulations such as the code for Buddhist monks and nuns is no exception. Every perspective functions within a certain field of methods and premises, and each perspective will yield a certain result. Paradoxically, all the results may be "true" within their respective fields yet mutually exclusive. To give an example: seen from the religious, i.e., the Buddhist, perspective, the Vinaya contains the word of the Buddha, and as such it represents a collection of rules and their respective interpretations that go back to the lifetime of the Buddha and were gathered together shortly after his death. However, seen from an academic perspective, the Vinaya is an anonymous compendium of literature that was continuously changed, adapted, and enlarged during many centuries by an unknown number of authors and redactors. Its nucleus is the *Prātimokṣa-sūtra*, the confession formula, which in itself already reveals signs of historical development and amalgamation of older and younger parts. Altogether, six complete versions of the Vinaya have survived until today, although there were probably more when Buddhism still flourished in India. All of them show that the Vinaya must have originated at a time when the community of monks was a group of homeless ascetics wandering around throughout the year, with the sole exception of the rainy season, when travel was both difficult and potentially harmful to other living beings. On the other hand, in the same Vinaya we find all sorts of regulations for buildings, even up to such facilities as toilets. As scholars looking from the historical point of view, we understand this seeming discrepancy between homeless wandering ascetics and monks residing in permanent dwellings as a slow historical process taking several centuries, a process that continuously necessitated the introduction of new rules in order to adapt to the changing lifestyle of the community of monks and nuns. The old rules were kept and new rules were added, until this development reached a standstill around the middle of the first millennium C.E. and the texts of the various Vinayas became more or less fixed and finalized. In our view, this reflects a process of constant adaptation carried out by countless unknown Vinaya masters who added the new rules whenever necessary, authorizing them via the same guidelines that were used earlier for the rules proclaimed by the Buddha himself.

Historically, there can be no doubt that the Vinaya was continuously modified and enlarged by the monks. Today three Vinayas are fully or partly preserved in Indian languages; they differ with regard to the number and order of rules, and they use three different Indian languages (Pāli, Sanskrit, and the so-called Buddhist Hybrid Sanskrit heavily influenced by Middle Indian). It is not likely that the Buddha himself proclaimed these different versions, and therefore the differences can only be explained as historical developments. It is evident that Vinaya masters in India, living many centuries after the Buddha, felt the need and the right to adjust their sacred lore to changes within their community. Evidently it is possible today to accept the result of all those changes as authoritative, but then it should perhaps also be possible to emulate the Vinaya masters of old and do what they did, namely adjust sacred lore to present-day needs.

At first sight, the two views, the academic and the religious, do not seem really compatible, and to argue from an academic standpoint against a Buddhist view or vice versa may lead to a futile dispute between positions marked by either belief or rationality. Interestingly enough, an inner-Buddhist variant of such a dispute seems to underlie the present considerations on the integrity of the various Vinaya lineages. Today, three traditions are still alive, the Theravāda in South and Southeast Asia, the Mūlasarvāstivāda in Tibet, and the Dharmaguptaka in China and Korea, and each of them takes the integrity of its own lineage for granted. When we look at such a lineage from the historical point of view, we find that its integrity can be doubted or even falsified. However, it is absolutely impossible to prove a tradition's integrity, since historical research will never be able to provide enough reliable data for excluding the possibility of a break in the lineage at some point in the past. Integrity cannot be reliably and convincingly established over a long period of time. This holds true for any given lineage, be it Tibetan, Chinese, or Southeast Asian. Therefore, when some Tibetan Vinaya masters assert the unbroken continuity of their own ordination lineage while casting doubt on the integrity of the Chinese tradition, they mix the two perspectives and employ rationality and belief at the same time, but for different ends—rationality for doubting the other tradition and belief for accepting their own.

This implies a methodological problem, and it raises the question of whether it is reasonable to expect legally applicable results from the ongoing research into the legitimacy of Vinaya lineages. In my opinion, all such endeavors will by necessity be futile, because the desired result—some kind of positive proof—is *a priori* unobtainable for a historical process that spans 2,500 years. When I read such sentences as "The *bhikṣu* lineage in China can be documented all the way back to the Buddha," and even "The *bhikṣuṇī* lineage in China can be documented from the time of Ching Chien (Jing-jian), the first Chinese *bhikṣuṇī*, in 357 C.E." in a research paper on the lineage of bhikṣuṇī ordination,[2] I cannot help regarding such statements as wishful thinking. China is an extremely historically minded culture with a tremendous number of historical records, but I would never expect reliable documentation to go back continuously until the year 357 C.E.; in India, without any historical records at all, it is completely out of the question, and such validity claims can be based on nothing but belief.

A third point I would like to make is that the Buddha apparently was a pragmatist. There are countless examples in the scriptures that illustrate how, in each case, the Buddha considered the specific situation of his audience and how he taught according to the needs and faculties of his listeners.

2. The Committee of Western Bhikṣuṇīs, "Research Regarding the Lineage of Bhikṣuṇī Ordination: A Response to Necessary Research Regarding the Lineage of Bhikṣuṇī Vinaya" (unpublished manuscript), 7.

Such pragmatism has not been limited to the Buddha himself; even without drawing attention to such concepts as upāya, it is easy to see a certain pragmatic attitude as a hallmark of Buddhism. Doubtless, this has been one of the reasons for the tremendous success of this religion all over Asia and now in the West. This pragmatism permitted, first of all, the necessary local adaptations when Buddhism began to spread all over India and beyond, and it allowed, secondly, innovation through continuous modification of the received set of beliefs and practices. For more than a thousand years after the death of the Buddha, the monks must have been very pragmatic when it came to modifying their rules and regulations. This explains, for example, why monks in Tibet wear robes very different from those worn by Sinhalese or Chinese monks. It also explains why certain rules of the Vinaya were kept but no longer enforced, even without the explicit consent of the Buddha. One of the better-known examples would be the clear-cut prohibition against a monk accepting gold and silver, i.e. money, with his own hands.[3] Quite often there is a notable difference between the contents of some of the rules and their implementation, between the normative and the factual, a divergence that is by now a time-honored and generally accepted practice.

The observation of such divergences appears to have a bearing on some of the legal problems seen as obstacles to the reintroduction of the order of nuns. One example could be the question whether a bhikṣuṇī ordination has to be performed by the monks alone or by both saṅghas; another example could be the question whether monks and nuns belonging to different Vinaya traditions are allowed to join in performing a valid ordination. As far as I can see, both questions will have to be answered from a pragmatic point of view because no absolutely satisfying legal solution is offered in the existing Vinayas. It is also not very likely that additional scholarly research will cut such Gordian knots since to date hardly a stone has been left unturned by scholars, but to no avail, I am afraid.

One of the needs strongly felt in postmodern societies is gender equality, and deficiencies in this regard are easily, and often justly, targeted by critics.

3. See Rosen 1959: 103 for the version of the Sarvāstivāda Vinaya and page 44 for references to the corresponding rule in the other Vinayas. This prohibition is rather differently observed today—very strictly in Thailand but much less so or even not at all in other parts of the Buddhist world.

Buddhism is no exception here; it will have to remedy these deficiencies if it is to survive. There is the well-known and oft-cited prophecy, put in the mouth of the Buddha himself, that the duration of Buddhism will be shortened by the introduction of the order of nuns.[4] Today, however, it may turn out that not introducing the order will prove harmful in such societies where the demand for equal opportunities does not hesitate to insert itself in the domain of religious specialists, be they priests, monks, or otherwise.

4. Cf. Hüsken 2000 and 2006.

Sects and Sectarianism

The Origin of the Three Existing Vinaya Lineages: Theravāda, Dharmaguptaka, and Mūlasarvāstivāda[1]

Bhikkhu Sujato

PERFORMANCE OF *upasampadā* by East Asian bhikkhunīs within either the Theravāda or Tibetan traditions depends on the belief that the ordination lineages are essentially compatible. The basic reason for assuming that they are compatible is simple: we are all sons and daughters of the Śākyan sage, and all the ordination lineages descend from the allowances granted by the Buddha himself in the Vinayas. The problem is that the Vinayas also envisage certain circumstances whereby it is not possible for formal saṅgha acts, such as ordination, to be performed by different saṅgha groups together. In particular, this applies if there has been a formal schism (*saṅghabheda*), narrowly defined as the performance of separate *uposatha*s within the same monastic boundary (*sīmā*). While this is the critical issue in the Vinayas themselves, other questions become relevant in considering the overall historical picture; for example the nature of the transmission in any particular lineage; or indeed the very notion of lineage itself. These questions are considered in other papers at this congress. For now I will focus on just one question: did the existing ordination lineages arise through schism?

1. This article is a summary of some threads in *Sects & Sectarianism: The Origins of Buddhist Schools*, a fully referenced book available for free download and in a print edition via http://santipada.googlepages.com.

Theravāda vs. Mahāsaṅghika: A False Lead

The traditional Theravādin answer to this question is a resounding "Yes!" The Theravādin view would have it that the bhikkhunīs in existence today are "Mahāyāna." Mahāyāna is believed to have descended from the Mahāsaṅghikas, the root schismatics. According to the earliest Sri Lankan chronicle, the *Dīpavaṃsa*, the Mahāsaṅghikas are none other than the "evil" Vajjiputtakas, who advocated the use of money by monks, and who were defeated at the Second Council, but who later reformed and held a new recitation where they invented new scriptures. In following these, the Mahāyāna is representative of a tradition whose fundamental principle was laxity in Vinaya. The *Dīpavaṃsa* explicitly states that the other seventeen schools apart from the Theravāda are schismatic and "thorns" in the *sāsana.* It is therefore impossible to accept them as part of the same communion or to perform any acts of *saṅghakamma* together, including ordination. The Mahāyāna are no more than disreputable distant cousins of the pristine Theravāda, which alone retains the original teachings and practice of the historical Buddha. Thus runs the thinking of conservative Theravāda.

Unfortunately for the conservative position, almost none of these claims holds water. The Mahāyāna is not descended in any direct or simple way from the Mahāsaṅghika, but rather emerged as a broad-based movement drawing on the teachings of many early schools, including but not limited to Mahāsaṅghika. The *Dīpavaṃsa*'s claim that the Mahāsaṅghikas were the Vajjiputtakas of the Second Council cannot stand: it finds no support anywhere else, and crucially it contradicts the Mahāsaṅghika's own texts. Furthermore, there is no evidence that laxity in Vinaya was a characteristic of Indian Mahāyāna; many Mahāyāṇa texts strongly emphasize Vinaya, and the reports of the Chinese pilgrims show how the various sects all maintained compatible standards of Vinaya.

It must also be noted that apart from the *Dīpavaṃsa*, most of the historical accounts of sect formation do not refer to the Sthavira/Mahāsaṅghika split as "schism" (*saṅghabheda*). This is true even in the case of the Mahāvibhāṣā's notorious demolition of the reviled "Mahādeva," who according to this version founded the Mahāsaṅghika. He is accused of murdering his father, sleeping with and then murdering his mother, and murdering an arahant, which are three of the five "deadly sins" (*ānantarika kamma*). But the accounts are unanimous that he did not commit the "deadly sin" of causing a schism. So even this, one of the most aggressively polemical passages in all of Buddhism, does not accuse the founder of the Mahāsaṅghikas of schism.

The *Dīpavaṃsa*'s claims regarding the Sthavira/Mahāsaṅghika split have virtually no historical credibility, and both traditional Theravādins and academics bewitched by the supposed superior historicity of the Pāli texts have led us astray here. It is far more plausible to treat the *Dīpavaṃsa*'s account as a portrayal of the situation at the time the *Dīpavaṃsa* or its sources was composed, when the Sri Lankan Mahāvihāra was in deep and protracted conflict with the Mahāsaṅghika schools in Andhra. This situation was backdated to the time of the root split, providing mythic authority for the Mahāvihāra.

The Three Lineages

The reality is that there has never been a distinctively "Mahāyāna" Vinaya or ordination lineage. Rather, some bhikkhus and bhikkhunīs, having ordained in one of the early schools, choose to study and practice certain texts and spiritual ideals known as "Mahāyāna." This was the case in ancient India, and it remains the case today. The bhikkhus and bhikkhunīs of the East Asian traditions (China, Korea, Vietnam, Taiwan, etc.) follow the Vinaya of the Dharmaguptaka school, while the Central Asian traditions (Tibet, Bhutan, Mongolia, Nepal, etc.) follow the Mūlasarvāstivāda. Both the Dharmaguptaka and the Mūlasarvāstivāda descend from the Sthavira (Skt.) or Theriya (Pāli) group of schools, as does the Theravāda. There is no existing Vinaya lineage descended from the Mahāsaṅghika. If we wish to understand the relationship between the existing saṅghas, then we must start by investigating these early schools of Buddhism.

I might note that I am here representing the perspectives from inside the schools themselves. It is extremely difficult, probably impossible, to determine whether these lineage claims are in fact correct, or even if the notion has any meaning, given the frequent interchange of monks and nuns from different traditions in India and beyond. Probably the best we can do is to take the schools' own self-perception and see what this entails.

One way of doing this is to examine the origins of the schools in question.

Here we enter into the swirling and uncertain world of mythology, where interpretation is all, and sectarian bias is not merely expected, but is the driving motivation. Given the contradictory, incomplete, and doubtful nature of the sources, it is unclear whether we can expect to find even a glimmer of truth. If we are to do more than merely present evidence, we must make inferences, and these inferences can be questioned. But our surest conclusions derive from the happy coincidence of the historical/mythic accounts and archaeological findings, and it is here that we begin our search.

The Aśokan Missions

One of the fullest accounts of the origination of any school is found in the *Sinhalese Vinaya Commentary*, which exists in a Pāli version as the *Samantapāsādikā*, and in an ancient Chinese translation as the *Sudassanavinayavibhāsā* (善見律毘婆沙*Shan-Jian-Lu-Pi-Po-Sha*, T 1462). This recounts several decisive events that took place in the time of Aśoka. Corrupt, non-Buddhist heretics entered the saṅgha disrupting the *uposatha*. They were expelled by Aśoka together with the elder Moggaliputtatissa, following which the "Third Council" was held to reaffirm communal identity. Subsequently Moggaliputtatissa organized the sending out of "missionaries" to various parts of India, an event that has often been compared with Aśoka's sending out of Dharma ministers as recorded in his edicts. The main purpose of this narrative is to establish the credentials of the Sinhalese school founded by Aśoka's son Mahinda and his daughter Saṅghamittā. Today we call the descendants of this school "Theravāda"; however I will refer to the archaic school by the more historically accurate term, the Mahāvihāravāsins (Dwellers in the Great Monastery).

There are two major pieces of epigraphic evidence from the early period of Indian Buddhism: the reliquaries at Vedisa and the Aśokan edicts. Strikingly, both of these confirm the evidence found in the *Sinhalese Vinaya Commentary*. When the Vedisa inscriptions were uncovered and deciphered, scholars were astounded to find they mentioned the names of several monks who the *Sinhalese Vinaya Commentary* says were sent as missionaries to the Himalaya soon after the "Third Council." The coincidence of these names in such widely separated sources is regarded by scholars as one of the bedrock findings of modern Buddhist studies.

Our second prime archaeological evidence is Aśoka's so-called "schism edict" (which actually states that the saṅgha is unified, not schismatic!). This mentions an expulsion of corrupt bhikkhus, which many scholars have identified with the events prior to the "Third Council." Unlike the Vedisa findings, the identification here is disputed among scholars; however the similarities are so far-reaching that it seems perverse to insist that they are unrelated, even if the exact nature of that relationship is not entirely clear.

I might note as an aside here that, while all other scholars I have read have assumed that the sectarian period began before Aśoka, my own review of the evidence has convinced me that the split between the Sthaviras and Mahāsaṅghikas did not take place until several generations after Aśoka. However, this does not directly affect the matter at hand.

The Sinhalese archaeological record, while not as decisive, tends to support the validity of the *Sinhalese Vinaya Commentary*'s account of the general date and place of arrival of Buddhism in Sri Lanka. The Indian archaeological record generally, while even less specific, also tends to agree as far as we can identify the geographic spread of the schools. This broad correspondence between epigraphic and textual evidence encourages us to take the missions account of the *Sinhalese Vinaya Commentary* seriously.

In the current context, it is worth recalling the mission of Soṇa and Uttara to Suvaṇṇabhūmi. This is believed by Burmese to refer to Burma, and Thais to refer to Thailand; scholarly opinion lacks such reassuring certainty. While it is doubtful whether any mission actually took place in the time of Aśoka, the story to this day forms a crucial narrative of self-identity for Buddhists in these regions. The mission was said to result in the ordination of 1,500 women. Thus bhikkhunī ordination is intrinsic to Southeast Asian Buddhism from the beginning.

Dharmaguptaka Origins

One of the major missionaries was Yonaka Dhammarakkhita. He was, as his name indicates, a Greek monk, native of "Alasanda" (Alexandria). He features in the Pāli tradition as a master of psychic powers as well as an expert on Abhidhamma. After inspiring King Aśoka's brother Tissa to become a monk and acting as his preceptor, he went to the Greek-occupied areas in the west of India.

Long ago Przyluski, followed by Frauwallner, suggested that Dhammarakkhita be identified with the founder of the Dharmaguptaka school, arguing that *dhammarakkhita* and *dhammagutta* have identical meaning, and synonyms can be easily substituted in Indic words, even proper names. Since that time two pieces of evidence have come to light that make this suggestion, to my mind, highly plausible. One is the positive identification of very early manuscripts belonging to the Dharmaguptakas in the Gandhāra region, exactly where we expect to find Yonaka Dhammarakkhita, and appearing only a couple of hundred years after the initial mission. The second is that the phonetic rendering of his name in the *Sudassanavinayavibhāsā* employs the regular Chinese term for "Dharmagupta" rather than "Dhammarakkhita." We also note that several texts say that the Dharmaguptaka was founded by a certain "Moggallāna." While this is traditionally identified with the great disciple of that name, I think it is more likely a reference to Moggaliputtatissa, the patriarch of the Third Council, who is also regarded by the Mahāvihāravāsins as their founder. We are thus justified as seeing the Mahāvihāravāsins and the Dharmaguptakas not as warring schismatic parties but as long-lost siblings parted only by the accidents of history and the tyranny of distance.

While this proposal as to the foundation of the Dharmaguptaka must remain speculative, our textual evidence attesting the close relation between these schools is quite unambiguous. Remarkably, even Buddhist scholars are in full agreement over this point: the Dharmaguptakas were very close in every respect with the Mahāvihāravāsins. Textually, we posses their Vinaya, *Dīrgha-āgama*, and *Śāriputrābhidharma* in Chinese translation, and a growing body of manuscript finds in Gandhārī. None of these show any significant doctrinal or Vinaya divergences from the corresponding Mahāvihāravāsin texts. Indeed, the Mahāvihāravāsin *Kathāvatthu Commentary*, although it discusses literally hundreds of heretical doctrines of the different schools, nowhere mentions the Dharmaguptakas as holding any divergent opinions.

Vasumitra's work on the doctrines of the schools, however, does mention a few minor points of divergence. The most serious is that the Dharmaguptakas regard offerings given to the Buddha as more meritorious than those given to the saṅgha, while the Mahāvihāravāsins hold the opposite view. May the Dhamma experts decide this matter!

Finally, we should notice that the *Sudassanavinayavibhāsā*, which I have referred to above as a Chinese version of the *Sinhalese Vinaya Commentary*, differs from the Pāli *Samantapāsādikā* in that it includes many features distinctive of the Dharmaguptaka, such as twenty-six training rules (*sekhiya*) regarding conduct around a stūpa. It is unclear whether the Dharmaguptaka influence was part of the original text or was the result of the adaption of the Sinhalese text within the Chinese Dharmaguptaka tradition. In any case it is clear that the Vinaya masters of old regarded these two schools as following Vinayas so closely related they could draw upon the same commentarial traditions.

Mūlasarvāstivāda Origins

With regard to the third of our schools, the Mūlasarvāstivādins, the history is even murkier. The name Mūlasarvāstivāda is not attested until very late (about 700 C.E.). Almost everything about the early history of the school is contested among scholars: Are the Mūlasarvāstivādins identical with the Sarvāstivādins or not? Was their original home Mathura or Kaśmīr? Were they doctrinally aligned with the Sautrāntikas? Did they really emerge so late, or did they simply change their name? And so it goes.

In my opinion the most persuasive theory for the origin of this school was again provided by Frauwallner, who argued that the Mūlasarvāstivāda Vinaya shows a close connection with Mathura, and the passages linking the school with Kaśmīr were a later interpolation. This aligns the Mūlasarvāstivādins closely with the famous arahants of Mathura, Śāṇakavāsin, and Upagupta.

Śāṇakavāsin features in the all Vinaya accounts of the Second Council as a revered Elder and Vinaya master. He is said to have established a major forest monastery near Mathura, which is called Urumuṇḍa in the northern sources and Ahogaṅga in the Pāli. Later on, it was to this very monastery, renowned as the finest place in all India for meditation, that Moggaliputtatissa resorted for retreat. The spiritual power Moggaliputtatissa derived from his time in Śāṇakavāsin's forest monastery was decisive in convincing Aśoka to entrust him with the task of purifying the saṅgha and organizing the missions. Thus the establishment of the Mahāvihāravāsins and Dharmaguptakas is closely associated with the Śāṇakavāsin lineage.

Mathura is not mentioned in the missions account, not because it was the resort of heretics, but because it was an already long-established orthodox center. Far from being associated with schism, it is precisely the place Moggaliputtatissa went to to avoid the politics and corruption he found in the capital.

It is even possible that Soṇaka, the preceptor of Moggaliputtatissa's preceptor, is simply a misspelling for Śāṇaka(-vāsin), in which case the Mahāvihāravāsin ordination lineage would be directly descended from Śāṇakavāsin and the forest tradition of Mathura.

It is true that there are serious doctrinal differences between the Mahāvihāra/Dharmaguptaka and the (Mūla-)Sarvāstivādins, especially the existence of the dharmas in the three periods of time; but the accounts of how this doctrine evolved attribute its formulation to a series of elders who lived after Aśoka. Indeed, the doctrine itself does not make much sense except in light of the later Abhidharma theory of dharmas. Thus the doctrinal difference was subsequent to the emergence of geographically distinct schools. Probably in the time of Aśoka these matters were debated as various perspectives were clarified, but they were fixed and formulated as definite sectarian positions some time later.

Finally, it should be noted that one of the other missionaries was Majjhantika, Mahinda's ordination teacher, who went to Kaśmīr and established the school later known as the Sarvāstivādin Vaibhāṣikas. It is a point of contention whether this school has any connection as a Vinaya lineage with the Mūlasarvāstivāda, or whether they simply share some similar doctrines. In any case, this school is also depicted as having emerged from geographical dispersion rather than schism. The Majjhantika/Mahinda link attests to the close connections between the Kaśmīr and Sinhalese lineages.

Conclusion

Summing up, there is little to no evidence that the process of sect formation in ancient India was driven by formal schism (*saṅghabheda*). In my opinion, this was inevitable, since following Devadatta, all Buddhists have been terrified that if they caused a schism they would go to hell. The schools emerged gradually, primarily due to geographical dispersion, and over time doctrinal differences hardened into sectarian postures. The existing lineages all spring from the ancient Sthaviras, and there is no serious evidence anywhere of schism between these schools.

The Dharmaguptakas in particular are extremely close to the Theravāda, and might be regarded as virtually the northwest branch of the same school. The Mūlasarvāstivāda, while doctrinally distinct from the other two, was closely associated with them, as the seat of the Mūlasarvāstivāda in Mathura was also the meditation retreat of the Dharmaguptaka/Theravāda patriarch, Moggaliputtatissa.

We are blessed that the schools through which our ordination lineages were transmitted were so intimately linked. A closer attention to the question of bhikkhunī ordination has pressed myself, and I hope others as well, to examine and understand better our complex shared heritage. Rather than fearing this as a threat to the integrity of our own traditional school, we should embrace it as an expansion of our communion to better reflect both our shared past and also our shared future as custodians of the Dhamma in this small world.

Some Remarks on the Status of Nuns and Laywomen in Early Buddhism

Gisela Krey

THE STORY OF the foundation of the bhikkhunī saṅgha as told in *Cullavagga* 10[1] has increasingly become a focus of critical scholarly attention. While some scholars are interested in the problem of relative chronology within the story itself, others are drawn to analyze inconsistencies with other canonical statements and the like.[2] Attempts have been made to establish the foundation story as the product of a specific socio-historical constellation, one that may have constructed the story in order to legalize what already existed. According to this theory, the eight heavy rules (Pāli, *garudhamma*; Skt., *gurudharma*) had to be justified to secure the subordination of the nuns to the bhikkhus. Liz Williams, whose argumentation I will engage in this paper, is one such scholar.[3] She makes the following three claims: First, there may have been bhikkhunīs before Mahāpajāpatī's request for ordination (*pabbajjā*). Second, the same rather informal way of

1. Cv X.1, Vin II: 253–56, almost identical with the *Mahāpajāpatī-sutta* AN IV (LI): 274–79. In quoting the canonical sources I always refer to the Pali Text Society edition if no further details are given.

2. Edward J. Thomas, author of an oft-reprinted biography of the Buddha, judges: "It [i.e., the story of Mahāpajāpatī] is just the kind of legend that would be added to the historical fact of the establishment of the Order" (Thomas 1927: 110), while M. E. Lulius van Goor ("De Buddhistische Non") had entirely rejected the legend as early as 1915. For a detailed research review, see Hüsken 1997: 30–36.

3. Williams 2000.

ordination—by the use of the *ehi* formula—has existed for women as well as for men right from the early days of the Buddha's ministry. Third, the Buddha was not reluctant to ordain women.

I

To substantiate the first claim, Williams advances two arguments: The first is that there were bhikkhunīs and the bhikkhunī saṅgha even when Mahāpajāpatī was still a laywoman. Williams refers to the *Dakkhiṇāvibhaṅga-sutta*, the "Exposition of Offerings" (MN 142). On the one hand Mahāpajāpatī is depicted as still being a laywoman on the level of a stream-enterer. For, like a patron, she offers a set of clothes, spun and woven by herself, as a gift to the Buddha, and she is said to keep (only) five precepts while the members of the saṅgha had to keep at least ten. On the other hand, the same sutta deals with the degrees of karmic fruitfulness gained by offerings depending on the receivers, among which are mentioned bhikkhunīs and the order of bhikkhunīs. This reveals an inconsistency with the account of the foundation of the bhikkhunī saṅgha in the *Cullavagga* according to which Mahāpajāpatī was the first nun.

Contrary to Williams' view, the reference to bhikkhunīs and the bhikkhunī saṅgha in the *Dakkhiṇāvibhaṅga-sutta* could be seen as merely an anachronism caused by the editors' negligence. According to this view "the original discourse was later modified after the founding of the Bhikkhunī Sangha to bring the latter into the scheme of offerings to the Sangha."[4] This kind of text, containing the enumeration of distinct possible receivers of gifts, would easily allow for some modification. Nonetheless, it seems strange that monks who carefully adhered to the tradition over such a long time did not notice this discrepancy earlier. There is another anachronism in the text besides: According to the recognized tradition, Mahāpajāpatī's ordination and the foundation of the bhikkhunī saṅgha took place about five years after the Buddha's enlightenment,[5] and Ānanda is said to have become the Buddha's atten-

4. From the footnote of Bhikkhu Bodhi in Ñāṇamoli and Bodhi 1995 (2001): 1356n1291.

5. See the commentarial literature on this event. Mahāpajāpatī became a nun most probably after the death of her husband Suddhodana.

dant only in the twentieth year of the Buddha's preaching.[6] Yet Ānanda in the story is depicted as advocating bhikkhunī ordination to the Buddha on Mahāpajāpatī's behalf.

Another attempt to explain this inconsistency is to consider the accounts not as historical fact but rather to suppose that names were regarded as symbolizing certain roles: Mahāpajāpatī as a relative and the Buddha's foster mother is chosen to characterize someone who insists on giving a personal gift to the Buddha, while the role of a mediator and supporter in favor of women is typical of Ānanda.[7] Besides, it was Ānanda's job to handle the clothes offered to the saṅgha by laypeople.[8] A classification like this might have been applied without regard to chronology. Some even think it possible that the whole sutta as such is an interpolation, since it repeats Ānanda's pleading for Mahāpajāpatī's cause in *Cullavagga* 10.[9]

Alternatively, the account of Ānanda's intervention in this sutta (MN 142) may be original, because here, in contrast to the *Cullavagga*, the request does not have any real effect and seems to have been used only to indicate that in general gifts offered to the whole saṅgha are of greater value than personal gifts. There is no obvious reason why the episode of Ānanda's intervention should have been borrowed from another story. If we look at the tradition of the Mahāsāṅghika-Lokottaravādin, we even find more passages incorporated into the story of Mahāpajāpatī containing material found in the *Dakkhiṇāvibhaṅga-sutta* and in other Pāli suttas.[10]

One could add that, in the Mūlasarvāstivāda tradition, the Sanskrit

6. *Theragāthā* vv. 1039ff.

7. It even seems to me that Ānanda should be understood as an advocate of an integrative line of Buddhism, while Mahākassapa is the voice of the hardliners, and that both strains have been competing since Buddhism's earliest times. According to Nyanaponika and Hecker (1997: 154), Ānanda was especially solicitous for the welfare of all four classes of disciples. In some cases Mahākassapa heavily reproached him for his attitude.

8. Vin I: 287.

9. See Norman 1983: 48.

10. See the edition by Gustav Roth (1970), who lists several Pāli parallels on pages 4–21, and for our purposes here, especially pages 14–15, where the Blessed One tells Ānanda at length how much Mahāpajāpatī owes to him. In MN 142, this same complex collection of phrases is put into the mouth of Ānanda, although they make more sense when spoken by the Buddha. Generally speaking, the account of the founding in Roth 1970 corresponds very closely to the Pāli version.

version of the *Bhikṣuṇī-Karmavācanā*[11] contains a less elaborate, simplified parallel account compared to that of the *Cullavagga*. In this text, which seems to be closer in wording and meaning to a supposed original version, at least in some respects,[12] the role of Ānanda is generally less prominent. Ānanda's very first request is successful, so apparently it is not necessary for him to point to the special merits of Mahāpajāpatī (Skt., Mahāprajāpatī) as the Buddha's foster mother. Compared to this version, the Pāli version is fleshed out more dramatically, and the obstacles to admission appear to be deliberately emphasized.

In the *Bhikṣuṇī-Karmavācanā*, the Ānanda episode is directly connected with Mahāprajāpatī's third request. She repeats her request for the admission of women although she herself had been successful with her very first request. Not only is Mahāprajāpatī allowed to live the monastic life (*brahmacarya*), but she is even encouraged by the Buddha to do so, equipped with the signs of a nun (wearing robes and shaven head). The Buddha advises her "to live the holy life"[13] without any reservation or hindrance and without imposing any requirements on her. Instead he praises the benefits she would receive if she adopted this way of life. Perhaps this personal encouragement might be read as a tacit acknowledgement that single nuns did in fact exist before the community was confronted with problems arising from institutionalization and formalization.[14] However, despite receiving this personal privilege, Mahāprajāpatī left saddened and disappointed, because in her mind she had intended the general admission

11. *Bhikṣuṇī-Karmavācanā*, fol. 3ff., according to the 1920 edition by Ridding and La Vallée Poussin, translated by Frances Wilson in Paul 1979: 82ff., esp. pp. 83–86. Now this text is available in a new edition by Michael Schmidt (1993), esp. pp. 242–48, fol. 3a1–7b1.

12. See Sponberg 1992, to whom the Pāli version, dated by him around 200 B.C.E., "appears to show significant development over the Sarvāstivādin Sanskrit version," which he suggests to be based on a second of at least two Sthavira traditions. He also assumes that the more developed Pāli version represents the story as "one tailored to serve specific needs" (pp. 32–33, nn. 15 and 17).

13. Literally, *brahmacaryañ cara* (Schmidt 1993: 242), "live the holy life." This formula reminds one of the words that, according to the *Mahāvagga*, were spoken by the Buddha when ordaining the first monks, e.g., Vin I: 12.

14. See Hüsken 1997: 474, who deduces from material given in Cv X.2–7 that there must have been an early period in which women were admitted to the order before a separate institution was established.

of women to the order. (According to other traditions like the *Cullavagga*, she was accompanied by numerous Sakyan women—as many as five hundred according to some sources.)[15] When she received no answer at all from the Buddha on this fundamental point, neither positive nor negative, she met Ānanda who, in order to help Mahāprajāpatī, repeated her request only once and, having received a positive answer, did not need to make use of any tactics or special strategies to persuade the Buddha.[16]

Therefore in the Mūlasarvāstivāda version there is no reference to the merits of Mahāprajāpatī regarding the Buddha's youth as found in *Cullavagga* 10 or in the *Dakkhiṇāvibhaṅga-sutta*. Furthermore, women's general capability of leading a holy and celibate life was included even in the first positive advice given to Mahāprajāpatī herself encouraging her to adopt this way of life. According to that tradition, Ānanda's request has never been refuted either, since he immediately succeeded in receiving the positive answer, however restricted, as we know from the *Cullavagga*: On condition of accepting the eight heavy rules for overcoming obstacles, women are permitted to leave their homes in order to be ordained as nuns.

Considering the rules, which are the same in both sources though in different order, it seems quite clear that not all of them were formulated at the very beginning when the women's order was founded; initially, there may have been only a few, since as we know, the other Vinaya rules were established only after a need arose in response to a particular act.

But I agree with Norman, according to whom it is "not unlikely that a general code of conduct for mendicant orders already existed at the time of the Buddha"[17] and, apart from that, precepts could be added or substituted without any problem in precanonical times.

15. See, for example, the tradition of Mā-L (Roth 1970: 6), where four women called by name are added to the five hundred Sakyan women. Five hundred signifies no specific number but only—as in the so-called prophecy of decline—a large one. In the second section of the Pāli version there is only mention of a vague "many" (*sambahulā*).

16. On this most significant difference in the Sanskrit version, see Sponberg 1992: 33n20.

17. Norman 1983: 20. That may be proven by Cv X.3, where Mahāpajāpatī asks the Buddha to revise the first garudhamma and replace it with the principle of seniority. The Buddha refuses, explaining that adherents of non-Buddhist sects will not greet women at all. See Sponberg 1992: 35n24: "The allusion is no doubt to the Jains, who had split into two irreconcilable factions over the question of whether women could become liberated as women rather than first being reborn as male monks."

Williams states that there is evidence, as an argument from silence, that bhikkhunīs must have existed before the garudhammas were established, and thus before the double ordination as well. For neither in the *Therīgāthā*, which is generally believed to be a rather early testimony[18] and to have been recited originally—at least in parts—by bhikkhunīs, nor in the *Therīgāthā* commentary of Dhammapāla, which at least partially seems to be based on early material, is there any mention of a double ordination as prescribed by one of the eight rules of *Cullavagga* 10.[19] The therīs' ordination (*pabbajjā* as well as *upasampadā*) as reflected in the *Therīgāthā* and its commentary only refers to bhikkhunīs or the bhikkhunīs' monastery (*vihāra*) as ordination place (although the decision to pursue monastic life could have been inspired by a Dhamma talk of a bhikkhu or the Buddha himself).

Following Sponberg, one could add: "Chronologically Pajāpatī is not the most likely candidate [to have been the first nun]...she became a nun only after the death of her husband, King Suddhodana, by which time the Buddha already is supposed to have had many women followers."[20]

However, one could possibly raise the following objection: According to all Buddhist traditions, Mahāpajāpatī doubtlessly was the first ordained nun and is, therefore, listed in the *Aṅguttara-nikāya* (I: 25) as the foremost bhikkhunī of those of long standing (*ratta-ññūnam*, i.e., in seniority).[21] Perhaps it means, however, that she was the first bhikkhunī with a leading and organizing function, since the legend reports that she brought five hundred Sakyan women with her. In the tradition of the Mahāsāṅghika-Lokottaravādin, Mahāpajāpatī is more highly appreciated and plays an even more important role than in, for example, the Theravāda tradition. For after the admission of women the Buddha explicitly calls her the head of the order of the nuns: "the (one) responsible for the sangha, the superior of the sangha, the leader of the sangha."[22] Why was Mahāpajāpatī chosen for the

18. With fair probability these "verses of the therīs" can be dated between the fifth and the third century B.C.E. (Norman 1983: 90).

19. An exception is the classification of nuns at the end of Dhammapāla's commentary; see Pruitt 1998: 379–80.

20. Sponberg 1992: 32n14.

21. Or "great in experience"; see Pruitt 1998: 180n2.

22. Roth 1970: 21 and 74: "saṃgha-sthavirīm, saṃgha-mahattarīm, saṃgha-parināyikām."

role of founder? Mahāpajāpatī is said to have had a lot of women followers, some who had become like widows after their husbands had become monks and followed the Buddha and others who had lost their husbands in the war against the Koliyans. Mahāpajāpatī's role as a founder may have been due to her position as a queen and to her influence as a person of authority. Among all the therīs, it is only her name that bears the prefix *mahā-* or "great."

But it may also be that this story of Mahāpajāpatī and her role as founder has become legendary and mythologized. That it conceivably was a monastic invention may be concluded from its similarity to the story about the establishment of the nuns' order told in Jainism, where the founder and leader is said to have been Mahāvīra's aunt (or cousin), Ajja Chandana, who was also purportedly Mahāvīra's first female disciple.[23] Since one needed a person of authoritative rank to be the founder, it would have been difficult to ignore Mahāpajāpatī, queen of the Sakyas and a close relative of the Buddha. In order to reach a conclusive decision on this question of influence or dependence, one would, however, need to be sure that the Jaina version is of an earlier date.

II

In order to prove her second point—on the existence in Buddhism's earliest days of a bhikkhunī equivalent to the *ehibhikkhu*, "Come bhikkhu," style of ordination—Williams refers to the verses of the therī Bhaddā Kuṇḍalakesā (Thī 107–11) and Dhammapāla's commentary on them.[24] Bhaddā tells in her poem how she met the Buddha and how, having paid homage to him, she stood face to face (*saṃmukhā*) with him and was ordained. In verse 109, she literally remembers her ordination. It is stated very clearly: "'Come, Bhaddā,' did he say, and that was my full ordination."[25] Similarly, in the *Apadāna* quoted by Dhammapāla, the nun Bhaddā says: "I requested the going forth [and] full ordination. Then the Leader said, 'Come, Bhaddā!' Then after my ordination...."[26] I agree with Williams that this invitation

23. See Horner 1930: 102, Sponberg 1992: 3n14, and Murcott 1991: 61.

24. Williams 2000: 172–73.

25. Verse 109 c–d: "ehi bhadde 'ti avaca sā me ās' ūpasampadā."

26. Pruitt 1998: 140.

should be taken as an example of the *ehi* formula for the ordination of women, in other words, as the formula for full ordination as expressed by the Buddha himself, although there is a small but noticeable difference between this formula and the formula used for men, as she is not addressed as "bhikkhunī" but by her individual name "Bhaddā." Yet this feature is neither unusual nor atypical of the Buddha. Compared with the formula as handed down in the *Mahāvagga*,[27] this is an abridged version, probably because it is part of a poem. The fact that there existed some kind of simple, direct ordination not only for men but for women, too, is supported by the *Bhikkhunī-vibhaṅga*, where different types of nuns are categorized, among them those designated as a nun by the words "Come, bhikkhunī."[28]

In spite of this unambiguous textual evidence, Dhammapāla as well as his translator, who follows Dhammapāla's argumentation, deny the existence of such a form of ordination. Dhammapāla interprets "Come, Bhaddā" as an order by the Buddha to go to the residence of the bhikkhunīs and to go forth and receive full ordination in the presence of the bhikkhunīs,[29] an implausible reading that is not substantiated by the text. According to Dhammapāla, the phrase "That was my ordination" means that being addressed by the Buddha was merely the impulse that led her to go receive ordination. But even in his interpretation, one finds no reference to a double ordination.

Concerning the reference in the *Bhikkhunī-vibhaṅga* to *ehi*-formula nuns, Dhammapāla argues that the expression "Come, bhikkhunī-nun"

27. For the complete version, see, e.g., Vin I: 6.32, 6.34, 6.37, 7.15, 9.4, 10.4, 14.5, 20.19 and 21, and 24.4: "ehi (etha) bhikkhū (bhikkhavo) 'ti bhagavā avoca / svākkhāto dhammo / cara (caratha) brahmacariyaṃ sammā dukkhassa anta-kiriyāyā 'ti / sā 'va tassa (tesam) āyasmato (āyasmantānam) upasampadā ahosi." This specific kind of ordination is also mentioned in Sanskrit sources, e.g., in the *Saṅghabhedavastu*, *Mahāparinirvāṇa-sūtra*, *Mahāvastu*, *Avadānaśataka*, and *Divyāvadāna*. See Edgerton 1953: 157: "ehi-bhikṣukā."

28. Vin IV: 214: "ehi bhikkkunīti bhikkhunī." The female equivalent of the *ehibhikṣu* ordination is also mentioned in the *Divyāvadāna* (616), where the ordination of the Caṇḍāla girl Prakṛti is described with the words: "ehi tvaṃ bhikṣuṇi cara brahmacaryam"; see also Edgerton 1953: 157: "ehibhikṣuṇī-vāda."

29. Cf. Pruitt 1998: 142 and 380. Pruitt also does not assume this formula to be the equivalent of an *ehi-bhikkhunī* ordination (140n1 and 142n2). He agrees with the commentary's explanations, according to which the meaning of the verse is: "He said to me, [i.e.,] he ordered me. 'Come, Bhaddā!' [i.e.,] 'Go to the residence of the bhikkhunīs and in the presence of the bhikkhunīs go forth and be fully ordained.' 'Because the Teacher's order to me was the cause of my full ordination' [is the meaning of] 'it became my full ordination.'"

refers to something that had been possible theoretically without ever having been put into practice.[30] In his view, all nuns were ordained by monks, with the exception of Mahāpajāpatī, and for him, the only ones who did not receive a double but a single ordination, namely by monks, were the five hundred Sakyan women of Mahāpajāpatī's entourage. Williams says of Dhammapāla, who probably lived in the sixth century in South India: "His views of and attitude towards women are obviously coloured by the socio-historical context in which he was writing."[31] It was the time when "the order of nuns in India had already virtually disappeared from the official record,"[32] although convents continued to exist beyond the seventh century. Dhammapāla's attitude may be subsumed to what Alan Sponberg calls "institutional androcentrism." In this attitude—which, according to him, only arose after the period of early Buddhism—it is accepted that women pursue a religious life, "but only within a carefully regulated institutional structure" that secures female subordination to male authority.[33]

It may be noted that the only case in the Pāli canon in which this formula is used for (the ordination of) a woman is the one of Bhaddā. Generally, however, we have to consider that female beings, even colleagues, were not a focus of the monks' attention and interest.

Separately, the case of Bhaddā also supports the first point concerning the existence of women who had taken up an ascetic and homeless religious life (*pabbajjā*) prior to Mahāpajāpatī's ordination. According to the legendary tradition, Bhaddā Kuṇḍalakesā was a fascinating if not emancipated figure. Before becoming a Buddhist nun, she is said to have been a member of the Jain order (a *nigaṇṭhī*) and to have adhered to the severest asceticism.[34] The explanation of her name Kuṇḍalakesā ("Curly Haired")

30. Dhammapāla discusses this matter at length and in a very sophisticated manner, which seems to indicate the importance of this question to him. He supposes that the Blessed One did not say this formula to any woman because there had been none "suitable for admission as a bhikkhunī" and "because none of them had done the appropriate meritorious acts" (Pruitt 1998: 380–81).

31. Williams 2000: 173.

32. This marginalization was initiated in the third century (Sponberg 1992: 18).

33. Sponberg 1992: 13.

34. Among the verses recited by her, allusions to practices of the Jains can be found (Pruitt 1998: 141). I have translated (anachronistically?) *nigaṇṭha* by "Jain." To my knowledge, it is

refers to one of the austerities of the initiation into the Jain order wherein her hair was not simply shaven but torn out; after this torture the new hair grew in very curly.

She can be seen as an example of a wandering wise woman at the Buddha's time who taught herself and engaged in religious and philosophical debates. If we rely on the material contained in Dhammapāla's commentary, we see that it was not impossible for women to live as wandering mendicants. She did so after having mastered all Jain teachings and, unsatisfied by them, having left that saṅgha in search of someone wiser than herself. Finally, she met the General of the Doctrine, Sāriputta, who defeated her in debate and taught her the doctrine. At the end of a verse, spoken by the Buddha and handed down in the *Dhammapada* (verse 101), she immediately attained arhatship. According to the commentary, Sāriputta, before this attainment, had "sent word to the bhikkhunīs to ordain her."[35] This means, in contrast to my interpretation of *Therīgāthā* verses 107–11, she was ordained by the nuns and not by the Buddha himself.

A similar career is ascribed by Dhammapāla to the therī Nanduttarā, who is also said to have gone forth as a Jain and, being intent on disputation, to have wandered all over India, until she met Mahāmoggallāna. After he defeated her in debate, she was instructed by him in the Dhamma and soon attained arhatship.[36] Both examples elucidate that, in the time of early Buddhism, it was not unusual for women to lead an ascetic life as wandering nuns.

To sum up Williams' first and second points, then: The existence of bhikkhunīs before either the nuns' order or the garudhammas were established is quite probable and can be substantiated by arguments without having to refer to the content of the *Dakkhiṇāvibhaṅga-sutta* (MN 142).

---

generally accepted that the Jaina order existed prior to Nātaputta, the Buddha's contemporary; and according to the *Kalpa-sūtra*, the predecessor of Nātaputta, Pārśva, already had nun disciples.

35. For this report and the quotation, see Pruitt 1998: 135–37. There is also a further version (p. 140) according to which Bhaddā first attained arhatship, and then, after getting the permission (to go forth) from the Buddha, she went to the nuns' monastery and went forth. She is also listed by the Buddha among the thirteen foremost nuns (AN I: 25).

36. See Pruitt 1998: 115 (on Thī 87–91).

III

Concerning Williams' third thesis, I agree with her that the Buddha was not reluctant to ordain women, and neither did he give in only after Ānanda's strategy of persuasion.[37] She refers to the recognized "canonical tradition of repeating a request three times before being accepted." This tradition, not peculiar to Mahāpajāpatī's request, does not necessarily signify reluctance; sometimes these refusals can be explained as tests of resolve and are followed by an ultimate acceptance.[38] The present case, however, at least in the Pāli version, is different from such occasions, for neither Mahāpajāpatī's nor Ānanda's third request is accepted.[39] The tradition of the Mūlasarvāstivāda, on the other hand, mentions three requests of Mahāpajāpatī and one of Ānanda. But no matter how many repetitions are counted—leaving aside the questionable eight heavy rules that clearly relegate women to a secondary status—"we should not interpret this event as showing discrimination against women by Gautama because he never even as much as hinted that a woman had not the same chance as a man to become an arhat."[40]

In accordance with Ute Hüsken's view, one can also argue that the Buddha's answer appears to be gently formulated:[41] "mā te rucci..." i.e., "let it not please you..." instead of "anavakāso yaṃ..." i.e., "it is impossible that..."[42] This means that the Buddha does not support, but rather advises against, Mahāpajāpatī's intention or perhaps even transfers the responsibility,

37. On the question of the Buddha's reluctance, see Williams 2000: 168.

38. Examples given at Williams 2000: 169n3.

39. To be precise, it is the seventh attempt on the whole and the fourth by Ānanda that is successful. If we compare the parallel accounts of other Buddhist traditions, the Theravāda tradition shows the most repetitions of the request and thereby (as well as by other literary means) emphasizes the importance of the Buddha's ensuing decision most explicitly. See the two accounts in the appendices following this article.

40. Kajiyama 1989: 60.

41. Hüsken 2000: 44n2: "Thus it is not an explicitly negative answer by the Buddha, but rather that he advises Mahāpajāpatī Gotamī against her request—without giving a reason." For she has translated the Buddha's answer "mā te rucci..." in the same manner as I do: "Let it not please you..." (ibid.). Surprisingly, the Buddha used the same moderate formula even toward Devadatta when he intended to take over the leadership of the order (Vin II: 188) or to split it (Vin II: 198).

42. See Cv X.3.

leaving the decision more or less up to her. Mahāpajāpatī herself, however, clearly interprets this answer as a refusal. According to the *Cullavagga*, she says to Ānanda: "…the Blessed One does not allow…."[43]

In the Sanskrit version of the Mūlasarvāstivāda, which may be closer to the supposed basic text, the Buddha tells Mahāprajāpatī, already after her first request, to practice the monastic life, without giving a concrete response to her entreaty on behalf of women in principle. Nothing here indicates that he is reluctant.

However, common to all the traditions of this story is the appearance on the part of the Blessed One of hesitation or reservation toward the admission of women rather than outright reluctance. Originally, this hesitation seems not to have been an expression of discrimination against women but rather a concern for the problems of organization foreseen by him or, as suggested by Sponberg, the dilemma between maintaining sufficient distance between the two orders on the one hand and the social unacceptability of a distinct autonomous community of women on the other.[44] As one can imagine, it took some deliberation to find a way out of this dilemma of closeness and distance. With the exception of *Cullavagga* 10 (and the almost identical *Mahāpajāpatī-sutta* in AN IV), no other canonical passages testify to the Buddha's reservation against women's admission.[45]

Many different theories have been put forth to explain the Buddha's hesitation. I will not deal with the larger discussion about the premature decline of the Dhamma and the brahmacariya that the ordination of women is said to incur;[46] I restrict myself to some explanations by the commentator Buddhaghosa (ca. fifth century).

In his commentary on the *Aṅguttara-nikāya* Buddhaghosa explains the Buddha's hesitancy by saying that the Buddha ascribed only little insight to women ("*itthiyo nāma paritta-paññā*")[47] and feared that the doctrine, if

43. Hüsken 2000: 45n4: "na bhagavā anujānāti" corresponds to the *Bhikṣuṇī-Karmavācanā*'s "na labhate mātṛgrāmaḥ," i.e., "…women do not attain…."

44. Sponberg 1992: 17.

45. Horner 1930: 105.

46. On this question, see Williams 2002.

47. In places in the Pāli canon, a belief in women's limited intelligence as an innate quality is portrayed as a display of Māra that women must reject, for accepting this prejudice may dis-

given to them directly, would not be sufficiently honored by them. And, to be sure that the doctrine would be honored, the Buddha only gave permission after the threefold rejection, although he himself was willing to grant it.[48] A similar explanation is given in the commentary on *Cullavagga* X.1.1 in the *Samantapāsādikā*:

> Why does he reject? Don't all the Buddhas have four assemblies? The Buddha, though wishing to permit [the going forth] (*anujānitu-kāmo*), attributes importance to it and so [firstly] rejects it. For he thinks: "These [women] desire [the going forth] but lack it. If the going forth (*pabbajjā*) is only permitted after they have repeated the request many times, they will keep it carefully in the right way, thinking: 'It was hard for us to get this [permission].'"[49]

This presumption of biological difference is Buddhaghosa's way of understanding why, even though the same soteriological path is open to both women and men, certain constraints are imposed on women alone.

A second line of Williams' argument against the assumption that the Buddha was reluctant is based on the importance of all four classes of disciples. She refers to the famous *Mahāparinibbāna-sutta* (DN 16) as one of the most impressive examples of this view. Māra reminds the Buddha before his final nibbāna of his vow, uttered immediately after his awakening,[50] "that he

---

courage them from following the path. See, e.g., the bhikkhunī Somā's dialogue with Māra in SN I: 129 and—slightly modified—in Thī 60–62.

48. Mp IV: 134.13–20 on AN IV (LI): "saṭṭhā pi itthiyo nāma paritta-paññā, eka-yācita-mattena pabbajjāya anuññātāya na me sāsanaṃ garuṃ katvā gaṇhantī 'ti tikkhattuṃ paṭikkhipitvā idāni garuṃ katvā gāhāpetu-kāmatāya 'sace Ānanda Mahāpajāpatī...' āha." This is quoted and translated in Hüsken 1997: 345n17.

49. See Sp 1290.26–1291.2, quoted and translated in Hüsken 1997: 342n9 (see also Hüsken 2000: 44n2).

50. The initial incident at Uruvelā does not occur elsewhere in Theravāda canonical sources, but it is contained in the *Lalitavistara* as well as in the Tibetan and Chinese Vinayas (CPS 92–95). For the Mūlasarvāstivādin Vinaya, in addition to the CPS (pp. 92 and 94) see also SBV I: 125. In the CPS we find an inconsistency within the sūtra itself: First the Buddha utters his vow not to go to nirvāṇa until all his disciples, bhikṣus, bhikṣuṇīs, upāsakas, and upāsikās, have been well trained and instructed (p. 94), but later he hesitates to preach the Dharma at all and has to be asked by Brahmā Sabhāpati to do so (pp. 108–20). The same inconsistency occurs in the SBV (pp. 125 and 129) and in the Lalitavistara (pp. 377–78 and 392–93).

will not enter parinibbāna until all four classes of disciple[s] are well versed in the teachings and can teach them to others."[51] This vow, which included bhikkhunīs as well as laywomen, implies that the Buddha, since the time of his awakening, had known that there would be bhikkhunīs.

Because of its importance and its view of "soteriological inclusiveness" (a term coined by Sponberg), I will quote this passage liberally:

> I will not take final nibbāna until I have nuns and female disciples who are accomplished, trained, skilled, [secure from bondage,] learned, knowers of the Dhamma, trained in conformity with the Dhamma, correctly trained and walking in the path of the Dhamma, who will pass on what they have gained from their Teacher, teach it, declare it, establish it, expound it, analyze it, make it clear; until they are able by means of the Dhamma to refute false teachings that have arisen and teach the Dhamma of wondrous effect.

And further:

> I will not take final nibbāna until this holy life has been successfully established and flourishes, is widespread, well known far and wide, well proclaimed among devas and humans.[52]

51. Williams 2000: 168.

52. Adapted from the translation in Walshe 1996: 246–47. See also Waldschmidt 1951: 208–11. The same passage occurs elsewhere in the canon, e.g., SN V: 261–62 (*Cāpāla-sutta*), AN IV: 310–11, and Ud, pp. 63–64. See especially the slightly modified version at Ud, p. 63: "na tāv' āhaṃ pāpima parinibbāyissāmi, yāva me bhikkhū na sāvakā bhavissanti viyattā vinītā visāradappattā yogakkhemā [better: *visāradā pattayogakkhemā*, according to SN V: 261 and AN IV: 310–11; see also DN III: 123–25] bahussutā dhamma-dharā dhamma-anudhamma-paṭipannā sāmīci-paṭipannā anudhamma-cārino, sakam ācariyakaṃ uggahetvā ācikkhissanti desissanti paññapessanti paṭṭhapessanti vivarissanti vibhajissanti uttāni-karissanti, uppannaṃ parappavādaṃ saha dhammena suniggahitan niggahetvā sappāṭihāriyaṃ dhammaṃ desissantī 'ti," etc. This is repeated referring to bhikkhuniyo, upāsakā, and upāsikā, all of whom shall be teaching the Dhamma to others. The Buddha's vow ends with the words (p. 64): "na tāv' āhaṃ pāpima parinibbāyissāmi, yāva me idaṃ brahmacariyaṃ na iddhaṃ ca bhavissati phītaṃ ca vitthārikaṃ bahujaññaṃ puthubhūtaṃ yāva devamanussehi suppakāsitan ti." I prefer this version because of its interpretation of the last words. It reads *yāva devamanussehi* (p. 64 line 16) "among devas and humans." This interpretation emphasizes the universal character (or spirit) of the words, while the reading of the DN: *yāvad eva manussehi* seems to indicate a limitation

In this sutta and its parallels the Buddha's answer to Māra shows that now all the conditions for his final nibbāna have been fulfilled[53] and that it will take place in three months' time. The nondiscriminative view of women in this passage seems to be due to the ideal of universal salvation, which includes the complete fourfold community. The Buddha has come for the benefit of all beings of all spheres, and for this universal mission it is necessary not to exclude women. Corresponding to that view, this statement contains the mission for both genders and for both kinds of followers—ordained and lay—to teach the Dhamma.

One of the most well-known sūtras in Sanskrit bears the title *Sūtra of the Four Assemblies* (*Catuṣpariṣat-sūtra*), and at the end of this sūtra the Blessed One sends his disciples in all directions to teach divine and human beings to their benefit and happiness. In the tradition of Mahāsāṅghika-Lokottaravādin, the fourfold community plays an important role in the story of Mahāpajāpatī. It is used as a main argument for why women should be permitted to become nuns. Asked by Ānanda the Buddha has to confirm that all former Buddhas had four assemblies.[54]

A further example of such an integrative view is the *Mahāvacchagotta-sutta* (MN 73), where the Buddha assures the wandering ascetic (*paribbājako*) Vacchagotta that there are not only far more than five hundred bhikkhus but also far more than five hundred bhikkhunīs who had reached the true goal, and that the number of male lay followers (*upāsakas*) equals the number of female lay followers (*upāsikās*) who will inevitably, after a spontaneous (re)birth in the pure abodes, attain final nibbāna.[55] We hear that the holy life would be deficient if within any one of the four classes—bhikkhus or bhikkhunīs, upāsakas or upāsikās—no accomplished ones

---

to the region of human beings. (Cf. the discussion under *yāva* in the PED, p. 555.) The "universal" interpretation is supported by parallels; see, e.g., AN IV: 311 and Buddhaghosa's commentary on SN V: 261 and II: 107 (Spk III: 253 and II: 118–19); it occurs also in Sanskrit sources, see, e.g., Divy 202 and 208: *yāvad deva-manuṣyebhyaḥ*.

53. The *Pāsādika-sutta* (DN III: 123–26) deals in detail with the fulfillment of these conditions and the perfection of the holy life.

54. Roth 1970: 12 and 14. See also Sp IV: 1290.

55. See the translation at Ñāṇamoli and Bodhi 1995: 596–99. To be precise, the classes of male and female lay followers in their white garments (*odāta-vasanā*) are subdivided into those who live a celibate life (*brahmacārino*/*brahmacāriniyo*) and those who enjoy sensual pleasures (*kāmabhogino*/*kāmabhoginiyo*).

were to be found. To put it in a positive way, each of the four classes of disciples contributes to the accomplishment of the holy life.[56]

In this sutta it is remarkable that it is not the Buddha nor one of his bhikkhus who deals with the four classes and their importance for the whole community but the ascetic Vacchagotta, before having converted to Buddhism. Does this mean that the idea of the fourfold assembly was inspired by another sect? In the religion of the Jains, the four communities were probably established as in early Buddhism. The *Upāli-sutta* (MN 56) mentions two classes of Jain followers, *nigaṇṭhas* and *nigaṇṭhīs*, who used to come to the house of Upāli, a chief patron and lay devotee of the Jains before his conversion.[57] It has been shown that the Jain sect of Śvetāmbaras (split off probably about 300 B.C.E.) considered women to be able to receive release (*nirvāṇa*).[58] Horner even presupposes that Jain nunneries already existed,[59] which the Buddha must have been aware of because both orders had their center in the same region (Bihar) reigned by King Bimbisāra, a well-known patron of debates between adherents of various sects. From later sources we hear that at Mahāvīra's death,[60] which apparently took place before the Buddha's parinibbāna, there were even more nuns (36,000) and laywomen (318,000) than monks (only 14,000) and laymen (159,000).[61] So it appears plausible that the Buddha's agreement to admit women into the order may have been influenced by the Jains' attitude toward women.

Perhaps one could agree with Horner and say that if Buddhist women

56. See MN I: 492–93: "idaṃ brahmacariyaṃ aparipūraṃ abhavissa ten' aṅgena" and the corresponding positive formulation: "idaṃ brahmacariyaṃ paripūraṃ ten' aṅgena." In the *Pāsādika-sutta* (DN III: 122–26), the Buddha explains the same subject to the novice Cunda just after Nātaputta died and the Nigaṇṭhas were split into two parties [an indication of doubtful chronology]. *Aṅga* can mean a constituent part of a whole. A similar statement is found in the DN 33 (*Saṅgīti-sutta*), where nine unfortunate, inopportune conditions for leading the holy life are enumerated by Sāriputta, the sixth of which is to be "born in the border regions among foolish barbarians where there is no access for monks and nuns, or male and female lay-followers" (Walshe 1996: 506–7).

57. See Ñāṇamoli and Bodhi 1995: 485–87.

58. The aphorism "asti strī-nirvāṇaṃ puṃ-vat," i.e., "there is the highest goal for women as for men," is even ascribed to Nātaputta's predecessor Parśvanātha (Murcott 1991: 60).

59. Horner 1930: 108.

60. The date of Mahāvīra's death given by Murcott (1991: 59) is 468 B.C.E.

61. See under "Mahāvīra" in Bowker 2003: 625–26. See also Murcott 1991: 60.

had been more highly appreciated and Gotama had "also organized his lay-devotees, men and women, as thoroughly as Mahāvīra did, Buddhism would not have declined in the land of its birth, but would have continued, even though diminished, as Jainism has done, down to the present day."[62]

If, as this paper has argued, the Buddha had no intention of exluding women from the path of going forth and held their ultimate liberation to be a central element of the fulfillment of his own awakening vow, then one could claim that reviving the fourfold community would actually be reviving the real spirit of the Buddha.

In concluding, I'll recite the same words as those that conclude the Dhamma talk between Vacchagotta and the Buddha: "Just as the river Ganges inclines toward the sea, slopes toward the sea, flows toward the sea, and merges with the sea, so too Master Gotama's assembly with its homeless ones and its householders inclines toward nibbāna, slopes toward nibbāna, flows toward nibbāna, and merges with nibbāna."[63]

62. Horner 1930: 116.

63. Adapted from Ñāṇamoli and Bodhi 1995: 599 (MN I: 493). This simile is found in many places elsewhere in the suttas, too, but put in the mouth of the Buddha and referring only to the bhikkhus.

APPENDIX 1:
THE STORY OF THE ESTABLISHMENT OF THE ORDER OF NUNS ACCORDING TO THE THERAVĀDA TRADITION

Passages from *Cullavagga* X.1 (Vin II: 253–56) with a tentative translation from Pāli:

Mahāpajāpatī Gotamī to the Blessed One (three times):
sādhu bhante labheyya mātugāmo tathāgata-ppavedite dhamma-vinaye agārasmā anagāriyaṃ pabbajjan ti.

"It would be good, Venerable Sir, [if] women could have [the opportunity of] going forth from home into homelessness in the doctrine and discipline proclaimed by the Tathāgata."

The Blessed One to Mahāpajāpatī Gotamī (three times):
alaṃ gotami, mā te rucci mātugāmassa tathāgata-ppavedite dhamma-vinaye agārasmā anagāriyaṃ pabbajjā ti.

"Enough, Gotamī, let it not please you, the going forth of women from home into homelessness in the doctrine and discipline proclaimed by the Tathāgata."

Mahāpajāpatī Gotamī, her wish unfulfilled, follows the Buddha from Kapilavatthu to Vesālī with shaven head and the robes of a monk[64] and accompanied by [a deputation of] many (*saṃbahula*) Sakyan women....

Ānanda to the Blessed One:
esā bhante mahāpajāpatī gotamī sunehi pādehi...rudamānā bahi dvārakoṭṭhake ṭhitā, na bhagavā anujānāti mātugāmassa tathāgata-ppavedite dhamma-vinaye agārasmā anagāriyaṃ pabbajjan ti:

"Venerable Sir, this Mahāpajāpatī Gotamī is standing in front of the gateway with her feet swollen...crying and saying: 'The Blessed One does not allow the going forth of women from home into homelessness in the doctrine and discipline proclaimed by the Tathāgata':

64. "kese chedāpetvā kāsāyāni vatthāni acchadetvā."

(three times):
sādhu bhante labheyya mātugāmo tathāgata-ppavedite dhamma-vinaye agārasmā anagāriyaṃ pabbajjan ti.

"It would be good, Venerable Sir, [if] women could have [the opportunity of] going forth from home into homelessness in the doctrine and discipline proclaimed by the Tathāgata."

The Blessed One to Ānanda (three times):
alaṃ ānanda, mā te rucci mātugāmassa tathāgata-ppavedite dhamma-vinaye agārasmā anagāriyaṃ pabbajjā ti.

"Enough, Ānanda, let it not please you, the going forth of women from home into homelessness in the doctrine and discipline proclaimed by the Tathāgata."

Ānanda's deliberation:
yan nūnāhaṃ aññena pi pariyāyena bhagavantaṃ yāceyyaṃ mātugāmassa tathāgata-ppavedite dhamma-vinaye agārasmā anagāriyaṃ pabbajjan ti.

"What about asking the Blessed One in another way for the going forth of women from home into homelessness in the doctrine and discipline proclaimed by the Tathāgata?"

Ānanda to the Blessed One:
bhabbo nu kho bhante mātugāmo tathāgata-ppavedite dhamma-vinaye agārasmā anagāriyaṃ pabbajitvā sotāpatti-phalaṃ vā sakadāgāmi-phalaṃ vā anāgāmi-phalaṃ vā arahattaṃ vā sacchikātun ti.

"Now, Venerable Sir, are women able, after having gone forth from home into homelessness in the doctrine and discipline proclaimed by the Tathāgata, to realize the fruit of stream-entering or the fruit of once-returning or the fruit of non-returning or arhatship?"

The Blessed One to Ānanda:
bhabbo ānanda mātugāmo tathāgata-ppavedite dhamma-vinaye agārasmā anagāriyaṃ pabbajitvā sotāpatti-phalam pi sakadāgāmi-phalam pi anāgāmi-phalam pi arahattam pi sacchikātun ti.

"Women, Ānanda, having gone forth from home into homelessness in the doctrine and discipline proclaimed by the Tathāgata, are able to realize the fruit of stream-entering as well as the fruit of once-returning, the fruit of non-returning, and arhatship."

Ānanda to the Blessed One (his fourth request):

sace bhante bhabbo mātugāmo tathāgata-ppavedite dhamma-vinaye agārasmā anagāriyaṃ pabbajitvā sotāpatti-phalam pi sakadāgāmi-phalam pi anāgāmi-phalam pi arahattam pi sacchikātuṃ, bahūpakārā bhante mahāpajāpatī gotamī bhagavato mātucchā āpādikā posikā khīrassa dāyikā bhagavantaṃ janettiyā kālaṃkatāya thaññaṃ pāyesi: sādhu bhante labheyya mātugāmo tathāgata-ppavedite dhamma-vinaye agārasmā anagāriyaṃ pabbajjan ti.

"If, Venerable Sir, women, having gone forth from home into homelessness in the doctrine and discipline proclaimed by the Tathāgata, are able to realize the fruit of stream-entering as well as the fruit of once-returning, the fruit of non-returning, and arhatship, [then since], Venerable Sir, Mahāpajāpatī Gotamī, the Blessed One's aunt, [was] very helpful, having served him, fed him, gave him milk, suckled the Blessed One with milk of her breast after his mother's death,[65] it would be good, Venerable Sir, [if] women could [have the opportunity of] going forth from home into homelessness in the doctrine and discipline proclaimed by the Tathāgata."

The Blessed One to Ānanda:

sace ānanda mahāpajāpatī gotamī aṭṭha garudhamme paṭigaṇhāti, sā 'v' assā hotu upasampadā...[the eight garudhammas, beginning with the rule concerning salutation and ending with that which concerns the addressing of monks by nuns].

"If, Ānanda, Mahāpajāpatī Gotamī accepts eight heavy rules, just that shall be her full ordination[66]...[the eight garudhammas]."

Ānanda to Mahāpajāpatī Gotamī:

sace kho tvaṃ gotami aṭṭha garudhamme paṭigaṇheyyāsi, sā 'va te bhavissati upasampadā...[the eight garudhammas].

65. This phrase seems to have been taken over from MN 142 (*Dakkhiṇāvibhaṅga-sutta*), whose context it fits better. There Ānanda continues his speech beginning with the same word "very helpful (*bahūpākaro*)..." as used in the preceding sentence, whereas here this sentence seems to interrupt Ānanda's outline of arguing, which began with a conditional phrase.

66. This reply does not harmonize very well with the request.

"If you now, Gotamī, would accept eight heavy rules, just that will be your full ordination...[the eight garudhammas]."

Mahāpajāpatī Gotamī to Ānanda:
(her joyful acceptance of the eight rules expressed by a metaphorical image)

Ānanda to the Blessed One:
(report of Gotamī's acceptance of the eight rules)

The Blessed One to Ānanda:
sace ānanda nālabhissa mātugāmo tathāgata-ppavedite dhamma-vinaye agārasmā anagāriyaṃ pabbajjaṃ, cira-ṭṭhitikaṃ ānanda brahmacariyaṃ abhavissa, vassa-sahassaṃ sad-dhammo tiṭṭheyya. yato ca kho ānanda mātugāmo tathāgata-ppavedite dhamma-vinaye agārasmā anagāriyaṃ pabbajito, na dāni ānanda brahmacariyaṃ cira-ṭṭhitikaṃ bhavissati, pañc' eva dāni ānanda vassa-satāni sad-dhammo ṭhassati...

[three similes ending with the same formula:] *evam eva kho ānanda yasmiṃ dhamma-vinaye labhati mātugāmo agārasmā anagāriyaṃ pabbajjaṃ, na taṃ brahmacariyaṃ cira-ṭṭhitikaṃ hoti...*

[the analogy of prophylaxis:] *evam eva kho ānanda mayā paṭigacc' eva bhikkhunīnaṃ aṭṭha garudhammā paññattā yāvajīvaṃ anatikkamanīyā 'ti.*

"If, Ānanda, women had not gotten [the opportunity of] going forth from home into homelessness in the doctrine and discipline proclaimed by the Tathāgata, the holy life, Ānanda, would have lasted long, the true doctrine would continue for a thousand years, but now, Ānanda, since women have gone forth from home into homelessness in the doctrine and discipline proclaimed by the Tathāgatha, now, Ānanda, the holy life will not last long, now, Ānanda, the true doctrine will continue only for five hundred years...

[three similes ending with the same formula:] "Just so, Ānanda, in which doctrine and discipline women get [the opportunity of] going forth from home into homelessness, that holy life will not last long...

[the analogy of prophylaxis:] "Just so, Ānanda, are the eight heavy rules for nuns pronounced by me as a precaution, not to be transgressed all their lives."

APPENDIX 2:
THE STORY OF THE ESTABLISHMENT OF THE ORDER OF NUNS ACCORDING TO THE MŪLASARVĀSTIVĀDA TRADITION

Passages excerpted from the *Bhikṣuṇī-Karmavācanā* (Schmidt 1993: 242–46), with a tentative translation from Sanskrit:[67]

Mahāprajāpatī Gautamī to the Blessed One (three times):

[saced bhadantāsty avakāśo][68] *mātṛgrāmasya caturthasya śrāmaṇya-phalasyādhigamāya labheta mātṛgrāmaḥ svākhyāte dharmma-vinaye pravrajyām upasampadaṃ bhikṣuṇī-bhāvañ, caren mātṛgrāmo bhagavato ntike brahmacaryam iti.*

"[If it is possible, Venerable Sir,] women, in order to attain the fourth fruit of asceticism, should get the [opportunity of] going forth (into homelessness), [of] full ordination, [of] becoming a nun in the well-proclaimed[69] doctrine and discipline;[70] women should practice the holy life in the presence of the Blessed One."[71]

The Blessed One to Mahāprajāpatī Gautamī (three times):

evam eva tvaṃ gautami muṇḍā saṃghāṭī-prāvṛtā yāvajjīvaṃ kevalaṃ

67. This differs from Frances Wilson's translation in Paul 1979: 82ff.

68. Supplement to the text according to Schmidt 1993: 242n10.

69. *Svākhyāte* can also be translated "proclaimed by yourself," corresponding to the Pāli *tathāgata-ppavedite*. But I prefer "well-proclaimed" because the same expression is used in Ānanda's report to Mahāprajāpāti. Besides, *svākhyāte dharmma-vinaye* occurs very often in the *Bhikṣuṇī-Karmavācanā* (e.g., Schmidt 1993: 260) and seems to correspond to *svākhāto dhammo* ("the Doctrine is well proclaimed") in the *Mahāvagga* (e.g., CPS II: 206).

70. *Dharmma-vinaye* has to be considered a *dvandva*, one described as "the teaching of the Buddha in its completeness" (PED p. 623 "vinaya"). The refererence to *vinaya* seems in fact to be an anachronism.

71. "should get...in the presence of the Blessed One": This phrase is very similar to that one used, according to the CPS, by the early disciples when asking for their ordination (CPS II: 204): "labhemahi vayaṃ bhadanta svākhyāte dharma-vinaye pravrajyām upasaṃpadaṃ bhikṣu-bhāvam / carema vayaṃ bhagavato 'ntike brahmacaryam /." Cf. the SBV I: 147, 148, 206 and II: 141.

paripūrṇṇaṃ pariśuddhaṃ paryavadātaṃ brahmacaryañ cara, tat tava bhaviṣyati dīrgha-rātram arthāya hitāya sukhāyeti.

"Just so! You, Gautamī, practice all your life, with shaven head and clad in monastic robes,[72] the entirely,[73] fully perfect, fully pure, fully clean holy life! That will serve you well for a long time, to your benefit and happiness."

Ānanda to the Blessed One (only once):

saced bhadantāsty avakāśo mātṛgrāmasya caturthasya śrāmaṇya-phalasyādhigamāya labheta mātṛgrāmaḥ svākhyāte dharmma-vinaye pravrajyām upasampadaṃ bhikṣuṇī-bhāvañ, caren mātṛgrāmo bhagavato ntike brahmacaryam.

"If it is possible, Venerable Sir, women, in order to attain the fourth fruit of asceticism, should get the [opportunity of] going forth (into homelessness), [of] full ordination, [of] becoming a nun in the well-proclaimed doctrine and discipline, women should practice the holy life in the presence of the Blessed One."

The Blessed One to Ānanda (only once):

mā te ānanda mātṛgrāmasya svākhyāte dharmma-vinaye pravrajyā rocatāṃ mā upasampan mā bhikṣuṇī-bhāvaḥ. tat kasmād dhetor.[74] *yasminn ānanda dharmma-vinaye mātṛgrāmaḥ pravrajati nāsau dharmma-vinayaś cira-sthitiko bhavati...*

[three similes ending with the same formula:] *evam ev ānanda yasmin dharmma-vinaye mātṛgrāmaḥ pravrajati nāsau dharmma-vinayaś cira-sthitiko bhavati. api tv aham ānanda mātṛgrāmasyāṣṭau gurudharmmān*

72. In the Pāli canon *saṅghāṭī* is one of the three robes of the monks allowed by the Blessed One. It designates the outer robe or cloak, perhaps made of pieces of cloth sewn together (patchwork) (see, e.g., Vin I: 287 and 289). A similar combination of the words *muṇḍa* and *saṅghāṭī-prāvṛta* occurs also in the account of Upāli's ordination (SBV I: 206) and of Śroṇakoṭiviṃśa's ordination (SBV II: 141). Both monks are ordained by means of the *ehibhikṣu* formula.

73. *Kevalam* is also translated with "[you]" alone (cf. F. Wilson's translation, which is based on the previous edition by Ridding and La Vallée Poussin), but with regard to its position within this phrase it could better be taken as one of the attributes belonging to *brahmacaryam* (SWTF 2003: 123) or as an adverb added to *paripūrṇṇam...*, with the meaning: "absolutely," "in its entirety" (see PED p. 226: *kevala-paripuṇṇa* "fulfilled in its entirety" and Vin I: 11.1: *kevala-paripuṇṇam...brahmacariyam*).

74. Correction according to Schmidt 1993: 243n29.

prajñapayāmy āvaraṇāyānatikramaṇāya yatra mātṛgrāmeṇa yāvajjīvaṃ śikṣā karaṇīyā / ...

[the analogy of prophylaxis:] *evam ev ānanda mātṛgrāmasyāṣṭau gurudharmmān prajñapayāmy āvaraṇāyānatikramaṇāya yatra mātṛgrām-eṇa yāvajjīvaṃ śikṣā karaṇīyā* / ...[the eight gurudharmas].

saced ānanda mahāprajāpatī gautamī imān aṣṭau gurudharmmān samādāya varttiṣyate saiva tasyāḥ pravrajyā saivopasampat sa eva bhikṣuṇī-bhāvaḥ.

"Let it not please you,[75] Ānanda, the women's going forth [into homelessness] in the well-proclaimed doctrine and discipline, not their full ordination, not their becoming a nun. Why? The doctrine and discipline, Ānanda, in which women go forth [into homelessness] does[76] not last long...

[three similes ending with the same formula]: "Just so, the doctrine and discipline, Ānanda, in which women go forth [into homelessness] does not last long. And yet, Ānanda, I pronounce eight heavy rules for women for [their] restraint and not-transgressing, in which the women have to train themselves all their lives...

[the analogy of prophylaxis:] "Just so, Ānanda, I pronounce eight heavy rules for women for [their] restraint and not-transgressing, in which the women have to train themselves all their lives...[the eight gurudharmas, beginning with the rule concerning ordination ending with that concerning salutation].

"If, Ānanda, Mahāprajāpatī Gautamī will accept these eight heavy rules and live [according to them], just that [will be] her going forth, just that her full ordination, just that her becoming a nun."

Ānanda to Mahāprajāpatī Gautamī:

labdhavān gautami mātṛgrāmaḥ svākhyāte dharmma-vinaye pravrajyām upasampadaṃ bhikṣuṇī-bhāvam. api tu gautami bhagavatā mātṛgrām-asyāṣṭau gurudharmmāḥ prajñaptāḥ āvaraṇāyānatikramaṇāya yatra mātṛgrāmeṇa yāvajjīvaṃ śikṣā karaṇīyā. / ...[the eight gurudharmas].

"Women, Gautamī, have the [opportunity of] going forth (*pravrajyā*) [into homelessness], [of] full ordination, [of] becoming a nun in the well-

75. Or: "It may not please you," "please, do not [request]." It is the same word as in Cv X.1.

76. Grammatically singular: "does" because *dharma-vinaya* is understood to be a unity.

proclaimed doctrine and discipline. And yet, Gautamī, the Blessed One has pronounced eight heavy rules for women for [their] restraint and not-transgressing, in which the women have to train themselves all their lives... [the eight gurudharmas]."

Here the Sanskrit text breaks off.

Women's Renunciation in Early Buddhism:

THE FOUR ASSEMBLIES AND THE FOUNDATION OF THE ORDER OF NUNS

Anālayo[1]

Introduction

THIS CHAPTER seeks to examine selected early canonical texts that portray the Buddha's attitude toward the order of nuns. In the first part of the essay a number of passages are taken up that show the importance of the order of nuns as one of the four assemblies, followed by surveying several instances that testify to the outstanding accomplishments of the early nuns. The second part turns to the account of the foundation of the order of nuns, examining the prediction of decline the Buddha is reported to have pronounced on this occasion, the eight special rules, Ānanda's intervention, and finally what the texts indicate to have been the motivation behind the Buddha's initial refusal to permit Mahāprajāpatī Gautamī's going forth.

The Four Assemblies

For an assessment of the Buddha's attitude toward the order of nuns according to the canonical texts, a passage of particular significance can be found in the *Mahāparinirvāṇa-sūtra* preserved in Pāli, in Sanskrit fragments, in Tibetan translation, and in four Chinese translations. According to this passage, soon after his awakening the Buddha made an explicit

1. I am indebted to Bhikkhu Bodhi, Bhikkhu Pāsādika, Bhikkhunī Tathālokā, and Ken Su for comments on an earlier draft of this article.

proclamation that it was his plan to establish and train four assemblies of disciples: monks, nuns, male lay followers, and female lay followers. The background to this proclamation was a suggestion by Māra, the Evil One in Buddhist literature, who had insinuated that the time for the Buddha's passing away had already come. In the *Mahāparinibbāna-sutta* of the Pāli canon, the Buddha's statement reads:

> I will not pass away until I have nun disciples who are wise, well trained, self-confident, and learned.[2]

The *Saṅghabhedavastu* of the (Mūla-)sarvāstivāda Vinaya, preserved in Sanskrit, Tibetan, and Chinese, indicates that this suggestion by Māra took place when the Buddha had been afflicted by disease after partaking of his first meal after awakening.[3]

The implication of this passage, preserved in each of the major Buddhist languages and by a range of different Buddhist schools, would be that soon after his awakening the Buddha had decided to establish an order of nuns. From the perspective of the *Buddhavaṃsa*, a later work in the Theravāda canon, this is not at all surprising, since other past Buddhas also had nun

2. DN 16 at DN II: 105,8: *na ... parinibbāyissāmi yāva me bhikkhuniyo na sāvikā bhavissanti viyattā vinītā visāradā bahussutā*. The parallel Sanskrit fragment 361 folio 165 R2–3 in Waldschmidt 1950: 53 similarly refers to the establishment of nuns in wisdom: *yāvan-me śrāvakā paṇḍit[ā] bhaviṣyaṃti vyaktā medhāvinaḥ ... bhikṣuṇya*; the same is the case for the Tibetan parallel in Waldschmidt 1951: 209,23: *dge slong ma dang ... mkhas pa gsal ba shes rab tu ldan pa*. Of the Chinese parallels, while DĀ 2 at T I: 15c4 mentions their teaching abilities in particular: 為人導師，演布經教，顯於句義 ... 諸比丘尼; T 6 at T I: 180b27 refers to their wisdom: 比丘尼，令皆智慧; and T 7 at T I: 191b28 describes their ability to overcome opponents, 比丘尼 ... 降伏諸餘外道 (an ability also mentioned in the other versions). T 5 at T I: 165a19 refers to the nuns only implicitly by speaking of the wisdom and attainment of the path by the four types of disciples: 須我四輩弟子黠慧得道. The corresponding passage in the (Mūla-)sarvāstivāda Vinaya T 1451 at T XXIV: 387c27 also speaks of the wisdom of the nuns: 若我聖眾聲聞弟子，未有智慧通達聰明 ... 苾芻尼; as is the case for a record of this statement in the *Divyāvadāna* in Cowell and Neil 1886: 202,10: *śrāvakāḥ paṇḍitā bhaviṣyanti vyaktā vinītā viśāradāḥ ... bhikṣuṇya*. In addition to being found in DN 16, the same statement recurs in the Pāli canon in SN 51.10 at SN V: 261,18; AN 8.70 at AN IV: 310,32; Ud 6.1 at Ud 63,32. Another occurrence in the Chinese canon is T 383 at T XII: 1010c29.

3. Gnoli 1977: 125,10; with its Tibetan parallel at *'Dul ba gzhi*, Kangyur Q ('dul ba) *ce*, 35a8; and its Chinese parallel T 1450 at T XXIV: 125c16.

disciples.[4] From this it would follow that for a Buddha to establish an order of nuns is a natural course of events.

Other early canonical passages concur with the indication given in the *Mahāparinirvāṇa-sūtra* that the order of nuns is an integral part of the Buddhist community. According to the *Mahāvacchagotta-sutta* of the *Majjhima-nikāya* and its Chinese parallels in the two extant *Saṃyukta-āgama* translations, even those outside of the Buddhist order perceived the existence of proficient Buddhist nuns as indispensable for the completeness of the Buddha's dispensation. The Pāli and Chinese versions of this discourse report that the wanderer Vacchagotta had inquired about the degree to which the four assemblies of Buddhist disciples had reached accomplishment in the Buddha's teaching. In reply, the Buddha clarified that each of the four assemblies had indeed reached accomplishment, and as far as the assembly of nuns was concerned, over five hundred nuns had attained the final goal. On hearing this reply, Vacchagotta expressed his admiration and satisfaction, proclaiming that without accomplished nuns, the Buddha's teaching would be deficient. In the Pāli version, this proclamation reads:

> If in this teaching only Master Gotama and the monks were accomplished, but there would not be accomplished nuns, then this holy life would be deficient in that respect.[5]

4. Skilling 2000: 56 notes that the *Buddhavaṃsa* records the names of the two outstanding nun disciples of each Buddha of the past, cf. verses 2.213 at Bv 23,5; 3.31 at Bv 28,3; 4.24 at Bv 30,21; 5.27 at Bv 33,25; 6.22 at Bv 36,18; 7.22 at Bv 39,15; 8.23 at Bv 42,19; 9.22 at Bv 45,17; 10.24 at Bv 48,19; 11.25 at Bv 51,23; 12.24 at Bv 54,19; 13.26 at Bv 57,23; 14.21 at Bv 60,13; 15.20 at Bv 63,11; 16.19 at Bv 66,11; 17.19 at Bv 69,11; 18.22 at Bv 72,17; 19.20 at Bv 75,11; 20.29 at Bv 78,29; 21.21 at Bv 81,15; 22.24 at Bv 84,21; 23.21 at Bv 87,13; 24.23 at Bv 90,19; 25.40 at Bv 94,23. The same is also reflected in *Therī-apadāna* verse 20.4 at Ap 557,23, where Padumuttara Buddha proclaims the outstanding accomplishment of one of his nuns. According to the *Divyāvadāna* in Cowell and Neil 1886: 61,18, the future Buddha Maitreya will also have nun disciples, as the queen at that time will go forth under him, together with her entourage. Harvey 2000: 385 notes that the *Buddhavaṃsa* also predicts the names of Gautama Buddha's foremost nun disciples (verse 2.67 at Bv 13,16), concluding that, from the perspective of the Buddhist tradition, it would have been "impossible for the Buddha not to have agreed finally to Gotamī's request."

5. MN 73 at MN I: 492,4: *sace ... imaṃ dhammaṃ bhavañc' eva gotamo ārādhako abhavissa bhikkhū ca ... no ca kho bhikkhuniyo ārādhikā abhaviṃsu, evam idaṃ brahmacariyaṃ aparipūraṃ abhavissa ten' aṅgena*. The parallel statements are SĀ 964 at T II: 247a9: 若沙門瞿曇成等正覺 ... 比丘尼 ... 不得如是功德者，則不滿足; and SĀ^2 198 at T II: 446c9: 瞿曇，汝於菩提，已得正覺 ... 比丘尼 ... 不具道行，便為支不滿足.

The *Mahāvacchagotta-sutta* and its Chinese parallels continue by recording that the completeness of the Buddha's teaching was inspiring enough for Vacchagotta to request ordination as a Buddhist monk. This is remarkable insofar as other discourses depict the same wanderer Vacchagotta as someone who on numerous occasions approached the Buddha or his senior disciples with questions on various philosophical matters.[6] The message conveyed by the *Mahāvacchagotta-sutta* and its Chinese parallels is that the Buddhist order's possession of accomplished disciples in each of the four assemblies, including the nuns, achieved what endless discussions on philosophical matters had not been able to bring about. It was this completeness of the Buddhist order that provided sufficient inspiration for an outside wanderer to desire to become a member of this Buddhist order himself. The texts also indicate that his inspiration was well founded, since the *Mahāvacchagotta-sutta* and its Chinese parallels record that he eventually became an accomplished disciple himself by reaching the final goal of total liberation.[7]

According to a discourse in the *Saṃyukta-āgama*, the Buddha also expected the four assemblies to serve as a source of inspiration for each other. This discourse reports how on one occasion a monk went begging with a scattered mind and in an unrestrained manner. While walking for alms he saw the Buddha from afar, which immediately caused him to collect himself. Back at the monastery, the Buddha advised the monk to collect himself in the same manner when seeing a monk, a nun, or a lay follower on the streets of the town.[8] This discourse shows that seeing a nun could serve as a source of inspiration for a monk. A discourse in the *Ekottarika-āgama* then presents the same theme from the perspective of a lay follower, reporting that for King Pasenadi to see any member of the four assemblies served as a source of inspiration.[9]

6. The Pāli Nikāyas contain over sixty discourses that deal with Vacchagotta's questions, e.g., MN 71–72 at MN I: 481–89; SN 33.1–55 at SN III: 257–63; SN 44.7–11 at SN IV: 391–402; and AN 3.57 at AN I: 160–62.

7. MN 73 at MN I: 496,31; SĀ 964 at T II: 247b28; and SĀ² 198 at T II: 447a22.

8. SĀ 1080 at T II: 283a6: 若見比丘，亦應自攝持，若復見比丘尼，優婆塞，優婆夷，亦當如是攝持諸根.

9. EĀ 23.1 at T II: 611b15: 我若見比丘，比丘尼，優婆塞，優婆斯，歡喜心意向如來者.

Thus a Buddhist community that lacks an order of accomplished nuns is deficient and unable to arouse the type of inspiration that, according to the *Mahāvacchagotta-sutta* and its parallels, had motivated a wanderer caught up in philosophical speculation to go forth as a Buddhist monk and become an arahant. In fact, according to a discourse in the *Aṅguttara-nikāya* and its *Madhyama-āgama* parallel, as well as a quotation in Nāgārjuna's *Sūtrasamuccaya* preserved in Tibetan, being reborn in a border country of the type where the four assemblies, including the nuns, are not found is a most unfortunate condition.[10]

The theme of the completeness of the Buddhist order comes up again in the *Pāsādika-sutta*, according to which the successfulness of the Buddha's teaching can be seen in its possession of four assemblies, including senior nuns, nuns of middle standing, and recently ordained nuns.[11] The Chinese parallel to the *Pāsādika-sutta* does not distinguish between nuns of different ordination age, but simply states that the holy life proclaimed by the Buddha is complete as each of the four assemblies, including the assembly of nuns, benefits from the Dharma, and is able to teach it to others.[12] In a similar vein, another discourse in the *Dīrgha-āgama* proclaims that one of the outstanding qualities of the Buddha is his being endowed with four assemblies of disciples, including an assembly of nuns. In this respect, he was considered superior to anyone else, whether past, present, or future.[13]

The *Lakkhaṇa-sutta* of the *Dīgha-nikāya* relates the Buddha's possession of all four assemblies of disciples to one of his thirty-two superior bodily marks. This discourse explains that the wheel marks on the soles of the Buddha's feet foretold his destiny of being surrounded by a large retinue

10. AN 8.29 at AN IV: 226,8: *paccantimesu janapadesu paccājāto hoti ... yatha n' atthi gati bhikkhūnaṃ bhikkhunīnaṃ upāsakānaṃ upāsikānaṃ* (see also DN 33 at DN III: 264,12); MĀ 124 at T I: 613b11: 生在邊國夷狄之中 ... 若無比丘，比丘尼，優婆塞，優婆夷; Pāsādika 1989: 6,15: *mtha' 'khob kyi mi ... dge slong dang, dge slong ma dang, dge bsnyen dang, dge bsnyen ma mi 'ong ba'i nang du skyes pa yin no.*

11. DN 29 at DN III: 125,25: *santi kho pana me ... etarahi therā bhikkhuniyo sāvikā ... majjhimā bhikkhuniyo sāvikā ... navā bhikkhuniyo sāvikā ... etarahi kho pana me ... brahmacariyaṃ iddhañca phītañca vitthārikaṃ bāhu jaññaṃ puthubhūtaṃ yavad eva manussehi suppakāsitaṃ.*

12. DĀ 17 at T I: 73c25: 自獲己利，復能受法為人說法 ... 比丘，比丘尼，優婆塞，優婆夷皆亦如是.

13. DĀ 3 at T I: 31a1: 如來大眾成就，所謂比丘，比丘尼，優婆塞，優婆夷，不見過去，未來，現在大眾成就，如佛者也.

that included an assembly of nuns.[14] The significance given to this bodily mark in the *Lakkhaṇa-sutta* further enforces the impression that, from the perspective of the early canonical texts, an order of nuns is intrinsic to the condition of being a Buddha.

The degree to which the existence of nuns is an integral requirement for the welfare of the Buddha's dispensation and for its stability is highlighted in a discourse in the *Saṃyutta-nikāya*. This discourse points out that for ensuring the long duration of the Dharma and preventing its disappearance, all four assemblies, including the nuns, should dwell with respect toward their teacher, the teaching, the community, the training, and the development of concentration.[15] This passage considers the existence of nuns an integral requirement for the welfare and stability of the Buddha's dispensation.

The theme of respect is broached from a slightly different angle by a discourse in the *Aṅguttara-nikāya*, according to which the four assemblies should be respectful toward their teacher, the teaching, the community, the training, and toward each other. Notably, this discourse treats in particular the conditions that lead to the continuity of the Dharma after the Buddha's passing away.[16]

Though the contrast in these discourses is between dwelling with and without respect, the explicit mention of the nuns makes it clear that they are considered an integral part of the Buddhist community, and their proper conduct is perceived as an important contribution to the stability and duration of the Dharma.[17] In fact, since for security reasons the nuns

14. DN 30 at DN III: 148,18: *mahāparivāro hoti, mahā 'ssa hoti parivāro bhikkhū bhikkhuniyo upāsakā upāsikāyo.*

15. SN 16.13 at SN II: 225,8: *bhikkhū bhikkhuniyo upāsakā upāsikāyo satthari ... dhamme ... saṅghe ... sikkhāya ... samādhismiṃ sagāravā viharanti sappaṭissā. Ime kho ... pañca dhammā saddhammassa ṭhitiyā asammosāya anantaradhānāya saṃvattanti.* A Chinese parallel to this discourse, SĀ 906 at T II: 226c15, mentions only the monks. Another Chinese parallel, SĀ[2] 121 at T II: 419c6, speaks of respect without specifying the subject, so that in this case it is open to conjecture whether only the monks are intended or all four assemblies.

16. AN 5.201 at AN III: 247,20: *bhikkhū bhikkhuniyo upāsakā upāsikāyo satthari ... dhamme ... saṅghe ... sikkhāya ... aññamaññaṃ sagāravā viharanti sappaṭissā. Ayaṃ kho ... paccayo yena tathāgate parinibbute saddhammo ciraṭṭhitiko hoti*; see also AN 6.40 at AN III: 340,13 and AN 7.56 at AN IV: 84,22.

17. According to Suvimalee 2005: 225, "all four components of the Buddhist society are mentioned as having equal value and responsibility in establishing the dhamma in society."

were not able to live in secluded spots in the way this was undertaken by the early monks, one would expect the nuns to have had closer relationships with the Buddhist laity. Such closer association with the laity and the activities of nuns as teachers and spiritual guides for lay disciples could well have been an important factor for the growth of the early Buddhist community.[18] From this perspective, then, we might look to the order of nuns as one of the central factors that helped to firmly establish the Buddha's teachings and thereby contributed to ensuring its survival until the modern day.

That the nuns were an integral part of the early Buddhist monastic community can also be deduced from a list of gift recipients in the *Dakkhiṇāvibhaṅga-sutta* and its *Madhyama-āgama* parallel. These two discourses indicate that a gift given to the community of monks and nuns together is superior to a gift given only to the community of monks.[19] Hence from the perspective of merit, the absence of a community of nuns would also result in a deficiency of the order in its function as a recipient of gifts. In addition to being treated together as superior recipients of offerings, monks and nuns are also reckoned together when it comes to receiving teachings, as they constitute the superior field for the Buddha's instructions.[20]

A discourse in the *Aṅguttara-nikāya* is quite explicit with respect to the role to be played by Buddhist nuns, as it proclaims that a nun who is wise, disciplined, and self-confident, who is learned and practices according to the Dharma, will illuminate the whole community. The same is stated with respect to a member of each of the other three assemblies, after which the discourse concludes with the following verse:

> A monk who is endowed with ethical conduct,
> a nun who is learned,
> a male lay disciple who has confidence,

18. Barua 1997: 75 suggests that "the rapid expansion of Buddhism was carried on by the preaching of the nuns"; see also Willis 1985: 77 on the importance of the support given by women in general for the prospering of early Buddhism.

19. This is implicit in a listing of altogether seven types of gifts in MN 142 at MN III: 255,28, MĀ 180 at T I: 722a22, T84 at T I: 904a16, and *Mgon pa'i bstan chos*, Tengyur Q *tu*, 290a8..

20. SN 42.7 at SN IV: 315,18: *seyyathāpi ... khettam aggam evam eva mayhaṃ bhikkhu-bhikkhuniyo*; SĀ 915 at T II: 231a17: 如彼沃壤肥澤田者，我諸比丘，比丘尼亦復如是 (adopting 壤 from the original simile at line 9); and SĀ[2] 130 at T II: 424b1: 上田，如我弟子，諸比丘，比丘尼.

and a confident female lay disciple:
these illuminate the community,
these are the community's illuminations.[21]

It is noteworthy that this listing should treat male and female lay disciples in the same manner but differentiate between the monastic disciples by highlighting ethics in the case of a monk and learnedness in the case of a nun. Precisely the same presentation recurs in the verses at the end of a *Saṃyukta-āgama* parallel and an *Ekottarika-āgama* parallel to this discourse.[22] This is not to say that the nuns would not illuminate the community by way of their ethical conduct, which is stated explicitly in another discourse in the *Aṅguttara-nikāya*.[23] But apparently their learnedness was outstanding enough for the concluding verse of three versions of this discourse to highlight this particular aspect.

Outstanding Nuns

That the early Buddhist nuns were quite learned is highlighted repeatedly in the Pāli Vinaya, which records that the nuns Thullanandā and Bhaddā Kāpilānī were learned and experts at preaching the Dharma.[24] According to the *Therīgāthā*, the similarly learned and virtuous nun Sumedhā was an expert at teaching;[25] and the learned and virtuous nun Jinadattā was an

21. AN 4.7 at A II: 8,22: *bhikkhu ca sīlasampanno, bhikkhunī ca bahussutā, upāsako ca yo saddho, yā ca saddhā upāsikā, ete kho saṅghaṃ sobhenti, ete hi saṅghasobhanā.*

22. SĀ 873 at T II: 220c11: 比丘持淨戒，比丘尼多聞，優婆塞淨信，優婆夷亦然; EĀ 27.7 at T II: 645c29: 比丘戒成就，比丘尼多聞，優婆塞有信，優婆斯亦爾.

23. AN 4.211 at AN II: 226,1: *bhikkhunī ... sīlavatī kalyāṇadhammā parisa-sobhaṇā*. In fact, the commentary on the verses in AN 4.7, Mp III: 7,17 explains that the qualities mentioned in relation to one or the other of the disciples should be understood to apply to all of them.

24. The nun Thullanandā is introduced as *bahussutā bhāṇikā visāradā paṭṭhā dhammiṃ kathaṃ kātuṃ* at Vin IV: 254,4; Vin IV: 255,4; Vin IV: 256,23; Vin IV: 285,18; Vin IV: 290,4; Vin IV: 292,14; and Vin IV: 302,21; epithets accorded at Vin IV: 290,6 and Vin IV: 292,14 also to the nun Bhaddā Kāpilānī.

25. Thī 449 introduces her as *sīlavatī cittakathikā bahussutā buddhasāsane vinītā*. According to Findly 2000: 142, Sumedhā and several other outstanding early nuns "continue to be models for women educators in all traditions of Buddhism."

expert in the Vinaya.[26] The *Ekottarika-āgama* concludes a meeting between the Buddha and Mahāprajāpatī Gautamī with the Buddha proclaiming her as outstanding among his disciples for her wide knowledge.[27] A discourse in the *Saṃyutta-nikāya* records the reputation of the nun Khemā for her wisdom and her capability as a speaker.[28] According to another discourse in the *Saṃyutta-nikāya*, together with its *Saṃyukta-āgama* parallel and a passage in the Mahāsāṅghika Bhikṣuṇīvinaya preserved in Sanskrit, Sukkā was such an outstanding nun that even spirits would roam the roads of the town and chastise all those who did not come to listen to her teachings.[29]

Not only the Buddhist canonical scriptures, but also inscriptions in ancient India testify to the learnedness of Buddhist nuns. One of these inscriptions indicates that a nun had performed the impressive deed of memorizing the entire *Tripiṭaka*.[30]

The *Divyāvadāna* also speaks of nuns who had committed the Tripiṭaka to memory,[31] and the *Dīpavaṃsa* similarly reports that nuns in Ceylon had memorized the Vinaya, the five Nikāyas, and the seven works of the Abhidhamma.[32]

The remarkable abilities of the early nuns in matters of memorization is again highlighted in the *Avadānaśataka*, which reports that the nun Somā performed the amazing feat of committing the entire code of rules

26. Thī 427 qualifies her as *vinayadharī bahussutā sīlasampannā*.

27. EĀ 18.8 at T II: 592c26: 我聲聞中第一弟子廣識多知，所謂大愛道是.

28. SN 44.1 at SN IV: 374,23: *paṇḍitā viyattā medhāvinī bahussutā cittakathī kalyāṇapaṭibhānā*. Skilling 2001: 143 notes that she also receives praise for her great wisdom and eloquence in the *Avadānaśataka* in Speyer 1970: 50,9: *eṣā 'grā ... mahāprājñānāṃ mahāpratibhānānaṃ*.

29. SN 10.9 at SN I: 212,27: *kim me katā rājagahe manussā, madhupītā va acchare ye, sukkaṃ na payirūpāsanti, desentim amataṃ padaṃ* (cf. also Thī 54); SĀ 1327 at T II: 365b1: 王舍城人民，醉酒眠睡臥，不勤供養彼，叔迦比丘尼 ... 善說離垢法，涅槃清涼處; Roth 1970: 112,22: *kiṃ rājagṛhe manuṣyā, madhu-mattāvatiṣṭhanti, ye śuklān na paryupāsanti daivasikān dharmān uttamā*.

30. Inscriptions no. 38 and 925 in Lüders 1973: 8 and 94 refer to the nun Buddhamitrā as a *trēpiṭikā*. For a survey of inscriptional references to nuns, see Skilling 1993/94; on references to nuns in the Sāñchī inscriptions in particular, see Barnes 2000 and Khan 1990.

31. Cowell and Neil 1886: 493,8: *bhikṣuṇyas tripiṭā dhārmakathikā*; see also Skilling 1994: 50.

32. Dīp verse 18.13 in Oldenberg 1879: 97,6; see also Skilling 2000: 64.

to memory after a single hearing from the Buddha.[33] This feat sets a noteworthy contrast to another discourse in which the same nun appears. The altogether three versions of this discourse, found in the *Saṃyutta-nikāya* and in the two extant Chinese translations of the *Saṃyukta-āgama*, report that Somā had been accosted by Māra with the suggestion that due to her innate lack of wisdom, a woman is incapable of reaching realization.[34] In reply, Somā not only clarified that sex is irrelevant once the mind has reached deeper concentration but also told Māra that it would be better for him to go with such talk to those who are still caught up in identifications of being a man or a woman.[35]

A record of a profound exposition on various intricate points of doctrine delivered by the nun Dhammadinnā can be found in the *Majjhima-nikāya*, preserved also in Chinese and Tibetan. When this exposition was reported to the Buddha, according to the three versions of this discourse, he lauded her exposition to the extent of declaring that he would have presented the matter in just the same way.[36] It is no wonder that the listing of eminent disciples in the *Aṅguttara-nikāya* and its counterpart in the

33. Speyer 1970: 22,4; see also the *Karmaśataka* summarized in Skilling 2001: 146.

34. SN 5.2 at SN I: 129,15: "what is to be attained by seers ... that a woman with her two finger wisdom cannot attain," *yaṃ taṃ isīhi pattabbaṃ ... na taṃ dvaṅgulapaññāya, sakkā pappotuṃ itthiyā*, a statement recurring in similar terms in the parallels SĀ 1199 at T II: 326b1 and SĀ² 215 at T II: 454a5. While in SĀ 1199 Māra also speaks of a woman's "two-finger wisdom," 二指智, in SĀ² 215 he instead refers to her "despicable and dirty wisdom," 鄙穢智. The reference to a woman's "two-finger wisdom" may have been a popular saying, as it recurs in a different context in the *Mahāvastu* in Senart 1897: 391,19 and 392,13; see also Kloppenborg 1995: 154 for an examination of the Pāli commentarial gloss on this imagery.

35. SN 5.2 at SN: I 129,24: *itthibhāvo kiṃ kayirā, cittamhi susamāhite ... yassa nūna siya evaṃ, 'itthāhaṃ' 'puriso 'ti vā ... taṃ māro vattum arahati*. After indicating in a similar way that womanhood is irrelevant once concentration has been developed, according to the two Chinese parallels she explained that such a statement was due to having the "perception of 'man' or 'woman,'" SĀ 1199 at T II: 326b8: 若於男女想, which in SĀ² 215 at T II: 454a10 reads: 若有男女相, where 相 appears to be an error for 想.

36. MN 44 at MN I: 304,36: *aham pi taṃ evam evaṃ byākareyyaṃ yathā taṃ Dhammadinnāya bhikkhuniyā byākataṃ*. MĀ 210 at T I: 790b1: 問我者， 我為 ... 亦以此義， 以此句， 以此文而答彼也; *Mngon pa'i bstan chos*, Tengyur Q (mngon pa) *tu*, 12a8: *nga yang don 'di nyid dang tshig dang yi ge 'di nyid kyis bstan pa bzhin du lung bstan par bya'o*. According to AN 10.28 at AN V: 58,24, the nun Kajaṅgalikā received the same confirmation from the Buddha for an exposition given by her. As noted by Harris 1999: 58, such instances involve a clear approval of women teaching men.

Ekottarika-āgama reckon Dhammadinnā as outstanding for her ability to expound the teachings.[37]

Dhammadinnā is not the only nun in this listing, which in each of its two versions, found in the *Aṅguttara-nikāya* and in the *Ekottarika-āgama*, covers a number of accomplished nun disciples that were outstanding for qualities like wisdom, meditative expertise and powers, abilities at teaching, and adherence to strict ethical conduct, comprising also the observance of ascetic practices.[38]

In addition to these listings of eminent disciples, a whole *saṃyutta* is dedicated to the nuns, the *Bhikkhunī-saṃyutta* of the *Saṃyutta-nikāya*, which has its counterpart in similar discourses found in both of the *Saṃyukta-āgamas* that have been preserved in Chinese translation.[39] Paeans of joy at having attained full awakening uttered by some of the Buddhist nuns are moreover collected in the *Therīgāthā*, a remarkable textual testimony to the degree to which some of the early Buddhist nuns had reached the acme of perfection in their practice of the Dharma.[40]

The *Ekottarika-āgama* depicts the extent to which some nuns had developed their meditative powers. A discourse in this collection reports that once, when the six heretical teachers had proclaimed their superiority to the

37. AN 1.14 at AN I: 25,21 and EĀ 5.2 at T II: 559a13.

38. AN 1.14 at AN I: 25,17 and EĀ 5.2 at T II: 558c26. Falk 1989: 161 notes that the listing in AN 1.14 "unquestionably carries a strong positive image of the nun." Skilling 2000: 55 highlights that the *Ekottarika-āgama* lists nearly four times as many outstanding nuns as its Pāli counterpart (in the case of monks the ratio is considerably less, as the *Ekottarika-āgama* lists only twice as many outstanding monks as the *Aṅguttara-nikāya*). A reference to this listing in an Uighur fragment in Gabain 1954: 55 also has a slightly higher number of outstanding nuns than AN 1.14.

39. SN 5.1–10 at SN I: 128–35; with its counterparts SĀ 1198–1207 at T II: 325c–329a and SĀ[2] 214–23 at T II: 453b–456b.

40. Blackstone 2000: 1 notes that the *Therīgāthā* may well be "the only canonical text in the world's religions that is attributed to female authorship and that focuses exclusively on women's religious experience." Though Chinese or Tibetan counterparts to this collection do not appear to have been preserved, a listing of texts in SĀ 1321 at T II: 362c11 refers to the "sayings of the nuns," 比丘尼所說; a reference also found in the (Mūla-)sarvāstivāda Vinaya in Dutt 1984: iv.188,9: *sthavirīgāthā*; and in *'Dul ba gzhi*, Kangyur Q ('dul ba) *khe*, 249b1 and *nge*, 214b5: *gnas brtan ma'i tshigs su bcad pa*. The Chinese translation T 1448 at T XXIV: 11b6, however, only lists the verses spoken by monks, 諸上座頌. Nevertheless, the Chinese canon has preserved a testimony to the outstanding accomplishment of Chinese nuns, the 比丘尼傳, T 2063 at T L: 934a–948a, translated in Tsai 1994.

Buddha, a nun who had overheard them rose up in the air through her supernormal powers and silenced them with a set of verses.[41] Another nun even performed various miracles and permutations before passing away.[42] Miraculous feats before passing away were according to yet another *Ekottarika-āgama* discourse also carried out by Mahāprajāpatī Gautamī together with an assembly of five hundred arahant nuns. A particularly noteworthy aspect of this discourse is that it portrays Mahāprajāpatī Gautamī passing away in a manner similar to the passing away of the Buddha.[43] According to the *Ekottarika-āgama* discourse, Mahāprajāpatī Gautamī entered successively the four absorptions, then the four immaterial attainments, and finally the attainment of cessation. After this she went through the same series of attainments in descending order, followed by again entering the four absorptions successively in an upward order until reaching the fourth absorption, at which point she passed away, an event accompanied by a great earthquake.[44] A similar report of Mahāprajāpatī Gautamī's passing away can also be found in the (Mūla-)sarvāstivāda Vinaya and in the *Apadāna*, a later text in the Theravāda canon.[45] According to the *Apadāna* account, the Buddha himself had asked Mahāprajāpatī Gautamī to perform a miracle in order to remove the wrong views of those fools who had doubts about women's ability to realize the Dharma.[46]

In sum, then, a survey of relevant instances and passages shows that according to the canonical texts, the Buddha had already planned right after his awakening to establish an order of nuns. The texts further indi-

41. EĀ 38.11 at T II: 728a6.

42. EĀ 42.3 at T II: 750c8.

43. For the Buddha's passing away, see DN 16 at DN II: 156,4; Waldschmidt 1951: 394; DĀ 2 at T I: 26b21; T 6 at T I: 188b19; and T 7 at T I: 205a3.

44. EĀ 52.1 at T II: 822a10.

45. T 1451 at T XXIV: 248c15 and Ap 540,7 (verses 17.145–48), which differ from the description in EĀ 52.1 insofar as they do not mention the attainment of cessation. T 1451 differs from the other accounts inasmuch as after having ascended and descended the eight attainments, she passes away from the first absorption (for yet others account of this event see, e.g., T 144 at T II: 868a10 or T 201 at T IV: 335b23). Murcott 1991: 18 comments that "clearly, the early sangha judged Pajapati to have been a remarkable person." On the significance of these *Apadāna* verses, see also Walters 1994: 372–76.

46. Ap 535,24 (verse 17.79): *thīnaṃ dhammābhisamaye, ye bālā vimatiṃ gatā, tesaṃ diṭṭhipahānatthaṃ, iddhiṃ dassehi gotamī*; see also Dhirasekera 1967: 157–58.

cate that the existence of this order of nuns as one of the four assemblies is an integral and indispensable requirement for the welfare and prosperity of the Dharma, and right from its beginning this order of nuns could count an impressive range of highly accomplished members.

The Foundation of the Order of Nuns

A different perspective emerges when one turns to the account of the foundation of the order of nuns. According to this account, a request made by Mahāprajāpatī Gautamī to be allowed to go forth was refused by the Buddha. Together with a group of like-minded women, Mahāprajāpatī Gautamī then shaved off her hair and put on robes, followed the Buddha from Kapilavastu to Vaiśālī, and repeated her request, which he again refused. At this point Ānanda intervened and convinced the Buddha to accede to her request. The Buddha finally gave his permission by stipulating eight special conditions to be observed, predicting that this permission will shorten the duration of his dispensation.

This account is found with some minor variations in the different Vinayas and also in several discourses. The agreement of the different Vinayas on the chief elements of this narration also extends to the Mahāsāṅghika-Lokottaravāda Vinaya, where a Sanskrit version of this account has been preserved.[47] In what follows, the different parts of the account of the foundation of the order of nuns will be examined in the reverse sequence of their original occurrence, starting from the prediction of decline, followed by examining the eight special rules, Ānanda's intervention, and finally the Buddha's refusal.

47. Roth 1970: 4–21. The Chinese version T 1425 at T XXII: 471a25 and T XXII: 514b4 is abbreviated and does not offer a full account, though a reference to the Buddha's refusal can be found in T 1425 at T XXII: 492a22 (on the relation between the Chinese and Sanskrit versions, see also de Jong 1974: 65). For a critical examination of the suggestion by Laut 1991 that an alternative account of the foundation of the order of nuns can be found in the *Maitrisimit* (see Geng 1988: 170–209), see Anālayo 2008: 106–8 and the remark by Hüsken 2000: 46n9.

The Prediction of Decline

The prediction that the existence of an order of nuns would shorten the duration of the Dharma stands in contrast to the passages examined so far. When evaluating the credibility of this prediction against the way other canonical texts portray the Buddha, it is difficult to believe that he could have been convinced to do anything detrimental to the duration of his own teaching. It also seems rather strange for the Buddha to attribute decline to the mere existence of nuns. After considering the different versions of the *Mahāparinirvāṇa-sūtra* that state the Buddha's intention to have an order of nuns, as well as other canonical texts reinforcing the idea that the existence of an order of nuns is an integral and indispensable part of the assembly of disciples of a Buddha, one would be at a loss to explain how and why the same condition should reduce the duration of the Buddha's dispensation by half.

The mere presence of women who had shaved their hair and donned robes with the determination to live a celibate life would not pose such a threat to monks that the lifetime of the whole dispensation would be diminished to such a degree. The real challenge may instead be seen in the presence of attractive laywomen, whom a monk would meet regularly on his daily alms rounds or during invitations for meals. Though instances of misconduct between monks and nuns are reported in the Vinayas, a perusal of the relevant regulations gives the impression that the most prominent cause for such problems should be attributed to relations with laywomen, not with nuns.[48]

Other discourses consistently relate decline and deterioration to mental qualities. This in fact represents a general feature of the early Buddhist teachings, in that the emphasis is on internal mental states or conditions as the determining factors for progress or regress, not on externals such as caste, race, or sex.[49] The factor mentioned most frequently in relation to a future

48. Gross 1993: 45 points out that "neither monks or nuns are tempted by each other, with very few exceptions. The real struggle is between monastics and laypeople."

49. Kabilsingh 1984: 36 comments that one of "the greatest contributions of Buddhism as a world religion lies in the fact that it raises itself above petty barriers of nation, caste, sex or colour."

decline of the Dharma is careless transmission of the teachings;[50] or such problems as lack of proper practice, lack of properly teaching the Dharma to others, and lack of respect for elders together with slackness in the practice and resistance to being admonished. Other passages, already discussed above, mention lack of respect toward the teacher, toward the teaching, and toward the training as causes for the decline of the Dharma.[51]

The need for a proper transmission of the teachings in order to avoid the decline of the Dharma is also the rationale behind a long listing of categories provided in the *Saṅgīti-sutta* and its parallels.[52] The *Mahāparinirvāṇa-sūtra* and its parallels mention in particular the mental qualities and practices conducive to awakening, which should be well remembered and undertaken in order to prevent the decline of the Dharma;[53] an injunction that is given for the same purpose in the *Pāsādika-sutta* as well.[54] Other passages highlight the importance of mindfulness practice for preventing the decline of the Dharma,[55] or attribute its decline to the presence of unwholesome mental states such as negligence and laziness.[56]

Hence to associate the decline of the Dharma with an external factor, such as the establishment of an order of nuns, stands in contrast to what other passages envisage as possible factors for such decline. This contrast is especially prominent in the case of those discourses that explicitly mention the nuns as one of the four assemblies whose proper conduct ensures

50. AN 2.3 at AN I: 59,1; AN 4.160 at AN II: 147,19; AN 5.154 at AN III: 176,18; AN 5.155 at AN III: 177,5; AN 5.156 at AN III: 178,24; to which Vin III: 8,5 adds that in the case of some former Buddhas a cause for a quicker disappearance of their dispensation was that they had not given sufficient teachings to be transmitted.

51. SN 16.13 at SN II: 225,8; AN 5.201 at AN III: 247,20; AN 6.40 at AN III: 340,13; and AN 7.56 at AN IV: 84,22.

52. DN 33 at DN III: 211,3; DĀ 9 at T I: 49c18; and the restored Sanskrit version in Stache-Rosen 1968: 45; cf. Schmidt 1997: 304 and Waldschmidt 1955: 314.

53. DN 16 at DN II: 119,25. While DĀ 2 at T I: 16c10 does not explicitly relate this to the duration of the Dharma, Sanskrit fragment S 360 folio 180 V2–3 in Waldschmidt 1950: 23 has preserved such a reference: *yath-edaṃ brahma[caryaṃ] cirasthitikaṃ syāt*; as does the Tibetan parallel in Waldschmidt 1951: 225,3: *ji ltar tshangs par spyod pa de 'dir yun ring du gnas shing.*

54. DN 29 at DN III: 127,14; where the parallel DĀ 17 at T I: 74a14 does not explicitly relate this to the duration of the Dharma.

55. SN 47.23 at SN V: 173,13 and SN 47.25 at SN V: 174,16; see also Williams 2002: 45.

56. AN 1.10 at AN I: 17,30.

the duration of the Dharma. One would not expect these discourses to mention well-behaved nuns as a factor required for the duration of the Dharma if, at the time when these discourses came into existence, the mere existence of nuns was already considered as causing a more rapid decline of the Dharma.

Besides, the prediction that the Dharma would only last for five hundred years has by now turned out to be incorrect.[57] Archaeological evidence shows that nuns were quite active in India even until the fourth century C.E.,[58] and for even longer in other countries.[59] In spite of that, or perhaps precisely because of that, the Dharma has survived even until today. The difficulty that arises from this unfulfilled prophecy has led to various strategies, such as extending the timespan[60] or reinterpreting this prediction to imply only a deterioration of the quality of the Dharma.[61]

57. Williams 2005: 11 highlights the "indisputable fact that time has refuted the prediction that the 'true Dhamma' would only last for five hundred years after the ordination of women." Here it needs to be noted that the suggestion by Law 1927: 87 that "Buddha's prediction was fulfilled when many troubles arose on account of the frequent meetings between the bhikkhus and the bhikkhunīs and [between] the bhikkhunīs and the lay people, as we find in the case of Thullanandā and Dabba the Mallian and also Abhirūpanandā and Sāḷho" does not appear to be correct, since the prediction does not speak about "troubles arising" right after the foundation of the order of nuns (to which it could be added that similar troubles arose between monks and laywomen after the foundation of the order of monks), but of the true Dharma lasting for five hundred years instead of a thousand years.

58. Schopen 1997: 248–50; see also Kieffer-Pülz 2000: 302–3. Law 1940: 31 notes that Aśoka's schism pillar edict envisages "schisms in the Saṅgha fomented by *bhikṣus* as well as *bhikṣuṇīs*," concluding that "the *bhikṣuṇīs* had at that time to be reckoned with as equally powerful factors in the matter of unity or division in the Buddhist Fraternity." Skilling 2000: 73 concludes that the inscriptions from the second century B.C.E. to the third century C.E. show not only that the nuns played an active role in the establishing of *caitya*s and *vihāra*s, but also that during this time they had the social status and economic means that enabled them to play such an active role.

59. Cf. Barnes 1996: 263 and Skilling 1993/94.

60. Nattier 2004: 211 notes that "early in the first millennium C.E., however, as the Buddhist community became aware that this initial figure of five hundred years had already passed, new traditions extending the life span of the dharma beyond this limit began to emerge." A detailed study of different time spans for the decline of the Dharma has been undertaken by Nattier 1991: 27–64, see also Yuyama 1992.

61. Mp I: 87,3 envisages that during five successive periods of a thousand years each, the ability to attain the paths and fruits and so on will disappear, followed by the disappearance of the keeping of the precepts; of the Tripiṭaka; of the external marks of monasticism; and of the relics. Notably, this commentarial gloss is made in relation to a discourse that has no

A problem with the first suggestion is that the relevant texts agree closely on predicting that the Buddha's teaching will last for only five hundred years.[62] There seems to be little scope for extending the time span beyond five hundred years.

To interpret the prediction to only mean a deterioration of the quality of the Dharma also does not fit the original statements, which clearly contrast the duration of the true teaching with its cessation.[63] In other contexts, the

---

relationship to the five hundred years prediction but instead treats other causes for the decline of the Dharma, such as misrepresentation of the teachings by monks.

62. The proclamation that due to permitting nuns to go forth the Buddha's teaching will last only five hundred years instead of a thousand can be found in (what could be, according to Lamotte 1958: 212, the) "Haimavata" Vinaya T 1463 at T XXIV: 803b17 (cf. also 818c5); in the Mahāsāṅghika Vinaya in Roth 1970: 16,14; in the Mahīśāsaka Vinaya T 1421 at T XXII: 186a14; in the (Mūla-)sarvāstivāda Vinaya T 1451 at T XXIV: 352a22; in the Theravāda Vinaya at Vin II: 256,9; and in the following discourses: AN 8.51 at AN IV: 278,16; MĀ 116 at T I: 607b9; T 60 at T I: 857c29; T 156 at T III: 153c25; T 196 at T IV: 159b8; and T 1478 at T XXIV: 949b12. The Sarvāstivāda Vinaya, T 1435 at T XXIII: 290c23, only refers to this event, without giving a full account of it. Since the *Madhyama-āgama* collection is generally held to stem from the Sarvāstivāda tradition (Enomoto 1984; Lü 1963: 242; Mayeda 1985: 98; Minh Chau 1991: 27; Waldschmidt 1980: 136; and Yinshun 1983: 703), the account given in MĀ 116 can be taken to represent the Sarvāstivāda position in this respect. The Sanskrit fragment in Schmidt 1993: 243,29 (= Ridding and La Vallée Poussin 1920: 125,16), which according to Schmidt 1994 stems from the (Mūla-)sarvāstivāda Vinaya (cf. Chung 1998: 420 and Roth 1970: 5n3b), does not specify the time, but only indicates that the Dharma will not endure for a long time. The Tibetan translation of the (Mūla-)sarvāstivāda Vinaya mentions that the Buddha's teachings will no longer remain unimpaired for one thousand years, without, however, referring to five hundred years, *'Dul ba phran tshegs kyi gzhi*, Kangyur Q ('dul ba) *ne*, 116b5. Another variant seems to occur in the Dharmaguptaka Vinaya, T 1428 at T XXII: 923c10, which reads: 若女人不於佛法出家者， 佛法當得久住五百歲. Nattier 1991: 30n12 translates this passage as: "if women had not become nuns [lit. 'left home in the Buddha-Dharma'], the Dharma would have lasted long, [i.e.] five hundred years," and takes it to be "the result of an error in textual transmission." Kajiyama 1982: 57 similarly understands the passage to mean that the Dharma "would have remained in this world for 500 years" and concludes that it may preserve an earlier version than the other texts. Judging from the syntax of the second part of this passage, however, the intended meaning could also be that "the Buddha-Dharma would have lasted five hundred years longer." On adopting this sense, T 1428 would agree with the other versions that the Dharma will last five hundred years less because women have been allowed to go forth, differing only inasmuch as it does not explicitly refer to the thousand years it would have lasted if an order of nuns had not been founded.

63. The Dharmaguptaka Vinaya T 1428 at T XXII: 923c10 speaks of the duration of the Buddha's teaching, 佛法當得久住; the "Haimavata" Vinaya T 1463 at T XXIV: 803b17 of the cessation of the true teaching, 滅 … 正法; the Mahāsāṅghika Vinaya in Roth 1970: 16,14 of the duration of the true teaching, *sad-dharmo sthāsyati*; the Mahīśāsaka Vinaya T

expression "true teaching" stands for the Buddha's teaching;[64] in fact several versions explicitly refer to the Buddha's teaching in this context. The Buddha's teaching is clearly still in existence today and thus has not ceased after five hundred years.

In view of the numerous canonical passages that stand in contrast to this inaccurate prediction, the possibility that this particular passage is the result of later influences has to be seriously taken into consideration.[65]

The Eight Special Rules

The hypothesis that the prediction of decline might be a later addition can claim support from the circumstance that other aspects of the account of the foundation of the order of nuns also suggest later developments. One such aspect concerns the eight special rules, the gurudharmas,[66] which,

1421 at T XXII: 186a14 of the duration and cessation of the Buddha's true teaching, 佛之正法住 . . . 滅; the Theravāda Vinaya at Vin II: 256,15 of the long duration of the holy life and the duration of the true teaching, *brahmacariyaṃ ciraṭṭhitikaṃ ... saddhammo ṭhassati* (same terms are used in AN 8.51 at AN IV: 278,23). The Chinese (Mūla-)sarvāstivāda Vinaya T 1451 at T XXIV: 352a22, however, speaks of a decrease in purity of the Buddha's teaching which, had it not been for the going forth of women, would have remained pure and undefiled for a thousand years: 我之教法滿一千年，具足清淨無諸染污; see also its Tibetan counterpart *'Dul ba phran tshegs kyi gzhi*, Kangyur Q ('dul ba) *ne*, 116b6: *nga'i bstan pa lo stong tshang bar nyes pa med cing nyams pa med par gnas par 'gyur ro*. The corresponding section has not been preserved in the Sanskrit fragment, though at an earlier point in Schmidt 1993: 244,4 the Sanskrit version speaks of the long duration of the teaching and discipline, *dharmmavinayaś cirasthitiko*. MĀ 116 at T I: 607b9 also speaks of the duration of the true teaching, 正法當住; T 60 at T I: 857c29 of the duration of the legacy of the teaching, 遺法當住; T 156 at T III: 153c25 of the cessation of the true teaching, 正法 … 滅; T 196 at T IV: 159b8 of the decay of the Buddha's true teaching, 佛之正法 … 衰微; and T 1478 at T XXIV: 949b12 of the duration and cessation of the Buddha's true teaching, 佛之正法當住 … 滅.

64. Geiger and Geiger 1920: 53–54.

65. According to Basham 1980: 23n2, "these cannot be the authentic words of Buddha himself." The negative attitude underlying this prediction and its dubious authenticity have been highlighted by several scholars that have examined the role of women in Buddhism; see, e.g., Bancroft 1987: 82; Church 1975: 54; Falk 1974: 106; Sponberg 1992: 13; Sumala 1991: 116; Williams 2002; and Wilson 1995: 49.

66. For a survey of the gurudharmas in different Vinayas, see Heirman 1997: 35n7 and Hirakawa 1982: 48n6.

according to the canonical accounts, the Buddha imposed as a condition for allowing Mahāprajāpatī Gautamī to go forth.[67]

A problem here is that several of these eight gurudharmas presuppose an already existing order of nuns and thus cannot have been promulgated at a point in time when the order of nuns was just about to be founded. This can be seen in the background story given in the Theravāda Vinaya to *pācittiya* rules that correspond to gurudharmas. The background stories already refer to nuns, indicating that nuns were already in existence when these rules were promulgated.[68]

A particularly striking case is one of the gurudharmas found in several Vinayas according to which a two-year probation period must be observed before taking ordination from both orders (of monks and nuns).[69] The same Vinayas also treat the problem that arose from ordaining a pregnant woman.[70] Such a problem could never have arisen if from the outset there had

67. In the Mahīśāsaka Vinaya T 1421 at T XXII: 185c19 and the Theravāda Vinaya at Vin II 255,4, the Buddha imposed these rules on Mahāprajāpatī Gautamī as the condition for her ordination; while the other Vinayas more explicitly state that women in general have to undertake these rules if they wish to go forth; cf. the "Haimavata" Vinaya T 1463 at T XXIV: 803b12; the Dharmaguptaka Vinaya T 1428 at T XXII: 923a27; the Mahāsāṅghika Vinaya in Roth 1970: 16,19; the (Mūla-)sarvāstivāda Vinaya T 1451 at T XXIV: 350c26; and MĀ 116 at T I: 605c29 (representative of the Sarvāstivāda tradition).

68. This is the case for the second garudhamma at Vin II: 255,9 and the narration to the equivalent *pācittiya* rule 56 at Vin IV: 313,13; for the third garudhamma and *pācittiya* rule 59 at Vin IV: 315,22; for the fourth garudhamma and *pācittiya* rule 57 at Vin IV: 314,9; for the sixth garudhamma and *pācittiya* rule 63 at Vin IV: 319,33 (the formulations differ slightly); and for the seventh garudhamma and *pācittiya* rule 52 at Vin IV: 309,7. For a detailed study of these inconsistencies, see Hüsken 1997: 347–60.

69. This is gurudharma no. 4 in the Dharmaguptaka Vinaya T 1428 at T XXII 923b8; gurudharma no. 2 in the Mahāsāṅghika Vinaya in Roth 1970: 17,5 or T 1425 at T XXII 471b11; gurudharma no. 4 in the Mahīśāsaka Vinaya T 1421 at T XXII 185c23; and gurudharma no. 6 in the Theravāda Vinaya at Vin II 255,19.

70. See the Dharmaguptaka Vinaya T 1428 at T XXII: 754b12 (cf. Heirman 2002b: 81); the Mahāsāṅghika Vinaya T 1425 at T XXII: 380a23 (though this Vinaya only speaks of going forth, which unlike full ordination would not conflict with the probationary period); the Mahīśāsaka Vinaya T 1421 at T XXII: 92a24; the Theravāda Vinaya at Vin IV 317,20. A ruling on the same problem can also be found in the (Mūla-)sarvāstivāda Vinaya T 1443 at T XXIII: 1005c26 and T 1455 at T XXIV: 514c12 (both instances only refer to going forth); and a reference to the same predicament in the Sarvāstivāda Vinaya T 1435 at T XXIII: 326b16. See also the discussions in Heirman 1997: 60–61; Hüsken 1997: 353; and Juo-Hsüeh Shi 2000: 420.

been a two-year probation period, requiring the candidate to observe complete celibacy.[71]

Additional evidence can be found in references to nuns being ordained with the simple formula "come nun." This rather simple ordination by the Buddha himself has its counterpart in the "come monk" ordination, apparently used for monks during the earliest years of the Buddhist monastic community. This then seems to have been followed by ordination through administering the three refuges, which in turn was succeeded by a full-fledged ordination ceremony by a monastic community. If nuns always had to seek ordination by both monastic communities, as suggested by the gurudharma above, a reference to a nun ordained through the simple formula "come nun" should never have occurred.

Yet, the Dharmaguptaka, Saṃmatīya, and Theravāda Vinayas explicitly refer to nuns who received the "come nun" ordination.[72] The "Haimavata" and Sarvāstivāda Vinayas use the same expression in an actual report of such an ordination.[73] An instance of such an ordination conferred on a nun by the Buddha himself is mentioned in the *Therīgāthā*,[74] and altogether seven instances occur in the *Avadānaśataka* collection preserved in Chinese.[75] Notably, the Sanskrit counterpart to this *Avadānaśataka* collection, which appears to be later than the one translated into Chinese,[76] reports the

71. See Vin IV: 319,26.

72. Dharmaguptaka Vinaya T 1428 at T XXII: 714a17: 善來比丘尼; Saṃmatīya Vinaya T 1461 at T XXIV: 668c21: 善來比丘尼; Theravāda Vinaya at Vin IV: 214,6: *'ehi bhikkhunī'ti bhikkhunī.*

73. "Haimavata" Vinaya T 1463 at T XXIV 803b26 and Sarvāstivāda Vinaya T 1435 at T XXIII 426b12.

74. Thī 109: *'ehi bhadde 'ti avaca, sā me ās' ūpasampadā*; see also Ap II 563,23 (21.44); though according to the commentary Thī-a 107 (references to Thī-a are to the digital edition by VRI) this should be understood to mean that she was sent off to the nuns' quarters to receive the going forth and higher ordination there. Skilling 2001: 154 comments that "the *Therīgāthā-aṭṭhakathā* goes to great length to deny that the '*ehī* ordination'—direct ordination by the Buddha himself—was ever used for nuns, but there is tantalizing evidence to the contrary."

75. T 200 at T IV: 238c5, 239a15, 239b25, 240a5, 240b16, 241a10, 241b18 report the "come nun" ordination for the nuns Suprabhā, Supriyā, Śuklā, Somā, Kuvalyā, Kāṣikasundarī, and Muktā. An instance of the "come nun" ordination is also recorded in the discourse on the wise and the fool, T 202 at T IV: 383b11. Skilling 1994: 55n36 points out a reference to the *ehi bhikṣuṇī* ordination in the *Divyāvadāna* in Cowell and Neil 1886: 616,19.

76. Bagchi 1945: 57 and Pachow 1953: 2.

same ordinations in a different manner, without mentioning in any of these seven instances the "come nun" ordination.[77]

The evidence of nuns being ordained by the "come nun" formula conflicts with the canonical account that at the time of the founding of the nuns' order, the Buddha pronounced that nuns should only be ordained by both communities.

These inconsistencies suggest that the gurudharmas, in the form we have them now, were probably not promulgated when Mahāprajāpatī Gautamī went forth. In fact, such a promulgation would violate a basic Vinaya principle, according to which rules are only set forth when a corresponding case has arisen.[78] The gurudharmas are the only instance that does not accord with this Vinaya principle, making it more likely that they were promulgated at a later time and then added to the account of the foundation of the order of nuns.

It also seems rather curious that several Vinayas report how Mahāprajāpatī Gautamī accepts the eight gurudharmas, one of which requires a nun of senior standing to pay respects to a junior monk, but then these Vinayas continue by reporting that she went to see the Buddha in order to get a ruling against the need for senior nuns to respect junior monks.[79] Since the same form of conduct was apparently observed among other contemporary

77. According to the Sanskrit version in Speyer 1970: 4,9; 8,7; 16,11; 21,6; 26,5; 33,5; 37,12, Suprabhā received the lower and higher ordination from Mahāprajāpatī; Supriyā and Śuklā just went forth (without further specification on how this happened); Somā went forth under Mahāprajāpatī; Kuvalyā went forth under the Buddha; Kāṣikasundarī went forth under Mahāprajāpatī; and Muktā just went forth. Muktā, Somā, and Śuklā are also mentioned in the *Therīgāthā*, where Thī-a 14 just says that Muttā went forth, Thī-a 66 says that Somā received ordination from the nuns, and Thī-a 58 says that Sukkā went forth under Dhammadinnā.

78. Vin III: 9,28: *na tāva ... satthā sāvakānaṃ sikkhāpadaṃ paññāpeti ... yāva na idh' ekacce āsavaṭṭhāniyā dhammā saṅghe pātubhavanti*; T 1425 at T XXII: 227c2: 如來不以無過患因緣而為弟子制戒立說波羅提木叉法; see also T 2121 at T LIII: 70a11. Kusuma 2000: 8 highlights another unusual aspect of this procedure, in that elsewhere "Vinaya rules are pronounced on *bhikkhus* and *bhikkhunīs*, but the garudhammas were pronounced on Mahāpajāpatī while she was still a laywoman."

79. The Mahīśāsaka Vinaya T 1421 at T XXII: 186a9; the (Mūla-)sarvāstivāda Vinaya T 1451 at T XXIV: 352a8; MĀ 116 at T I: 607a10 (representative of the Sarvāstivāda tradition); and the Theravāda Vinaya at Vin II: 257,29 agree that in spite of having happily accepted the gurudharmas, Mahāprajāpatī Gautamī attempted to get the Buddha to approve that junior monks should respect senior nuns.

groups, such as the Jains,[80] a perhaps more straightforward presentation would be to assume that after the founding of the nuns' order the monks did not show any respect to the nuns and expected even senior nuns to be respectful toward junior monks, in keeping with such customs. Such an issue would only have manifested itself at a time when the first generation of nuns had reached some seniority. Once this had happened several times, the nuns might then have decided to approach the Buddha to get clarification about this matter. This incident, and the Buddha's reaction to it, could then have been the starting point for a process of textual growth that eventually incorporated the whole set of gurudharmas, integrating various regulations pronounced by the Buddha in response to different situations that arose when the order of nuns was already in existence.

Ānanda's Intervention

Another difficulty with the account of the foundation of the order of nuns relates to the intervention by Ānanda in favor of Mahāprajāpatī Gautamī's request to be granted the going forth. This intervention is not only found in the actual account of the foundation of the order of nuns but also comes up in the records of the so-called First Council, during which Ānanda was upbraided for having intervened and convinced the Buddha to grant Mahāprajāpatī Gautamī's request.[81] Moreover, the Chinese pilgrims Faxian (法顯) and Xuanzang (玄奘) report from their visits to India in the fifth and seventh centuries respectively that the Indian nuns made regular offerings

80. Jaini 1991: 168. The existence of such a custom among the Jains would have been known to the Buddhists, since the Jain order of nuns appears to have been already in existence when the Buddhist order of nuns was founded. This suggests itself from a reference in the *Jinacaritra* 161–62 in Jacobi 1879: 69 (noted by Kabilsingh 1984: 29) to nun disciples of Pārśva, the predecessor of Mahāvīra. The same would also follow from the circumstance that Bhaddhā, who according to Thī 109 was ordained with the *ehi* formula and thus must have gone forth at a very early stage of the Buddhist monastic order, appears to have been a Jain nun before her conversion to Buddhism; cf. Thī 107 and Thī-a 101.

81. Dharmaguptaka Vinaya T 1428 at T XXII: 967b27; Mahāsāṅghika Vinaya T 1425 at T XXII: 492a22 (where the accusation is levied by Upāli); Mahīśāsaka Vinaya T 1421 at T XXII: 191b14; (Mūla-)sarvāstivāda Vinaya T 1451 at T XXIV: 404c25; Sarvāstivāda Vinaya T 1435 at T XXIII: 449c8; Theravāda Vinaya at Vin II: 289,25. Tilakaratne 2005: 250 comments that "this charge strongly suggests that the majority of the senior members of the Saṅgha did not like the existence of the Bhikkhunī Order."

at stūpas dedicated to Ānanda in gratitude for his intervention on their behalf.[82]

A problem with this intervention by Ānanda, however, is of a chronological nature. In keeping with the general ancient Indian disinterest in precise historical dates, most of the canonical accounts of the foundation of the order of nuns do not give this event an explicit placing in time. According to the Pāli commentarial tradition, Mahāprajāpatī Gautamī made her request to be allowed to go forth when the Buddha had come to visit his home country after having spent the fifth rain in Vaiśālī.[83] The Mahīśāsaka Vinaya seems to agree with this placing.[84]

Such an early dating seems reasonable in view of the fact that, according to tradition, Mahāprajāpatī Gautamī was the Buddha's foster mother and nourished the infant bodhisattva with her own milk when the Buddha's mother passed away soon after giving birth. This would imply that Mahāprajāpatī Gautamī was considerably older than the Buddha. Yet, the Pāli Nikāyas and the Chinese Āgamas report several meetings between her and the Buddha after she had gone forth.[85] Particularly prominent appears

82. T 2085 at T LI: 859b24 and T 2087 at T LI: 890b16. Deeg 2005: 142 notes that the worship paid by the nuns to the memory of Ānanda is also recorded in the Mahāsāṅghika Vinaya; cf. Roth 1970: 314,27.

83. Mp I: 341,12, Thī-a 3, and Thī-a 141 report that Mahāpajāpatī Gotamī requested the going forth after her husband had passed away and the Buddha had settled a quarrel regarding the use of the water of the river Rohiṇī. According to Jordt 1988: 31, "there is general agreement among historians that the Buddha established an order of nuns about five years after he had established an order of monks"; see also Malalasekera 1995: 796 and Ñāṇamoli 1992: 104. Mp IV: 132,1, however, places her request already at the time of the Buddha's first visit to Kapilavatthu. On the general agreement among various sources that the Buddha spent the fifth rains retreat after his awakening at Vaiśālī, see Mochizuki 1940: 41.

84. T 1421 at T XXII: 185b25 places Mahāprajāpatī Gautamī's request after the stream-entry of her husband, based on which Jing 2006: 282 concludes that "the Vinaya of the Mahīśāsakas records that during the fifth year after the Buddha's enlightenment five hundred Śākya ladies headed by Mahāprajāpatī were permitted to enter the Order."

85. MN 142 at MN III: 253,2 and its parallels MĀ 180 at T I: 721c24 and T 84 at T I: 903b28 record a visit paid by her to the Buddha, where the mention of the order of nuns later on in these discourses gives the impression she was already ordained at that time; in fact T 84 at T I: 903b28 explicitly qualifies her as a nun. MN 146 at MN III: 270,10; Sanskrit fragment SHT VI: 1226 folio 5–6 in Bechert 1989: 22; SĀ 276 at T II: 73c16; and T 1442 at T XXIII: 792a23 report that, together with a group of nuns, she approached the Buddha for instruction. AN 8.53 at AN IV: 280,10 (see also the parallel Sanskrit fragment SHT III 994 folio V3–R2 in Waldschmidt 1971: 255 and Vin II: 258,25) reports her visiting the Buddha at Vesālī

to have been her role as a spokeswoman for the nuns during meetings with the Buddha, reported in the different Vinayas.[86] For her to still have had repeated meetings with the Buddha once she had gone forth, her ordination must have taken place at a comparatively early stage of the Buddha's teaching career.

An early existence of the order of nuns is also implicit in the above-discussed references to nuns ordained by the simple "come nun" ordination, a way of ordaining only used during the earliest stage of development of the monastic order, when ordination was still given by the Buddha personally.

A problem with placing the foundation of the order of nuns at such an early period, however, is that Ānanda does not yet seem to have been ordained at this stage. Though according to the Dharmaguptaka, Mahīśāsaka, and Theravāda Vinayas, Ānanda was ordained together with other Śākyans at the time of the Buddha's first visit to Kapilavastu,[87] other canonical passages give the impression that Ānanda may have only been ordained about twenty years after the Buddha had begun to teach. In his verses in the *Theragāthā*, Ānanda proclaims that he had been a disciple in higher training (*sekha*) for twenty-five years.[88] According to a discourse in the *Saṃyutta-nikāya* and its *Saṃyukta-āgama* parallel, Ānanda's stream-entry took place soon after his ordination,[89] and according to the Vinaya accounts of the so-called First Council, he became an arahant only after the Buddha's passing away.[90] From this it would follow that he became a

---

and receiving an instruction, due to which according to Mp IV: 137,28 she became an arahant. Her attainment and the location at Vesālī suggest that she was already a nun by the time of this instruction. EĀ 52.1 at T II: 821c9 records how she requested the Buddha to allow her to pass away. For a critical examination of the suggestion by von Hinüber 2008 that the order of nuns was only founded after the Buddha's demise, see Anālayo 2008: 110–25.

86. A detailed survey of references to such meetings can be found in Anālayo 2008: 139n59.

87. T 1428 at T XXII: 591b20; T 1421 at T XXII: 17a8; Vin II: 182,25; cf. also T 1465 at T XXIV: 902c17.

88. Th 1039 and Th 1040: *paṇṇavīsativassāni sekhabhūtassa me sato.*

89. SN 22.83 at SN III: 106,3 and its parallel SĀ 261 at T II: 66b4. Vin II: 183,21 confirms that he became a stream-enterer soon after his ordination.

90. His attainment of full awakening after the Buddha's demise is reported in the Dharmaguptaka Vinaya T 1428 at T XXII: 967a24; in the Mahāsāṅghika Vinaya T 1425 at T XXII:

monk only about twenty-five years before the Buddha's passing away, and therewith twenty years after the beginning of the Buddha's ministry.[91] Thus he would have ordained considerably later than the time when the order of nuns appears to have been founded, even though the accounts of the foundation of the order of nuns introduce him as a monk.

According to the *Saṅghabhedavastu* of the (Mūla-)sarvāstivāda Vinaya, Ānanda was only born at the time when the Buddha attained awakening.[92] In this case, he would still have been a child at the time when Mahāprajāpatī Gautamī requested the going forth. When appointing Ānanda as his attendant, according to the *Saṅghabhedavastu*, the Buddha refused the offer of several other monks to act as his attendant because they were as old as himself and thus rather in need of having attendants themselves, a presentation that further highlights the comparatively young age of Ānanda.[93]

Contrary to the suggestion made in the *Saṅghabhedavastu*, the Pāli commentarial tradition holds that Ānanda was born at the same time as the bodhisattva.[94] In the *Lalitavistara* the two also appear to be of similar age, as this work describes how Ānanda took part in an exhibition of prowess together with the bodhisattva when both were still princes.[95]

Discourses found in the Pāli Nikāyas and their counterparts in the Chinese Āgamas, however, give the impression that Ānanda was considerably younger than the Buddha. A discourse in the *Saṃyutta-nikāya* and its *Saṃyukta-āgama* parallels report that, after the Buddha's demise, Mahākāśyapa treated Ānanda as a youngster, in reply to which Ānanda

---

491b1; in the Mahīśāsaka Vinaya T 1421 at T XXII: 190c15; in the (Mūla-)sarvāstivāda Vinaya T 1451 at T XXIV: 406a12; and in the Theravāda Vinaya, Vin II: 286,11.

91. Witanachchi 1965: 529 concludes that Ānanda "was ordained in the twentieth year after the enlightenment."

92. Gnoli 1977: 120,10 (cf. also Gnoli 1978a: 52,27) with its Chinese counterpart T 1450 at T XXIV: 165a18 and its Tibetan counterpart *'Dul ba gzhi*, Kangyur Q ('dul ba) *ce*, 32b5. The same is also suggested in the *Mahāprajñāpāramitā-śāstra*, T 1509 at T XXV: 84a12.

93. Gnoli 1978a: 60,13+25.

94. See Horner 1979: 116 on the doubtful nature of this suggestion.

95. The *Lalitavistara* in Lefmann 1902: 152,12 and 154,6 reports that Ānanda wrestled and competed in archery with the bodhisattva; cf. also T 190 at T III: 710b23; Bu ston's history of Buddhism in Obermiller 1986: 19; and Lamotte 1981: 230n3.

pointed to gray hairs on his head.[96] This exchange between the two monks would not make sense if Ānanda had been of the same age as the Buddha.[97] Similarly, the *Mahāparinirvāṇa-sūtra* and its parallels indicate that at a time shortly before his passing away the Buddha described how his body had been affected by old age to Ānanda, a description that would have been redundant if Ānanda had been of the same age as the Buddha.[98]

Thus these texts give the impression that Ānanda was considerably younger than the Buddha,[99] which in turn implies that his going forth would have taken place at a considerably later time than the time to which the Pāli commentaries allocate the foundation of the order of nuns. To attempt to solve this contradiction by shifting the foundation of the order of nuns to a later time, when Ānanda had already become a monk, would also not offer a satisfactory solution. By then the Buddha would have been approaching his sixties, hence his foster mother Mahāprajāpatī Gautamī would in turn have been in her late seventies or even in her eighties. For her to have gone forth at such an advanced age seems improbable in view of her many activities as a nun recorded in the different Vinayas.

The Buddha's Refusal

So far, then, different elements in the account of Mahāprajāpatī Gautamī's request appear to be problematic, namely the prediction of future decline, the promulgation of the eight special rules, and the presence of the monk

96. SN 16.11 at SN II: 218,24; SĀ 1144 at T II: 303a7; and SĀ² 119 at T II: 418a6 (where instead of pointing to his gray hair Ānanda only affirmed that he was no longer a child).

97. Bodhi 2000: 804n296 explains that "commentarial tradition holds that Ānanda was born on the same day as the Bodhisatta...if this were true, however, he would now be over eighty years of age and thus would hardly have to point to a few grey hairs to prove he is no longer a youngster."

98. See DN 16 at DN II: 100,13; SN 47.9 at SN V: 153,28; DĀ 2 at T I: 15b2; T 5 at T I: 164c15; T 6 at T I: 180a26; T 1451 at T XXIV: 387b12; and a reconstruction of the relevant Sanskrit fragments together with the Tibetan version in Waldschmidt 1951: 198–99. Bodhi 2000: 1921n141 comments that "this passage would hardly make sense if the commentaries were right in holding that Ānanda was born on the same days as the Bodhisatta, for the Buddha would not need to insist on the frailties of old age if Ānanda too was an old man."

99. Neumann 1995: 1113n228 describes sculptural representations of Ānanda as a young monk who mourns the Buddha's death, which suggests that he was held to have been considerably younger than the Buddha.

Ānanda. In the light of the numerous passages indicating the importance of the order of nuns and the Buddha's plan to have such an order immediately after his awakening, it would also seem problematic that the Buddha should refuse to establish such an order when requested to do so.[100]

Had the Buddha really been reluctant to have an order of nuns at all,[101] it would be difficult to imagine why he should have decided otherwise. Several accounts of the foundation of the order of nuns report that Ānanda asked if women are capable of attaining the four stages of liberation, a question often combined with a reminder to the Buddha of his debt of gratitude to his foster mother.[102] Yet, the Buddha would not have needed to be

100. According to Gross 1993: 33, "the Buddha's reluctance to ordain women...seems so antithetical to the basic message of Buddhism." Horner 1990: 109 comments that "the circumstance which appears to require the more explanation is not that Gotama allowed women to enter the Order, but that he appears to have hesitated." In regard to the formulation of the Buddha's refusal at Vin II: 253,9, Wijetunge 2005: 281 notes that the Buddha does not totally reject her proposal, but rather says "enough, may it not please you," *alaṃ, gotamī, mā te rucci*, whereas a complete rejection should according to Wijetunge have used *na* or *abhabba*. However, the same *mā te rucci* is used by the Buddha not only when rejecting a proposal by Mahāmoggallāna (Vin III 7,15) or by Sāriputta (Vin II 201,2) but also when telling Devadatta that he should not split the monastic community, Vin II: 198,10: *alaṃ, devadatta, mā te rucci saṅghabhedo* (cf. also Vin II: 188,32), a context where the expression can safely be assumed to carry rather strong undertones.

101. The report of the Buddha's refusal in the different Vinayas makes it clear that this refusal is concerned with allowing women in general to go forth, as Gautamī's request in the Dharmaguptaka Vinaya T 1428 at T XXII: 922c9 refers to "women" in general, 女人; as is the case for the Mahāsāṅghika Vinaya in Roth 1970: 5,6: *mātṛgāmo*; the Mahīśāsaka Vinaya T 1421 at T XXII: 185b25: 女人; the (Mūla-)sarvāstivāda Vinaya in T 1451 at T XXIV: 350b14: 女人; MĀ 116 at T I: 605a27: 女人 (representative of the Sarvāstivāda tradition); and the Theravāda Vinaya at Vin II: 253,7: *mātugāmo*. A different formulation can be found in the "Haimavata" Vinaya, T 1463 at T XXIV: 803a24, according to which she asked: "can we women receive the going forth in the Buddha's Dharma?" 我等女人於佛法中得出家不. This appears to be the only instance that could be interpreted to support the suggestion by Wijayaratna 1991: 22 that Mahāprajāpatī Gautamī's request was not for a foundation of an order but only for herself and her group of women to go forth, "à proprement parler, Mahā-Pajāpatī Gotamī n'a pas sollicité la fondation d'un ordre des moniales...elle voulut simplement obtenir pour elle et pour son groupe d'entrer dans la vie religieuse." Yet, the same Vinaya continues with the Buddha replying to this request by refusing to allow women in general to go forth, which makes it more probable that her request is meant to stand for women in general; T 1463 at T XXIV: 803a25: "I do not wish to allow women to go forth," 吾不欲聽女人出家.

102. This is the case in the Dharmaguptaka Vinaya T 1428 at T XXII: 923a22; in the "Haimavata" Vinaya T 1463 at T XXIV: 803b9; in the Mahīśāsaka Vinaya T 1421 at T XXII: 185c16; and in the Theravāda Vinaya at Vin II: 254,29. On the theme of the Buddha's indebtedness to his foster mother, see also Ohnuma 2006.

reminded that women are capable of awakening in order to convince him to establish an order of nuns. Nor would he have needed a reminder of his debt of gratitude to his foster mother, which he had already settled anyway by leading her to stream-entry.

In the (Mūla-)sarvāstivāda Vinaya and the Sarvāstivāda version, it is in fact Mahāprajāpatī Gautamī herself who brings up the point of women's ability to attain the four stages of awakening, and she already does so when making her first request for permission to go forth.[103] Nevertheless, her request meets with the Buddha's refusal, so that in these versions the argument of women's abilities to reach awakening is clearly not the factor that motivates the Buddha to permit them to go forth. According to the Mahāsāṅghika Vinaya, the Buddha decided to grant her request with the thought that otherwise Ānanda would become confused and forget the teachings he had heard, which the Buddha wanted to avoid even at the cost of his teachings lasting only for five hundred years.[104] This seems hardly convincing as a reason that would persuade the Buddha to do what he did not want to do and what was going to seriously affect the duration of his dispensation.[105]

The contrast between the Buddha's original plan to have an order of nuns and his subsequent refusal is particularly prominent in the (Mūla-) sarvāstivāda and the Theravāda traditions, which both report the Buddha's decision to found an order of nuns (as part of his intention to have four assemblies) and his refusal to establish an order of nuns (when requested to do so by Mahāprajāpatī Gautamī) within a single textual collection, in the (Mūla-)sarvāstivāda *Kṣudrakavastu* and the Theravāda *Aṅguttara-nikāya*

103. T 1451 at T XXIV: 350b15; MĀ 116 at T I: 605a13; the same is the case for T 60 at T I: 856a11 and T 196 at T IV: 158a25.

104. Roth 1970: 16,14: *mā haivānandasya gautamī-putrasya bhavatu cittasyānyathātvaṃ mā pi se śrutā dharmā sammoṣaṅ gaccha[n]tu, kāmaṃ pañcāpi me varṣa-śatāni sad-dharmo sthāsyati* (notably, in this Vinaya Ānanda is referred to as the son of Mahāprajāpatī Gautamī).

105. Horner 1990: 107 points out that for the Buddha "it would have been in complete discordance with his character to have let people's wishes and desires, however lofty, supplant or overcome what he knew to be right. Nor was he likely to take any step which might strike at the integrity of the Order."

respectively.[106] Faced with this evident contradiction, both traditions had to find ways to resolve it.

The (Mūla-)sarvāstivāda Vinaya does so in its account of the so-called First Council, where Ānanda was reprimanded for his intervention in favor of the nuns. When accused for this intervention, Ānanda argues that former Buddhas also had four assemblies. In reply, Mahākāśyapa explains that in the case of former Buddhas, the existence of an order of nuns was possible because at that time people were not under the influence of desire to the extent they were at the time of the present Buddha.[107]

This attempt to resolve the difficulty does not work well, since another passage in the same Vinaya indicates that the Buddha knew about the condition of beings already when he decided to found an order of nuns soon after his awakening and not only when he was requested to do so by Mahāprajāpatī Gautamī. This is the account of his decision to teach at all given in the (Mūla-)sarvāstivāda Vinaya and in a range of other sources, where after an intervention by Brahmā the Buddha surveys the condition of beings in the world in order to ascertain if some of them would be able to understand his teachings.[108] Hence if the degree to which human beings were under the influence of desire had been the cause for the Buddha's unwillingness to allow Mahāprajāpatī Gautamī to go forth, the same condition should have prevented him from planning to have an order of nuns at all. Instead, it seems as if his decision to have four assemblies of disciples, including an order of nuns, was the outcome of his survey of the condition of beings in the world. This decision would have been based on knowing the degree to which beings were under the influence of desire.

106. In the case of the (Mūla-)sarvāstivāda tradition, the Buddha's decision to have four assemblies can be found in T 1451 at T XXIV: 387c27 and his refusal in T 1451 at T XXIV: 350b18; in the case of the Theravāda tradition his decision can be found in AN 8.70 at AN IV: 310,32 and his refusal in AN 8.51 at AN IV: 274,7.

107. T 1451 at T XXIV: 405a9: 又云我聞過去諸佛皆有四眾，望佛同彼者，於曩昔時人皆少欲，於染瞋癡及諸煩惱悉皆微薄，彼合出家，今則不然.

108. The Buddha's surveying the world is described in the *Saṅghabhedavastu* in Gnoli 1977: 130,1 and in T 1450 at T XXIV: 126c18; cf. also the *Catuṣpariṣat-sūtra* fragment M 480 R1–3 in Waldschmidt 1952: 43–44 and its Tibetan counterpart in Waldschmidt 1957: 117,11. Other references to this survey are MN 26 at MN I: 169,6; T 189 at T III: 643a20; T 190 at T III: 806c12; T 191 at T III: 953a15; the Dharmaguptaka Vinaya T 1428 at T XXII: 787a20; the *Mahāvastu* in Senart 1897: 318,1; and the Mahīśāsaka Vinaya T 1421 at T XXII: 104a4.

The Theravāda commentary on the *Aṅguttara-nikāya* tries to resolve the same conflict by suggesting that the Buddha's hesitation was merely a teaching device in order to instill respect among the nuns for the opportunity they got by being allowed to go forth, since in truth and fact the Buddha wanted to have an order of nuns right from the outset.[109]

The line of thought opened up by the Pāli commentary is worth considering further, in the sense that the Buddha's refusal need not be attributed to a negative attitude toward having an order of nuns at all. A passage preserved in several accounts of the foundation of the order of nuns offers an intriguing indication in this respect, suggesting that the Buddha's refusal may have been related to the particular circumstances of her request. This passage is found in the account of the foundation of the order of nuns given in the *Madhyama-āgama*, in an individual translation, in the Mahīśāsaka Vinaya, and in the (Mūla-)sarvāstivāda Vinaya preserved in Sanskrit, Chinese, and Tibetan. According to this passage, when refusing her request to be allowed to go forth, the Buddha told Mahāprajāpatī Gautamī that she may nevertheless shave her hair and don robes to live a celibate life.[110] The two discourses contrast this instruction to going forth from home into the homeless life,[111] and the two Chinese Vinayas explicitly indicate that Mahāprajāpatī Gautamī should undertake this celibate life while living at home.[112]

109. Mp IV: 133,2 *anuññātukāmo paṭikkhipi*.

110. MĀ 116 at T I 605a17: 瞿曇彌，如是汝剃除頭髮，著袈裟衣，盡其形壽，淨修梵行; T 60 at T I: 856a14: 汝瞿曇彌，常可剃頭被袈裟，至竟行清淨梵行; T 1421 at T XXII: 185b27: 在家剃頭著袈裟衣勤行精進 (which introduces this as a way of practice observed by women under past and future Buddhas); the (Mūla-)sarvāstivāda Sanskrit version in Schmidt 1993: 242,5: *evam eva tvaṃ gautamī muṇḍā saṃghāṭīprāvṛtā yāvajjīvaṃ...bra[h](maca)ryañ cara* (the translation by Wilson in Paul 1985: 83 as "just you alone, O Gautamī," adopted also by Ohnuma 2006: 883, does not fully do justice to the original, which does not explicitly restrict this injunction to her "alone"); with its Tibetan counterpart in *'Dul ba phran tshegs kyi gzhi*, Kangyur Q ('dul ba) *ne*, 98b4: *khyod kyis 'di ltar 'di bzhin du nam 'tsho'i bar du mgo bregs te sbyar ma gyon la... tshangs par spyad pa spyod cig*. A slightly different presentation can be found in the Chinese version T 1451 at T XXIV: 350b16: 汝應在家著白衣服，修諸梵行純一圓滿清淨無染, according to which she should wear "white robes." Yet, the same text continues by reporting that she and her companions put on monastic robes, making it probable that the Buddha's original instruction intended the same, T 1451 at T XXIV: 350b21: 皆著赤色僧伽胝衣.

111. MĀ 116 at T I: 605a16: 捨家，無家, and T 60 at T I: 856a13: 出家，棄家.

112. T 1421 at T XXII: 185b28: 在家 and T 1451 at T XXIV: 350b16: 在家.

For the Buddha to tell Mahāprajāpatī Gautamī to live a semi-monastic life by shaving her hair and donning robes, but without setting out wandering as a mendicant nun, would provide a meaningful background to ensuing events. It would explain why Mahāprajāpatī Gautamī and her group shaved their hair and donned robes when following the Buddha up to Vaiśālī after the first refusal of their request to be allowed to go forth.[113] Such a reaction would not make much sense if the Buddha had simply been unwilling to have nuns at all. It should be kept in mind that, according to the canonical texts, Mahāprajāpatī Gautamī was already a stream-entrant by the time of her first request, making it highly improbable that she would openly defy the Buddha and challenge him by going forth against his wish. But for her to shave her hair and don robes in accordance with the Buddha's instructions, and then to follow him in order to demonstrate that she and her friends were capable of adapting to the difficult conditions of a homeless life, would be perfectly understandable.

On the interpretation suggested by this episode, the Buddha's initial refusal would then simply have been an expression of his concern that for Mahāprajāpatī Gautamī and the other Śākyan ladies, used as they were to living in relatively protected conditions at home, it would prove too difficult to follow the life of a wandering mendicant in ancient India.[114] Such hesitation would be understandable if this initial request had come at a

113. This is reported in the Dharmaguptaka Vinaya T 1428 at T XXII: 922c18; in the "Haimavata" Vinaya T 1463 at T XXIV: 803a29; in the Mahāsāṅghika Vinaya in Roth 1970: 6,12; in the Mahīśāsaka Vinaya T 1421 at T XXII: 185c4; in the (Mūla-)sarvāstivāda Vinaya T 1451 at T XXIV: 350b20; and in the Theravāda Vinaya at Vin II: 253,23.

114. Kabilsingh 1984: 24 suggests that "the Buddha was reluctant to accept women into the Order primarily because he was aware that it was not simply a question of the admission of women, but that there were many other problems involved thereafter. The immediate objection was possibly Mahāpajāpatī herself. Since she used to live a luxurious life in the palace and had never been acquainted with the experience of hardship, it was almost unimaginable to see the queen going from house to house begging for meals. It might be out of pity and compassion that the Buddha refused her request to join the Order, because he could not bring himself to the point of letting her undergo such a hard and strenuous life." Wijayaratna 1991: 25 similarly reasons that the Buddha may have initially refused because he anticipated that Mahāprajāpatī Gautamī and the other women, coming from well-to-do backgrounds, might not be able to adjust to the tough living conditions of wandering mendicants, "il est donc possible que le Bouddha ait pensé que les femmes, notamment celles venant de familles aisées, ne seraient pas capables de pratiquer un mode de vie aussi dur...comme la vie errante." See also Kajiyama 1982: 60, who suggests that the Buddha may have hesitated to ordain women

time when the Buddhist monastic order was still in its beginning stages, a time when support by the laity for the Buddhist order was still in its incipient stages and lodgings were few.[115] During this early period with limited lodgings and uncertain support, for ancient Indian women to go forth would indeed have been quite a demanding undertaking, an undertaking the Buddha perhaps was hoping to launch only at a somewhat later period when living conditions were better established.

In sum, the Buddha's initial hesitation to grant Mahāprajāpatī Gautamī's request need not be interpreted as an expression of a general reluctance to have an order of nuns. Understood in this way, the Buddha's initial refusal would also not stand in contrast to his earlier decision to have an order of nuns. Moreover, this interpretation would make it understandable why he later consents to Mahāprajāpatī Gautamī's request, since once Mahāprajāpatī Gautamī and her companions had shown that their sincere motivation to go forth was strong enough to enable them to brave the hardships of a mendicant life,[116] the cause for the Buddha's initial hesitation would have been overcome.

Conclusion

Given that all we have at our disposition are textual records that have been orally transmitted over long periods of time, the possibilities of reconstructing "historical truth" are rather dim. Though the time and manner in which the order of nuns was founded remains uncertain, it seems nevertheless safe to conclude that the elements in the canonical accounts that express a negative attitude toward nuns seem to stem from a later textual layer. These stand in direct contrast to the numerous canonical texts that present the

"because he had to deliberate on problems which might arise" (though Kajiyama thinks in particular of problems between the two orders).

115. That to provide sufficient lodgings for nuns was a problem even later on can be seen from *pācittiya* regulations 82 and 83 at Vin IV: 336,9+29, according to which ordaining too frequently had to be curtailed because there were insufficient lodgings to accommodate the newly ordained nuns.

116. According to Sharma 1977: 250, the chief motivation of the early Buddhist nuns for going forth appears to have been a sincere interest in the Dharma, and the wish to escape from personal, familial, or social problems played only a secondary role.

Buddha's attitude toward the order of nuns in a positive light, indicating that he wanted an order of nuns, whose existence should be reckoned as one of the prerequisites for the duration of his teachings.

In the light of the modern situation, from the above-examined passages it would follow that the existence of an order of nuns in each of the Buddhist traditions would provide ideal conditions for the growth and spread of the Dharma. Any effort directed in support of the establishing and continuity of such an order could thus safely be assumed to be in accordance with what the canonical sources present as the Buddha's original intentions.

The Revival of Bhikkhunī Ordination in the Theravāda Tradition

Bhikkhu Bodhi[1]

Officially sanctioned bhikkhunī ordination disappeared from the Theravāda Buddhist tradition centuries ago. The last evidence for the existence of the original bhikkhunī saṅgha in a country following Theravāda Buddhism dates from Sri Lanka in the eleventh century. Beginning in the late 1990s, however, a revival of the bhikkhunī ordination has been underway in the Theravāda world, spearheaded by monks and nuns from Sri Lanka. With the support of a number of learned monks,[2] Sri Lankan women have sought to restore the long-vanished order of nuns not only to a place in their nation's heritage but to the religious life of international Theravāda Buddhism.

The first ordination in the contemporary revival movement took place at Sarnath, India, in December 1996, when ten Sri Lankan women were ordained as bhikkhunīs by Sri Lankan monks from the Mahābodhi Society assisted by Korean monks and nuns. This was followed by a grand

1. Several ideas in this paper originally developed out of correspondence with Bhikṣuṇī Jampa Tsedroen, Bhikṣuṇī Thubten Chodron, Bhikkhunī Tathālokā, and Bhikṣuṇī Shiu-Sher. I also thank Bhikkhu Anālayo for his comments on an earlier draft of the paper.

2. These include the late Ven. Talalle Dhammāloka Anunāyaka Thera of the Amarapura Nikāya, Ven. Dr. Kumburugamuve Vajira Nāyaka Thera, former vice-chancellor of the Buddhist and Pāli University of Sri Lanka, and Ven. Inamaluwe Srī Sumaṃgala Nāyaka Thera of the historic Rangiri Dambulla Vihāra. The first practical steps in resuscitating the bhikkhunī saṅgha were taken by Ven. Dodangoda Revata Mahāthera and the late Ven. Mapalagama Vipulasāra Mahāthera of the Mahābodhi Society in India.

international ordination at Bodhgaya in February 1998, conferred on women from many countries. It was held under the auspices of the Taiwan-based Fo Guang Shan organization and was attended by bhikkhus from different Buddhist countries following both the Theravāda and Mahāyāna traditions along with bhikkhunīs from Taiwan. From 1998 on, bhikkhunī ordinations have been held regularly in Sri Lanka, and at present over five hundred women on the island have been ordained. But while the ordination of bhikkhunīs has won the backing of large numbers of bhikkhus as well as lay devotees, to date it still has not received official recognition from either the Sri Lankan government or the *mahānāyaka theras*, the chief prelates of the fraternities of monks. In other Theravāda Buddhist countries, notably Thailand and Myanmar, resistance to a revival of the bhikkhunī saṅgha is still strong. In those countries, the conservative elders regard such a revival as contrary to the Vinaya and even as a threat to the longevity of Buddhism.

In this paper I intend to focus on the legal and moral issues involved in the revival of the Theravāda bhikkhunī saṅgha. My paper will be divided into three parts. In part 1, I will review the arguments presented by Theravādin traditionalists who see a revival of bhikkhunī ordination as a legal impossibility. In part 2, I will offer textual and ethical considerations that support the claim that bhikkhunī ordination should be resuscitated. Finally, in part 3, I will respond to the legal arguments presented by the traditionalists and briefly consider how the restoration of bhikkhunī ordination might be harmonized with the stipulations of the Vinaya.

The Case Against the Revival of Theravāda Bhikkhunī Ordination

While monastic ordination has never been an absolute requirement for spiritual practice and attainment in Buddhism, through the centuries the lifeblood of the Buddhist tradition has flowed through its monasteries and hermitages. Even today, in this age of electronic commerce and high technology, the call to the simple monastic life still inspires many, women as well as men. Yet in most countries that follow the Theravāda tradition, women are allowed only subordinate forms of renunciant life. The heritage of formally sanctioned monastic ordination prescribed in the ancient canonical texts is denied them.

Monastic ordination as a bhikkhunī involves three stages: (1) *pabbajjā*, the "going forth" into homelessness or novice ordination; (2) the *sikkhamānā* training, which prepares the candidate for full ordination; and (3) *upasampadā*, or full ordination. Conservative Theravādin Vinaya experts posit hurdles at all three stages. Each merits its own discussion.

(1) *Pabbajjā*. The first step of entry into the renunciant life, pabbajjā, transforms the woman aspirant from a lay devotee into a sāmaṇerī or novice. The Vinaya Piṭaka itself does not explicitly state who is entitled to give pabbajjā to a female aspirant for ordination, but the Theravāda tradition unequivocally understands that it is a bhikkhunī who assumes this role. Of course, in the earliest phase of the bhikkhunī saṅgha, this procedure had to be managed differently. According to the account found in the *Cullavagga*, the Buddha ordained Mahāpajāpatī Gotamī by giving her eight principles of respect and then allowed bhikkhus to ordain the other women.[3] The bhikkhus then gave upasampadā to the five hundred Sakyan women directly. It seems that at this point the distinction between pabbajjā as novice ordination and upasampadā had not yet arisen. But thereafter it became the duty of a bhikkhunī to give pabbajjā to a female aspirant, who would become her pupil, to be trained by her for eventual full ordination.

Once a full-fledged bhikkhunī saṅgha came into being, one never finds in the Pāli canon or its commentaries an instance of a bhikkhu giving pabbajjā to a woman. But we can still ask whether there is any prohibition against a bhikkhu doing so. Though no Vinaya rule forbids this, conservative Theravādins hold that the pabbajjā must always be given by a bhikkhunī. They point out that in the texts and commentaries, when a woman asks the Buddha to admit her to the saṅgha, the Buddha does not give her pabbajjā himself or send her to any of the senior monks for ordination but always instructs her to go to the bhikkhunīs. Later texts, neither canonical nor commentarial, explicitly state that it is prohibited for a bhikkhu to give pabbajjā to a woman. Thus the *Mahāvaṃsa*, the "Great Chronicle" of Sri Lankan history, relates the story of the elder Mahinda's arrival in Sri Lanka and his conversion of the royal court to the Dhamma.

3. Vin II: 255.

> But the queen Anulā, who had come with five hundred women to greet the elders, attained to the second stage of salvation [once-returning]. And the queen Anulā with her five hundred women said to the king: "We wish to receive the pabbajjā ordination, your Majesty." The king said to the elder, "Give them the pabbajjā!" But the elder replied to the king: "It is not allowed (to us), O great king, to bestow the pabbajjā on women. But in Pāṭaliputta there lives a nun, my younger sister, known by the name Sanghamittā. She, who is ripe in experience, shall come here bringing with her the southern branch of the great Bodhi-tree of the king of ascetics, O king of men, and (bringing) also bhikkhunīs renowned (for holiness); to this end send a message to the king my father. When this elder-nun is here she will confer the pabbajjā upon these women."[4]

While waiting for Sanghamittā to arrive, the queen Anulā, together with many women of the royal harem, accepted the ten precepts and wore ochre robes. That is, they observed the same ten precepts that a sāmaṇerī observes and wore the robes of a renunciant (probably not cut up into patches), but they had not received any formal ordination; they were the equivalents of the *dasasilmātās* of present-day Sri Lanka. They left the palace and went to reside in a pleasant convent built by the king in a certain part of the city. It was only after Sanghamittā and the other bhikkhunīs arrived from India that they could take pabbajjā.

(2) *The Sikkhamānā Training*. The second legal obstacle to a woman's ordination, according to the conservative Vinaya experts, is imposed by the sixth garudhamma. This rule states that before she can take upasampadā, a woman candidate must live as a sikkhamānā, or "probationer," training in six rules for a period of two years. She receives the status of sikkhamānā through a *saṅghakamma*, a legal act of the saṅgha. Now this act is performed by the bhikkhunī saṅgha, not by the bhikkhu saṅgha,[5] and therefore, in the absence of a bhikkhunī saṅgha, a female candidate for ordination has no way to

4. *Mahāvaṃsa*, XV.18–23, as translated in Geiger 1912: 98. I have slightly modernized Geiger's archaic English and translated some words he left in Pāli.

5. Bhikkhunī *pācittiya* 63; Vin IV: 318–20.

become a sikkhamānā. Without becoming a sikkhamānā, it is said, she will not be able to fulfill the prescribed training (*sikkhā*) leading to upasampadā. Further, after completing her training in the six rules, the sikkhamānā must obtain an "agreement" (*sammati*) from the saṅgha, an authorization to take upasampadā, and this agreement too is given by a bhikkhunī saṅgha.[6] Thus these two steps along the way to upasampadā—namely, (1) the agreement to train in the six rules, and (2) the agreement confirming that the candidate has completed the two years' training in the six rules—both have to be conferred by a bhikkhunī saṅgha. In the absence of a Theravāda bhikkhunī saṅgha, the Vinaya experts say, a candidate for bhikkhunī ordination cannot pass through these two steps, and without passing through these two steps, she will not be qualified for full ordination.

The last book of the Pāli Vinaya Piṭaka, known as the *Parivāra*, is a technical manual dealing with fine points of Vinaya observance. One section of this work called *Kammavagga* (Vin V: 220–23), devoted to legal acts of the saṅgha, examines the conditions under which such acts "fail" (*vipajjanti*), i.e., grounds on which such acts are invalidated.[7] Among the stipulations of the *Parivāra*, an upasampadā can fail on account of the candidate (*vatthuto*); on account of the motion (*ñattito*); on account of the announcement (*anussāvanato*); on account of the boundary (*sīmāto*); and on account of the assembly (*parisato*). Applying these requirements to the case of the female candidate for upasampadā, conservative Vinaya experts sometimes argue that a woman who has not undergone training as a sikkhamānā is not a qualified candidate, and thus upasampadā given to her will be invalid.

(3) *Upasampadā*. In the eyes of the Vinaya conservatives, the most formidable barrier to reviving the bhikkhunī saṅgha concerns the upasampadā, the full ordination. In the case of bhikkhu ordination, the ordination of a monk, upasampadā is administered by an act known as "ordination with a motion as the fourth" (*ñatticatutthakammūpasampadā*). First the spokesman for the saṅgha makes a motion (*ñatti*) to the saṅgha to give ordination to the candidate with a certain senior monk as preceptor. Then he

6. Bhikkhunī *pācittiya* 64; Vin IV: 320–21.

7. This section is expanded upon in the *Samantapāsādikā* (Sp VII: 1395–1402) as well as in the *Vinayasaṃgaha*, or "Compendium of the Vinaya," a topical anthology from the *Samantapāsādikā* composed by the twelfth-century Sri Lankan elder, Sāriputta (chap. 33, VRI ed.: pp. 363–84).

makes three announcements that the saṅgha ordains the candidate with the senior monk as preceptor; any monk present who disapproves is invited to voice objection. And finally, if no monk has objected, he concludes that the saṅgha has given ordination to the candidate with the senior monk as preceptor.

When the bhikkhunī saṅgha was first established, the same method must have been used to ordain women as bhikkhunīs. After the bhikkhunī saṅgha gained maturity, however, this method was replaced by another that involved the participation of both the bhikkhunī saṅgha and the bhikkhu saṅgha. Both ordain the candidate by separate processes following in close succession, each with a motion and three announcements. The method is therefore called ordination through eight proclamations (*aṭṭhavācikūpasampadā*). The sixth garudhamma, which Mahāpajāpatī Gotamī reportedly accepted as a condition for ordination, already states that after training as a sikkhamānā for two years in the six rules, a woman should seek upasampadā from a dual saṅgha, that is, from both the bhikkhunī saṅgha and the bhikkhu saṅgha.[8] The same principle is described more fully in the *Cullavagga* section of the Vinaya in its explanation of the *upasampadā* rite, where the candidate first takes ordination from the bhikkhunī saṅgha and then comes before the bhikkhu saṅgha to undergo the second ordination involving another motion, three announcements, and confirmation.[9]

The main legal objection that conservative Vinaya legalists raise against a revival of bhikkhunī ordination is that it must be given by an *existing* bhikkhunī saṅgha, and to be a purely Theravāda ordination it must come from an existing Theravāda bhikkhunī saṅgha. This leads to a conundrum, for in the absence of an existing Theravāda bhikkhunī saṅgha, a legitimate Theravāda bhikkhunī ordination cannot be granted. The ordination cannot be self-generated but must be the continuation of an existing tradition. Therefore, the argument runs, when that tradition has been disrupted, it cannot be reconstituted even with all the goodwill in the world. For monks to attempt to reconstitute a broken bhikkhunī saṅgha, it is said, is to claim

8. Vin II: 255: *Dve vassāni chasu dhammesu sikkhitasikkhāya sikkhamānāya ubhatosaṅghe upasampadā pariyesitabbā.*

9. Vin II: 272–74.

a privilege unique to a perfectly enlightened Buddha, and no one but the next Buddha can claim that.

Those who favor reviving the bhikkhunī ordination cite a statement by the Buddha in the *Cullavagga*: "Bhikkhus, I allow bhikkhus to give upasampadā to bhikkhunīs,"[10] rightly pointing out that the Buddha never revoked that allowance. However, it would be *incorrect* to say that the Buddha gave permission in perpetuity to the bhikkhus to ordain bhikkhunīs on their own. As long as there were no bhikkhunīs in existence, that is, at the very inception of the bhikkhunī saṅgha, it was only natural that the Buddha's allowance to the bhikkhus to ordain bhikkhunīs would be applied in this way, for there was simply no other way it could be applied. Thereafter the allowance continued, but it did not mean that bhikkhus *on their own* could ordain bhikkhunīs. The Buddha did not revoke this allowance because the allowance was necessary after the dual-saṅgha ordination procedure was initiated. If the Buddha had revoked the permission he had earlier given to bhikkhus to ordain bhikkhunīs, then the bhikkhu saṅgha would not have been entitled to give ordination after the bhikkhunī saṅgha gave its ordination. However, the bhikkhus retained this privilege, except now it was part of a two-stage system of ordination. When the new procedure was introduced, with the bhikkhunī saṅgha conferring ordination first, the allowance to the bhikkhus to ordain bhikkhunīs was integrated into the new two-stage ordination. So the permission remained intact, except that now the bhikkhus did not act alone. The upasampadā they were entitled to confer followed upasampadā conferred by the bhikkhunīs.

This requirement for dual-saṅgha ordination became integral to the Theravāda tradition's conception of the bhikkhunī. In the Pāli Vinaya Piṭaka, we encounter a standard description of a bhikkhunī that reads thus:

> *Bhikkhunī*: one who is a mendicant; one who arrives on almsround; one who wears a robe made of cut-up patches; one who has the designation of a bhikkhunī; one who claims to be a bhikkhunī; a "come, bhikkhunī" bhikkhunī; a bhikkhunī ordained by going to the three refuges; an excellent bhikkhunī; a bhikkhunī by essence; a trainee bhikkhunī; a bhikkhunī beyond

10. Vin IV: 255: *Anujānāmi, bhikkhave, bhikkhūhi bhikkhuniyo upasampādetuṃ.*

> training (i.e., an arahant bhikkhunī); a bhikkhunī fully ordained *by a dual sangha in harmony*, through an act that is unshakable and able to stand, consisting of a motion and three announcements. Among these, what is intended in this sense as a bhikkhunī is one fully ordained *by a dual sangha in harmony*, through an act that is unshakable and able to stand consisting of a motion and three announcements.[11]

From the time the bhikkhunī saṅgha reached maturity until its demise, the dual-saṅgha ordination was regarded in Theravāda countries as mandatory. We find in the Vinaya Piṭaka occasional mention of an *ekato-upasampannā*, "one ordained on one side," and we might suppose this means that some bhikkhunīs continued to be ordained solely by the bhikkhu saṅgha. This, however, would be a misinterpretation of the expression. The expression *ekato-upasampannā* refers to a woman who has received ordination solely from the bhikkhunī saṅgha but not yet from the bhikkhu saṅgha. It denotes a woman in the intermediate stage between ordinations by the two wings of the "dual saṅgha." The Pāli Vinaya Piṭaka is scrupulously consistent in restricting the use of the word "bhikkhunī" to those who have fulfilled the dual-saṅgha ordination. In the *Suttavibhaṅga* section of the Vinaya, whenever the text has occasion to gloss the word *bhikkhunī*, it states: "A bhikkhunī is one who has been ordained in the dual saṅgha" (*bhikkhunī nāma ubhatosaṅghe upasampannā*).

Thus, in the light of the *Parivāra*'s criteria, the Vinaya legalists argue that when the rules for ordination specify a dual-saṅgha upasampadā, and when a bhikkhunī is legally defined as one ordained by a dual saṅgha, if a single saṅgha performs the ordination, the assembly is defective because valid ordination requires the participation of the two assemblies, of bhikkhus and bhikkhunīs. The motion and announcements are also defective, since

11. Vin IV: 214: *Bhikkhunīti bhikkhikāti bhikkhunī; bhikkhācariyaṃ ajjhupagatāti bhikkhunī; bhinnapaṭadharāti bhikkhunī; samaññāya bhikkhunī; paṭiññāya bhikkhunī; ehi bhikkhunīti bhikkhunī; tīhi saraṇagamanehi upasampannāti bhikkhunī; bhadrā bhikkhunī; sārā bhikkhunī; sekhā bhikkhunī; asekhā bhikkhunī; samaggena ubhatosaṅghena ñatticatutthena kammena akuppena ṭhānārahena upasampannāti bhikkhunī. Tatra yāyaṃ bhikkhunīsamaggena ubhatosaṅghena ñatticatutthena kammena akuppena ṭhānārahena upasampannā, ayaṃ imasmiṃ atthe adhippetā bhikkhunīti.*

only one motion and three announcements have been recited, whereas valid ordination requires two procedures, each with its own motion and three announcements. Starting from these premises, since a Theravāda bhikkhunī saṅgha no longer exists, the legalists arrive at the inevitable conclusion that there is simply no possibility of reviving the Theravāda bhikkhunī saṅgha. Bhikkhunī ordination will remain out of reach throughout the duration of the present Buddha's dispensation.

The Case for a Revival of Theravāda Bhikkhunī Ordination

Now that I have sketched the legal arguments that conservative Theravāda Vinaya authorities raise against restoring the bhikkhunī ordination to the Theravāda tradition, I want to look at some factors, textual and ethical, that favor its restoration. These factors can be distributed into two groups: one might be called *ancient mandate*, the other, *compelling contemporary circumstances.*

The primary *ancient mandate* is the Buddha's own decision to create a bhikkhunī saṅgha as a counterpart to the male bhikkhu saṅgha. We should note that when the five hundred women headed by Mahāpajāpatī Gotamī came to the Buddha with their heads shaved, wearing ochre robes, they did not ask the Buddha to establish an order of nuns. They simply asked him "to permit women to go forth from the household life into homelessness in the Dhamma and Vinaya proclaimed by the Tathāgata."[12] Although, according to the canonical record, the Buddha at first denied this request, he finally acquiesced. In yielding, however, he did not simply agree to allow women to go forth in some secondary role, for example, as ten-precept nuns; rather, he allowed them to take full ordination as bhikkhunīs, the female counterpart of the bhikkhus. Further, he constituted renunciant women into a distinct *order*, a society governed by its own rules and regulations. Though he subordinated this order to the bhikkhu saṅgha with respect to certain functions, he still made it largely autonomous.

In the canonical record, the Buddha is shown giving a dire prediction

12. Vin II: 253; AN IV: 274: *Sādhu, bhante, labheyya mātugāmo tathāgatappavedite dhammavinaye agārasmā anagāriyaṃ pabbajjaṃ.*

about the effect this step would have on the lifespan of the spiritual life (*brahmacariya*) or the good Dhamma (*saddhamma*). He says that because women have received the going forth, the spiritual life will not last the full thousand years that it was originally destined to last but will instead endure only five hundred years.[13] This prediction is one of the major stumbling blocks that conservative Theravādins raise against attempts to revive the bhikkhunī saṅgha. It is beyond my purpose here to determine whether this passage is authentic or not, but regardless of the truth value of the story, we should still note a significant fact about the version that has come down in the Pāli canon (and, I believe, in all the other Vinayas that have been preserved except that of the Mahīśāsakas): namely, that the Buddha is shown making this prophecy *only after* he has agreed to allow women to go forth. If he truly wanted to prevent women from going forth, he would have made this prophecy while Ānanda was still launching his appeal on behalf of the Sakyan women. In such a case, Ānanda would probably have desisted from his effort and a bhikkhunī saṅgha would never have gotten off the ground.

There is little evidence that the permission granted to women to go forth contributed in any way to shortening the lifespan of the teaching, and the time frame mentioned in the text is also difficult to reconcile with the facts of Buddhist history insofar as we can ascertain them. The text may be suggesting that the reason for the Buddha's hesitancy was concern that close contacts between bhikkhus and bhikkhunīs would contribute to a situation whereby intimate feelings between the two would arise, and this would lead to many disrobings, or to the rise of a married clergy such as we find among the Buddhist priests of Japan. But the historical record contains no indications that this happened in the course of Indian Buddhism—certainly not around the dreaded date (approximately the first century C.E.). Other suttas speak about different causes for "the decline and disappearance of the good Dhamma," and these seem to me to point to factors that might play a greater role in the decline of the Dhamma than the conferring of ordination on women. For example, a sutta in the *Aṅguttara-nikāya* says the good Dhamma declines when the four assemblies dwell without respect for the Buddha, the Dhamma, the Saṅgha, the training, *samādhi*, and heedful-

13. Vin II: 256; AN IV: 278.

ness.[14] We should note that in this prediction the bhikkhunīs will also be around when the good Dhamma declines and disappears, which shows that in the view of the texts, the Buddha did not expect the bhikkhunī saṅgha to die out before the bhikkhu saṅgha did.

One way to interpret the Buddha's hesitancy to permit the going forth of women is to see it as a means of giving special emphasis to the need for caution in the relations between bhikkhus and bhikkhunīs. Consider a parallel: Shortly after his enlightenment, the Buddha pondered the question whether or not to teach the Dhamma to the world. According to the texts, he first decided *not* to teach, to keep silent and dwell at ease.[15] The deity Brahmā had to come down from his celestial abode and persuade the Buddha to take up the task of proclaiming the Dhamma to the world. Can we really believe that the compassionate Buddha actually decided not to teach, to pass the rest of his life dwelling quietly in the forest? This hardly seems conceivable in the light of other texts that suggest his career as a world teacher was already pre-ordained.[16] But this dramatic scene can be seen as a way of emphasizing how hard it was for the Buddha to come to a decision to teach, and a message emerges that we have to revere and treasure the Dhamma as something precious. Similarly, because the Buddha hesitated to admit women to the saṅgha, from fear that it would shorten the lifespan of the teaching, we can draw out the message that bhikkhus and bhikkhunīs have to be heedful in their dealings with one another and not indulge in frivolous socializing. The Buddha might also have hesitated because he foresaw that the creation of a bhikkhunī saṅgha would have placed on the bhikkhus the burden of educating and protecting the nuns, responsibilities that could have obstructed their own progress.

Positive statements of support for the existence of bhikkhunīs can be gathered from the Sutta Piṭaka. I will briefly mention three.

(1) The first is the well-known statement in the *Mahāparinibbāna-sutta* (DN 16), which the Buddha is said to have made to Māra, when, shortly

14. AN III: 340.

15. MN I: 167–69; SN I: 135–37; Vin I: 4–7.

16. For example, AN 5.196 (III: 240–42) relates that the Bodhisatta had five dreams shortly before his enlightenment, several of which foretold his role as a great teacher with many disciples, both monastics and householders.

after his enlightenment, the tempter urged him to pass straightaway into final nibbāna without teaching others:

> Evil One, I will not pass into final nibbāna until I have bhikkhunī disciples who are competent, well trained, confident, learned, upholders of the Dhamma, practicing in accordance with the Dhamma, practicing properly, conducting themselves in accordance with the Dhamma, who have learned their own teacher's doctrine and can explain it, teach it, describe it, establish it, disclose it, analyze it, elucidate it, and having thoroughly refuted rival doctrines in accordance with reason, can teach the compelling Dhamma.[17]

According to this text, then, the Buddha considered well-trained bhikkhunī disciples one of the pillars of the teaching.

(2) Another passage, less well known, comes from the *Mahāvacchagottasutta* (MN 73). In this discourse, the wanderer Vacchagotta asks the Buddha whether he alone has achieved realization of the Dhamma or whether he has disciples who have also achieved realization. The wanderer inquires in turn about each class of disciple: bhikkhus, bhikkhunīs, celibate male householders, non-celibate male householders, celibate female householders, and non-celibate female householders. With each inquiry, the Buddha confirms that he has "not merely five hundred, but many more disciples than that" who have attained the highest realization appropriate to their particular status. When the questioning is finished, Vacchagotta exclaims, in words with which the Buddha himself would surely have agreed: "If the Venerable Gotama (the Buddha) had attained success in this Dhamma, and if there were bhikkhus who had attained success, but there were no bhikkhunīs who had attained success in this Dhamma, then this spiritual life would be incomplete with respect to this factor. But because, besides the Venerable Gotama and the bhikkhus, there are also bhikkhunīs who

17. DN II: 105: *Na tāvā'haṃ, pāpima, parinibbāyissāmi, yāva me bhikkhuniyo na sāvikā bhavissanti viyattā vinītā visāradā bahussutā dhammadharā dhammānudhammappaṭipannā sāmīcippaṭipannā anudhammacāriniyo, sakaṃ ācariyakaṃ uggahetvā ācikkhissanti desessanti paññapessanti paṭṭhapessanti vivarissanti vibhajissanti uttānikarissanti, uppannaṃ parappavādaṃ sahadhammena suniggahitaṃ niggahetvā sappāṭihāriyaṃ dhammaṃ desessanti.*

have attained success, this spiritual life is complete with respect to this factor."[18] For bhikkhunīs the highest success is arahantship, the same as for the bhikkhus.

(3) The saṅgha is known as "the field of merit for the world," and while this epithet applies preeminently to the "ariyan saṅgha," it also extends to the monastic saṅgha as the visible representation of the ariyan saṅgha in the world. Therefore, in the *Dakkhiṇāvibhaṅga-sutta* (MN 142), the Buddha discusses seven types of gifts that can be made to the saṅgha. Most of these include bhikkhunīs among the recipients, namely: (1) a gift to the dual saṅgha headed by the Buddha; (2) a gift to the dual saṅgha after the Buddha has passed away; (4) a gift specifically for the bhikkhunī saṅgha; (5) a gift for a selection of bhikkhus and bhikkhunīs taken to represent the saṅgha; and (7) a gift for a selection of bhikkhunīs taken to represent the saṅgha. The only two types of gifts excluded are those specifically for the bhikkhu saṅgha (3) and for a selection of bhikkhus taken to represent the saṅgha (6). Yet today, in Theravāda lands, these latter two types of gifts for the saṅgha are the only two that are possible; the other four are excluded by the absence of a viable bhikkhunī saṅgha.

Besides these passages, the *Aṅguttara-nikāya*, Ekanipāta, includes a series of suttas in which the Buddha is shown appointing various bhikkhunīs to the position of "most eminent" in different domains of the spiritual life; for example, the bhikkhunī Khemā was most eminent in wisdom, Uppalavaṇṇā in psychic potency, Bhaddakaccānā in great spiritual penetrations.[19] The compilers of the Pāli canon also collected the verses of the elder nuns into a work called the *Therīgāthā*, which offers us deep insights into the yearnings, striving, and attainments of the earliest generations of Buddhist women renunciants.

Quite apart from specific texts, an even more powerful argument based upon ancient precedent would appeal to the spirit of the Dhamma itself, which by its very nature is intended to disclose the path to liberation from

18. MN I: 492: *Sace hi bho gotama imaṃ dhammaṃ bhavañ c'eva gotamo ārādhako abhavissa, bhikkhū ca ārādhakā abhavissaṃsu, no ca kho bhikkhuniyo ārādhikā abhavissaṃsu, evam idaṃ brahmacariyaṃ aparipūraṃ abhavissa ten'aṃgena. Yasmā ca kho bho gotama imaṃ dhammaṃ bhavañ c'eva gotamo ārādhako, bhikkhū ca ārādhakā, bhikkhuniyo ca ārādhikā, evam idaṃ brahmacariyaṃ paripūraṃ ten'aṃgena.*

19. AN I: 25.

suffering to all humankind. When the Buddha first consented to teach, he declared: "Open to them are the doors to the deathless: Let those who have ears release faith."[20] Obviously, he did not intend this invitation to apply only to men but to all who would be willing to listen to his message of deliverance from suffering. He compares the Dhamma to a chariot, and says "One who has such a vehicle, *whether a woman or a man*, has by this vehicle drawn close to nibbāna."[21] The poet-monk Vaṃgīsa confirms that the Buddha's enlightenment was intended to benefit bhikkhunīs as well as bhikkhus:

> Indeed, for the good of many
> the Sage attained enlightenment,
> for the bhikkhus and bhikkhunīs
> who have reached and seen the fixed course.[22]

In the suttas, we see that the Buddha often included the bhikkhunīs as the recipients of his teaching. When he compares himself to a farmer cultivating different fields, he likens the bhikkhus and bhikkhunīs jointly to the most excellent field for his teaching.[23] In the simile of the ancient city, he says that after he had followed the noble eightfold path and penetrated the links of dependent origination, "I explained them to the bhikkhus, the bhikkhunīs, the male lay followers, and the female lay followers, so that this spiritual life has become successful and prosperous, extended, popular, widespread, well proclaimed among gods and humans."[24] When Sāriputta devises a teaching that elucidates the path that all Buddhas take to arrive at full enlightenment, the Buddha urges him to expound this teaching to the bhikkhus and bhikkhunīs as well as to the male and female lay devotees.[25]

Though many people will not be mature enough to tread this path to its

20. MN I: 169, SN I: 138, Vin I: 7.

21. SN I: 33.

22. SN I: 196. The parallel verses at *Theragāthā* 1256–57 extend this to laymen and laywomen as well.

23. SN IV: 315.

24. SN II: 107.

25. SN V: 161.

end, in principle no one should be hindered from doing so merely by reason of his or her gender. Yet this is precisely what is happening when women are prevented from taking full ordination. While defenders of the present system say that women can make just as much progress by taking up some surrogate female renunciant lifestyle as they could by becoming bhikkhunīs, the plain fact is that these subordinate renunciant roles do not meet their aspirations or give them access to the complete training laid down by the Buddha. Nor did the Buddha ever design for women renunciants such subordinate roles as that of the *dasasilmātā*, the *thilashin*, or the *maechi*, who all technically still belong to the assembly of upāsikās. The one position that the Buddha intended for those who leave the homeless life was that of a fully ordained bhikkhunī. Further, in Asian Buddhist societies, nuns who have settled for such surrogate positions usually do not command the reverence from the Buddhist lay communities that bhikkhunīs could inspire. Thus they seldom take on leadership roles or give guidance in religious activities and social services but linger on the margins, often appearing timid and self-conscious.

This line of thinking leads directly to reflection on the *contemporary conditions* that support a resuscitation of bhikkhunī ordination. I will note two such conditions.

(1) The first arises out of the realization that has been thrust upon Theravādins, beginning around the middle of the twentieth century, that they are not the only Buddhists who preserve a monastic system guided by a Vinaya traceable to the early saṅgha. As communications have improved between different parts of the Buddhist world, more knowledgeable Theravādin Buddhists (especially in Sri Lanka) have come to learn that the monks and nuns of East Asia—in Taiwan, China, Korea, and Vietnam, though not Japan—while following Mahāyāna teachings and practices, are still governed by a Vinaya with a body of rules largely identical with those laid down in the Pāli Vinaya Piṭaka. This Vinaya, which derives from the Dharmaguptaka school, is strikingly similar in many details with the Pāli Vinaya. The Tibetan Buddhist monastic system is also guided by a Vinaya derived from another early school, the Mūlasarvāstivādins. In recent years prominent Tibetan lamas have encouraged some of their student-nuns to receive full ordination in East Asian countries, and many would support

officially starting a bhikkhunī saṅgha within Tibetan Buddhism. Thus, when the Buddhist traditions of East Asia and Tibet have (or may one day have) orders of officially sanctioned bhikkhunīs, the absence of a recognized bhikkhunī saṅgha in South Asian Theravāda Buddhism will be conspicuous, a glaring gap. Educated people around the world—even educated Theravādin lay followers, both men and women—will find it difficult to empathize with the refusal of the Theravādin monastic order to grant full ordination to women, and will compare Theravāda unfavorably with the other forms of Buddhism.

(2) Such an exclusive attitude would receive strong public disapproval today because of the vast differences between the social and cultural attitudes of our age and those of India in the fifth century B.C.E., when the Buddha lived and taught. Our own age has been shaped by the ideas of the European Enlightenment, a movement that affirmed the inherent dignity of the human person, led to the rise of democracy, ushered in such concepts as universal human rights and universal suffrage, and brought demands for political equality and equal justice for all under the law. In today's world, all discrimination based on race, religion, and ethnicity is regarded as unjust and unjustifiable, the remnant of primal prejudices that we are obliged to cast off in the realization that all human beings, by virtue of their humanity, are entitled to the same rights that we assume for ourselves, including the right to fulfill their highest religious aspirations. The great project of the contemporary world, we might say, has been the dissolution of privilege: without a sound reason, no one is entitled to special privileges denied to others.

One of the most basic grounds for distinguishing people into the privileged and the deprived, the superiors and the subordinates, has been gender. Men have historically been in the privileged position, with women in the subsidiary position and denied those privileges claimed by men. From the mid-nineteenth century on, discrimination based on gender came to be perceived as arbitrary and unjust, a system that had been imposed on society simply because of the dominant roles that men had played in eras when social stability depended on physical strength and military force. Thus women came to claim the right to work at professional jobs, the right to vote, the right to equal salaries, the right to serve in the military, even the right to hold the highest position in the land. As far back as 1869, John

Stuart Mill wrote in the opening paragraph of his tract, *The Subjection of Women*: "An opinion which I have held from the very earliest period when I had formed any opinions at all on social political matters...is that the principle which regulates the existing social relations between the two sexes—the legal subordination of one sex to the other—is wrong itself, and now one of the chief hindrances to human improvement; and that it ought to be replaced by a principle of perfect equality, admitting no power or privilege on the one side, nor disability on the other."[26] The 130 years since these words were written have witnessed, in the progressive countries of the West, a sustained effort to translate this conviction into practice in various domains of both private and public life.

Now that discrimination based on gender has been challenged almost everywhere in the secular sphere, it is time for its role in religious life to come up for serious scrutiny. For religion, unfortunately, remains one of its most persistent strongholds, and Buddhism is no exception to this. It is true that the Vinaya makes bhikkhunīs subordinate to bhikkhus and the bhikkhunī saṅgha subordinate to the bhikkhu saṅgha, but we have to remember that the Buddha lived and taught in India in the fifth century B.C.E. and had to conform to the social expectations of the period. While certain practices that pertain to etiquette may need to be evaluated in the light of altered social and cultural conditions insofar as they do not touch on the basics of monastic discipline, in this paper I am not concerned with rules governing the relationship between monks and nuns but solely with the question of ordination. When we contemplate what line of action would be appropriate for us to take on this issue, we should not ask what the Buddha did twenty-five centuries ago but what he would want us to do today. If people see Theravāda Buddhism as a religion that includes male renunciants but excludes female renunciants, or that admits them only through some type of unofficial ordination, they will suspect that something is fundamentally askew, and defensive arguments based on appeals to arcane principles of monastic law will not go very far to break down distrust. This will be an instance of the type of behavior that we meet so often in the Vinaya where

26. Mill 1869.

"those without confidence do not gain confidence, while among those with confidence, some undergo vacillation."[27]

On the other hand, by showing that they have the courage to restore to women the right to lead a full religious life as instituted by the Buddha, that is, by reviving the bhikkhunī saṅgha, Theravādin elders will enable their form of Buddhism to take its place in the modern world, firmly and proudly, while still upholding a path that is timeless and not subject to the vagaries of changing fashions. To take this step does not mean, as some might fear, that we are "meddling" with the Dhamma and the Vinaya just to fit people's worldly expectations; the truths of the Dhamma, the principles of the path, the guidelines of the Vinaya, remain intact. But it would show that we know how to apply the Dhamma and the Vinaya in a way that is appropriate to the time and circumstances, and also in a way that is kind and embracing rather than rigid and rejecting.

Addressing the Legalist Challenge

Nevertheless, while there might be strong textual and ethical grounds favoring a revival of the Theravāda bhikkhunī saṅgha, such a step would not be possible unless the legal objections to such a movement can be addressed. The legalists object to resuscitating bhikkhunī ordination not so much because of bias against women (though some might have such a bias), but because they see such a measure as a legal impossibility. To restore the Theravāda bhikkhunī saṅgha, the three challenges posed by Theravāda Vinaya legalists would have to be overcome. These are the challenges based on: (1) the problem of pabbajjā (novice ordination); (2) the problem of sikkhamānā ordination and training; and (3) the problem of upasampadā.

Before I deal with these problems individually, however, I first want to note that Theravāda jurisprudence often merges stipulations on legal issues that stem from the canonical Vinaya texts, the *aṭṭhakathās* (commentaries), and the *ṭīkā*s (subcommentaries) with interpretations of these stipulations that have gained currency through centuries of tradition. I do not want to undervalue tradition, for it represents the accumulated legal expertise

27. *Appasannānañceva appasādāya pasannānañca ekaccānaṃ aññathattāya.* See Vin III: 20, III: 21, etc.

of generations of Vinaya specialists, and this expertise should certainly be respected and taken into account in determining how the Vinaya is to be applied to new situations. But we also must remember that tradition should not be placed on a par with the canonical Vinaya or even with the secondary authorities, the *aṭṭhakathās* and *ṭīkās*. These different sources should be assigned different weights of authority according to their different origins. When our understanding of the Vinaya is strongly grounded in tradition, however, without realizing it we may become entangled in a web of traditionalist *assumptions* that obstructs our ability to distinguish what derives from the canonical Vinaya from what is prescribed by tradition. Sometimes simply changing the assumptions can recast the principles of the Vinaya in a whole new light.

I will illustrate this point with an analogy from geometry. A straight line is drawn through a point. As this line is extended, the distance between its two ends widens. It is thus obvious that the two ends will never meet, and if anyone expresses doubts about this, I would almost question their rationality. But this is so only because I am thinking within the framework of traditional geometry—Euclidean geometry—which held sway over mathematics up until the twentieth century. When, however, we adopt the standpoint of spherical geometry, we can see that a line drawn through a particular point, if extended far enough, eventually encounters itself. Again, in traditional geometry we are taught that a triangle can have at most only one right angle and that the sum of the angles of a triangle must be 180 degrees, and this can be proven with absolute rigor. But that is so only in Euclidean space. Give me a sphere, and we can define a triangle with three right angles whose angles make a sum of 270 degrees. Thus, if I break away from my familiar assumptions, a whole new range of possibilities suddenly opens up to my understanding.

The same applies to our thinking about the Vinaya, and I write from personal experience. During my years in Sri Lanka, I shared the traditional conservative Theravādin view about the prospects for bhikkhunī ordination. This was because the monks that I consulted on this issue were Vinaya conservatives. Thinking the question of bhikkhunī ordination too abstruse for me to understand myself, I asked them about it and simply deferred to their judgment. When I finally decided to examine the canonical and commentarial sources on the subject, I did not find anything to disprove what they had said. They were quite learned in the Vinaya, and so I found that they had indeed been speaking about straight lines and triangles, not about bent lines and hexagons. But what I found was that they were framing their judgments against a background of traditionalist assumptions; they were locating their straight lines and triangles in a Vinaya version of Euclidean space. And the questions occurred to me: "Is it necessary to frame these lines and triangles in Euclidean space? What happens if we transfer them to a Vinaya version of curved space? What happens if we detach the pronouncements of the Vinaya from the background of traditionalist premises and look at them using the Buddha's original intention as a guide? What happens if we acknowledge that the Vinaya Piṭaka, as it has come down to us, did not anticipate the division of the original saṅgha into different schools with their own ordination lineages or the disappearance of the bhikkhunī saṅgha in one particular school? What happens if we acknowledge that it simply gives us no clear guidance about what should be done in such a situation? What if we then try to guide ourselves by the question, 'What would the Buddha want us to do in such a situation as we find ourselves in today?'" When we raise these questions, we can see that the procedures for bhikkhunī ordination laid down in the Vinaya Piṭaka were never intended to preclude the possibility of reviving a defunct bhikkhunī saṅgha. They were simply proposed as the norm for conducting an ordination when the bhikkhunī saṅgha already exists. When this understanding dawns, we then enter a new space, a new framework that can accommodate fresh possibilities unimagined within the web of traditionalist assumptions.

For conservative theory, the two fundamental assumptions are: (1) that the dual-saṅgha ordination was intended to apply under all circumstances and admits of no exceptions or modifications to accord with conditions; and (2) that the Theravāda is the only Buddhist school that preserves an authentic Vinaya tradition. For those who favor revival of the bhikkhunī saṅgha, the fundamental starting point is the Buddha's decision to create the bhikkhunī saṅgha. Although the Buddha may have hesitated to take this step and did so only after the intercession of Ānanda (according to the *Cullavagga* account), he eventually did establish an order of bhikkhunīs and gave this order his wholehearted support. The procedure of ordination was merely the legal mechanics to implement that decision. From this standpoint, to block the implementation of that decision because of a legal technicality is to hamper the fulfillment of the Buddha's own intention. This is not to say that the proper way to implement his intention should violate the guidelines of the Vinaya. But within those broad guidelines the two assumptions of conservative legalism can be circumvented by holding either or both of the following: (1) that under exceptional circumstances the bhikkhu saṅgha is entitled to revert to a single-saṅgha ordination of bhikkhunīs; and (2) that to preserve the form of dual-saṅgha ordination, the Theravāda bhikkhu saṅgha can collaborate with a bhikkhunī saṅgha from an East Asian country following the Dharmaguptaka Vinaya.

This approach to ordination may not satisfy the most rigorous demand of conservative Theravāda Vinaya legal theory, namely, that it be conducted by Theravāda bhikkhus and bhikkhunīs who have been ordained by Theravāda bhikkhus and bhikkhunīs in an unbroken lineage. But to make that impossible demand the uncompromising requirement for restoring the bhikkhunī saṅgha would seem unreasonably stringent. Admittedly, those who insist on the dual ordination do so, not because they take some special delight in being stringent, but out of respect for what they see as the integrity of the Vinaya. However, the strictest interpretation of the Vinaya may not necessarily be the only one that is valid, and it may not necessarily be the one that best serves the interests of Buddhism in the modern world. In the view of many learned Theravāda monks, mainly Sri Lankan, adopting either of the above routes will culminate in a valid bhikkhunī ordination and at the same time will grant to women—half the Buddhist population—the chance to live the spiritual life as fully ordained bhikkhunīs.

I will now turn to the three hurdles posed at the beginning of this section—pabbajjā, the sikkhamānā training, and upasampadā—taking each individually. Since functional bhikkhunī saṅghas already exist, these discussions are partly anachronistic, but I think it is still important to bring them up to address the concerns of the legalists. Hence I will be giving not explanations of how a bhikkhunī ordination can be revived but justifications for the procedures that have already been used to revive it. I will begin with the upasampadā, since this is the most critical step in the whole ordination process. I will then continue in reverse order through the sikkhamānā training back to pabbajjā.

(1) In the Pāli Vinaya Piṭaka, *upasampadā* for bhikkhunīs is prescribed

as a two-step process involving separate procedures performed first by a bhikkhunī saṅgha and then by a bhikkhu saṅgha. To restore the extinct bhikkhunī saṅgha two methods have been proposed. One is to allow Theravāda bhikkhus on their own to ordain women as bhikkhunīs until a bhikkhunī saṅgha becomes functional and can participate in dual-saṅgha ordinations. This method draws upon the authorization that the Buddha originally gave to the bhikkhus to ordain women during the early history of the bhikkhunī saṅgha. Such a procedure must have held for some time before the dual-saṅgha ordination was instituted, after which it was discontinued in favor of dual-saṅgha ordination. However, because the Buddha's permission to bhikkhus to ordain bhikkhunīs was not actually abolished, advocates of this method contend that it can become operative once again during a period when a bhikkhunī saṅgha does not exist. On this view, the original process by which the bhikkhus, on the Buddha's command, created a bhikkhunī saṅgha serves as a viable model for reviving a defunct bhikkhunī saṅgha. The original allowance could be considered a legal precedent: just as, in the past, that allowance was accepted as a means of fulfilling the Buddha's intention of creating a bhikkhunī saṅgha, so in the present that allowance could again be used to renew the bhikkhunī heritage after the original Theravāda bhikkhunī saṅgha disappeared.

The other route to reestablishing the Theravāda bhikkhunī saṅgha is to conduct the dual-saṅgha ordination by bringing together Theravāda bhikkhus and bhikkhunīs from an East Asian country such as Taiwan. This method, the one generally preferred, could be combined with a single-saṅgha ordination by Theravāda bhikkhus in two successive steps. This was the procedure used at the grand ordination ceremony at Bodhgaya in February 1998, held under the auspices of Fo Guang Shan, and it had certain advantages over either taken alone.

The grand ordination ceremony assembled bhikkhus from several traditions—Chinese Mahāyāna, Theravāda, and Tibetan—along with Taiwanese and Western bhikkhunīs to conduct the full dual ordination in accord with the Chinese tradition. The women who were ordained included Theravāda nuns from Sri Lanka and Nepal as well as Western nuns following Tibetan Buddhism. One might think that this was a Mahāyāna rite that made the nuns Mahāyāna bhikkhunīs, but this would be a misunderstanding. While the Chinese monks and nuns were practitioners of

Mahāyāna Buddhism, the monastic Vinaya tradition they observe is not a Mahāyāna Vinaya but one stemming from an early Buddhist school, the Dharmaguptakas, which belonged to the same broad Vibhajyavāda tradition to which the southern Theravāda school belongs. They were virtually the northwest Indian counterpart of the Theravāda, with a similar collection of suttas, an Abhidharma, and a Vinaya that largely corresponds to the Pāli Vinaya.[28] Thus the upasampadā ordination performed by the Chinese saṅgha at Bodhgaya conferred on the candidates the bhikkhunī lineage of the Dharmaguptakas, so that in Vinaya terms they were now full-fledged bhikkhunīs inheriting the Dharmaguptaka Vinaya lineage.[29]

However, the bhikkhunīs from Sri Lanka wanted to become heirs to the Theravāda Vinaya lineage and to be acceptable to the Theravāda bhikkhus of Sri Lanka. The Sri Lankan bhikkhus who sponsored their ordination, too, were apprehensive that if the nuns returned to Sri Lanka with only the Chinese ordination, their co-religionists would have considered their ordination to have been essentially a Mahayanist one. To prevent this, shortly afterward the newly ordained bhikkhunīs traveled to Sarnath, where they underwent another upasampadā conducted in Pāli under Theravāda bhik-

28. See Heirman 2002a.

29. In the course of the Chinese transmission of the Dharmaguptaka ordination lineage, the bhikkhunī ordination has often been conferred solely by a bhikkhu saṅgha rather than by a dual saṅgha, which could open the ordination to a strict Theravādin objection that valid transmission has been broken. The account of bhikkhunī upasampadā in the Vinaya texts of the Dharmaguptakas, as preserved in Chinese (at T 22: 925a26–b17; 1067a28–c2), does describe it as a dual-saṅgha ordination, very much as in the Pāli Vinaya. Vinaya masters in the Chinese tradition have explicitly discussed this problem. An early Vinaya master from Kashmir, Guṇavarman, who in the fifth century presided over the ordination of Chinese bhikkhunīs by a bhikkhu saṅgha alone, expressed the opinion: "As the *bhikṣuṇī* ordination is finalized by the *bhikṣu saṅgha*, even if the 'basic dharma' (i.e., the ordination taken from the *bhikṣuṇī saṅgha*) is not conferred, the *bhikṣuṇī* ordination still results in pure vows, just as in the case of Mahāprajāpatī." And Tao-Hsuan (Dao-xuan), the seventh-century patriarch of the Chinese Dharmaguptaka school, wrote: "Even if a *bhikṣuṇī* ordination is transmitted directly from a *bhikṣu saṅgha* without first conferring the 'basic dharma,' it is still valid, as nowhere in the Vinaya indicates otherwise. However, the precept masters commit an offence." Both quotations are from Heng-Ching 2000: 523, 524. These opinions suggest that, from the internal perspective of this school (or at least according to several important Vinaya commentators), ordination solely by the bhikkhu saṅgha, though not in full conformity with the prescribed procedure, is still valid. If this fault were considered serious enough to invalidate ordination through a lineage of Chinese bhikkhunīs, ordination could still be sought from Vietnamese bhikkhunīs, who have preserved the dual ordination through the centuries.

khus from Sri Lanka. This ordination did not negate the earlier dual ordination received from the Chinese saṅgha but gave it a new direction. While recognizing the validity of the upasampadā they received through the Chinese saṅgha, the Sri Lankan bhikkhus effectively admitted them to the Theravāda saṅgha and conferred on them permission to observe the Theravāda Vinaya and to participate in *saṅghakammas*, legal acts of the saṅgha, with their brothers in the Sri Lankan bhikkhu saṅgha.

While dual-saṅgha ordination should certainly prevail whenever conditions make it feasible, a case—admittedly, a weaker one—can also be made to justify ordination solely by a saṅgha of Theravāda bhikkhus. Although we speak of "a bhikkhu saṅgha" and "a bhikkhunī saṅgha," when a candidate applies for ordination, she actually applies simply to be admitted *to the saṅgha*. This is why, during the earliest phase in the history of the bhikkhunī saṅgha, the Buddha could permit the bhikkhus to ordain women as bhikkhunīs. By giving women the upasampadā, what the bhikkhus do is admit them to the saṅgha. It is then by reason of the fact that they are women that they become bhikkhunīs and thereby members of the bhikkhunī saṅgha.

According to the *Cullavagga*, preliminary ordination by bhikkhunīs was introduced because the candidate has to be questioned about various obstructions to ordination, among them issues relating to a woman's sexual identity. When the bhikkhus asked women candidates these questions, they were too embarrassed to reply. To avert this impasse, the Buddha proposed that a preliminary ordination be held by the bhikkhunīs, who would first question the candidate about the obstructions, clear her, give her a first ordination, and then bring her to the bhikkhu saṅgha, where she would be ordained a second time by the bhikkhus.[30] In this arrangement, it is still the bhikkhu saṅgha that functions as the ultimate authority determining the validity of the ordination. The unifying factor behind most of the garudhammas is the granting of formal precedence in saṅgha affairs to the bhikkhus, and we can thus infer that the point of the sixth garudhamma, the principle of respect that requires that a sikkhamānā obtain upasampadā from a dual saṅgha, is to ensure that she obtain it from the bhikkhu saṅgha.

30. See Vin II: 271.

We can therefore claim that there are grounds for interpreting this sixth principle to imply that under extraordinary conditions upasampadā by a bhikkhu saṅgha alone is valid. We can readily infer that under the exceptional circumstances when a Theravāda bhikkhunī saṅgha has vanished, Theravāda bhikkhus are entitled to take as a precedent the original case when there was no bhikkhunī saṅgha and revive the allowance that the Buddha gave to the bhikkhus to ordain bhikkhunīs on their own. I have to emphasize that this is an interpretation of the Vinaya, a liberal interpretation, and it is far from compelling. But while Vinaya conservatives might have reservations about this way of interpreting the text, we would ask them to consider carefully whether their views are rooted in the text or in traditional interpretation. If our attitude is open and flexible, there seems no reason to deny that under these pressing conditions an upasampadā given by a bhikkhu saṅgha alone, being used for a purpose in harmony with the Buddha's intention, is sufficient to elevate a woman to the stature of a bhikkhunī.

Further, if we pay close attention to the wording of the Vinaya passage concerned with bhikkhunī ordination,[31] we would notice that the text does not lock this rite into a fixed and immutable form sealed with inviolable imperatives: "You must do it in this way and never in any other way." In fact, grammatically, the Pāli passage uses not the imperious imperative but the gentler gerundive or optative participle, "it should be done thus." But grammar aside, the text is simply describing the *normal and most natural way* to conduct the ordination when all the normal requisite conditions are at hand. There is nothing in the text itself, or elsewhere in the Pāli Vinaya, that lays down a rule stating categorically that, should the bhikkhunī saṅgha become extinct, the bhikkhus are prohibited from falling back on the original allowance the Buddha gave them to ordain bhikkhunīs and confer upasampadā on their own to resuscitate the bhikkhunī saṅgha.

To me this seems to be the crucial point: Only if there were such a clear prohibition would we be entitled to say that the bhikkhus are overstepping the bounds of legitimacy by conducting such an ordination. In the absence of such a decree in the text of the Vinaya Piṭaka and its commentaries, the judgment that an ordination by bhikkhus is in violation of the Vinaya is only an interpretation. It may be at present the dominant interpretation; it

31. Vin II: 272–74.

may be an interpretation that has the weight of tradition behind it. But *it remains an interpretation*, and we can well question whether it is an interpretation that needs to stand unquestioned. I myself would question whether it is the interpretation that properly reflects how the Buddha himself would want his monks to act under the critical conditions of our own time, when gender equality looms large as an ideal in secular life and as a value people expect to be embodied in religious life. I would question whether it is an interpretation that we should uphold when doing so may well "cause those without confidence not to gain confidence and those with confidence to vacillate."[32] Perhaps, instead of just resigning ourselves to a worst-case scenario, i.e., the absolute loss of the Theravāda bhikkhunī saṅgha, we should assume that the Theravāda bhikkhu saṅgha has the right, even the obligation, to interpret the regulations governing bhikkhunī ordination with the flexibility and liberality needed to bring its sister saṅgha back to life.

The Buddha himself did not regard the Vinaya as a system fixed immutably in stone, utterly resistant to interpretative adaptations. Before his passing, he taught the saṅgha four principles to help deal with novel situations not already covered by the rules of discipline, situations the monks might meet after his *parinibbāna*. These are called the four *mahāpadesā*,[33] "the four great guidelines," namely:

1. If something has not been rejected by me with the words "This is not allowed," if it accords with what has not been allowed and excludes what has been allowed, that is not allowed to you.
2. If something has not been rejected by me with the words "This is not allowed," if it accords with what has been allowed and excludes what has not been allowed, that is allowed to you.
3. If something has not been authorized by me with the words "This is allowed," if it accords with what has not been allowed and excludes what has been allowed, that is not allowed to you.
4. If something has not been authorized by me with the words "This is

32. See above, p. 106.

33. *Samantapāsādika* I 231.

> allowed," if it accords with what has been allowed and excludes what has not been allowed, that is allowed to you.[34]

Applying these guidelines to the question of whether the saṅgha has the right to revive the bhikkhunī saṅgha in either of the two ways discussed (or their combination), we can see that such a step would "accord with what has been allowed" and would not exclude anything else that has been allowed. Thus this step could clearly gain the support of guidelines 2 and 4.

It might be surprising to learn that the revival of the bhikkhunī saṅgha was advocated over half a century ago by a distinguished authority in one of the most conservative bastions of Theravāda Buddhism, namely, Burma. The person I refer to is the original Mingun Jetavan Sayadaw, the meditation teacher of the famous Mahasi Sayadaw and Taungpulu Sayadaw. The Jetavan Sayadaw composed, in Pāli, a commentary to the *Milindapañha* in which he argues for a revival of the bhikkhunī saṅgha. I have translated this part of the commentary and include it as an appendix to the present paper. Writing in the heartland of Theravāda conservatism in 1949, the Jetavan Sayadaw unflinchingly maintains that bhikkhus have the right to revive an extinct bhikkhunī saṅgha. He contends that the dual-saṅgha ordination was intended to apply only when a bhikkhunī saṅgha exists and that the Buddha's permission to the bhikkhus to ordain bhikkhunīs regains validity at any period of Buddhist history when the bhikkhunī saṅgha becomes nonexistent. I do not agree wholly with the Sayadaw's argument, particularly with his contention that the Buddha had foreseen with his omniscience the future extinction of the bhikkhunī saṅgha and intended his permission to bhikkhus to ordain bhikkhunīs as a remedy for this. I see this permission in its historical context as a measure designed to deal with an immediate problem arisen during the Buddha's own time; but I also regard it as one that we can employ as a legal precedent to solve our present problem. Nevertheless, I believe the Jetavan Sayadaw's essay is a refreshing reminder that a current

34. Vin I: 251: *Yaṃ bhikkhave, mayā "idaṃ na kappatī" ti apaṭikkhittaṃ, taṃ ce akappiyaṃ anulometi, kappiyaṃ paṭibāhati, taṃ vo na kappati. Yaṃ bhikkhave, mayā "idaṃ na kappatī" ti apaṭikkhittaṃ, taṃ ce kappiyaṃ anulometi, akappiyaṃ paṭibāhati, taṃ vo kappati. Yaṃ bhikkhave, mayā "idaṃ kappatī" ti ananuññātaṃ, taṃ ce akappiyaṃ anulometi, kappiyaṃ paṭibāhati, taṃ vo na kappati. Yaṃ bhikkhave, mayā "idaṃ kappatī" ti ananuññātaṃ, taṃ ce kappiyaṃ anulometi, akappiyaṃ paṭibāhati, taṃ vo kappatī ti.*

of thought sympathetic to the revival of the bhikkhunī saṅgha could flow through the Theravāda world even sixty years ago. Moreover, we can see from his essay that the idea that the bhikkhunī saṅgha can be revived was a hotly discussed topic of his time, and it is likely that a positive attitude toward the issue was shared by a sizeable section of the Burmese saṅgha.

Now, however, that a Theravāda bhikkhunī saṅgha exists in Sri Lanka, the question of how to revive it is no longer relevant. Any woman who wants to be ordained as a bhikkhunī in the Theravāda tradition can go to Sri Lanka to receive full ordination there. Of course, she will first have to fulfill the preliminary requirements, and in my view it is important to restore the observance of the sikkhamānā training to the preliminary requirements for bhikkhunī ordination.

(2) I next come to the *sikkhamānā* training. In the first section of this paper, I presented an argument sometimes posed by conservative Vinaya theorists. To recapitulate: Sikkhamānā training is a prerequisite for valid bhikkhunī ordination. Authorization to undertake this training, and confirmation that one has completed it, are both conferred by a bhikkhunī saṅgha. Without an existing Theravāda bhikkhunī saṅgha, this training cannot be given nor can one be confirmed as having completed it. Full ordination given to women who have not gone through these two steps is invalid. Hence there can be no valid Theravāda bhikkhunī ordination, and thus no revival of the Theravāda bhikkhunī saṅgha.

I want to look more closely at this issue, for if this contention is true, this would mean in effect that all the upasampadās given to all women in all Buddhist schools who have not undergone the sikkhamānā training are invalid. The question we are addressing is the following: Is bestowal of sikkhamānā status an absolutely necessary condition for valid upasampadā? Is the upasampadā conferred on a sāmaṇerī who has not gone through the formal sikkhamānā training valid or invalid, legal or illegal?

First, let us be clear that the Vinaya requires that a woman undertake the sikkhamānā training before undergoing upasampadā. To do so is one of the eight garudhammas. It is on this basis that the Vinaya legalists maintain that the upasampadā is valid only when given to a candidate who has trained as a sikkhamānā. Here, however, we are concerned not with what is prescribed by the texts but with a question of strict legality.

The "variant cases" sections attached to bhikkhunī *pācittiyas* 63 and 64 establish that upasampadā given to a woman who has not undergone the sikkhamānā training, though contrary to the intention of the Vinaya, is still valid. According to these rules, the preceptor receives a *pācittiya* offense for conducting the upasampadā, while the other participating bhikkhunīs receive *dukkaṭa* offenses, but the ordination itself remains valid and the candidate emerges a bhikkhunī. Bhikkhunī *pācittiya* 63 states: "If a bhikkhunī should ordain a probationer who has not trained for two years in the six dhammas, she incurs a *pācittiya*."[35] The "variant cases" section includes the following:

> When the act is legal, she ordains her perceiving the act as legal: a *pācittiya* offense. When the act is legal, she ordains her while in doubt [about its legality]: a *pācittiya* offense. When the act is legal, she ordains her perceiving the act as illegal: a *pācittiya* offense.[36]

According to this statement, the preceptor incurs a *pācittiya* if she gives the upasampadā to a candidate who has not trained in the six dhammas in three cases when the act is legal: she perceives it as legal, she is doubtful about its legality, and she perceives it as illegal. If, however, the act is illegal, she incurs only a *dukkaṭa*, even when she perceives it as legal. Interestingly, in describing these illegal cases, the text omits the word *vuṭṭhāpeti*, glossed by the word commentary as *upasampādeti*, "to fully ordain"; for in these cases, though the participants "go through the motions" of conferring full ordination, technically no act of ordination is performed.

Now since in the first three variants, the act is described as "legal" (*dhammakamma*), this implies that in the view of the compilers of the Vinaya, the upasampadā itself is valid and the candidate is legally ordained. Since the sixth garudhamma, as well as bhikkhunī *pācittiya* 63, are binding on the preceptor, she is penalized with a *pācittiya* for disobeying it; but disobedience, it seems, does not negate the validity of the upasampadā.

35. Vin IV: 319: *Yā pana bhikkhunī dve vassāni chasu dhammesu asikkhitasikkhaṃ sikkhamānaṃ vuṭṭhāpeyya pācittiyaṃ.*

36. Vin IV: 320: *Dhammakamme dhammakammasaññā vuṭṭhāpeti āpatti pācittiyassa. Dhammakamme vematikā vuṭṭhāpeti āpatti pācittiyassa. Dhammakamme adhammakammasaññā vuṭṭhāpeti āpatti pācittiyassa.*

We find the same set of variants for bhikkhunī *pācittiya* 64, which assigns a *pācittiya* to a bhikkhunī who gives the upasampadā to a sikkhamānā who has not received the authorization from a saṅgha; the implications are similar. Admittedly, there is an internal tension here between (1) the stipulation that the candidate must have undergone the sikkhamānā training and have had this authorized by the saṅgha before she is eligible to receive upasampadā, and (2) the fact that the ordination can be considered a "legal act" (*dhammakamma*) when given to a candidate who has not met these requirements. But it seems that failure to undertake or complete the sikkhamānā training does not negate the validity of the upasampadā. It might be noted, by way of contrast, that bhikkhunī *pācittiya* 65, which assigns a *pācittiya* to a preceptor for ordaining a *gihigatā*, a formerly married girl, below twelve years of age, does not have the variants in terms of legal acts and so forth attached to it. In this case there can be no legal ordination, for the ordaining of a *gihigatā* below the age of twelve can never be legal. Similarly for *pācittiya* 71, the parallel rule for ordination of a *kumāribhūtā*, i.e., a maiden, below the age of twenty. In this case, too, there are no variants expressed in terms of legal acts perceived as legal, as illegal, or doubted, for the ordination of a maiden below the age of twenty is always invalid.

I bring up these cases because they show that the Vinaya did not regard as invalid an upasampadā ordination that failed to fully conform to the procedures laid down in the eight garudhammas and even within the body of the *Suttavibhaṅga*; that is, women who received full ordination without having undergone the sikkhamānā training were still regarded as validly ordained bhikkhunīs as long as their ordination conformed to the other decisive criteria. How this would have been possible under a traditional system of bhikkhunī training is difficult to imagine, but the theoretical possibility at least is envisaged. Rather than declaring the ordination null and void, the *Suttavibhaṅga* allows it to stand while requiring that disciplinary offenses (*āpatti*) be assigned to the preceptor, the teacher, and the other bhikkhunīs who filled the quorum.

This example might be taken as an analogy for the case when upasampadā is given by a dual ordination with bhikkhunīs from another school followed by a single-saṅgha ordination by a community of Theravāda bhikkhus. Although the procedure might not fulfill the highest standards of legal perfection, one could contend that because it does conform to basic templates of ordination prescribed in the texts, it should be admitted as valid.

Let us return to our main issue. Since the agreement to undertake the sikkhamāṇā training is given by a saṅgha, in the absence of a bhikkhunī saṅgha, one would suppose that this task should fall to a bhikkhu saṅgha. This might seem odd, but in the Vinaya Piṭaka itself we find a passage that suggests that at a time when the canonical Vinaya was still in process of formation, departures from the standard practice of sikkhamānā appointment were recognized. In the *Mahāvagga*'s "*Vassūpanāyikakkhandhaka*," the "Chapter on Entering the Rains Retreat," there is a passage in which the Buddha is shown granting permission to a bhikkhu to leave his rains residence at the request of a sāmaṇerī who wishes "to undertake the training" (*sikkhaṃ samādiyitukāmā hoti*):

> But here, bhikkhus, a sāmaṇerī desires to undertake the training. If she sends a messenger to the bhikkhus, saying: "I desire to undertake the training. Let the masters come; I want the masters to come," you should go, bhikkhus, for a matter that can be done in seven days even if not sent for, how much more so if sent for, thinking: "I will be zealous for her to undertake the training." You should return before seven days.[37]

The *Samantapāsādikā*—the Vinaya commentary—comments on this amid a long list of occasions when a bhikkhu can leave his rains residence, and thus it has to string them all together and touch each one briefly. Therefore, in commenting on this passage, it says rather tersely:

> A bhikkhu can go visit a sāmaṇerī if he wants to give her the training rule (*sikkhāpadaṃ dātukāmo*). Together with the other reasons (i.e., she is ill, wants to disrobe, has a troubled conscience,

37. Vin I: 147: *Idha pana, bhikkhave, sāmaṇerī sikkhaṃ samādiyitukāmā hoti. Sā ce bhikkhūnaṃ santike dūtaṃ pahiṇeyya "ahanhi sikkhaṃ samādiyitukāmā, āgacchantu ayyā, icchāmi ayyānaṃ āgatan"ti, gantabbaṃ, bhikkhave, sattāhakaraṇīyena, appahitepi, pageva pahite—"sikkhāsamādānaṃ ussukkaṃ karissāmī"ti. Sattāhaṃ sannivatto kātabboti.*

> or has adopted a wrong view), there are these five reasons [for which the bhikkhu can go visit her during the rains].[38]

The commentary seems to be "normalizing" the passage by assigning the bhikkhu the task of re-administering to the sāmaṇerī her training rules, but the canonical text, in contrast, seems to be ascribing to him a key role in the transmission of the sikkhamānā training to a sāmaṇerī, a task normally assigned exclusively to the bhikkhunī saṅgha. Could we not see in this passage a subtle suggestion that under unusual circumstances the bhikkhu saṅgha can in fact give the sikkhamānā training to a female aspirant for upasampadā? It might be an elder bhikkhu eligible to give the "exhortation" (*ovāda*) to bhikkhunīs who would be considered fit to serve as preceptor for a sikkhamānā. Still, the best alternative would be for the aspiring sāmaṇerī to find a situation where she could receive authorization to train as a sikkhamānā from bhikkhunīs and actually train under their guidance for the full two-year period, until she is qualified to take full ordination.

(3) Finally we come to the problem of *pabbajjā*. Conservatives maintain that only a bhikkhunī can give a woman aspirant pabbajjā, that is, can ordain her as a sāmaṇerī. However, we should note that there is no stipulation in the Vinaya explicitly prohibiting a bhikkhu from giving pabbajjā to a woman. Such a practice is certainly contrary to established precedent, but we have to be careful not to transform established precedent into inviolable law, which, it seems, is what has happened in the Theravāda tradition. When the *Mahāvaṃsa* has the Elder Mahinda declare to King Devānampiyatissa, "We are not permitted, your majesty, to give the pabbajjā to women," we should remember that Mahinda is speaking under normal circumstances, when a bhikkhunī saṅgha exists. He therefore requests the king to invite his sister, Sanghamittā, to come to Sri Lanka to ordain the women of the court. His words should not be taken as binding under all circumstances. We should also remember that the *Mahāvaṃsa* is neither a canonical Vinaya text nor a Vinaya commentary; it is a partly mythical chronicle of Sri Lankan Buddhist history. Neither the canonical Vinaya nor any authoritative Vinaya commentary expressly prohibits a bhikkhu from giving pabbajjā to women. To do so would certainly be the less desirable

38. Sp V: 1069.

alternative, but in the hypothetical situation when a Theravāda bhikkhunī saṅgha does not exist at all or exists only in remote regions, this would seem to be justification for a departure from normal procedure.

One last issue that must be faced, which I can only touch on, concerns the strategy of implementing a revival of the bhikkhunī saṅgha. In particular, we must deal with the question: "Should individual saṅghas begin ordaining women as bhikkhunīs independently or should they first attempt to gain recognition of bhikkhunī ordination from the higher authorities of the saṅgha hierarchy?" This is an extremely delicate question that takes us into the heart of communal monastic life. It is also a partly dated question, since bhikkhunī ordinations have already started. But still, I think it is useful to reflect on this consideration to ensure that the bhikkhunī saṅgha will develop in healthy and harmonious integration with the bhikkhu saṅgha.

The very question raises other questions, almost unanswerable, about where exactly in the Theravāda monastic order authority begins and how far that authority extends. To try to settle the issue before us by obtaining a universal consensus among bhikkhus throughout the Theravāda world seems unfeasible, and it would also seem unfeasible to hold an international election among Theravāda bhikkhus. A council of prominent elders from the leading Theravāda countries would almost certainly represent the viewpoint that I have called conservative legalism, and they would again almost certainly decide that bhikkhunī ordination is unattainable. Since they are not an official authority, it would be an open question whether the entire Theravāda saṅgha need be bound by their decree, especially if they reach a decision without giving proponents of bhikkhunī ordination a chance to present their view. In my opinion bhikkhus who belong to an extended community, such as a *nikāya* or network of monasteries, should attempt to reach consensus on this issue within their community. It is only when serious, sincere, and prolonged attempts at persuasion prove futile that monks who favor restoring the bhikkhunī saṅgha should consider whether to hold bhikkhunī ordinations without such a consensus.

Although there might not be any such thing as a unified international Theravāda saṅgha, it seems to me that each monk has an obligation to act in conscience *as if* there were such an entity; his decisions and deeds should be guided by the ideal of promoting the well-being and unity of an integral saṅgha even if this saṅgha is merely posited in thought. On this basis, I would then have to say that when one group of bhikkhus decides to confer bhikkhunī ordination without obtaining the consent of the leadership of the saṅgha body to which they belong, or without obtaining a wide consensus among fellow bhikkhus in their fraternity, they risk creating a fissure within the saṅgha. While they are certainly not maliciously causing a schism in the saṅgha, they are still dividing the saṅgha into two factions that hold irreconcilable views on the critically important question of whether persons of a particular type—namely, women who have undergone the upasampadā procedure—actually possess the status of a fully ordained monastic. And this is surely a very serious matter. In short, while in principle I believe there are legal grounds for reintroducing bhikkhunī ordination in the Theravāda tradition and strongly support a revival of the bhikkhunī saṅgha, I also feel that this should be done in a cautious way that will preserve the tenuous unity of the saṅgha rather than divide it into two factions, a dominant faction that remains convinced the bhikkhunī saṅgha cannot be revived and a smaller faction that acknowledges the existence of a bhikkhunī saṅgha. But this concern also has to be balanced against concern that an established monastic old guard committed to preserving the status quo will persistently block all proposals to revive a bhikkhunī saṅgha, thus frustrating all attempts at transformation. In such a case, those committed to reviving the bhikkhunī saṅgha may well be entitled to obey the call of their own conscience rather than the orders of their monastic superiors. However, I believe, it would be far preferable for them to try to draw their monastic superiors into the process. This will call for patience and persistence, and will require all their powers of persuasion. But such an approach is more prudent than a rash action that may cause bitter divisions within the saṅgha. In Sri Lanka, at least, the attitudes of the senior monks have changed dramatically over the past ten years and many have become amenable to the idea of bhikkhunī ordination. Thus proponents of bhikkhunī ordination should give priority to meeting the leading elders of the saṅgha and patiently attempting to win their approval in a way that will, at the same time, enable them to preserve the dignity of their positions.

Conclusion

The disappearance of the Theravāda bhikkhunī saṅgha has presented us with a situation not explicitly addressed in the Vinaya and thus one for which there is no unambiguous remedy. When faced with such a contingency, naturally Vinaya authorities will hold different ideas about how to proceed, all claiming to accord with the purport of the Vinaya. As I see it, the Vinaya cannot be read in any fixed manner as either unconditionally permitting or forbidding a revival of the bhikkhunī saṅgha. It yields these conclusions only as a result of interpretation, and interpretation often reflects the attitudes of the interpreters and the framework of assumptions within which they operate as much as it does the actual words of the text they are interpreting.

Amid the spectrum of opinions that might be voiced, the two main categories of interpretation are the conservative and the progressive. For conservatives, bhikkhunī status absolutely requires a dual-saṅgha ordination with the participation of a Theravāda bhikkhunī saṅgha; hence, since no Theravāda bhikkhunī saṅgha exists, and for conservatives non-Theravādin bhikkhunīs cannot fill this role, the Theravāda bhikkhunī lineage is irreparably broken and can never be restored. For progressives, bhikkhunī ordination can be restored, either by permitting bhikkhunīs from an East Asian country to fulfill the role of the bhikkhunī saṅgha at a dual-saṅgha ordination or by recognizing the right of bhikkhus to ordain bhikkhunīs until a Theravāda bhikkhunī saṅgha becomes functional.

In my opinion, in deciding between the conservative and the progressive approaches to the bhikkhunī issue, the question that should be foremost in our minds is this: "What would the Buddha want his elder bhikkhu-disciples to do in such a situation, *now*, in the twenty-first century?" If he were to see us pondering this problem today, would he want us to apply the regulations governing ordination in a way that excludes women from the fully ordained renunciant life, so that we present to the world a religion in which men alone can lead the life of full renunciation? Or would he instead want us to apply the regulations of the Vinaya in a way that is kind, generous, and accommodating, thereby offering the world a religion that truly embodies principles of justice and nondiscrimination?

The answers to these questions are not immediately given by any text or tradition, but I do not think we are left entirely to subjective opinion either. From the texts we can see how, in making major decisions, the Buddha displayed both compassion and disciplinary rigor; we can also see how, in defining the behavioral standards of his saṅgha, he took account of the social and cultural expectations of his contemporaries. In working out a solution to our own problem, therefore, we have these two guidelines to follow. One is to be true to the spirit of the Dhamma—true to both the letter and the spirit, but above all to the spirit. The other is to be responsive to the social, intellectual, and cultural horizons of humanity in this particular period of history in which we live, this age in which we forge our own future destinies and the future destiny of Buddhism. Looked at in this light, the revival of a Theravāda bhikkhunī saṅgha can be seen as an intrinsic good that conforms to the innermost spirit of the Dhamma, helping to bring to fulfillment the Buddha's own mission of opening "the doors to the deathless" to all humankind, to women as well as to men. At the same time, viewed against the horizons of contemporary understanding, the existence of a bhikkhunī saṅgha can function as an instrumental good. It will allow women to make a meaningful and substantial contribution to Buddhism in many of the ways that monks do—as preachers, scholars, meditation teachers, educators, social advisors, and ritual leaders—and perhaps in certain ways that will be unique to female renunciants, for example, as counselors and guides to women lay followers. A bhikkhunī saṅgha will also win for Buddhism the respect of high-minded people in the world, who regard the absence of gender discrimination as the mark of a truly worthy religion in harmony with the noble trends of present-day civilization.

APPENDIX:
CAN AN EXTINCT BHIKKHUNĪ SAṄGHA BE REVIVED?
The Original Mingun Jetavan Sayadaw of Burma

From the *Milindapañha Aṭṭhakathā* (Rangoon: Haṃsāvatī Piṭaka Press, Burmese year 1311 [= 1949]), pp. 228–38. Translated from the Pāli by Bhikkhu Bodhi.

[228] In this problem [of the *Milindapañha*], a guideline can be said to be given for bhikkhus of the future.[39] What is this guideline that can be said to be given for bhikkhus of the future? "Bhikkhus, I allow bhikkhus to ordain bhikkhunīs." There is a passage beginning: "After completing her training in six rules for two years, a sikkhamānā should seek ordination from both saṅghas." The statement, "Bhikkhus, I allow bhikkhus to ordain bhikkhunīs," does not occur with reference to the subject[40] of [the statement]: "After completing her training in six rules for two years, a sikkhamānā should seek ordination from both saṅghas." And the statement, "After completing her training in six rules for two years, [229] a sikkhamānā should seek ordination from both saṅghas," does not occur with reference to the subject of [the statement]: "Bhikkhus, I allow bhikkhus to ordain bhikkhunīs." Although the latter does not occur [with that reference], still the subject referred to by the two statements, each taken by itself, is just a woman who is to be ordained.

One statement says that a woman who is to be ordained should be ordained by a bhikkhu saṅgha; the other, that a woman who is to be ordained should be ordained by a dual saṅgha. Now there will be future bhikkhus of wrong beliefs who will cling to their own conviction and for the purpose of promoting their wrong beliefs will argue thus: "Friends, if the Tathāgata said: 'Bhikkhus, I allow bhikkhus to ordain bhikkhunīs,' then

39. *Anāgatabhikkhūnaṃ nayo dinno nāma hoti.*

40. In the phrase *atthe nappavattati*, I understand the word *attha* to signify, not "meaning," but the referent of a statement. Thus the *attha* or referent of the statement "I allow bhikkhus to ordain bhikkhunīs" is a female aspirant for ordination at a time when no bhikkhunī saṅgha exists in the world; and the referent of the statement "a *sikkhamānā* should seek ordination from a dual saṅgha" is a sikkhamānā who has completed her training at a time when the bhikkhunī saṅgha exists in the world.

the statement: 'After completing her training in six rules for two years, a sikkhamānā should seek ordination from a dual saṅgha' is false. But if the Tathāgata said: 'After completing her training in six rules for two years, a sikkhamānā should seek ordination from a dual saṅgha,' then the statement: 'Bhikkhus, I allow bhikkhus to ordain bhikkhunīs' is false. Isn't it true that ordination by a dual saṅgha is excluded by [the injunction] that a bhikkhu saṅgha should give ordination to a woman? And isn't [the allowance to give] ordination by the bhikkhu saṅgha excluded by the injunction that a dual saṅgha should give ordination to a woman? Thus the two are mutually exclusive. A bhikkhu saṅgha giving ordination to a woman candidate is one; a dual saṅgha giving ordination to a woman candidate is another."

This is a dilemma. At present, when bhikkhus are unable to answer and resolve this dilemma, [other] bhikkhus sometimes come along and argue over it. Some say: "The bhikkhu saṅgha could ordain women only in the period before the bhikkhunī saṅgha arose. From the time the bhikkhunī saṅgha arose, women must be ordained by a dual saṅgha. Therefore, now that the bhikkhunī saṅgha has become extinct, women cannot be ordained by the bhikkhu saṅgha." But others argue: "They can be ordained." [230]

In this matter we say that the statement: "Bhikkhus, I allow bhikkhus to ordain bhikkhunīs" was made by the Exalted One, and this statement of the Exalted One concerns restriction [of the ordination solely by a bhikkhu saṅgha] to a period when the bhikkhunī saṅgha does not exist.[41] Hence there is a difference in both meaning and wording [between this statement and the other] explaining the procedure for a sikkhamānā. The statement: "After completing her training in six rules for two years, a sikkhamānā should seek ordination from a dual saṅgha" was spoken by the Exalted One, and it explains the procedure for a sikkhamānā. Hence there is a difference in both meaning and wording [between this statement and the other] restricting [the single-saṅgha ordination] to a period when the bhikkhunī saṅgha does not exist. One is a restriction [of the ordination solely by a bhikkhu saṅgha] to a period when the bhikkhunī saṅgha does

41. *Tañ ca pana bhagavato vacanaṃ ayaṃ bhikkhunīsaṅghassa abhāvaparicchedo.* I understand the last phrase to signify the limitation (*pariccheda*) of single-saṅgha ordination to a time when the bhikkhunī saṅgha is nonexistent (*bhikkhunīsanghassa abhāva*).

not exist, while the other explains the procedure for a sikkhamānā. The two are far apart in meaning; they are not speaking about the same thing and should not be mixed up. All the Exalted One's bodily deeds, verbal deeds, and mental deeds were preceded and accompanied by knowledge. He had unobstructed knowledge and vision regarding the past, the future, and the present. So what should be said of an arahant?[42]

Thus the Exalted One's statement: "Bhikkhus, I allow bhikkhus to ordain bhikkhunīs" concerned restriction [of the ordination solely by a bhikkhu saṅgha] to a period in the past when the bhikkhunī saṅgha did not exist; in the future, too, it will be restricted to a period when the bhikkhunī saṅgha will not exist; and at present it is restricted to a period when the bhikkhunī saṅgha does not exist. Since the Exalted One had seen [such situations] with his unobstructed knowledge and vision, that is, with his knowledge of omniscience, his statement should be allowed [to have such applications]. It should be admitted that the bhikkhu saṅgha had been allowed [to ordain bhikkhunīs] in the past, though restricted to a period when the bhikkhunī saṅgha did not exist; in the future too, though restricted to a period when the bhikkhunī saṅgha will not exist; and at present too, restricted to a period when the bhikkhunī saṅgha does not exist. Hence at present, or even now, though restricted to a situation in which the bhikkhunī saṅgha has become nonexistent, women can be ordained by the bhikkhu saṅgha.[43]

[*Question*:] Then, when Queen Anulā wanted to go forth, and the king said, "Give her the going forth," why did Mahinda Thera reply: "Great king, we are not permitted to give the going forth to women"?[44]

[*Reply*:] This was because the bhikkhunī saṅgha existed at the time, not because it was prohibited by the text (*sutta*). Thus to explain the meaning, Mahinda Thera said: [231] "My sister, the Therī Sanghamittā, is at Pāṭaliputta. Invite her." By this statement, the point being made is that he is not permitted [to ordain women] because of the restriction [of the ordination solely by a bhikkhu saṅgha] to a period when the bhikkhunī

42. The mention of an arahant here is difficult to account for, unless the Sayadaw is referring to Nāgasena, one of the two protagonists in the *Milindapañha*.

43. *Tato eva paccuppanne ca etarahi vā pana bhikkhunīsaṅghassa abhāvaparicchedan'eva bhikkhusaṅghena mātugāmo upasampādetabbo.*

44. The reference is to *Mahāvaṃsa* XV.18–23. See Geiger 1912: 98.

saṅgha does not exist, not because it is prohibited by the text. The text that states: "Bhikkhus, I allow bhikkhus to ordain bhikkhunīs" should not be rejected merely on the basis of one's personal opinion. One should not strike a blow to the Wheel of Authority of the omniscient knowledge. The wishes of qualified persons should not be obstructed. For now women are qualified to be ordained by the bhikkhu saṅgha.[45]

When [the Buddha] said: "If, Ānanda, Mahāpajāpatī Gotamī accepts these eight principles of respect, let that suffice for her ordination," he laid down these eight principles of respect as the fundamental regulations (*mūlapaññatti*) for bhikkhunīs at a time when bhikkhunīs had not yet appeared. One principle among them—namely, "After completing her training in six rules for two years, a sikkhamānā should seek ordination from a dual saṅgha"—was laid down as a fundamental regulation for a sikkhamānā to undertake as part of her training at a time even before the bhikkhunī saṅgha appeared. After the Buddha had laid down these eight principles of respect as the fundamental regulations for bhikkhunīs, ordination [initially] arose by [Mahāpajāpatī's] acceptance of them. When Mahāpajāpatī Gotamī then asked: "Bhante, how shall I act in regard to these Sakyan women?" the Exalted One did not see: "It is only now that the bhikkhunī saṅgha is nonexistent, [but it will not be so] in the future too."[46] He saw: "The bhikkhunī saṅgha is nonexistent now and in the future, too, it will be nonexistent." Knowing that when the bhikkhunī saṅgha is nonexistent the occasion arises for an allowance [given to] the bhikkhu saṅgha [to be used], the Buddha laid down a secondary regulation (*anupaññatti*) to the effect that women can be ordained by the bhikkhu saṅgha, that is: "Bhikkhus, I allow bhikkhus to ordain bhikkhunīs." But this secondary regulation did not reach a condition where it shared [validity] with any prior and subsequent prohibition and allowance that had been laid down.[47] Thus the

45. *Sabbaññutañāṇassa āṇācakkaṃ na pahārayitabbaṃ. Bhabbapuggalānaṃ āsā na chinditabbā. Bhikkhusaṅghena hi mātugāmo etarahi upasampādetuṃ bhabbo ti.*

46. I felt it necessary to add the phrase in brackets in order to give this sentence (which in the original is merely a clause in an extremely complex sentence) the meaning required by the context.

47. *Esā pana anupaññatti pure ceva pacchā ca paññattena paṭikkhepenāpi anuññātenāpi sādhāraṇabhāvaṃ na pāpuṇi.* The purport seems to be that this authorization is valid only as

Exalted One, the Worthy One, the Perfectly Enlightened One, who knows and sees, allowed women at present to be ordained in such a way.

In order to achieve success in [the recitation of] the enactment formula (*kammavācā*), the text of the enactment formula should be recited in full. A competent, able bhikkhu, who understands the Exalted One's intention, should inform the saṅgha: [232] "Bhante, let the saṅgha listen to me. This one of such a name seeks ordination under that one of such a name. She is pure with regard to the obstructive factors. Her bowl and robes are complete. This one of such a name asks the saṅgha for ordination with that one of such a name as sponsor (*pavattinī*). If the saṅgha finds it fitting, the saṅgha may ordain this one of such a name with that one of such a name as sponsor. This is the motion. Bhante, let the saṅgha listen to me. This one of such a name seeks ordination under that one of such a name. She is pure with regard to the obstructive factors. Her bowl and robes are complete. This one of such a name asks the saṅgha for ordination with that one of such a name as sponsor. The saṅgha ordains this one of such a name with that one of such a name as sponsor. Any venerable who agrees to the ordination of this one of such a name with that one of such a name as sponsor should remain silent; any venerable who does not agree should speak up. A second time I declare this matter...A third time I declare this matter [repeat above pronouncement]. This one of such a name has been ordained by the saṅgha with that one of such a name as sponsor. The saṅgha is in agreement; therefore it is silent. That is how I understand it."

At the conclusion of the enactment formula, the woman who was to be ordained by the bhikkhu saṅgha is now called "one ordained on one side [solely by a bhikkhu saṅgha]."[48] But in the commentary, the bhikkhus ordained the five hundred Sakyan women on the basis of the secondary regulation, "Bhikkhus, I allow bhikkhus to ordain bhikkhunīs." Without having them first select a preceptor, they ordained them making them pupils of Mahāpajāpatī, and thus, for the success of the enactment formula, they used the following proclamation: "Bhante, let the saṅgha listen to me. This

long as the Buddha does not issue another decree that implicitly annuls its validity, such as that stipulating a dual-saṅgha ordination.

48. *Ekato upasampanno*. The expression ends in the masculine termination *-o* because the subject of the sentence, *mātugāmo*, "woman," is a word of masculine gender.

one of such a name seeks ordination under Mahāpajāpatī," and so forth. Thus they too were all called "ordained on one side." There is no reference to them first selecting a preceptor. And since here the Exalted One had not yet authorized it, here there is nothing [233] about first selecting a preceptor, or about explaining the bowl and robes, or about requesting the ordination, or about inquiring into the twenty-four obstructive factors, or about explaining the three dependences and the eight strict prohibitions. Thus, even at the cost of life, bhikkhus do not lay down what has not been laid down and do not abrogate what has been laid down, but they take up and practice the training rules that have been laid down; such is the Exalted One's intention. By this very method, a bhikkhu saṅgha can give ordination [to constitute] a bhikkhunī saṅgha made up of those ordained on one side, and when a chapter of five [bhikkhunīs] has been constituted, it is proper for them to give ordination in the remote countries through a dual-saṅgha procedure. And in this case it is determined that a dual saṅgha has arisen.[49]

Then, if it is asked, "Why did the bhikkhus in the past ordain the five hundred Sakyan women?" the answer should be given: "Because the narrative gives the story of what had been allowed all as one."[50]

At this point, with the arising of a dual saṅgha, if a woman wishes ordination, she should acquire the going forth as a sāmaṇerī in the presence of bhikkhunīs, and it is only a bhikkhunī who should let her go forth. After they have let her go forth, only a bhikkhunī saṅgha should give her the agreement [to train] as a sikkhamānā. After she receives it, she should train in the six rules for two years. When the sikkhamānā has completed her training, she should then seek ordination from a dual saṅgha. And here, when it is said in the fundamental regulation, "After completing her training, a sikkhamānā should seek ordination from a dual saṅgha," the Exalted One laid down a particular sequence. He first had the sikkhamānā receive

49. *So eten'ev'upāyena bhikkhusaṅghena etarahi upasampādetabbo ekato upasampannabhikkhunīsaṅgho, pañcavagge pahonte paccantimesu janapadesu ubhatosaṅghena upasampādetuṃ yutto c'eva hoti. Ubhatosaṅgho ca uppanno ti idha ṭhātabbameva.*

50. *Atha kasmā pubbe bhikkhū pañcasatā sākiyāniyo upasampādentī ti pucchitā anuññātassa vatthuno ekato nidānattā ti vissajjetabbā.* Perhaps the point is: "Why did the bhikkhus go on to ordain *five hundred* women by a single-saṅgha ordination instead of ordaining five and then letting these five function as a bhikkhunī saṅgha that could help to ordain the others?" But I am not sure that I have caught the author's point.

ordination from a bhikkhu saṅgha and cleared [of obstructive factors by the bhikkhus]. Thereupon she would receive ordination by a bhikkhunī saṅgha, and thus she would be "ordained by a dual saṅgha." At a later time, however, the Exalted One laid down a secondary regulation, saying: "Bhikkhus, I allow a woman who has received ordination on one side and been cleared [of obstructive factors] by the bhikkhunī saṅgha to receive ordination by the bhikkhu saṅgha." Thus he enjoins a sikkhamānā who has completed her training to first receive ordination from a bhikkhunī saṅgha. When she has been ordained on one side and cleared [of obstructive factors] by the bhikkhunī saṅgha, she is subsequently to be ordained by the bhikkhu saṅgha. Thus he allowed her to become ordained by a dual saṅgha in a reversal of the preceding sequence[51] but did not reject one who previously had been ordained on one side by the bhikkhu saṅgha.[52] The one was too remote from the other for the two to be confused with one another. Also, imagining that a later secondary regulation negates a previously [234] laid down [regulation] occurs to blind foolish persons, not to those with insight, for the conclusion is seen in the narrative on the secondary regulation.[53]

This is the sequence in the text for the act of ordination of a sikkhamānā who has completed her training: First, she should be asked to choose her preceptor. After she has done so, the bowl and robes should be explained to her: "This is your bowl. This is your outer robe; this is your upper robe; this is your under robe; this is your blouse; this is your bathing cloth. Go, stand in that area."

[Pages 234–38 give the formulas for dual-saṅgha ordination found at Vin II: 272–74, starting with "*Suṇātu me, ayye, saṅgho, itthannāmā itthannāmāya ayyāya upasampadāpekkhā. Yadi saṅghassa pattakallaṃ, ahaṃ itthannāmā itthannāmaṃ anusāseyyaṃ*," and ending with "*Tassā tayo ca*

51. The earlier sentence, when explaining the procedure in which the bhikkhus give the ordination first, refers to the sequence as *anukkama*. I assume that the expression used here, *kamokkama*, means "a reversal of the preceding sequence," and translate accordingly.

52. The point seems to be that after introducing the dual-saṅgha ordination, the Buddha did not require the women who had previously received ordination by the bhikkhu saṅgha alone to undergo another ordination by the bhikkhunī saṅgha; he allowed their one-sided ordination to stand.

53. *Anupaññattiyā nidānena niṭṭhaṃgatadiṭṭhattā*. The point is not quite clear to me.

nissaye aṭṭha ca akaraṇīyāni ācikkheyyātha." The translation here resumes at the very end, on page 238.]

Thus the bhikkhu saṅgha described above should make a determined effort as follows: "Now that the bhikkhunī saṅgha has become extinct, we will revive the institution of bhikkhunīs! We will understand the heart's wish of the Exalted One! We will see the Exalted One's face brighten like the full moon!"[54] A bhikkhu motivated by a desire to resuscitate the institution of bhikkhunīs should be skilled in the subject praised by the Exalted One. But in this problem [set in the *Milindapañha*], this is the guideline given for bhikkhus of the future. So the question asked, "What is this guideline that is given for bhikkhus of the future?" has just been answered.

54. *Idāni bhikkhunīsaṅghe vaṃsacchinne mayaṃ bhikkhunīsāsanaṃ anusandhānaṃ karissāma, bhagavato manorathaṃ jānissāma, bhagavato puṇṇindusaṃkāsamukhaṃ passissāmā ti.*

The Eight Garudhammas

Ute Hüsken

PROPONENTS AS WELL as opponents to the concept of a bhikṣuṇī ordination repeatedly refer to one specific version of the account of the establishment of the bhikṣuṇī order in the Theravāda tradition given in the Vinaya Piṭaka. The events depicted there do not allow for drawing a coherent picture of the events and the underlying attitude toward nuns during the time of the Buddha, leaving the historical event, along with the current debate, up for further discussion.

This legend forms the content and context of the eight so-called "heavy rules" (*garudhamma*) mentioned in the *Cullavagga*. It shall be demonstrated, on the basis of internal evidence, that diverse and at times even conflicting agenda are voiced in this canonical account. This leads to the more general question of what can be the touchstone of authenticity and authority when it comes to evaluating a tradition. Thus, although the texts analyzed in this paper do not stem from the Tibetan Buddhist tradition, our reflections may have some relevance for the issue as to whether, and how, a nuns' order in the Tibetan tradition can be established.

Apart from the *Bhikkhunīvibhaṅga*, few passages in the Vinaya Piṭaka exclusively or specifically relate to women. The tenth chapter of the *Cullavagga*, however, provides direct and indirect evidence regarding the Buddha's attitude toward the establishment of a nuns' order. His attitude is depicted as ambivalent, to say the least. According to the *Cullavagga*, although the Buddha in the end agreed to establish a bhikkhunī saṅgha, he:

1. only hesitatingly accepted women as members of the order;
2. admitted that women are capable of salvation;
3. compared women to diseases and weakening factors for the saṅgha and for the duration of the dharma; and
4. announced as a precondition for any woman's ordination the acceptance of the eight "heavy rules" (*garudhamma*).

These eight rules serve not only as admission criteria but also as rules that are to be observed for life by every nun. It is therefore striking that this set of rules in the Pāli Vinaya is not part of the *Bhikkhunīpāṭimokkha*. However, seven of these rules do in fact have parallels either in word or in content with other rules stated in the *Bhikkhunīpāṭimokkha*. Moreover, it is remarkable that these eight rules, although depicted as a precondition for ordination, are not at all mentioned in the ordination formulas for nuns, as given elsewhere in the *Cullavagga*. It is therefore possible that the eight garudhammas are a list of those rules that were deemed most important to later monastics who were in charge of transmitting the texts and became a significant aspect of the account during the editing process. At the same time, additional weight might have been attributed to this set of eight rules, as the number eight also seems to echo the eight *pārājika* rules for nuns.

Let us begin with a discussion of the fifth of these eight rules, as it directly hints at a general inconsistency regarding the garudhammas and the rules of the *Bhikkhunīpāṭimokkha*.

The fifth garudhamma stipulates that a nun who has broken one of the garudhammas must undergo fourteen days of *mānatta* (a probation period) before both orders. This garudhamma is the only one out of the eight rules without equivalent among the *pācittiya* rules of the *Bhikkhunīvibhaṅga*. The penalty for transgressing a garudhamma corresponds to that imposed on a nun when she breaks a *saṃghādisesa* rule: she has to spend a two-week probation period isolated from the main group of nuns along with another nun who is assigned to her as a companion for the probation period. This penalty, however, differs from the result of a breach of a *pācittiya* rule, which requires a simple confession. Listing identical rules as garudhamma (with two weeks probation) and as *pācittiya* (resulting in confession), as is the case with garudhammas 2, 3, 4, and 7 (these are identical to *pācittiya* 56, 59, 57, and 52), is an obvious inconsistency—given that the term garudhamma does not refer to "saṃghādisesa" in garudhamma 5.

Garudhammas 1, 7, and 8 deal with the relationship of individual nuns to individual monks. The first of the eight heavy rules makes quite clear that a nun is always beneath a monk in rank: "A nun, even if she has been ordained for a hundred years, is to greet respectfully, to stand up, to salute with joined palms, and to carry out other acts of homage toward a monk, even if he has been ordained only on that very day." This is not the only rule emphasizing the general subordination of individual nuns under individual monks. *Pācittiya* 94 of the *Bhikkhunīvibhaṅga*, for example, states that a nun may not sit in the presence of a monk, and *Cullavagga* VI.6.5 states that women (including nuns, presumably) are not to be greeted by monks. The rule that nuns must greet monks, but not the other way around, is also emphasized later on in this section in the *Cullavagga* when Mahāpajāpatī Gotamī asked the Buddha to rescind garudhamma 1, which he explicitly and vehemently rejects, with reference to the customs prevalent among other ascetics.

Garudhamma 7 states that a nun is in no way allowed to insult or disparage a monk, and garudhamma 8 says that a nun may not address a monk (or admonish monks), whereas monks may address (or admonish) nuns.

Three more garudhammas regulate the relationship between the bhikkhunī saṅgha and the bhikkhu saṅgha. Garudhamma 2 fixes one aspect of the general dependence of the bhikkhunī saṅgha on the bhikkhu saṅgha: a nun may not spend the rainy season in a residential district where there is no monk. The reason given for this is that instruction, to be delivered by monks, and legal actions to be performed by the bhikkhunī saṅgha would not be possible otherwise. Implicitly, this rule presupposes a development described only later in the *Cullavagga*, specifically that the *kammas* to be performed by nuns are to be supervised by monks. At this stage, namely before any woman is accepted as a nun and before any of the formal procedures have been regulated, this rule seems slightly out of place, or premature.

Garudhamma 3 further states that a nun must ask the bhikkhu saṅgha for instruction and for the *pāṭimokkha* date twice a month. The nuns thus have to comply with the monks' calculation of the date and, in that respect, remain dependent upon them. One aspect should however be noted: later in the *Cullavagga* (X.6) a gradual development is described. At first the monks recited the *pāṭimokkha* formula for the nuns, but then this task was handed over entirely to the nuns. So the "asking for *pāṭimokkha*," regulated in this garudhamma, is there depicted as the result of a development.

Garudhamma 4 again refers to legal acts of the saṅgha: the nuns must perform the *pavāraṇā* ceremony before both orders. Later in the same section of the *Cullavagga*, there is a description in which we read that at first the nuns did not perform the *pavāraṇā* ceremony at all, while later they performed it only within their own orders. So if the garudhamma prescribing the *pavāraṇā* ceremony before both orders had existed from the beginning, such a misunderstanding as described there would certainly not have happened.

However, the garudhamma that most conspicuously breaks the timeframe of the account is garudhamma 6, according to which a woman must live two years as a sikkhamānā before receiving full ordination. During this time she must follow six rules. Her full ordination then is to be performed by both orders. This rule partly corresponds to *pācittiya* 63 and 64 of the *Bhikkhunīvibhaṅga*, which deal with the special two-year probationary period for women. It is remarkable that the Buddha, at the very moment of granting the establishment of a Buddhist nuns' order, uses the term *sikkhamānā* without giving further explanation, although he evidently never used it before. The events leading to the institution of a sikkhamānā's probation period are described differently in rules *pācittiya* 61 and 62 of the *Bhikkhunīvibhaṅga*: the two-year probation period was set up after pregnant and breastfeeding women had been ordained, designed to prevent difficulties arising from such situations. In the *Bhikkhunīvibhaṅga*, it is taken for granted that especially these rules stem from a time when the Buddhist order of nuns was already a permanent part of the Buddhist monastic community.

This is also suggested by the further events related in the *Cullavagga*. When Mahāpajāpatī accepted the eight garudhammas without hesitation, the Buddha expressed his misgivings about the admission of women into the Buddhist order and pointed out the negative consequences for the duration of the existence of the dhamma in this world. Women were equated with diseases, and their admission into the order was assumed to bring about an earlier decline of the Buddhist teachings. The Buddha made this statement not as the reason he is against the ordination of women but *after* he had already agreed to it. These statements are difficult to reconcile with the passage in which the Buddha had admitted without hesitation that women have the ability to attain enlightenment and that he eventually assented to the establishment of a bhikkhunī saṅgha. This inconsistency might reflect the Buddha's personal ambivalence: accepting women as monastics certainly was a radical step, one bound to lead to conflicts within the wider social milieu. However, I am convinced that this inconsistent account is not a reflection of the Buddha's personal ambivalence, which we cannot now know, but rather gives expression to the fact that diverse and sometimes even contradictory currents prevalent at the time of the redaction of these texts are expressed.

This is even more likely if we take a closer look at the remaining passages of this section in the *Cullavagga*. There, immediately after Mahāpajāpatī Gotamī's acceptance of the garudhammas, a development of the Buddhist nuns' ordination is depicted: first the Buddha announces that nuns are to be ordained by monks. Later this procedure is modified again: in a next step women must be declared "pure" from the ordination obstacles (*antarāyikā dhammā*) by the nuns before they are ordained by the monks. Subsequently, a "double" initiation of women is decreed: first by the order of nuns, and then by the order of monks. This is depicted as a gradual development, which contradicts the account in the beginning of the tenth chapter of the *Cullavagga*, where the full-fledged form (double ordination) is proclaimed by the Buddha right from the beginning.

It is more than likely that the stories that explain how the individual *pāṭimokkha* rules came into being are younger than most of the rules themselves, and came into being possibly at the same time as *Mahāvagga* and *Cullavagga*. However, the discrepancy between the stories told in the *Bhikkhunīvibhaṅga* and in the tenth chapter of the *Cullavagga*, and the differences of the diverse accounts even within the tenth chapter of the *Cullavagga*, are striking. I am neither able to nor would I want to give precedence or attribute more authenticity to one or the other version. However, the simple fact that diverse accounts exist of one and the same event within a single text clearly shows that if we attribute authenticity to one story, the other definitely has to be rejected. In any case, we can assume that the establishment of the Buddhist nuns' order did not take place precisely as described here. It is much more likely that this textual passage has been extended gradually, and reflects rather the concerns of various editors who, moreover, did not have a uniform position. It is uncertain whether the Buddha himself formulated the eight garudhammas as preconditions for female ordination, and it might be even uncertain whether it was in fact the Buddha himself who founded the nuns' order, as Oskar von Hinüber convincingly argues.

Be this as it may, there is an important aspect that emerges from this analysis, which should be emphasized as a conclusion: the ordination of nuns is a ritual and a legal act at the same time. It derives part of its attributed efficacy (as ritual) and of its legal obligation (as legal act) from the fact that the Buddha himself is said to have laid down the procedure. However, the ordination procedures of the diverse Buddhist schools also derive their efficacy and legal obligation from practice and practicability. If, in the course of the long history of the Buddhist order, actual practice, and with it the texts, had not been adapted to the local, historical, cultural, political, and social contexts in which they are embedded, the ordination procedures would have lost their relevance and their connection with the living world. It might therefore be time to again adapt the ordination procedures to the urgent need—felt by many Buddhists—to establish (or reestablish) the ordination of women into the Tibetan tradition, with the help of specialists of the tradition, in theory as well as in practice.

A Need to Take a Fresh Look at Popular Interpretations of the Tripiṭaka: Theravāda Context in Thailand

Dhammananda Bhikkhunī

Having personally spent more than three decades researching the issue of ordination for Buddhist women in Thailand, I realize that there is an urgent need to reread the Tripiṭaka again. Often ideas passed on from generation to generation without checking the true meaning from the original text can eventually be taken to have equal authority to the text itself.

Social and Religious Background in Thailand

Buddhism was introduced to Thailand during the thirteenth century, most likely from Sri Lankan monks who practiced Theravādin Buddhism. Similar to Tibet, Thai Buddhism reflects other religious traditions, including Animism, Brahmanism, and Buddhism. And also similar to Tibetan Buddhism, Thai Buddhism has no tradition of women's ordination. There are currently around 300,000 members of the monastic community in Thailand. Roughly 10 percent of these members have a university level of education.

While the Sukhothai kingdom of the thirteenth century allowed for the freedom of religious practice for both male and female Buddhists, an ordination was never established. Instead, women renunciates were called *maechis*, white-robed women who shaved their heads and lead a somewhat religious lifestyle. The maechi practice may have been in existence as early as the Ayudhya period, at least some four hundred years ago, but it is difficult to gauge since they are neither supported nor recognized by the government. Nationwide, the number of maechis does not exceed ten thousand, as compared to the three hundred thousand monks already mentioned.

The first wave of bhikkhunīs came as late as 1928 when Narin Klueng, a Buddhist critic and politician, supported the revival of the traditional "fourfold Buddhists" (bhikkhus, bhikkhunīs, laymen, and laywomen) by ordaining his own daughters, Sara and Chongdi. Narin Klueng was very critical of the saṅgha. When the country was suffering from a severe economic crisis, he was imprisoned for controversial remarks about the government and greater saṅgha, and his daughters were eventually forced to give up their robes. In response to this, on June 18, 1928, the Sangharaja (Jinavornsirivatna) issued an order forbidding all Thai monks from giving ordination to women. This directly contradicted the allowance for women's ordination by the Buddha (*Vinaya Piṭaka, Cullavagga*) and has been the most significant stumbling block for any future progression of the bhikkhunī ordination in Thailand. The country came under a formal constitution in 1932, but this made no attempt to overturn the 1928 order of the Sangharaja against women's ordination.

Voramai Kabilsingh, my mother, started her monastic life in 1954 and went to Taiwan in 1970 to receive bhikkhunī ordination. Without a formal Thai saṅgha already in place to support her, she returned to Thailand only to be wholly ignored by the male monastic community. Despite this somewhat hostile environment, she worked to build and cultivate a nunnery and Buddhist educational foundation, educating the public in the core teachings of Buddhism rather than just popular Buddhism. Ven. Voramai Kabilsingh passed away at the ripe, full age of ninety-six in 2003 after seeing her daughter ordained as a bhikkhunī.

My own story of ordination begins in 2001 when I traveled to Sri Lanka and received lower ordination. I received full ordination two years later, in 2003. My first year was a very difficult period, as I was bombarded by endless criticism and underwent a thorough process of character assassination. After five years, more women who were initally uncertain about ordination started approaching other bhikkhunīs; these women went on to receive ordination both in Thailand and Sri Lanka. Now in the whole country there are six bhikkhunīs and sixteen sāmaṇerīs ordained in the Theravāda tradition.

Current Attitudes Toward the Ordination of Women

In November of 2004, the question of women's ordination became public and political. Senator Rabiebrat Pongpanit spent forty-five minutes questioning Deputy Prime Minister Visnu Krue-ngram on the legality of women's ordination. But the question was never fully answered, as it became clear that it must first be openly recognized by the saṅgha.

In response, the saṅgha quoted the Sangharaja's order of 1928 as the reason not to accept the bhikkhunī order. But the Thai Saṅgha Act of 1963, which instituted government authority over monastic ordination, made this point moot. Thai bhikkhunīs didn't simply need recognition from their male counterparts; the government was in a position to grant them authority as bhikkhunīs.

At present, ordained women are still not considered "valid" by the public. Bhikkhunīs must still go by the name "Mrs. So-and-So," as national identification card databases do not list the prefix "bhikkhunī." This is a certain sign of sex discrimination in Thai society.

Thai bhikkhunīs do have support, however, among the general public. The public who are not tainted by a patriarchal mentality generally express positive thoughts regarding the ordination of women. It is now the task of this initial group of ordained women to gain acceptance from the general public. The work is not easy, as there is neither official recognition nor support, but the mission is not impossible. By trusting that the bhikkhunī tradition is a noble heritage administered by the Buddha, these committed women will be able to take on the task.

Theravāda Buddhism

Some state that the argument against female ordination has its roots in the Theravāda tradition. The tradition is said to have originated with the so-called First Council, which took place three months after the passing of the Buddha. And it was only at the First Council that we start to see evidence of monks expressing their ideas against ordination of women. In order to understand the First Council thoroughly one needs to read the *Mahāparinirvāṇa-sūtra*, which provides us with the historical context and general attitudes surrounding the Buddha's death.

The *Mahāparinirvāṇa-sūtra* recorded the journey the Buddha took with Ānanda, his cousin and attendant. In the last meeting with the five hundred monks, Ānanda expressed sadness at the fact that the Buddha was going to pass away. He left the audience and went outside to gather himself. It was at this time that the Buddha chose to praise Ānanda for being the best of attendants (compared to the attendants of the previous Buddhas), who knew exactly how to handle people of different groups when they came to see the Buddha.

Ānanda had an exceptional memory, and was both the cousin and attendant of the Buddha. His memory recorded all of the Buddha's teachings, and at his passing, Ānanda was named the prime Dhamma holder. Kings and ministers are said to have sought out Ānanda for his assistance in their practice. While there is some debate over whether or not he was enlightened at the time of the First Council, he was present at the gathering.

Ānanda came under interrogation for several reasons at this First Council, one of the issues of greatest contention being that of female ordination. Ānanda reiterated that the ordination of Mahāpajāpatī, the Buddha's aunt who had nursed him as a child, was under the direction of the Buddha himself. But Ānanda confessed this as a wrongdoing, and further confessed a wrongdoing in his action of allowing women to pay respect to the body of the Buddha. While Ānanda argued that he did so only with the greatest security of the women in mind, he ultimately confessed this also as a wrongdoing. The *Mahāparinirvāṇa-sūtra* makes mention of Ānanda's memory as well as his welcoming personality, which leads one to wonder if this latter action was merely a reflection of those personality traits the Buddha himself had appraised. Regardless, the decision was made to adhere to the Vinaya code and not stray from it as a rulebook for daily life. There would be no revisiting of the rules.

The Need to Reread the Texts

There are countless myths surrounding the inclusion of women in the saṅgha, and any discussion of the ordination of women inevitably involves the promulgation of these myths. By supporting ourselves with a full understanding of the cultural context of these myths, we can work to use them to further a greater recognition for the ways in which women have played a vibrant, crucial role in the development of the religion.

The very first myth that we encounter involves the Queen Mahāpajāpatī, the Buddha's aunt and stepmother. She asked the Buddha for ordination, a request he refused. To show her dedication, she shaved her head and donned a robe herself, along with a large group of royal women of the Sakya clan who followed the Buddha on foot from Kapilavatthu to Vesālī. This time it was Ānanda who approached the Buddha on the women's behalf. The Buddha again refused, using exactly the same words without giving any reason, at least not one that was recorded. This led Ānanda to ask if the Buddha's refusal was because women could not gain enlightenment in the same way men could. Now the Buddha made a clear statement, "Ānanda, women can be enlightened through the four stages of enlightenment. They can see the truth (of enlightenment) with their own eyes." It was purely because of this equal spiritual ability that the Buddha allowed women to join the saṅgha, and the statement should be encouragement for Buddhist women everywhere.

Mahāpajāpatī was the only one who received ordination by accepting the eight garudhammas. The rest of the female followers were ordained by the bhikkhu saṅgha. Ānanda reported back to the Buddha of Mahāpajāpatī's acceptance of the eight garudhammas. But this led the Buddha to make a peculiar statement about the acceptance of women into the order. Using three different illustrations, the Buddha compared women's presence to worms in a paddy field that would eventually weaken the rice, likening women to worms who could plague healthy sugarcane, and finally noting their inability to protect themselves in the presence of bandits. He concluded with a fourth point, stating that the lifespan of Buddhism's teachings (*sāsana*) in this world will be shortened by five hundred years because of women having been ordained.

Those against the ordination of women always quote this saying with the three comparisons. But none have taken notice of, or all have purposely avoided, the last verse where the Buddha says very clearly that having recognized the results of women's entering the order, he is like a man knowing that there would be a flood and therefore builds a dam to prevent its destruction of his property. In this case, the Buddha put a prevention against the above four points above by laying down the eight garudhammas.

For centuries monks and scholars who have read only part of the text have been quoting the text out of context and hence caused a solid belief that ordination of women will weaken Buddhism. This myth has been passed on and concretized over the centuries. Now we have to deconstruct these unhealthy myths that have cast a shroud over the beauty of Buddhism for so long. Unveiling these myths will uplift Buddhism in the long run. Now this Theravāda attitude against women that has concretized over the centuries needs to be critically examined.

Before the great passing away of the Buddha, he asserted that in the future should the saṅgha find some of the minor rules troublesome, they can be eliminated. But because the saṅgha at the First Council could not decide as to which were the minor rules, Mahākāssapa proposed maintaining all of them without new additions or subtractions. Theravādins have taken this decision of Mahākāssapa over the statement of the Buddha.

In Thailand, to make things more complicated, due to the weakening of practice on the monks' part, particularly during the sack of Ayudhya in 1767, the king had to intervene by setting up a law to control the behavior of monks. As a result, now Thai monks not only follow the Dhamma Vinaya of the Buddha but also come under the Saṅgha Act of the Thai government.

The very first line of this Saṅgha Act defines "saṅgha" as a male saṅgha only. In light of this act, a bhikkhunī saṅgha and the ordination of bhikkhunīs is out of the legal boundary of the government. Apart from this act, there is also the infamous order of 1928 mentioned earlier, in which the Sangharaja forbade the Thai monks from giving any level of ordination to women.

Theravādins have had to take on the task of choosing between being a Theravādin first or Buddhist first. One must be reminded that prioritizing the meaning of these two words is important and crucial. All of us Buddhists, Theravādins or Mūlasarvāstivādins, must be Buddhists first of all: Buddhists who fully respect the Buddha and follow his teachings, fundamentally respecting his intentions. For the Buddha entrusted Buddhism to us, the fourfold Buddhists—bhikkhus, bhikkhunīs, laymen, and laywomen. In the details of our practices Theravādins and Mūlasarvāstivādins may differ, but we must be Buddhists first of all, and with that mentality we can be brothers and sisters upholding the *sāsana* together.

General Beliefs Against Ordination of Women and the Rereading of Texts

"The bhikkhunī lineage is dead and gone and cannot be revived."

This is one basic myth about the ordination of women that is a real stumbling block against any attempt to introduce bhikkhunī ordination. It is believed and emphasized that ordination must be done by a dual saṅgha, namely both a bhikkhunī and a bhikkhu saṅgha. This disregards the allowance of the Buddha as is written in the *Cullavagga* of the Vinaya Piṭaka that monks can give ordination to women. It is true that later the Buddha also allowed dual ordination with the reason quoted above, but the previous allowance for a single saṅgha was never lifted. In Thailand the situation has been worsened by the 1928 Sangharaja order. The education of monks in Thailand is still limited, as only two Buddhist monastic universities are available. In the standard textbook that the monks use for the highest *Nakdhamma* level, information given about bhikkhunīs states briefly that Sanghamitta Therī went to Sri Lanka in the third century B.C.E., but possibly she went alone and there were not sufficient bhikkhunīs to give ordination to bhikkhunīs in Sri Lanka.

However, this is an absurd conclusion, as Princess Sanghamitta went with at least eighteen learned bhikkhunīs (the *Dīpavaṃsa*, a fourth-century chronicle, provides full details of their names) and gave the proper ordination to Queen Anulā of Sri Lanka along with her retinue. Also the purpose of Princess Sanghamitta's trip to Sri Lanka was to give ordination, and there is no reason to think that she went alone and hence could not perform proper ordination. This example shows how prejudiced the mentality of the author was toward the issue of ordination of women. The young monks who follow this text are taught to think in only one way: that it is not possible to have bhikkhunī ordination in Thailand.

"The dual ordination existing in Taiwan is Mahāyāna."

Ven. Voramai Kabilsingh, who tried to comply with the need for dual ordination and went to receive her ordination in Taiwan in 1970, found upon her return to Thailand that her ordination was considered Mahāyāna. The saṅgha, at best, ignored her existence. We need to further understand that the ordination lineage as established and handed down by the Buddha was simply an ordination without label. Divisions into Theravāda, Mahāyāna, and Vajrayāna are all later developments. The ordination lineage for bhikkhus or bhikkhunīs should be considered complete as Buddhist ordinations and not otherwise.

"By admitting women to the saṅgha, the life of the sāsana will be shortened."

As mentioned above, this appeared in the conversation the Buddha had with Ānanda after admitting women to the order. Having made the statement, the Buddha followed with the laying out of the eight garudhammas for women to follow for prevention and protection, just like a man would build a dam for the prevention of a flood. Logically it would be absurd for the Buddha to establish the bhikkhunī order knowing full well that it would cause an early decline in the Buddhist teachings. Therefore this interpretation is the result of reading his statement out of context, causing such a myth to be sustained.

"By admitting women to the saṅgha, the social structure will be weakened."

This criticism came even during the Buddha's time when he gave ordination to the Sakyan women. Women are the heart of a family, and the happiness of a family depends greatly and chiefly on the role women play as mothers, wives, grandmothers, and so on. However, the Sakyan ladies who were the first batch to receive ordination were all considered widows, as their husbands had previously joined the order.

The life of an ordained person is neither easy nor comfortable, and the path will not be meant for women in general but only for a few dedicated and committed ones. Of Thailand's population of 62 million, only three hundred thousand are monks, less than half a percent, and monastic women would likely comprise a much smaller percentage of the overall population.

However, the point is about the opportunity that women should be offered, according to the establishment of the fourfold Buddhists as intended by the Buddha.

"By having too many women the saṅgha will be weakened."
This is an attitude taken by the Santi Asoke group in Thailand. This is also a misunderstanding and a quoting out of context the conversation the Buddha had with Ānanda at the acceptance of bhikkhunī ordination. As stated above, the Buddha compared women's ordination to a family with only women, one susceptible to thieves. The Santi Asoke group neither read nor included the last paragraph, again mentioned above, where the Buddha said that as a precaution against such a shortcoming he was just like a man expecting a flood and building a dam—in this case the eight garudhammas—to prevent it.

"Women are obstacles to monks' purity."
This is true, but again the statement is quoted incompletely. In the next line the Buddha also said that men are obstacles to women's practice. However, we get to hear only the first part of the passage because in Thailand we have only male monks teaching us. These monks quote only what is meant for them, but the result of this incomplete quotation creates another negative message. Women tend to look down upon themselves and have low self-esteem, causing them to put great emphasis on the value of male monks.

"The best form of merit-making is ordination,
and only men enjoy this."
In Thailand ordination is taken as the highest form of earning merit (that belief can also be open for discussion), and only men enjoy this as a birthright. Further, the value placed on sons is higher than that placed on daughters. In many families the sons are raised like princes while daughters have to take on many responsibilities. Research carried out in the northern part of Thailand showed that eldest daughters in families have often had "to go to work in Bangkok" so that the younger brothers could be ordained. Clearly, gender exploitation is a result of religious values and a wrong belief system within the religion itself.

The research revealed that the young women who went to work in

Bangkok felt bad about themselves, and to assure themselves a better lifestyle in their next birth, they would often make large donations to local temples when they returned annually to visit their villages. Beautiful, shiny temples in the north sometimes are not a reflection of the degree of faith alone but also of the number of women who have had to sacrifice their lives in the name of gratitude for their parents and the opportunity for their brothers to be ordained.

But of course the best form of merit-making, namely ordination, was made available to both men and women in the Buddha's time. We see examples of many bhikkhunīs who were enlightened and became leading disciples. The correct lineage is still alive and available, but it is we women who must come forward and take equal responsibility along with the other three parts of the fourfold Buddhists.

Suggestion for the Mūlasarvāstivāda Saṅgha

Vinaya masters tend to stick strictly to the Vinaya, which is true of both the Theravādin and Mūlasarvāstivādin traditions. With all my respect to the saṅgha, I would like to offer my humble suggestion that in order to preserve Buddhism we need to take into account that the Buddha reminded us on his death bed that it was the Dhamma and Vinaya that will be the lights upon ourselves. Do not insist blindly on only paying attention to the words of the Vinaya, as there is a great need to also apply Dhamma in order to provide us with an understanding of the Vinaya in its true spirit.

We must remember that the Vinaya is not an end of interpretation but only a means. In the beginning when Sāriputta brought this discussion about laying down monastic rules to the Buddha, the Buddha refused to establish what later became known as the Vinaya, as the early saṅgha consisted mostly of enlightened monks. Only when the saṅgha started to grow and there were many varieties of people joining it was the Vinaya introduced. The Vinaya was meant to be an instrument to bring about the peaceful existence of the saṅgha: for the promotion of good monks, for the restraint of those who were shameless, and for an increase in the faith of the laypeople.

I first discussed the ordination of women with H. H. the Dalai Lama in 1980 in Dharamsala. He was delighted that I did my research on bhikkhunī ordination, and I promised to send him my existing research so that, in his words, "We don't have to start from scratch." After my ordination, I met him again in 2005 in New York when we both attended a Peace Council meeting. He came straight to me and reassured me that on the Tibetan side "they are seriously researching it." Twenty-five years is a long time for any serious research.

His idea was to have all the saṅghas in the various Tibetan lineages agree and make a move together. However, it is too idealistic to wait for all of the senior Vinaya masters to come forward and voice themselves on an issue that might seem too farfetched for their concern. His Holiness can start a nucleus project from within the Geluk tradition, with he himself serving as *upajjhāya* for the first batch, and let the Vinaya masters go ahead with the instruction and training to prepare women (foreigners and locals) for a proper ordination.

Ordination must not be for the sake of ordination itself, again not an end, but only as a means to uplift women and to establish them according to the heritage given to them by the Buddha. This process can be taken as a true expression of respect for the Buddha.

Some senior Tibetan masters also pointed out that there was not yet a need for full ordination among the local Tibetan women and, as a result, there is no need to discuss the introduction of the bhikkhunī lineage in Tibetan Buddhism. This in fact is a reflection of how successfully Tibetan women have been kept in the dark about their roles and responsibilities within Buddhism. To bring about the fourfold Buddhists is to strengthen Buddhism so that it will be truly meaningful to all Buddhist practitioners.

Conclusion

The ordination of women cannot happen through women alone; the bhikkhu saṅgha must make it a reality. The bhikkhu saṅgha has to realize its responsibility in seeing to it that the bhikkhunī saṅgha is properly installed. The establishment of a bhikkhunī saṅgha is a sign of a prosperous Buddhist community. A country will not be a central country (*majjhimapadesa*) unless there is the complete set of the fourfold Buddhists.

Again we will remember that the Buddha prophesized that the growth or decline of Buddhism depends on the fourfold Buddhists and that they respect the Buddha, the Dhamma, the Saṅgha, the monastic code (*sikkha*), and meditation (*samādhi*) or practice. Elsewhere he said clearly that the decline of Buddhism will occur when the fourfold Buddhists do not respect each other.

By establishing Buddhism, the Buddha expected that those who follow it would study his teachings, put them into practice, and should there be outsiders who say otherwise, be able to defend and provide a correct understanding on particular issues related to his teachings. As long as the fourfold Buddhists are strong together, Buddhism will be prosperous. To establish the bhikkhunī ordination is to strengthen Buddhism so that it will prosper in the hearts and minds of all Buddhists, and eventually the world will reap the fruits.

In an international arena, it is hard to talk about compassion and the beauty of the teachings of the Buddha when within Buddhism itself there is so much suppression and exploitation in all forms at various levels. Worst still if the suppression is within the saṅgha. Ordination of both genders is one form of expression of true equality that was given to us by the Buddha; we only need to retain its essence and spirit to be true Buddhists.

A Lamp of Vinaya Statements

A CONCISE SUMMARY OF BHIKṢUṆĪ ORDINATION

Tashi Tsering[1]

To the Lord of Dharma, Buddha, the compassionate one;
to Śāriputra and the two Rāhulas,
Ācārya Nāgārjuna and Bhāvaviveka,
Śrīgupta and Jñānagarbha;

To the benevolent Dharma kings and the great abbot Śāntarakṣita,
the founder of Vinaya—through your kindness
the lineage of the abbots of the Mūlasarvāstivāda Vinaya tradition
has not been interrupted in this land of Tibet;

And especially to the incomparable lord of all sentient beings,
the great abbot, holder of the white lotus [Avalokiteśvara],
who manifests in saffron robes, possessing the threefold kindnesses:
To you all, I bow down at your feet with complete faith and respect.

I will explain the subjects of the three books [I composed]:
In clear and concise words, without any fabrication of my own,
I ask whether there is a way to bestow bhikṣuṇī ordination today
in accord with the Mūlasarvāstivāda Vinaya tradition.

1. Translated by Dr. Chok Tenzin Monlam and heavily revised by the editors. The author, who is also published under the name Acharya Geshe Thupten Jangchub, was unavailable to review final revisions. The Tibetan for this article was published in 2007 in a volume from the Department of Religion and Culture.

Having paid homage and made the commitment to compose this article, I would like to briefly introduce the results of the research done on bhikṣuṇī ordination up to this point.

Introduction

His Holiness the Fourteenth Dalai Lama has consistently been the model of love, compassion, and nonviolence, showing the right path to achieving the happiness and well-being of all sentient beings. To this end, he has focused great energy on the promotion of world peace, religious harmony, and the protection of the environment and its inhabitants in order to prevent social and global tragedies. Many consider him the helmsman of world peace for his great contributions to human society and to the lives of every sentient being.

For his endeavors, the Dalai Lama has gained many followers, both Buddhist and non-Buddhist. They recognize the exceptional qualities to be gained by practicing the paths he demonstrates, how through the wisdom of listening and contemplation, happiness is increased and suffering eliminated. Understanding the power of his position and the responsibilities it entails, His Holiness has created centers for education and religious cultivation around the world. By recognizing that men and women are equals, he has granted nuns (*btsun ma*) the opportunity to pursue geshema degrees, emphasizing since 1983 that Vinaya holders must recognize the possibility of bhikṣuṇī ordination in accordance with Vinaya traditions.

Following his instructions, the Department of Religion and Culture of the Central Tibetan Administration has conducted thorough research on the Vinaya texts to assess the possibility of bhikṣuṇī ordination. Utmost effort has been made to examine the ordination of bhikṣuṇīs in the Sthaviravāda (here: Theravāda) and the Dharmaguptaka Vinaya traditions, and we have examined in particular the texts of the Mūlasarvāstivāda Vinaya tradition of Nālandā University. In 1997, I researched the Dharmaguptaka Vinaya tradition in Taiwan and the possibility for validating the origin of that ordination lineage. In 1998, a conference in Dharamsala brought together Vinaya holders of the Sthaviravāda, Dharmaguptaka, and Mūlasarvāstivāda traditions to discuss whether there is an extant practice of bhikṣuṇī ordination in each of these traditions.

In 2000, the Department of Religion and Culture of the Central Tibetan Administration published three books on the research findings,[2] distributing copies to high lamas, Vinaya holders, nuns, and interested researchers with the request that they contribute critical research articles in response. Thirteen responses were published separately by the Department of Religion and Culture later that year and reflect the ideas and opinions of those closely connected with Vinaya discourse and philosophy. A 2006 meeting of Vinaya holders in Dharamsala considered whether there is a way to implement bhikṣuṇī ordination according to the Mūlasarvāstivāda tradition. This meeting produced thoughtful opinions and dialogue but did not result in a consensus.

In order to determine whether it is presently possible to give bhikṣuṇī ordination to Tibetan nuns in accordance with the Mūlasarvāstivāda Vinaya tradition, we must first consider the ways in which full ordination of both men and women existed during the lifetime of the historical Buddha. This will lead us to consider both the scriptural evidence as well as historical adaptations and interpretations.

Can the Three Methods of Bhikṣuṇī Ordination Be Applied Today?

According to the *Uttaragrantha*,[3] during the lifetime of the Buddha in general there were ten different means to full ordination:

1. Through self-arising
2. Through realizing truth
3. Through summoning
4. Through accepting the Teacher
5. Through pleasing (the Teacher) through questions
6. Through accepting the eight heavy rules (*gurudharma*)
7. Through messages/messengers

2. Ācārya Dge shes Thub bstan byang chub, Volume 1: *Dge slong ma'i 'byung khung*; Volume 2: *Rab gsal me long;* Volume 3: *Thub dbang zhal lung* (Dharamsala: Department of Religion and Culture, 2000).

3. *'Dul ba gzhung dam pa*, Kangyur D ('dul ba) *pa*, 234r6.

8. Through five [monks]: four bhikṣus and a Vinaya holder
9. Through an assembly of ten
10. Through taking refuge

In particular there were three methods of full ordination for women:[4]

1. Through accepting the eight heavy rules
2. Through messages/messengers
3. Through the saṅgha of both bhikṣus and bhikṣuṇīs

We first consider the eight heavy rules and their relevance to modern ordination. The *Kṣudrakavastu*[5] states:

> The Buddha pronounced, "Mahāprajāpatī and the five hundred Śākya women have gone forth [i.e., received *pravrajyā* ordination] and then were fully ordained and attained the entity of a bhikṣuṇī by accepting the gurudharmas. Other women should proceed gradually. Any bhikṣuṇī can approach the aspirant who wishes to become ordained and ask about her hindrances and accept her."

And the *Ekottarakarmaśataka*[6] also states:

> The Buddha pronounced, "Through accepting the gurudharmas, Gautamī Mahāprajāpatī and the five hundred Śākya women have gone forth, were fully ordained, and received the entity of a bhikṣuṇī. Other women should go forth and obtain the entity of a bhikṣuṇī gradually."

This makes it clear that today women cannot be fully ordained through simply accepting the gurudharmas. They should be ordained gradually by

4. *'Dul ba gzhung dam pa*, Kangyur D ('dul ba) *pa*, 235v6.

5. *'Dul ba phran tshegs*, Kangyur D ('dul ba) *da*, 105v1.

6. Guṇaprabha (ca. fifth–sixth century), *Las brgya rtsa gcig pa*, Tengyur D ('dul ba) *wu*, 117v2.

means of the present ceremonial rite (*karmavidhi*), beginning with the vow of an upāsikā.[7]

Concerning the second method, full ordination through messages or messengers, and whether its practice may be applied nowadays, Tsonawa Sherap Sangpo's Vinaya commentary states with reference to the *Vinayavibhaṅga*:[8]

> [The Buddha pronounced,] "With Prajāpatī as the abbess, send Utpalavarṇā as the messenger and fully ordain Dharmadattā." As stated, this [kind of] full ordination through a messenger can be done from outside by means of the present ceremonial rite. It was done in dependence on the [dual] saṅgha communities [of bhikṣus and bhikṣuṇīs] because the *Kṣudrakavastu* states, "The two saṅgha communities have sent Utpalavarṇā as a messenger." The method was performed in dependence on a ceremonial rite because the *Vinayamātṛkā* states, "As for [the use of ordination by] message, the reason why it came about in the case of virtuous ordinary beings such as Dharmadattā is because a messenger must be employed as a rite in cases where [such] an obstacle arises." And it also states in its commentary, "Give the precepts through the rite of messenger (*dūtavidhi*)." And furthermore it is said: "If, at that time, the recipient of the vow qualifies in terms of the three conditions—if that recipient is capable of attaining the paths of seeing and above, if the abbot and others know that the recipient is a fortunate being, and if that recipient is not able to come into the presence of the abbot and others—then the recipient is allowed to receive the ethical precepts through a message."

The *Vinaya Synopsis*[9] also states:

7. A more detailed explanation of the context is explained in Tsering 2000.

8. Mtsho sna ba Shes rab bzang po (thirteenth century), *'Dul ba mtsho ṭik nyi ma'i 'od zer* (Dharamsala: Sherig Parkhang, 1987), 48.

9. Shar chen Ngag dbang tshul khrims (nineteenth century), *'Dul sdom* (Sermé edition), 25.

> The three prerequisites for [bestowing vows through a message] are:
> the recipient is unable to come before the abbot and preceptor,
> the abbot and preceptor know [she is a suitable candidate],
> and the recipient is capable of attaining the path of seeing.

As these Vinaya citations establish, ordination of a bhikṣuṇī through messages must satisfy three criteria: the recipient (who depends on the two saṅgha communities) is unable to come before her preceptor and abbot; they recognize her nonetheless as a fortunate being; and she is capable of attaining the path of seeing in this lifetime.

Let us now consider bhikṣuṇī ordination through the saṅgha of both bhikṣus and bhikṣuṇīs, the third method, and examine some of the Vinaya citations on whether there is a way to give bhikṣuṇī ordination today through the two saṅgha communities. The *Kṣudrakavastu*[10] states:

> After a bhikṣu saṅgha comprised of a minimum of ten bhikṣus and a bhikṣuṇī saṅgha comprised of a minimum of twelve bhikṣuṇīs have all assembled and sat, [she] should be placed with folded hands on a swath of grasses or on a clean mat in front of the bhikṣu who leads the ceremonial rite. Then she should request both saṅghas—bhikṣus and bhikṣuṇīs—to bestow on her the full ordination.

The *Ekottarakarmaśataka*[11] also states:

> After that, in addition to the saṅgha of bhikṣuṇīs, in a central land ten or more bhikṣus should assemble; in the borderlands, where that is lacking, the bhikṣu saṅgha should add five or more Vinaya holders, and a bhikṣu should lead the ritual act. It should be known that the person who wants to be fully ordained should request to be fully ordained from both saṅghas.

10. *'Dul ba phran tshegs*, Kangyur D ('dul ba) *da*, 111v2; cited in Thub bstan byang chub 2000: 37.

11. Guṇaprabha, *Las brgya rtsa gcig pa*, Tengyur D ('dul ba) *wu*, 129v7; cited in Thub bstan byang chub 2000: 156.

After receiving the śikṣamāṇā and brahmacarya ordination vows, the candidate should receive the bhikṣuṇī ordination from the saṅgha of both bhikṣus and bhikṣuṇīs. Guṇaprabha's *Vinayasūtra*, his extensive autocommentary (*Vinayasūtravṛttyabhidhāna-svavyākhyāna*), and Tsonawa's commentary all agree on this point. Since we do not have bhikṣuṇīs of the Mūlasarvāstivāda tradition at this time, the bhikṣuṇī ordination through the dual saṅgha of bhikṣus and bhikṣuṇīs is not possible. This is demonstrated by the scriptural citations.

Can the Vinaya Traditions Be Intermingled?

Sakya Paṇḍita's *Ethics of Three Codes*[12] states:

> Sārvastivādins themselves obtain their vows
> through a [legal] act with the decision fourth [after] the motion,[13]
> but if adherents of the other schools were to follow that rite,
> they would lose their monkhood. [180]

And further it states:

> Therefore, whatever the task may be,
> it will end in success if performed in accord with its own system.
>   [197cd]
> But if done in some contrary way, it will not be successful,
> or even if it does succeed, it will be hard for it to turn out well.
> Similarly, all permissions and prohibitions will be successfully
>   achieved
> if observed according to their respective systems. [198]

His *Epistles to the Holy Beings*[14] also states:

12. Sa skya paṇḍi ta Kun dga' rgyal mtshan (1182–1251), *Sdom gsum rab dbye*, Gangs can rig mdzod 25 (Lhasa: Bod ljongs bod yig dpe rnying dpe skrun khang, 1992), 19. We follow here partly the translation in Rhoton 2002: 64.

13. According to Rhoton (2002: 79n47), the Mahāsāṅghika school is not supposed to accept the validity of ordination by the *jñāpticaturthakarma* (*gsol ba dang bzhi'i las*).

14. Sa skya paṇḍi ta, *Skyes bu dam pa rnams la spring pa'i yi ge*, Gangs can rig mdzod 25

> In particular, there are two traditions of prātimokṣa: that of the Śrāvakas and that of the Mahāyānists. That which was observed by the four basic orders of Śrāvakas was preserved in the four languages known as Sanskrit, Prākrit, Apabhraṃśa, and Paiśācī. Out of these orders emerged eighteen subschools, among which many mutually variant rules of permission and prohibition can be seen. I have explained that each of these schools must practice its initial acquiring of vows, observing them, categorizing rules of permission and prohibition, and relinquishing or repairing vows according to its own tenets, and that it is wrong to mix up one with another. [Of these], only the Vinaya of the Sarvāstivāda school was translated into Tibetan.

Panchen Sönam Drakpa's *Religious History of Vinaya*[15] states:

> All the [vow] lineages that flourished in Tibet were transmitted from the three abbots of the Mūlasarvāstivāda Vinaya tradition. The kings and ministers of Tibet decreed to not spread other Vinaya traditions [in Tibet] besides those of the Mūlasarvāstivāda. For that reason, although the great lord, Atiśa, who was from the Mahāsaṃghika Vinaya tradition, came to Tibet, no [vow] lineage was transmitted through him.

Can Full Ordination Be Bestowed on Women with the Bhikṣu Rite or on Men with the Bhikṣuṇī Rite?

The *Uttaragrantha*[16] says:

(Lhasa: Bod ljongs bod yig dpe rnying dpe skrun khang, 1992), 153. Translation follows Rhoton 2002: 232.

15. Bsod nams grags pa (1478–1554), *'Dul ba'i chos 'byung* (Dharamsala: Library of Tibetan Works and Archives, 1975), 24.

16. *'Dul ba gzhung bla ma*, Kangyur D ('dul ba) *na*, 240v1.

> "Noble One, if a male novice (*śrāmaṇera*) is ordained [as a bhikṣu] by the bhikṣuṇī ceremonial rite, is it considered being fully ordained?"
>
> "Upāli, it is called fully ordained; however, the performers of the ordination have infractions (*sātisāra*)."
>
> "Noble One, if a probationary nun (*śikṣamāṇā*) is ordained by the bhikṣu ceremonial rite, is it considered being fully ordained?"
>
> "Upāli, it is called fully ordained; however, the performers of the ordination have infractions."

Also the *Vinayasūtra*[17] says:

> It is not [an invalid act] if bhikṣus and bhikṣuṇīs perform each other's rite.

The *Vinayasūtra* autocommentary[18] states:

> "It is not [an invalid act] if bhikṣus and bhikṣuṇīs perform each other's rite" means if a bhikṣu is ordained by the bhikṣuṇī rite, it is not unaccomplished [i.e., not invalid], and if a bhikṣuṇī is ordained by the bhikṣu rite, it is not unaccomplished. Neither the rite for the full ordination of bhikṣus nor the rite for the full ordination of bhikṣuṇīs is ultimately the exclusive rite to be used for [its respective ordination alone]. When the bhikṣu saṅgha performs full ordination [for bhikṣus by means of the bhikṣuṇī rite] it is superior, and the bhikṣuṇī saṅgha, since it is merely a follower, is [only] staying close by. Likewise, since it is said that "from the bhikṣus the entity of a bhikṣuṇī must be bestowed when the bhikṣuṇī upasaṃpadā is performed [by means of the bhikṣu rite]," one comprehends accordingly. Such scriptural citations are stated in the *Kṣudrakavastu* and *Upālipariprcchā* [in the

17. Guṇaprabha, *Dul ba'i mdo*, Tengyur D ('dul ba) *wu*, 84v6.

18. Guṇaprabha, *Vinayasūtravṛttyabhidhāna-svavyākhyāna*, *'Dul ba'i mdo 'grel pa mngon par brjod pa rang gi rnam par bshad pa*, Tengyur D ('dul ba) *zu*, 197v6.

> *Uttaragrantha*]: "Noble One, if a male novice is ordained [as a bhikṣu] through the bhikṣuṇī ceremonial rite, is it considered being fully ordained? Upāli, it is called fully ordained; however, those who perform the ordination will be guilty (*sātisāro bhavati*)."

Rongtön's commentary on a Vinaya text[19] states:

> The *Upāliparipṛcchā* states, "It is appropriate to ordain a novice monk through the bhikṣuṇī ceremonial rite and to ordain a śikṣamāṇā through the bhikṣu ceremonial rite; however, the performers have infractions (*duṣkṛta*)."

Also the *Vinaya Synopsis*[20] states:

> Although in the charter stories (*nidāna*) of the Vinaya it is stated that [the act] is not accomplished if the vow is bestowed through the [other's] ceremonial rite, the *Upāliparipṛcchā* states that it is accomplished, but the performer has an infraction (*aparādha*).

Gorampa's *Supplement to Ethics of Three Codes*[21] says:

> It is stated in the *Karmavastu* itself
> that the ordination is accomplished
> by interchanging the two saṅghas
> and by interchanging the formulas of the rites.

Annotation to the Supplement to Ethics of Three Codes[22] states:

19. Rong ston Shākya rgyal mtshan (1367–1449), *'Dul ba me tog phreng rgyud kyi rnam 'grel*, middle vol. (Bir: Dzongsar College), 14r2.

20. Byams pa skal bzang (d. 1944?), *'Dul ba'i sdom tshig* (Sera Jé), 21r4.

21. Go rams Bsod nams seng ge (1429–89), *Sdom gsum rab dbye'i kha skong*, Sa skya pa'i bka' 'bum, vol. 14 (Tokyo: Toyo Bunko, 1969), 283.

22. Ngag dbang chos grags (1572–1641), *Sdom gsum rab tu dbye ba'i kha skong gi mchan 'grel gzhung don rab gsal* (Darjeeling: Gumsa Monastery), 22v5.

> It is stated in the *Karmavastu* itself that if during the actual supplication and the [legal] act with the decision fourth [after] the motion[23] the two saṅghas are interchanged, and the bhikṣu assembly uses the bhikṣuṇī rite and the bhikṣuṇī assembly uses the bhikṣu rite, the rite is accomplished for the one to be ordained; and if the formulas of the rite are interchanged and even a woman is given full ordination on the basis of the bhikṣu rite and a man on the basis of the bhikṣuṇī rite, it is accomplished. Commenting on the *Vinayavastu* the *Vinayasūtra* states: "Bhikṣus, with regard to bhikṣuṇīs using the others [i.e., the bhiksu's rite], it is not unaccomplished."

It is likewise explained in the following Vinaya commentaries: Dharmamitra's *Vinayasūtraṭīkā*; Prajñākara's *Vinayasūtravyākhyāna*; Tsonawa's Vinaya commentary and *Annotation to the Vinayasūtra*; the First Dalai Lama's *Precious Garland Vinaya Commentary*; the Eighth Karmapa's Vinaya commentary; Lochen Dharmaśrī's *Commentary to Ethics of Three Codes*; Shākya Chokden's *Sun Chariot Vinayasūtra Exegesis* and *Elucidation of the Ekottarakarmaśataka*; Mangthö Ludrup Gyatso's *Jewel Rosary Vinaya Exegesis*; Yangchen Khenpo Ngawang Chödrak's *Ornament of Beautiful Precious Jewels*, *Annotation to Ethics of the Three Codes*, and *General Survey on Vinaya*; Shenphen Chökyi Nangwa's *Tree of the White Lotus: Explanation of the Difficult Points of the Vinayasūtra*; and Thupten Chödrak's *Precious Garland: A Clear Commentary to Seventeen Fundamentals*. They all explain that if a woman is ordained by the bhikṣu rite or a man is ordained by the bhikṣuṇī rite, the performers of the full ordination have infractions or become guilty.[24]

23. Tib. *gsol ba dang bzhi kyi las*, Skt. *jñāpticaturthakarma*, Pāli *ñatticatutthakamma*. This refers, in case of full ordination, to a legal act whereby the motion to ordain is first formulated as a wish or supplication in the optative case and then is followed three times by a declaration of the content of the motion (in the indicative case), indicating it is accepted if none of the participants opposes. This in turn is followed with the decision to ordain as a fouth and final element following the motion.

24. I have not seen any cases in the history of ancient India where a bhikṣuṇī is ordained by the bhikṣu ceremonial rite or a bhikṣu is ordained by the bhikṣuṇī rite. However, there are records of bhikṣuṇīs being ordained by performing the bhikṣu ceremonial rite in fifteenth-century Tibet. Other records criticize the practice.

Is Brahmacarya Ordination Necessary for Bhikṣuṇī Ordination?

Some interpreters state that the brahmacarya ordination (*upasthāna*) is necessary prior to bhikṣuṇī ordination (*upasaṃpadā*), regardless of whether it is performed through the bhikṣu or the bhikṣuṇī ceremonial rite. Let us review these arguments. *Supplement to Ethics of Three Codes*[25] states:

> However, for a woman to receive full ordination
> through the present ceremonial rite,
> she must first receive the brahmacarya upasthāna
> or she will not become fully ordained.

Annotation to the Supplement to Ethics of Three Codes[26] states:

> "However, for a woman to receive full ordination through the present ceremonial rite, she must first receive the brahmacarya upasthāna or she will not become fully ordained," even if the actual ordination rite has been performed. It is so because the *Vinayasūtra* states, "If she has not obtained the vow of being close to the brahmacarya, she does not become fully ordained."

Through similarly quoting the *Vinayasūtra*, these commentaries on the Vinaya—Lochen Dharmaśrī's *Commentary to Ethics of Three Codes*, Mangthö Ludrup Gyatso's *Jewel Rosary Vinaya Exegesis*, Ngawang Chödrak's *Ornament of Beautiful Precious Jewels*, *Annotation to Ethics of the Three Codes*, and *General Survey on Vinaya*—also explain that the brahmacarya ordination is a prerequisite for bhikṣuṇī ordination, whether performed through the bhikṣu or the bhikṣuṇī ceremonial rite.

Other sources, however, say that the brahmacarya upasthāna is necessary for the bhikṣuṇī ordination performed through the bhikṣuṇī ceremonial rite but not for bhikṣuṇī ordination performed through the bhikṣu cer-

25. Go rams Bsod nams seng ge, op. cit., 284.

26. Ngag dbang chos grags, op. cit., 23r4.

emonial rite. For instance, *Extensive Ornament Commentary on Ethics of Three Codes*[27] states:

> [The Vinaya citation] "Even after two years [of probation as a śikṣamāṇā], without obtaining the brahmacarya upasthāna vow, she will not be fully ordained" is true if a woman is ordained through the bhikṣuṇī ceremonial rite but not if she is ordained through the bhikṣu ceremonial rite. Although it is accomplished, the performers become guilty.

The Eighth Karmapa's *Vinayasūtra* commentary[28] also states:

> When we said that the bhikṣuṇī vow is not accomplished if the brahmacarya upasthāna has not been bestowed, we meant that the bhikṣuṇī vow is not accomplished as flawless and perfect; but in terms of generated but faulty (*duṣkṛta*), we did not say that the bhikṣuṇī vow is not accomplished. Therefore there is no contradiction.

The First Dalai Lama's *Precious Garland Vinaya Commentary*[29] also states:

> If asked, can a śikṣamāṇā become fully ordained only after having practiced for two years? [Answer:] Since one practices pure chastity—brahmacarya—in order to accomplish pure nirvāṇa, if one has not obtained the vow that is close to full ordination, one does not become fully ordained. If asked, well then, if accordingly [the brahmacarya upasthāna vow is] not performed, does this necessarily mean that the vow of a bhikṣuṇī will not arise?

27. 'Brug chen Padma dkar po (1527–96), *Sdom gsum rgyan 'grel las le'u dang po*, Collected Works of Kun-mkhyen Padma-dkar-po, vol. 5 (Darjeeling : Kargyud Sungrab Nyamso Khang, 1973), 68.

28. Karma Mi bskyod rdo rje (1507–54), *'Dul ba mdo'i rgya cher 'grel* (Delhi: Rumtek Pel Choekhorling), vol. 1: 338.

29. Dge 'dun grub (1391–1474), *'Dul ṭīk rin chen phreng ba* (Varanasi: Geluk Association), vol. 2: 191.

> The answer is no, this doesn't necessarily follow. For it is stated that the bhikṣuṇī vow [also] arises if a woman is fully ordained by means of the bhikṣu ceremonial rite [which does not include the brahmacarya upasthāna], and because there were other cases [of women] who became fully ordained [merely] by accepting the eight gurudharmas. But if a full ordination is performed by means of the bhikṣuṇī rite and the brahmacarya upasthāna vow has not been obtained, [then yes,] the bhikṣuṇī vows are not generated.

Shākya Chokden's *Sun Chariot Vinayasūtra Exegesis*[30] also states:

> If asked: if the bhikṣuṇī vow is generated through performing the bhikṣu ceremonial rite, then how is it not contradictory to [the scriptural citation that states], "...without receiving the brahmacarya upasthāna vows, she does not become fully ordained"? This is true only if ordained on the basis of the bhikṣuṇī rite. If a woman is fully ordained on the basis of a bhikṣu rite, [the brahmacarya upasthāna] is not required, just as it is not necessary to obtain the śikṣamāṇā vow.

Other commentaries such as Paṇchen Lodrö Leksang's *Ornament of Precious Garland Commentary on the Vinayasūtra*; Jetsün Chökyi Gyaltsen's *Pearl Rosary: A Necklace for Scholars*; Paṇchen Delek Nyima's *Well-Expressed Garland of Precious Jewels*; Thupten Chödrak's *Precious Garland: A Clear Commentary to Seventeen Fundamentals*; and Tsongkhapa's *Essence of the Ocean of Vinaya* are also clear on this point that the brahmacarya ordination is required for the bhikṣuṇī rite but not for the bhikṣu rite.

30. Shākya mchog ldan (1428–1507), *'Dul ba mdo'i gnas rnam par bshad pa mdo'i snang byed nyi ma'i shing rta*, Collected Works of Panchen Shakya Chokden (Thimbu, Bhutan: Kusang Topgya, 1975), 21v2.

Must Brahmacarya Ordination Be Performed Only by the Bhikṣuṇī Saṅgha?

Some scriptural evidence suggests that the brahmacarya ordination may be performed only by the bhikṣuṇī saṅgha. The *Vinayasūtra*[31] states:

> After the secret interview, the saṅgha should impart it.

The *Vinayasūtra* autocommentary[32] also states:

> "After having performed the secret interview [i.e., questioning the śikṣamāṇā about hindrances to full ordination], the saṅgha should impart it" means the brahmacarya upasthāna vow should be imparted. If asked who should impart it, the saṅgha should. Since it is [required on] this occasion, the bhikṣuṇī saṅgha should impart it.

Supplement to Ethics of the Three Codes[33] offers the following interpretation on this citation:

> The brahmacarya upasthāna is imparted
> only by a female assembly, as stated in the scriptures.
>
> No exception is mentioned in this regard,
> and there are also no other proofs.
> Hence, performing such a ceremonial rite [by bhikṣus]
> is not justifiable and is messing with the doctrine.

Annotation to the Supplement to Ethics of the Three Codes[34] further states:

31. Guṇaprabha, *'Dul ba'i mdo*, Tengyur D ('dul ba) *wu*, 11v2.

32. Guṇaprabha, *Vinayasūtravṛttyabhidhāna-svavyākhyāna*, *'Dul ba'i mdo 'grel pa mngon par brjod pa rang gi rnam par bshad pa*, Tengyur D ('dul ba) *zhu*, 49v4; and cited in Thub bstan byang chub 2000: 201.

33. Go rams Bsod rnam seng ge, op. cit., 285.

34. Ngag dbang chos grags, op. cit., 23r6.

> The brahmacarya upasthāna vow should only be given by the bhikṣuṇī saṅgha, because Guṇaprabha's autocommentary states, "Since it is [required on] this occasion, the bhikṣuṇī saṅgha should impart it." Regarding necessity and the way to bestow it, no exceptions are given. And since there is no evidence that it is *not* required as a prerequisite, it would be just messing with the doctrine if, in a situation where bhikṣuṇīs are not available, the bhikṣu saṅgha alone gives full ordination to a woman, performing the rite in this way.

The commentaries *Ornament of Beautiful Precious Jewels* by Ngawang Chödrak, Mangthö Ludrup Gyatso's *Jewel Rosary Vinaya Exegesis*, Ngawang Chodrak's *Annotation to Ethics of the Three Codes*, Jetsün Chökyi Gyaltsen's *Pearl Rosary: A Necklace for Scholars*, and Ngawang Chödrak's *General Survey on the Vinaya* elaborate on this in a similar way. It also becomes clear from the detailed study in my *Clear Mirror*, the second of the three research books published by the Department of Religion and Culture in 2000.

Other scriptural citations state that the bhikṣu saṅgha *can* bestow the brahmacarya upasthāna vows. The *Vinayavastu*[35] states:

> What is to be done regarding the śikṣamāṇā is this: After having trained for two years in the six trainings and their six corollary trainings, this śikṣamāṃā should send a messenger to the bhikṣus by supplicating, "Noble ones, I request that you grant me full ordination." If the bhikṣus reply, "Come here," then they [the bhikṣus] bless [themselves and their articles allowing them to go outside] for up to seven days; and for the sake of what is to be done for the śikṣamāṇā they go out. This is what is to be done regarding the śikṣamāṇā.

The *Vinayasūtra*[36] also states:

35. *'Dul ba gzhi*, Kangyur D ('dul ba) *ka*, 244v1.

36. Guṇaprabha, *'Dul ba'i mdo*, Tengyur D ('dul ba) *wu*, 63r5.

It is also [similar] for śikṣamāṇās regarding the brahmacarya upasthāna vow and full ordination.

The *Vinayasūtraṭīkā*[37] states:

> The meaning of "It is also [similar] for the śikṣamāṇās regarding the brahmacarya upasthāna vow and full ordination" is: If a śikṣamāṇā wishes to receive the brahmacarya upasthāna vow and also full ordination and the śikṣamāṇā is outside the [retreat] boundary (*sīmā*), then to accomplish these two purposes for the benefit of the Dharma—to bestow the brahmacarya upasthāna vow and give full ordination—bhikṣus, even if they have accepted the rainy season and are inside the boundary, may leave the boundary for up to seven days after having done the requisite blessing stating that they will return within this time.

Tsonawa's Vinaya commentary[38] states:

> First of all, one should know that the brahmacarya upasthāna vow is received from the bhikṣuṇī saṅgha, consisting of the abbess, the instructor at a secret location, the master of ceremonies, and others. The bhikṣuṇī saṅgha should be comprised of twelve bhikṣuṇīs if in a central land, and six bhikṣuṇīs if in a borderland where twelve bhikṣuṇīs are not found. In the case that even this required number of bhikṣuṇīs doesn't exist, a saṅgha of four bhikṣuṇīs can bestow the brahmacarya upasthāna vow. The act is accomplished but there is a fault, since it is said "If fully ordained by an assembly of four [the act] is accomplished, though there is a fault." If one cannot find the required number of bhikṣuṇīs, it is appropriate for a bhikṣu saṅgha to bestow the brahmacarya upasthāna vow, since it is stated in the *Varṣāvastu* [section of the *Vinayasūtra*], "The brahmacarya upasthāna vow

37. Dharmamitra (dates unknown), *'Dul ba'i mdo'i rgya cher 'grel*, Tengyur D ('dul ba) *yu*, 138v5.

38. Mtsho sna ba Shes rab bzang po, op. cit., 209.

> for the śikṣamāṇā and...." And [Dharmamitra's] commentary states, "In order to accomplish this purpose to bestow the brahmacarya upasthāna [on a śikṣamāṇā], bhikṣus who have accepted the rainy season retreat, since they are in the boundary, should do a blessing [to return] within seven days."

The Eighth Karmapa's *Vinayasūtra* commentary[39] states much the same thing.

Conclusion

To sum up, then, we saw in citations from the *Kṣudrakavastu* and the *Ekottarakarmaśataka*[40] that bhikṣuṇī ordination should be bestowed on a woman by the saṅgha of both bhikṣus and bhikṣuṇīs after she has received the vows of the śikṣamāṇā and the brahmacarya ordination from the bhikṣuṇī saṅgha. Since a bhikṣuṇī lineage of the Mūlasarvāstivāda Vinaya tradition does not exist, all the Vinaya holders agree that there is no way to impart bhikṣuṇī ordination through the bhikṣuṇī ceremonial rite.

This led us to ask what would happen if the bhikṣuṇī ordination were bestowed through the bhikṣu ceremonial rite? We saw in citations from the *Uttaragrantha* and the *Vinayasūtra*[41] that it is generally accepted that bhikṣuṇī vows will be generated within a woman if the bhikṣu ceremonial rite is performed and bhikṣu vows will be generated within a man if the bhikṣuṇī ceremonial rite is performed. However, those who perform the ordination will get infractions.

After reviewing the Vinaya literature, the Vinaya holders were unable to come to an agreement on three questions:

1. Whether or not it is appropriate to bestow the bhikṣuṇī vow accompanied by an infraction through performing the bhikṣu ceremonial rite.

39. Karma Mi bskyod rdo rje, *'Dul ba mdo'i rgya cher 'grel nyi ma'i dkyil 'khor*, Collected Works of the Kagyü Tradition, vols. 10–11 (Ziling: Mtsho sngon mi rigs dpe skrun khang, 2004), 482.

40. See p. 156 above.

41. See p. 158–59 above.

2. Whether [in that case] the brahmacarya ordination is required beforehand.
3. Whether the brahmacarya ordination can only be bestowed by the bhikṣuṇī saṅgha or whether it may also be bestowed by the bhikṣu saṅgha when a [Mūlasarvāstivāda] bhikṣuṇī saṅgha cannot be found.

All matters related to the Vinaya rites of the saṅgha should be resolved in conformity with the Vinaya or without contradicting it through assembling the Vinaya holders as stated below. The Buddha said:[42]

> Oh bhikṣus! When I, your Teacher, pass into parinirvāṇa and become no more available, you may think, "Our great Teacher is missing." But you should refrain from such a view. This is why I have instructed you to recite the *Prātimokṣa-sūtra* twice a month. From now on this Teaching will be your great Teacher. Oh bhikṣus! For all the subtle points of the basic precepts and for minor matters, convene the saṅgha, discuss the issue, and resolve it to reach a peaceful decision.

Ācārya Guṇaprabha, the great Vinaya holder of India, said:[43]

> If [an act] goes against the ceremonial rite, then the act is not acceptable. Here, *ceremonial rite* refers to: the number of saṅgha members required, the uttering of the act, and the performer of the rite.

Lord Atiśa, the great Vinaya holder, said:[44]

> In India, whenever any important or controversial issue came up, we convened an assembly of upholders of the Tripiṭaka. Then

42. *Kṣudrakavastu*, *'Dul ba phran tshegs*, Kangyur D ('dul ba) *da*, 288r4.

43. *Vinayasūtra*, *'Dul ba'i mdo*, Tengyur D ('dul ba) *wu*, 81v4.

44. Cited in Tsong kha pa Blo bzang grags pa (1357–1419), *Lam rim chen mo* (Kaphuk, loose folio), 179r3.

> we sought to determine whether the issue was prohibited by the Tripiṭaka or contradicted by the Tripiṭaka, and in this way we came to a decision.

Tsongkhapa states that:[45]

> We should take the Vinaya, which teaches the precepts to be trained, as the substitute for the Teacher after the passing of the Buddha, just as it is stated in the *Vinayavibhaṅga:*[46]
>
> > "After my passing into parinirvāṇa,
> > this [*Prātimokṣa-sūtra*] will be your teacher."
> > Those gone forth should recite it with respect
> > in front of the bhikṣu saṅgha [listening] intently.
> >
> > Since [the Buddha] intended this Vinaya
> > to be the key to that prātimokṣa,
> > those who wish to be liberated
> > should respect and earnestly listen to it.

And so on, to the end:

> Whosoever does not have this bridle [of Vinaya]
> and does not wish for it to last forever
> will be troubled by the onslaught of afflictions,
> wandering forever with no place to hold.

The Dalai Lama has stated that:[47]

45. Tsong kha pa Blo bzang grags pa, *Dge slong gi bslab bya gnam rtse ldeng ma* (Kan su'u mi rigs dpe skrun khang), 78.

46. *'Dul ba rnam par 'byed pa*. The initial quote here within the verse is from a famous verse in the *Bhikṣu Prātimokṣa-sūtra*.

47. From a speech His Holiness gave at the 1993 bhikṣuṇī conference.

> Such matters related to these lineages, when vital for practice, should be discussed and decided collectively by the upholders of Tripiṭaka in general, and particularly by the Vinaya holders; there is no way an individual can make the decision on his or her own.

Three factors affect the possibility of reviving the Mūlasarvāstivāda bhikṣuṇī ordination in the twenty-first century:

1. The number of women taking interest in Buddhism and wishing to receive the bhikṣuṇī ordination has increased significantly in our time.
2. There are scriptural citations stating that the bhikṣuṇī vow is generated when imparted through the Mūlasarvāstivāda bhikṣu ceremonial rite.
3. The possibility of reviving the Mūlasarvāstivāda bhikṣuṇī ordination depends entirely on the Vinaya holders. If the Vinaya holders can reach a peaceful consensus, it would be of benefit both now and in future generations.

In this short article, I have attempted to present straightforward scriptural evidence to inform a final decision on the many questions surrounding the bhikṣuṇī ordination. May the merit acquired through this effort fulfill my prayers!

> May the spiritual masters who glorify the Dharma live long,
> may all who protect Dharma have good health,
> and may the Buddhadharma, the source of the happiness
> and well-being of all sentient beings, prevail forever.

May all be happy!

A Tibetan Precedent for Multi-Tradition Ordination

Thubten Chodron[1]

When I received śrāmaṇerikā ordination in Dharamsala, India, in 1977, I was told the story behind the blue cord on our monastic vest: it was in appreciation of the two Chinese monks who aided the Tibetans in reestablishing the ordination lineage when it was on the verge of extinction in Tibet. "Full ordination is so precious," my teachers instructed, "that we should feel grateful to all those in the past and present who preserved the lineage, enabling us to receive the vow today." When I received bhikṣuṇī ordination in Taiwan in 1986, the kindness of all the monastics that received, preserved, and passed on the Vinaya lineages became even clearer to me. Due to their efforts, so many of us have the precious opportunity to live as monastics today.

A bhikṣu saṅgha of three Tibetan and two Chinese monks ordained Lachen Gongpa Rapsal (Bla chen Dgongs pa rab gsal) after wide-scale persecution of the Buddhist saṅgha in Tibet. Led by the Tibetan king Langdarma, the persecution decimated the monasteries and monastic communities. Lachen Gongpa Rapsal was an exceptional monk, and his disciples, such as Lumé (Klu mes) and others, were responsible for restoring temples and monasteries in Central Tibet and ordaining many bhikṣus,

1. I am indebted to Bhikṣuṇī Tien-chang, a graduate student (now Ph.D.) in Asian Languages and Literature at the University of Washington, Seattle, for doing the bulk of the research for this paper. She also graciously answered my many questions and points for clarification as well as corrected the final draft of this paper.

thus spreading the precious Buddhadharma. His ordination lineage is the principal lineage found in the Geluk and Nyingma schools of Tibetan Buddhism today.[2]

Interestingly, thirty years after my ordination, I am returning to the story of Lachen Gongpa Rapsal's ordination and the reestablishment of the bhikṣu saṅgha in Tibet. Only now, I see his ordination is a precedent of multi-tradition ordination that could be used to establish the bhikṣuṇī ordination in Tibetan Buddhism in current times.

In recent years there has been discussion of the possibility of establishing the bhikṣuṇī saṅgha in countries where it either did not previously develop and or has died out. Everyone agrees that dual ordination by a saṅgha of bhikṣus and a saṅgha of bhikṣuṇīs is the preferable mode of giving the bhikṣuṇī ordination. However, in the absence of a Mūlasarvāstivādin bhikṣuṇī saṅgha to participate in such an ordination in the Tibetan community, new questions arise: Is it possible for the ordaining saṅgha to consist of Mūlasarvāstivādin bhikṣus and Dharmaguptaka bhikṣuṇīs? Could the Mūlasarvāstivādin bhikṣu saṅgha alone give the bhikṣuṇī ordination?

The ordination and activities of Bhikṣu Lachen Gongpa Rapsal provide precedents for both (1) ordination by a saṅgha consisting of members of different Vinaya lineages and (2) reasonable adjustment of Vinaya ordination procedures in exceptional circumstances. Let us examine this in more depth.

2. This ordination lineage was brought to Tibet by the great sage Śāntarakṣita in the late eighth century. At the time of the second propagation (*phyi dar*) of Buddhism in Tibet, it became known as the Lowland Vinaya (*smad 'dul*) lineage. During the second propagation, another lineage, which was called the Upper or Highland Vinaya (*stod 'dul*) lineage, was introduced by the Indian scholar Dharmapāla into western Tibet. However, this lineage died out. A third lineage was brought by Panchen Śākyaśrībhadra. It was initially known as the Middle Vinaya (*bar 'dul*) lineage. However, when the Upper lineage died out, the Middle lineage became known as the Upper Vinaya lineage. This lineage is the chief Vinaya lineage in the Kagyü and Sakya schools.

A Precedent in Tibetan History for the Ordaining Saṅgha to Consist of Mūlasarvāstivādin and Dharmaguptaka Members

Scholars have different opinions regarding the dates of Langdarma, Gongpa Rapsal, and the return of Lumé and other monks to Central Tibet. Craig Watson places Langdarma's reign at 838–42[3] and Gongpa Rapsal's life at 832–915.[4] I will provisionally accept these dates. However, the exact dates do not affect the main point of this paper, which is that there is a precedent for ordination by a saṅgha composed of Mūlasarvāstivādin and Dharmaguptaka monastics.

The Tibetan king Langdarma persecuted Buddhism almost to extinction. During his reign, three Tibetan monks—Tsang Rapsal, Yo Gejung, and Mar Śākyamuni—who were meditating at Chuḅori, took Vinaya texts and after traveling through many areas, arrived in Amdo, in northeast Tibet. Musu Salbar (a.k.a. Musuk Labar), the son of a Bön couple, approached them and requested the going-forth ceremony (*pravrajyā*). The three monks gave him novice ordination, whereafter he was called Gewa Rapsal or Gongpa Rapsal. The ordination took place in southern Amdo.[5]

Gongpa Rapsal then requested full ordination (*upasaṃpadā*) from these three monks. They responded that since there were not five bhikṣus—the

3. Watson 1980. Both Shakabpa 1976 and Snellgrove 1987 say Langdarma reigned 836–42. Dhongthog Rinpoche 1968 places Langdarma's persecution in 901 and his assassination in 902 or 906. The *Tibetan-Chinese Dictionary* (1993) is in accord with the 901–6 dates. Tibetans "number" years according to animals and elements that form sixty-year cycles. The uncertainty of the dates is because no one is sure to which sixty-year cycle the ancient authors were referring. Dan Martin (1998) says "the date of first entry of the monks of the Lowland Tradition [Gongpa Rapsal's Vinaya descendants] into Central Tibet is itself far from decided; in fact this was a conundrum for traditional historians, as it remains for us today."

4. According to the Third Thuken Losang Chökyi Nyima (1737–1802) in "Short Biography of Gongpa Rapsal," Gongpa Rapsal was born in the male water-mouse year, which could be 832 (Roerich 1979), 892 (Wang Seng 1997), or 952 (*Tibetan-Chinese Dictionary*). I assume Dan Martin would agree with the latter as he provisionally places the date of return of the Lowland monks to Central Tibet as 978, while Dhongthog Rinpoche places the return in 953. The Tibetan Buddhist Resource Center says Gongpa Rapsal lived 953–1035 but also notes, "the sources differ on the birthplace of dgongs pa rab gsal...and the year (832, 892, 952)."

5. Fazun 1979 identifies the area as nearby present-day Xining. Helga Uebach (1987: n729) identifies the place where the two Chinese monks were from as present-day Pa-yen, southeast of Xining.

minimum number required to hold an upasaṃpadā ceremony in an outlying area—the ordination could not be given. Gongpa Rapsal then approached Palgyi Dorjé, the monk who assassinated Langdarma, but he declined because he had killed a human being. Instead, Palgyi Dorjé searched for other monks who could participate in the ordination and brought two respected Chinese monks—Kewang and Gyiwang[6]—who joined the three Tibetan monks to give bhikṣu ordination to Gongpa Rapsal.

We are now faced with the question: Were these two Chinese monks ordained in the Dharmaguptaka or Mūlasarvāstivādin lineage? To answer this, let us examine the history of various Vinaya lineages in China.

According to Huijiao's *Biographies of Eminent Monks*, Dharmakāla traveled to China around 250 C.E. At that time, no Vinaya texts were available in China. Monks simply shaved their heads to distinguish themselves from the laity. On the request of the Chinese monks, Dharmakāla translated the prātimokṣa of the Mahāsāṅghika, which they used only to regulate their daily life. He also invited Indian monks to establish the ordination karma procedure and give ordination. This was the beginning of bhikṣu ordination taking place in the Chinese land.[7] This record does not specify the lineage of that ordination. However, in 254–55, a Parthian monk named Tandi, who was also versed in Vinaya, came to China and translated the Karmavācanā of the Dharmaguptaka school.[8] So it is clear that the karma procedure for ordination performed by the Chinese began with the Dharmaguptaka. For that reason, Dharmakāla is listed as one of the patriarchs of the Dharmaguptaka Vinaya lineage.[9]

For quite a while, the model for Chinese monks seemed to be that they were ordained according to the Dharmaguptaka ordination procedure, but their daily life was regulated by the Mahāsāṅghika prātimokṣa. Not until the fifth century did other Vinaya texts become available to them.

6. Different historical sources record their names with variations, such as Kowang (*ko bang*) or Gyimphak (*gyim phag*); see, eg., Szerb 1990: 59, Watston 1978: 269, Fazun 1979: 331–32, and Uebach 1987: 125. Tibetan historians such as Butön refer to them as *gyanak hashang* (*rgya nag hwā shang*) (Szerb 1990: 59); *gyanak* means China, and *hashang* is a respectful term used in Chinese Buddhism for monks whose status is equivalent to *upādhyāya* (abbot or preceptor).

7. *Gaoseng zhuan* 高僧傳, T 2059: 325a4–5.

8. T 2059: 325a8–9.

9. Yuan Liang 1987: 15.

The first Vinaya text introduced to Chinese communities was Sarvāstivādin, which together with its bhikṣu prātimokṣa was translated by Kumārajīva between 404–9. It was well received, and according to Sengyou (d. 518), a prominent Vinaya master and historian, the Sarvāstivādin Vinaya was the most widely practiced Vinaya in China at that time.[10] Soon after, the Dharmaguptaka Vinaya was also translated into Chinese by Buddhayaśas between 410–12. Both the Mahāsāṅghika and Mahīśāsaka Vinayas were brought back to China by the pilgrim Faxian. The former was translated by Buddhabhadra between 416–18, the latter by Buddhajīva between 422–23.

The Mūlasarvāstivādin Vinaya was brought to China much later by the pilgrim Yijing, who translated it into Chinese between 700–711. According to Yijing's observation in his *Record of Buddhist Practices Sent Home from the Southern Sea* (composed ca. 691), at that time in eastern China most people followed the Dharmaguptaka Vinaya. In the area around Guanzhong (i.e., Chang'an), in addition to the Dharmaguptaka Vinaya, the Mahāsāṅghika Vinaya was used in the earlier time.[11] The Sarvāstivādin was prominent in the Yangzi River area and farther south.[12]

For three hundred years after the four Vinayas—Dharmaguptaka, Mahāsāṅghika, Mahīśāsaka, and Sarvāstivāda—were introduced to China, from the fifth century until the early Tang period in the eighth century, different Vinayas were followed in different parts of China. Monks continued to follow the Dharmaguptaka Vinaya for ordination and to use another Vinaya to regulate their daily life. During 471–99 in the northern Wei period, the Vinaya master Facong advocated that monastics follow the same Vinaya for both ordination and regulating daily life.[13] He asserted

10. *Chu sanzangjiji* 出三藏記集 [The Collection of Records for Translation of the Tripiṭaka], T 2145: 19c26–27, 21a18–19.

11. According to Daoxuan 道宣 in his *Xu gaoseng zhuan* 續高僧傳 [*Continued Biographies of Eminent Monks*], the Guanzhong area followed the Mahāsāṅghika Vinaya alone (T 2060: 614b24).

12. Heirman 2002b: 21; Yijing 義淨, *Nanhai jigui neifa zhuan* 南海寄歸内法傳, T 2125: 205b27–28.

13. Gyōnen, *Risshū kōyō* 律宗綱要 [Outline of the Vinaya School], T 2348: 16a19–22. Facong 法聰 first studied the Mahāsāṅghika Vinaya but then realized that since the Dharmaguptaka Vinaya was used to give ordination in China, this Vinaya should be seriously studied. He then devoted himself to studying and teaching the Dharmaguptaka Vinaya. Unfortunately, little is known about his life, perhaps because he focused on giving oral, not written Vinaya teachings.

the importance of the Dharmaguptaka Vinaya in this regard because the first ordination in China was from the Dharmaguptaka tradition and the Dharmaguptaka was by far the predominant—and maybe even the only—tradition used for ordination after the first ordination.

The renowned Vinaya master Daoxuan (596–667) in the Tang period was Facong's successor. A very important figure in the history of Vinaya in Chinese Buddhism, Daoxuan is regarded as the first patriarch of the Vinaya school in China.[14] He composed several important Vinaya works that are still used today, and he thus laid the solid foundation of Vinaya practice for Chinese monastics. Among his Vinaya works, the most influential ones are *Sifenlu shanfan buque xingshichao* and *Sifenlu shanbu suijijeimo*, which no serious monastic in China neglects reading.[15] According to his *Continued Biographies of Eminent Monks*, Daoxuan observed that even when the Sarvāstivāda Vinaya reached its peak in southern China, still it was Dharmaguptaka procedure that was performed for ordination.[16] Thus, in line with Facong's thought, Daoxuan advocated that all of monastic life—ordination and daily life—for all Chinese monastics should be regulated by only one Vinaya tradition, the Dharmaguptaka.[17]

Due to Daoxuan's scholarship, pure practice, and prestige as a Vinaya master, northern China began to follow only the Dharmaguptaka Vinaya. However, all of China did not become unified in using the Dharmaguptaka until the Vinaya master Dao'an requested the Tang emperor Zhongzong to issue an imperial edict declaring that all monastics must follow the Dharmaguptaka Vinaya.[18] The emperor did this in 709, and since then Dharma-

---

As a result, his eminent successor Daoxuan could not include Facong's biography when he composed *Continued Biographies of Eminent Monks*.

14. If the list of Vinaya patriarchs includes Indian monks, then Dharmagupta in India is counted as the first patriarch. In that case, Daoxuan is the ninth patriarch (Gyōnen, *Risshū kōyō*, T 2348: 16a23–27). There are several ways of tracing back the Dharmaguptaka Vinaya masters. Gyōnen summarizes one of them : (1) Dharmagupta (in India), (2) Dharmakāla (who helped establish the ordination karma in China), (3) Facong, (4) Daofu, (5) Huiguang, (6) Daoyun, (7) Daozhao, (8) Zhishou, (9) Daoxuan.

15. 四分律刪繁補闕行事鈔 (T 1804) and 四分律刪補隨機羯磨 (T1808).

16. *Xu gaoseng zhuan*, T 2060: 620b6.

17. *Xu gaoseng zhuan*, T 2060: 620c7–8.

18. Ann Heirman, private correspondence; Zanning 贊寧 et al., *Song gaoseng zhuan* 宋高僧傳 [Biographies of Eminent Monks of the Song Dynasty], T 2061: 793c25–27.

guptaka has been the sole Vinaya tradition followed throughout China, areas of Chinese cultural influence, as well as in Korea and Vietnam.

Regarding the Mūlasarvāstivādin Vinaya tradition in Chinese Buddhism, the translation of its texts was done in the first decade of the eighth century, after Facong and Daoxuan had already recommended that all monastics in China follow only the Dharmaguptaka and the emperor was promulgating the imperial edict to that effect. Thus there was little opportunity for the Mūlasarvāstivādin Vinaya to become a living tradition in China.[19]

While the other Vinaya traditions are discussed in Chinese records, there is hardly any mention of the Mūlasarvāstivādin, and no evidence has been found that it was practiced in China. In the Vinaya section of Zanning et al.'s *Biographies of Eminent Monks of the Song Dynasty*, written circa 983, in historical records such as Zhipan's *Combined Annals of the Buddhas and Patriarchs* of 1269,[20] and in other texts, no reference to Mūlasarvāstivādin ordination is given. Furthermore, the Japanese monk Gyōnen (1240–1321) traveled extensively in China and recorded the history of Vinaya in China in his *Outline of the Vinaya School*. He noted four Vinaya lineages—Mahāsāṅghika, Sarvāstivādin, Dharmaguptaka, and Mahīśāsaka—existing in China and said, "Although these Vinayas have all spread, it is the Dharmaguptaka alone that flourishes in the later time."[21] His Vinaya text makes no reference to the Mūlasarvāstivāda Vinaya being followed in China.[22]

Let us return to the ordination of Lachen Gongpa Rapsal, which occurred in the second half of the ninth century (or possibly the tenth, depending upon which dates one accepts for his life), at least one hundred and fifty years after Emperor Zhongzong's imperial edict requiring the saṅgha to follow the Dharmaguptaka Vinaya. According to Nelpa Paṇḍita's *Flower Garland*, when Kewang and Gyiwang were invited to become part of the ordaining saṅgha, they replied, "Since the teaching is available in China

19. A living Vinaya tradition involves an established saṅgha living according to a set of precepts over a period of time and transmitting those precepts from generation to generation continuously. See Tsedroen 2008.

20. Zhipan 志磐, *Fozu tongji* 佛祖統紀, T 2035.

21. *Risshū kōyō*, T 2348: 16a17–18; see also Heirman 2002b: 22.

22. Dr. Ann Heirman, private correspondence.

for us, we can do it."[23] This statement clearly shows that these two monks were Chinese and practiced Chinese Buddhism. Thus they must have been ordained in the Dharmaguptaka lineage and practiced according to that Vinaya since all ordinations in China were Dharmaguptaka by that time.

For Kewang and Gyiwang to have been Mūlasarvāstivādin, they would have had to have taken the Mūlasarvāstivādin ordination from Tibetan monks. However, there were no Tibetan monks to give the ordination due to Langdarma's decimation of the Mūlasarvāstivādin ordination lineage. If Kewang and Gyiwang had received Mūlasarvāstivādin ordination from Tibetans in Amdo, it would indicate that there were other Tibetan Mūlasarvāstivādin monks in the area. In that case, why would the Chinese monks have been asked to join the three Tibetan monks to give the ordination? Surely Tsang Rapsal, Yo Gejung, and Mar Śākyamuni would have asked their fellow Tibetans, not the two Chinese monks, to participate in ordaining Gongpa Rapsal.

All evidence points to the two Chinese monks holding the Dharmaguptaka lineage, not the Mūlasarvāstivādin. Thus the saṅgha that ordained Gongpa Rapsal was a mixed saṅgha of Dharmaguptaka and Mūlasarvāstivādin bhikṣus. This is a clear precedent in Tibetan history for giving ordination with a saṅgha consisting of Dharmaguptaka and Mūlasarvāstivādin members. This precedent was not unique to Gongpa Rapsal's ordination. As recorded by Butön, after Lachen Gongpa Rapsal's ordination, the two Chinese monks again participated with Tibetan bhikṣus in the ordination of other Tibetans.[24] For example, they are said to have been the assistant monks during the ordination of ten men from Central Tibet, headed by Lumé.[25] Furthermore, among Gongpa Rapsal's disciples were Drum Yeshé Gyaltsen (Grum Ye shes rgyal mtshan) and Nupjen Chup Gyaltsen (Bsnub byan Chub rgyal mtshan) from the Amdo area. They, too, were ordained by the saṅgha that included the two Chinese monks.[26]

23. Uebach 1987.

24. Obermiller 1986: 202.

25. Butön and Losang Chökyi Nyima say that Lumé was a direct disciple of Gongpa Rapsal. Others say that one or two monastic generations separated them.

26. According to the *Dam pa'i chos byung* of Dkon mchog lhun grub (1497–57), Drum Yeshé Gyaltsen's ordination was performed by the same five-member saṅgha as Gongpa Rapsal's (i.e., it included two Chinese monks) (Fazun 1979).

A Precedent in Tibetan History for Reasonable Adjustment of the Vinaya Ordination Procedures in Exceptional Circumstances

In general, to act as preceptor in a full-ordination ceremony, a bhikṣu must have been ordained ten years or more. As recorded by Butön, Gongpa Rapsal later acted as the preceptor for the ordination of Lumé and nine other monks although he had not yet been ordained five years. When the ten Tibetan men requested him to be their preceptor (*upādhyāya, mkhan po*), Gongpa Rapsal responded, "Five years have not yet passed since I was ordained myself. I cannot therefore be a preceptor." Butön continues, "But Tsan [Tsang] said in his turn, 'Be such an exception!' Thus the Great Lama [Gongpa Rapsal] was made preceptor...with the Hva-cans [hashangs, i.e., Kewang and Gyiwang] as assistants."[27] In Losang Chökyi Nyima's account, the ten men first requested Tsang Rapsal for ordination, but he said he was too old and referred them to Gongpa Rapsal, who said, "I am unable to serve as the *upādhyāya* as five years have not yet elapsed since my own full ordination." At this point, Tsang Rapsal gave him permission to act as preceptor in the bhikṣu ordination of the ten men from Central Tibet. Here an exception was made to the standard bhikṣu ordination procedure.

In the Theravāda Vinaya and the Dharmaguptaka Vinaya, no provision can be found that allows someone who has been ordained fewer than ten years to act as the preceptor for a bhikṣu ordination. The only mention of "five years" is in the context of saying that a disciple must take dependence with his teacher, stay with him, and train under his guidance for five years. Similarly, in the Mūlasarvāstivādin Vinaya found in the Chinese canon, no provision for acting as a preceptor if one has been ordained fewer than ten years can be found. Such an exception is also not found in the Mahāsāṃgika, Sarvāstivāda, and other Vinayas in the Chinese canon.

The Tibetan Mūlasarvāstivādin Vinaya as well states that a monk should not do six things until he has been ordained for ten years,[28] one of which is that he should not serve as preceptor. The last of the six, however, is that he should not go outside the monastery until he has been a monk for ten years.

27. Obermiller 1986: 202.

28. *Vinayavastu, 'Dul ba lung gzhi*, Kangyur D ('dul ba) *ka*, ff. 70–71.

Regarding this last one, the Buddha said that if a monk knows the Vinaya well, he can go outside after five years. While there is no direct statement saying that after five years a monk can serve as preceptor, since all six activities that a monk is not supposed to do are in one list, most scholars say that what is said about one can be applied to the other five. This is a case of interpretation, applying what is said about one item in a list of six to the other five items. That is, if a monk who has been ordained five years is exceptionally gifted, upholds his precepts well, abides properly in the Vinaya code of conduct, has memorized sufficient parts of the Vinaya, and has full knowledge of the Vinaya—i.e., if he is equivalent to a monk who has been ordained ten years—and if the person requesting ordination knows that he has been a monk for only five years, then it is permissible for him to serve as preceptor. However, there is no provision for such a gifted monk to be a preceptor if he has been ordained fewer than five years.

Therefore, since Gongpa Rapsal acted as preceptor although he had been ordained fewer than five years, there is a precedent for adjusting the ordination procedure described in the Vinaya in extenuating conditions. This was done for good reason—the existence of the Mūlasarvāstivādin ordination lineage was at stake. These wise monks clearly had the benefit of future generations and the existence of the precious Buddhadharma in mind when they made this adjustment.

Conclusion

The ordination of Lachen Gongpa Rapsal sets a clear precedent for ordination by a saṅgha composed of monastics from two different Vinaya traditions. In other words, it would not be an unprecedented innovation for a bhikṣuṇī ordination to be given by a saṅgha consisting of Tibetan Mūlasarvāstivādin bhikṣus and Dharmaguptaka bhikṣuṇīs. The nuns would receive the Mūlasarvāstivādin bhikṣuṇī vow. Why? First, because the bhikṣu saṅgha would be Mūlasarvāstivādin, and Dharmamitra's extensive commentary and Guṇaprabha's autocommentary on the *Vinayasūtra* of the Mūlasarvāstivādin tradition both state that the bhikṣus are the main figures performing the bhikṣuṇī ordination. Second, because the bhikṣu and bhikṣuṇī vow are of one nature,[29] it would be suitable and consistent to say that the Mūlasarvāstivādin bhikṣuṇī vow and the Dharmaguptaka bhikṣuṇī vow of are one nature. Therefore, if the Mūlasarvāstivādin bhikṣuṇī ordination rite were used, even though a Dharmaguptaka bhikṣuṇī saṅgha would be present, the candidates would receive the Mūlasarvāstivādin bhikṣuṇī vow.

Applying the exception made for Gonpa Rapsal to the present situation of Mūlasarvāstivādin bhikṣuṇī ordination, it would seem that for the benefit of future generations and for the existence of the precious Buddhadharma, reasonable adjustments could be made in the ordination procedure. For example, the Tibetan Mūlasarvāstivādin bhikṣu saṅgha alone could ordain women as bhikṣuṇīs. After twelve years, when those bhikṣuṇīs are senior enough to become preceptors, the dual ordination procedure could be done.

Tibetan monks often express their gratitude to the two Chinese monks for enabling ordination to be given to Gongpa Rapsal, thereby allowing monastic ordination to continue in Tibet after the persecution of Langdarma. In both Gongpa Rapsal's ordination and the ordination he gave subsequently to ten other Tibetans, we find historical precedents for:

1. Giving full ordination by a saṅgha composed of members of both the Mūlasarvāstivādin and the Dharmaguptaka Vinaya lineages, with the candidates receiving the Mūlasarvāstivādin vow. Using this precedent, a saṅgha of Mūlasarvāstivādin bhikṣus and Dharmaguptaka bhikṣuṇīs could give the Mūlasarvāstivādin bhikṣuṇī vow.
2. Adjusting the ordination procedure in special circumstances. Using this precedent, a saṅgha of Mūlasarvāstivādin bhikṣus could give the Mūlasarvāstivādin bhikṣuṇī vow. After ten years, a dual ordination could be given with a Mūlasarvāstivādin bhikṣu and bhikṣuṇī saṅgha.

This research is respectfully submitted for consideration by the Tibetan bhikṣu saṅgha, upon whom rests the decision to establish the Mūlasarvāstivādin bhikṣuṇī saṅgha. Having bhikṣuṇīs in the Tibetan

29. See Tsedroen 2006.

tradition would enhance the existence of the Buddhadharma in the world. The fourfold saṅgha of bhikṣus, bhikṣuṇīs, and male and female lay followers would exist in the Tibetan community, thus fulfilling the Buddha's wish. It would give many women, in many countries, the opportunity to create great merit by upholding the bhikṣuṇī vows and progress toward enlightenment in order to benefit all sentient beings. In addition, from the viewpoint of the Tibetan community, Tibetan bhikṣuṇīs would instruct lay Tibetan women in the Dharma, thus inspiring many of the mothers to send their sons and daughters to monasteries. This increase in saṅgha members would benefit Tibetan society and the entire world. Seeing the great benefit that would unfold due to the presence of Tibetan nuns holding the Mūlasarvāstivādin bhikṣuṇī vow, I request the Tibetan bhikṣu saṅgha to do their utmost to make this a reality.

On a personal note, I would like to share with you my experience of researching this topic and writing this paper. The kindness of previous generations of monastics, both Tibetan and Chinese, is so apparent. They studied and practiced the Dharma diligently, and due to their kindness we are able to be ordained so many centuries later. I would like to pay my deep respects to these women and men who kept the ordination lineages and practice lineages alive, and I would like to encourage all of us to do our best to keep these lineages alive, vibrant, and pure so that future generations of practitioners can benefit and share in the tremendous blessing of being fully ordained Buddhist monastics.

A "Flawless" Ordination: SOME NARRATIVES OF NUNS' ORDINATIONS IN THE MŪLASARVĀSTIVĀDA VINAYA

Damchö Diana Finnegan

RECENT DISCUSSIONS regarding the possibility of full ordination for women in the Tibetan Buddhist traditions have focused largely on the possibility of identifying the correct rules and ritual procedures for female ordination in the Mūlasarvāstivāda monastic lineage that is followed by Tibetan Buddhists. Primary resources in this effort have been Guṇaprabha's fifth to seventh-century digest of the Vinaya and the many commentarial texts that interpret and elaborate on it.[1] I would like to introduce into these conversations an additional resource that has been

1. The dating of Guṇaprabha's literary production remains a matter of debate, with Gregory Schopen placing his dates some time during the fifth through seventh centuries C.E., while K. Sasaki narrows this range to 550 through 630 C.E. (Schopen 2004: 64–69; Yonezawa et al. 2001: 14). For discussions of what is known of his life and scholarly activities, see inter alia Schopen 1994: 63–64; and 2004: 64–69, 86n55, 126–28, and 312–18. For a Sanskrit edition of the *Vinayasūtra*, see Sankrityayana, 1981. Additionally, a Sanskrit edition of the *Vinayasūtra*'s chapter on ordination, the *Pravrajyāvastu*, has been published along with its autocommentary in Bapat and Gokhale 1982. The Tibetan translation can be found in the Dergé (*sde dge*) edition of the Tengyur at *'dul ba wu*, 1–100a. This and all subsequent references to Tibetan texts are to the Dergé (D) edition as reprinted in *The Sde-dge Mtshal-par Bka'-'gyur* (Situ Chos kyi 'byung gnas 1976–79). The overwhelming majority of commentarial works used by Tibetan Buddhist monastics draw primarily on the *Vinayasūtra*, rather than on the Mūlasarvāstivāda Vinaya (MSV) itself, for reasons too complex to elaborate here. Indeed, a full survey of the *Vinayasūtra*, the commentarial works associated with it, and their place in the history of the transmission of the MSV has yet to be published. The Study Group of Sanskrit Manuscripts in Tibetan at the Taishō University in Tokyo has been conducting a detailed study of the *Vinayasūtra* and the *Vinayasūtravṛtti* for some time.

underutilized in the recent discussions of women's ordination to date: the narratives of women's ordinations in the Mūlasarvāstivāda Vinaya, the root Vinaya text of the Mūlasarvāstivāda tradition.[2]

These and other stories are often omitted from the commentarial texts used with greatest frequency by Tibetan Buddhists, yet they offer rich resources for considering what was involved in turning individual women into bhikṣuṇīs or fully ordained nuns. Not only do these narratives help contextualize the ordination process, they are also of great value in assessing a permissible degree of flexibility in implementing the procedural rules for ordination. This paper takes up two such accounts from different sections of the root Vinaya text of the Mūlasarvāstivāda monastic lineage. (By root text here, I mean the actual Mūlasarvāstivāda Vinaya, as opposed to Guṇaprabha's highly abridged reorganization of that Vinaya material in his work entitled *Vinayasūtra* but often referred to by Tibetans as the *Root Sūtra*.)[3]

2. In its Tibetan translation, the Mūlasarvāstivāda Vinaya in its totality occupies the first thirteen volumes of the Tibetan *Kangyur*, filling 7,785 folio sides. This would be roughly comparable to 5,700 pages in book format in an English translation without footnotes. For the Dergé edition of the MSV, see Situ Chos kyi 'byung gnas 1976–79, volumes *ka* through *pa*. A large portion of the *Vinayavastu* is extant in its original Sanskrit and has been published in several editions. The major Sanskrit editions of the *Vinayavastu* are Dutt 1984, Gnoli 1977, and Gnoli 1978a. Bagchi 1967 is essentially a re-edition of Dutt in two volumes. Scattered fragments from other portions of the Vinaya in Sanskrit continue to come to light. See inter alia Vogel and Wille 1984. A partial Chinese version of the MSV also exists (T 1422–51). Yijing produced this rendering into Chinese between 700 and 712 C.E., but this is "not only incomplete, but also full of gaps," as Erich Frauwallner puts it (Frauwallner 1956). It is clear from a comparison of the Chinese and Tibetan versions of the Utpalavarṇā story that Yijing makes highly selective use of narrative details, skipping many and condensing others (see next note below).

3. This can be a point of considerable confusion, as Tibetans routinely refer to this abridgement by Guṇaprabha as the *mdo rtsa ba* or *Root Sūtra*. The term "root" text is usually contrasted to commentarial texts, and is thus reserved for texts that function as primary sources for knowledge on a certain area of study, with commentaries serving secondarily to interpret or control the meaning of the root texts. This appellation of "Root Sūtra" reflects the manner in which the *Vinayasūtra* is treated in Tibetan monastic studies, as if it were the "root" or ultimate source from which all knowledge on the Vinaya springs. However, calling it a "root text" can tend to efface the fact that the *Vinayasūtra* is itself fundamentally a derivative work, drawing on the Mūlasarvāstivāda Vinaya that it reorganizes and reworks in a highly condensed—and highly selective—form. While Guṇaprabha's *Vinayasūtra* does fit the classical Sanskrit sense of sūtra as a string of aphoristic statements, it is neither a sūtra in the usual Buddhist sense of a canonical discourse with the status of *buddhavacana* nor is it the root Vinaya itself. However, its aphorisms are so laconic as to be virtually unintelligible without the associated

Both stories in question depict women joining the community of fully ordained nuns, and both of these women were later publicly recognized by the Buddha as exemplary women in the nuns' order. One of the women was an aged servant woman who is said to have been Buddha's mother in many past lives. The other was a prominent courtesan with a highly checkered past, and in her case the Buddha urged particular care in making her ordination a "flawless" or "perfect" one. It may surprise us to learn that the concern for creating a "flawless" renunciate ordination seems to have nothing at all to do with following the established rules for ordination procedures but instead has to do with gaining social acceptance for that particular woman's entry into the nuns' order. We may also be surprised to see that in both these ordination narratives, Buddha Śākyamuni appears to simply entrust women to Mahāprajāpatī for ordination, a fact that hints at greater practical autonomy and responsibility for the nuns' community than comes to light elsewhere.

The Relation of Vinaya Narratives to Rules

First, though, we might ask what relation these stories in the Vinaya bear to the procedural rules governing ordination. Some stories in the Vinaya depict the first instance a precept or procedural rule was articulated. In these cases, the story serves as a sort of precedent for each rule, providing some context for later legal interpreters to draw on when seeking to implement the rules. However, in the case of the Mūlasarvāstivāda Vinaya, the narratives go far beyond a jurisprudential tool to aid in implementing Vinaya rules or procedures. This massive text includes a tremendous amount of narrative material that is entirely unconnected to any monastic rule or code of conduct. Instead, there are stories that purport to describe the comings and goings of the Buddha and his monastic assembly as they wandered from town to town, the deeds and misdeeds of various monks and nuns, and the biographies and past-life stories of monks and nuns and of the Buddha. The Mūlasarvāstivāda Vinaya's narratives thus offer an imaginative vision of a full and complex community life in which particular actions are thoroughly

---

commentaries, and thus the *Vinayasūtra* does ultimately stand as a root text in relation to the commentaries on it.

contextualized within an equally full and complex social world. As a result of the fullness of its narrative reach, the Mūlasarvāstivāda Vinaya runs to many thousands of pages in its Tibetan translation. Compared with other lineages, the root text of the Mūlasarvāstivāda Vinaya preserves a vastly greater body of narrative material, more perhaps than all the other Vinayas combined. In fact, when it comes to the life of the monastic community, it appears that the Mūlasarvāstivāda was a tradition that particularly valued narrative contextualization. In those stories that do depict the creation of behavioral guidelines, rules frequently prove inadequate as new situations arise. We therefore read of Buddha Śākyamuni revising the behavioral advice and rules he had previously given, qualifying them, limiting them, or even abandoning them outright as the shifting contexts require. What emerges in the narratives of the Mūlasarvāstivāda Vinaya is a community life evidently guided more by sensitivity to the particulars of each situation and responsiveness to changing contexts than by any concern for formulating universal rules or by a valuing of the sanctity of rules per se.

Nevertheless, in the centuries that followed, monastic communities generally preserved the precepts and other advice for community life in whatever form they were last stated by the Buddha according to the texts they considered canonical. They did so even as they preserved other canonical texts that quote Buddha Śākyamuni as saying that changes could be made to all but the most basic rules, in response to changing historical and cultural circumstances.[4] We may say that although the Buddha himself was a practitioner of situational ethics, the monastic institutions that followed him adhered to a rule-based understanding of the Vinaya.[5] The narratives of the Vinaya argue for a great deal of responsiveness and adaptability; even

4. This stance is not uncontested. Perhaps the best-known instance of this comes in the statement attributed to Buddha just before his passing into *mahāparinirvāṇa*, in which he authorizes the saṅgha to gather and make deliberations as to minor rules that can be changed. Ānanda is famously scolded later for not having asked Buddha to specify which rules were the minor ones that could be changed. In the Mūlasarvāstivāda Vinaya, this statement can be found in the *Kṣudrakavastu* at Kangyur D ('dul ba) *da*, 439b3.

5. This tendency to preserve advice in the form of inviolable, universal rules may itself be seen as a response to the context of increasing institutionalization of Buddhist monasticism and of the vast extension of that community over geographic space and historical time. This, of course, is a topic for a separate and much longer paper.

as commentarial traditions tend to identify and isolate the rules embedded in that mass of narratives.

The study of these narratives with their attention to particulars is rare in Tibetan monasteries, because the root Vinaya text that contains these narratives is no longer read by most Tibetan monks or scholars. Instead, Vinaya education and the regulation of monastic life are centered on Guṇaprabha's highly condensed interpretive digest and the vast commentarial tradition based on his work, along with local monastic constitutions, or *bca' yig*.[6] These secondary and derivative works have effectively replaced the root text (Mūlasarvāstivāda Vinaya) as the locus of authority for most discussions of Vinaya matters in the Tibetan lineages. However, as women explore possible ways to reinstate full ordination for women in the Mūlasarvāstivāda tradition, these narratives encourage us to ask how Buddha's monastic order might respond to the vastly different social circumstances in which we now find ourselves. Returning to the root texts helps us identify and contextualize the interpretive choices at work in the commentarial tradition, and therefore educates us as we Buddhist monastics seek to productively live according to the Vinaya in our very own, quite different context today.

The Story of Kacaṅgalā

The first of the two narratives under consideration is still extant in Sanskrit as well as in the Tibetan and Chinese translations of the Mūlasarvāstivāda Vinaya.[7] In this story, the Buddha sends his attendant Ānanda to seek out

6. Although these monastic texts are potential sources of invaluable information on the institutional formation of monasteries and monastic practices in Tibet, little work has been done on them to date. Ter Ellington's article is still the best introduction to this genre, with José Cabezón taking up the *bca' yig* of Sera Jé monastery (Ellington 1990; Cabezón 1997).

7. The story of Kacaṅgalā taken up here occurs in the *Bhaiṣajyavastu*, or "*Section on Medicine*," of the *Vinayavastu*. It can be found in Sanskrit at Dutt 1984: III.i.20–24. The corresponding Tibetan is located at Kangyur D ('dul ba) *kha*, 131b2–133b4, including a brief past-life story. A Sanskrit version of the story of Kacaṅgalā appears as narrative 78 in the *Avadānaśataka* and follows closely the version in the MSV (Speyer 1909: 41–44; Vaidya 1959: 192–93). León Feer has translated this version into French (Feer 1891: 290–93). The *Karmaśataka* also contains an even briefer telling of the tale, which Feer has also translated from Tibetan into French (Feer 1901: 262–63). The story of Kacaṅgalā is preserved in two Chinese iterations, according to Hubert Durt, who has undertaken a comparative study of the various versions of her story (Durt 2005). One is Yijing's rendering of the passage in the Chinese MSV (T 1448:

an old servant woman named Kacaṅgalā[8] and tell her that the Bhagavān is thirsty. He does so, and the old woman rushes to the Buddha to offer him water. The moment she first sees him, she is overwhelmed with motherly love. She throws up her arms, crying, "My son, my son," and rushes to embrace the Buddha. Although the monks move to stop her, the Buddha tells them to let her approach. This old servant had been his mother for five hundred lives, he says, and out of gratitude for her kindness and compassion for her, he clasps the old woman to his chest. When the Buddha then teaches the Dharma to her, Kacaṅgalā immediately attains the fruit of stream-entry. She later requests the necessary permission from her master to join the monastic order, which as a servant she needs before going forth. Having received it, Kacaṅgalā approaches the Buddha and asks for renunciate ordination and full ordination in the nuns' order. The text then states that the Buddha "entrusted her" to Mahāprajāpatī, who "gave her renunciate ordination and full ordination and instructed her."[9] As the story continues, Kacaṅgalā works hard, and despite having come to the Dharma at such a late age, she becomes an arhat or *arhantinī*.[10] Later the Buddha proclaims her to be foremost among his female disciples in terms of her skill at giving commentary on the collection of sūtras.

44a12–45a3); the other is a collection of narratives with a reconstructed Sanskrit title of *Vividharatnakośa* (T 203). An English translation of a Chinese reworking of the latter is found in Willemen 1994: 20–21. For this paper, I have consulted the Tibetan and Sanskrit versions and the translations of the Chinese renditions.

8. This woman's name itself is subject to some variation. In Pāli texts, she is known as Kajaṅgalā (Malalasekera 1938: 482). In his translation of the *Avadānaśataka* into French, Feer notes that the Nepali manuscripts of his Sanskrit text clearly render the name Kavaṅgalā, despite the similarly between the *va* and *ca* (Feer 1891: 290). The Tibetan and Sanskrit of the MSV both render her name as Kacaṅgalā.

9. Dutt 1984: III.i.22 for the Sanskrit and Kangyur D ('dul ba) *kha*, 132b2 for the Tibetan. Here the term I am translating as "renunciate ordination" is *pravrajyā* in Sanskrit or *rab tu 'byung ba* in Tibetan, which is sometimes translated as "going forth," and the term "full ordination" here translates as *upasaṃpadā* in Sanskrit or *bsnyen par rdzogs pa* in Tibetan, or *rdzogs par bsnyen pa*, as this particular Tibetan text sometimes renders it.

10. The MSV seems to be quite consistent in using the term *arhantinī* as the feminine form of *arhat*, although *arhatinī* is attested in other texts. For some examples, see Edgerton 1953: 67.

The Story of Utpalavarṇā

In another narrative, we hear of the ordination of Utpalavarṇā, a woman who went on to become preeminent among the nuns in terms of her extraordinary powers, or *ṛddhi* (Tibetan: *rdzu 'phrul*). The description of her ordination is embedded within a relatively detailed account of her life story.[11] The Sanskrit does not survive for this portion of the text, but in the Tibetan edition, Utpalavarṇā's story takes up a full seventeen folio sides. Her life story in the Mūlasarvāstivāda Vinaya differs significantly from the presentation in the Pāli canon.[12] As presented in the Mūlasarvāstivāda, Utpalavarṇā's biography contains much that shocks and saddens. As a young woman, Utpalavarṇā learns that her husband is having an affair with her mother, who lives with them. She leaves home, only to end up sharing a man with her own daughter.

Her life's painful path then leads to a long career as a courtesan. She becomes the chief courtesan in the city of Rājagṛha and unknowingly enters into an incestuous relationship with her own son, whom she had abandoned at birth. The tale twists further when a second daughter whom she had similarly abandoned at birth is married to that son. When Venerable Mahāmaudgalyāyana sees that it is her time to be tamed, he goes to meditate in a park where she is offering sexual services to a group of five hundred men. Upon hearing a single Dharma teaching from him, she instantly attains the first fruit of stream-entry and asks at once to be given renunciate ordination and full ordination. Venerable Mahāmaudgalyāyana responds to her request by instructing her to go to ask her various "husbands" for

11. The story of Utpalavarṇā falls within the *Bhikṣuvibhaṅga* of the MSV. The Tibetan translation is located at Kangyur D ('dul ba) *nya*, 216a3–224b4, followed by a past-life story. Yijing's Chinese translation appears in the Taishō collection at T 1442: 897a23–899b16, including Buddha's explanations of the past-life story. Apart from the omission or transformation of numerous details, the Chinese follows the major movements of the narrative as it appears in Tibetan.

12. When read against the account in the MSV, Pāli narratives present a dramatic sanitization of the more sordid tale presented here. Utpalavarṇā, there called Uppalavaṇṇā, is an exceptional beauty who followed her father's suggestion that she ordain as a nun to spare him the difficulty of having to select from among the many powerful men who sought her hand. For a discussion of the Uppalavaṇṇā's career in Pāli texts and list of citations, see Horner 1952: III.53n5 and Malalasekera 1938: 418ff.

permission to go forth.[13] She does so, and Venerable Mahāmaudgalyāyana next takes her request to the Buddha. The Buddha's reply here is crucial, and may be translated either as "a flawless renunciate ordination would be good," or "it would be good for the renunciate ordination to be flawless."[14] This story thus offers a particularly potent example for exploring what constitutes a flawless renunciate ordination. It also echoes a concern that has been expressed often in the recent discussions surrounding full ordination for women in the Tibetan tradition: the process should be beyond reproach in order to withstand the objections of those critics who so strongly oppose it. In the case of the potentially controversial ordination of Utpalavarṇā, what the narrative tells us Buddha did was compose a message to send to Mahāprajāpatī, the head of the nuns' order, who was then staying in Śrāvastī. While he was doing so, King Bimbisāra arrived and expressed his contempt for Utpalavarṇā. As the text states:

> When the Bhagavān was composing the message, King Bimbisāra came and said, "Bhagavan, why has this prostitute[15] come here?"
>
> The Bhagavān said, "Great King, do not say that. She is your Dharma sister and seeks renunciate ordination, full ordination, and bhikṣuṇī-hood in this well-spoken Dharma Vinaya."
>
> "Bhagavan, to whom are you composing the message?"
>
> "Great King, to Mahāprajāpatī in Śrāvastī."
>
> "Bhagavan, I myself will have it conveyed to her."
>
> "Great King, [that would be] perfect (or flawless)."[16]

13. Kangyur D ('dul ba) *nya*, 223b6–7. The Chinese version omits this point entirely. The Tibetan does not specify whether the "husbands" from whom she must attain permission refers to her son and the other men with whom she cohabited exclusively at various periods, or whether we are to understand the entire male community of the town to whom she was a "co-wife" in the sense of an object of their sexual enjoyment. Like many other moments in the MSV, this vignette points both toward wider social expectations of the normative sort we find outlined in dharmaśāstra material and toward the Buddhist attempt to create a monastic society that sits well with those expectations. An effort to adequately situate this exchange within that context would carry us well beyond the bounds of this present paper.

14. Tibetan: *ma nyes kyis rab tu 'byung ba legs so*; Kangyur D ('dul ba) *nya*, 224a2. The Chinese omits this point as well.

15. The term used by the king here is *'jud mthun ma* (Kangyur D ['dul ba] *nya*, 224a3).

16. Echoing the earlier recommendation by the Buddha that the ordination be flawless or

> The king ordered it to be conveyed to her. Utpalavarṇā took it and went to Śrāvastī. Mahāprajāpatī Gautamī gave her renunciate ordination and fully ordained her.[17]

With this, King Bimbisāra has effectively placed his own seal of approval on the ordination, a move that would likely silence any public objections. Thus we see that in the view of this text a "flawless renunciation" has less to do with adherence to the established rules for ordination and more to do with gaining social acceptance for that ordination. After ordaining Utpalavarṇā, Mahāprajāpatī gives her personal instruction, and Utpalavarṇā soon realizes the truth and becomes an arhat. She is later singled out as chief among female disciples of the Buddha in terms of her spiritual powers.[18]

Nuns Caring for Nuns

This narrative raises two major issues bearing on the discussions of full ordination for women today: first, the role of the nuns' order in accepting women and training them after they renounce; and second, the relative indifference to ordination procedures or rules. The Buddha is presented as simply composing a message and sending Utpalavarṇā off to Mahāprajāpatī for ordination. Similarly, we saw him "entrusting" his past-life mother to Mahāprajāpatī for ordination and training. The term I am translating as "entrust" here is *saṃnyastā* in Sanskrit and *gtad pa* in Tibetan, which is the same term used for Buddha's entrusting of the Dharma to his disciples after his *mahāparinirvāṇa*. In both stories, we note the suggestion that Mahāprajāpatī herself was responsible for fully ordaining the women. The Tibetan here reads *skye dgu'i bdag mo chen mo gau ta mis de rab tu phyung rdzogs par bsnyen par byas te*,[19] or as it had said in the case of Kacaṅgalā, *de rab tu phyung bsnyen par rdzogs par byas*.[20] We have the Sanskrit version of

perfect (*ma nyes*) ordination, he uses the same term here to describe the king's intervention to make it so (Kangyur D ['dul ba] *nya*, 224a5).

17. Kangyur D ('dul ba) *nya*, 224a2–5.

18. Kangyur D ('dul ba) *nya*, 224b4.

19. Kangyur D ('dul ba) *nya*, 224a5.

20. Kangyur D ('dul ba) *kha*, 132b2.

the Kacaṅgalā story, which reads *tayā pravrājitā, upasaṃpāditā* and thus has a causative sense.[21] Both the Sanskrit and Tibetan can mean either "she gave her renunciate ordination and fully ordained her" or "she had her given renunciate ordination and full ordination." In both instances it is left unclear whether the primary agent of the ordination was Mahāprajāpatī or whether Mahāprajāpatī was directing others to perform the ordination. But in either case, the narrator presents the matter as if, for all intents and purposes, Mahāprajāpatī is the main agent ensuring that Kacaṅgalā is fully ordained. Monks may or may not have been present, the point being simply that the stories do not bother to tell us. This contrasts greatly with recent discussions of women's ordination, where the issue of who is present at the ordination, who actually confers the vows, and what their lineage is has been the source of a tremendous amount of attention, and indeed anxiety. Apparently the narrator of the root Vinaya does not consider these issues important enough to merit any narrative details whatsoever. The focus is directed instead at the work of gaining broad social support for that ordination. Elsewhere in the Mūlasarvāstivāda Vinaya, in passages explicitly concerned with ordination procedure, it is specified that the full ordination of women requires the presence of both fully ordained monks and fully ordained nuns.[22] In this story, if monks are indeed present at the ordination, they are there at Mahāprajāpatī's bidding. This hints at a greater effective self-determination for the nuns' community, especially when it comes to granting full ordination, than appears to be the case when we focus on monks' ritual role in the ordination ceremonies.

The Importance (or Lack Thereof) of Procedural Rules

Given the Buddha's comment that it would be good for this to be a flawless ordination, we might expect here an increased care to follow established procedures. But there is no mention of any of the ritual aspects of drawing

21. Dutt 1984: III.i.22.

22. A most clear specification of this point occurs in the Mūlasarvāstivāda Vinaya in the *Kṣudrakavastu* at Kangyur D ('dul ba) *da*, 168a2ff., where it is embedded within instructions as to how to proceed in offering full ordination to women.

of boundaries, convoking the assemblies of monks and nuns, or other procedural formalities. Instead, the Buddha acts to build consensus to overcome possible objections to the ordination. After all, Utpalavarṇā is a courtesan with a history of highly deviant sexual behavior: sex with her own son, sharing men with her mother and her daughters, and acting as a consort to hundreds of men at a time. Social resistance is to be expected. In this instance, the Buddha utilizes what commentators will identify as a new form of ordination, ordination by messenger. But in the story itself, this "ordination by messenger" looks more like a device to galvanize and demonstrate high-level public support for the ordination than a means of actually conferring ordination. The implication is that gaining consensus was important to make the ordination flawless, rather than any particular adherence to established procedures. It should be clear that this account presents some intriguing parallels to women seeking ordination in the Mūlasarvāstivāda Vinaya tradition today. They too face the resistance of some members of Tibetan society, both lay and monastic.

In the face of potential social resistance to Utpalavarṇā's ordination, Buddha acts to make clear his own complete support. He chides the king when he treats Utpalavarṇā in ordinary social terms once she had requested acceptance into the monastic community, and creates a situation with the message whereby the king himself is given a role in facilitating Utpalavarṇā's ordination. Later, Buddha simply leaves the details of the manner of conferring ordination to Mahāprajāpatī to handle. After he has ensured that they will not have to bear public censure for accepting this woman as a renunciate, we see the Buddha effectively handing her to the nuns' order to care for, ordain, and train.

These ordination narratives shed some interesting light on the rules stipulating that fully ordained nuns be present at the full ordination of other women. This requirement has been a key point of contention in the debate over reinstating full ordination for women in the Mūlasarvāstivāda lineage, since no women currently hold full ordination in the Mūlasarvāstivāda lineage. But these narratives raise the possibility that the Buddha stipulated that fully ordained nuns must participate in the full ordination of other women not so much out of a concern with the maintenance of unbroken lineage as out of a concern that there be communities of experienced nuns to train and support newly ordaining women. If so, it may be time for the conversations about reinstating women's full ordination to include discussions of the creation of communities of fully ordained nuns practicing in the Tibetan tradition: communities in which novice nuns can be trained and supported.

Concluding Comments

These and other accounts of women's ordination in the Mūlasarvāstivāda Vinaya are set in a social environment where granting ordination to women is imagined to have potentially jeopardized the acceptance of the Buddhist order. Today we find ourselves in a contrary position, as now it is the denial of full ordination to women that stands to place Buddhism in a compromised position in the modern societies of today.

In conclusion, we note that in a narrative in which the Buddha urges special care to make the renunciate ordination faultless, he shows no concern whatsoever for procedure or ritual formalities. Instead, he simply acts to overcome social resistance to the ordination. As such, the story suggests that the technical details that have garnered so much attention in current discussions about full ordination for women may not be the most important aspect of the process. An approach in which rigid adherence to established procedures is a marker of an authentic Buddhist ordination is certainly not the approach we see the Buddha adopting in the narratives of the Vinaya itself. Instead, the narrative vision shows us a high degree of flexibility and responsiveness to the particulars of changing situations. In the face of public qualms over an ordination, we see the Buddha building consensus and then entrusting women to the senior nuns, rather than clinging to procedural correctness. If the accounts of the Buddha's own behavior in the Mūlasarvāstivāda Vinaya are indeed a model for monastic communities to live by across the centuries, then perhaps it is time we attended as much to the responsive living method it portrays the Buddha actually practicing as we do to the static procedural rules that his followers attempted to derive from it.

Buddhist Women's Role in the Saṅgha

Lobsang Dechen

WOMEN HAVE always had the opportunity to participate in religious life in the history of Buddhism in Tibet. Some of the most loved and colorful personalities of the Tibetan Buddhist pantheon are women, such as Machik Lapdrön in the eleventh century and Shuksep Jetsün Rinpoché in the nineteenth century. The fifteenth-century princess Chökyi Drönmé was recognized as an embodiment of the deity Vajravārahī. After renouncing worldly life, she became a nun known as Samding Dorjé Phakmo and was one of the highest-ranking nuns in Tibet. As an abbess, her successive incarnations presided over monks (the twelfth reincarnation is currently in Tibet). While the first instance of a male reincarnation lineage in Tibet begins with the First Karmapa Düsum Khyenpa in the twelfth century, Samding Dorjé Phakmo is the first instance of a female recognized reincarnation.

Many modern adherents would say that Tibetan Buddhism in its essence does not and should not discriminate against gender, caste, race, or any other attribute. The Dalai Lama himself has highlighted the need, and strengthened the opportunity, for both men and women to study and practice the Dharma.

To a certain extent, the lack of bhikṣuṇī ordination in Tibetan Buddhism can be seen as a reflection of Tibet's geographical isolation. Only a few Indian bhikṣus were able to cross the mountain border between India and Tibet and, as far as we know, no Indian bhikṣuṇīs came to Tibet. Historical instances of bhikṣuṇī ordination in Tibet must therefore have been given by a bhikṣu saṅgha only, and the practice did not survive.

Tibetan nuns have traditionally concentrated on reading, memorizing prayers, and ritual practices, as well as meditation, which is taught by senior nuns responsible for two or three younger nuns. Generally, they did not study philosophy, but at His Holiness the Dalai Lama's urging and with his enouragement, a study program in Buddhist philosophy has been introduced in the Tibetan nunneries in exile. This program has been hugely successful.

Very few nuns escaped Tibet during the first years of Chinese occupation, and upon arrival in India they were scattered throughout the exile community as opposed to living collectively in a nunnery. Those whose families could not support them found work in the community, from manual labor to domestic positions. Gradually communities of nuns were formed in order to practice and learn together. As interest in the Dharma increased among young women, many of them became nuns. During the 1980s, a greater number of young nuns escaped Tibet and joined the poorly provided for and already overcrowded nunneries in exile. New nunneries were thus established to accommodate them, and the older ones were expanded. Under the guidance of His Holiness the Dalai Lama, a proper education program for nuns was introduced at that time, equivalent to the monks' program and specifically focusing on Buddhist philosophy and related sciences such as medicine. In the twenty years since this formal study was begun, an increasing number of well-educated and trained nuns have emerged to become leaders in the community. They teach in Tibetan schools and work as Tibetan doctors. They are a competent and vital aspect of the Tibetan community in exile.

While a number of nuns have reached the level at which it is traditional to study the Vinaya, the lack of full ordination creates a problem in that they are not permitted to study the Vinaya beyond the introductory level. In order to attain the geshé and khenpo degrees, a Geluk student must study the five great topics, which include the Vinaya, while in the Nyingma, Sakya, and Kagyü lineages, students must study the thirteen great topics. Some people say that without this extended study of the Vinaya, a nun cannot gain the geshé or khenpo degree.

It is a commonly held view that Tibetan nuns are not interested in receiving bhikṣuṇī ordination; they seem to be very content with the way things are. In my experience, this is a misconception. We are also human beings who do not want suffering and seek happiness. However, because nuns have been unable to study all the Vinaya texts, they have often lacked confidence when discussing the possibilities for bhikṣuṇī ordination. We have been dependent on expert Tibetan Vinaya holders to help us research the Vinaya texts and to find a proper way to give the bhikṣuṇī ordination. The method of implementation needs to be appropriate and correct, both for the nuns and the larger saṅgha community, in order that the lineage thus introduced will endure for the benefit of the Buddhadharma and future generations.

There are now a great number of Tibetan nuns who are educated and understand the importance of bhikṣuṇī ordination. Full ordination will allow us to complete our studies and become fully qualified teachers for the perpetuation of the Dharma, and there is no better time than the present to achieve this goal. Our interest in receiving bhikṣuṇī ordination is not driven by a concern for our status as women but by a wish to work most effectively toward liberation from cyclic existence for the benefit of all beings. We will gain respect not through receiving ordination but through how our behavior accords with the precepts. Our motivation is to work sincerely for the benefit of the Buddhadharma and of all beings throughout the world, in this generation as well as for generations to come. If the bhikṣuṇī lineage were restored to the Tibetan tradition, then the Tibetan Buddhist community would be strengthened by the existence of all four classes of practitioners and Tibet would be regarded from a Buddhist perspective as a central land.

Monks have sometimes discouraged nuns from considering bhikṣuṇī ordination by assuring them that it is not necessary. I believe that most often the advice was given sincerely, out of a belief that they were protecting nuns or assuring the longevity of the Dharma. They might have thought it would only be an encumbrance to nuns and lead to too many downfalls. But it is clear that Tibetan nuns, and women in general, have often been underestimated in the debate over changing procedure and policy. When we first started the Buddhist philosophy classes in the nunneries, many well-intentioned people did not believe that nuns would succeed in these arduous studies. They thought women would not be able to focus on the classes and endure the years of intensive study required. Now, after twenty years, monks and laypeople alike appreciate the quality of the nuns' learning and their achievements. This is particularly apparent during the annual one-month inter-nunnery debate session, when guests witness the nuns' debating. It is now apparent that the nuns are ready and able to receive bhikṣuṇī ordination and hold the vows, if a means of conferring them can be found in accordance with the Vinaya.

During the 1998 conference on bhikṣuṇī ordination held at the Norbulingka Institute, only one person put forward a small quotation in support of the bhikṣuṇī ordination. All the rest in attendance were opposed. Now, many years of research and a series of meetings has created a greater awareness of the bhikṣuṇī issue. There are now many Vinaya holders seriously engaged in this research, and the numbers of its proponents has increased significantly. This shows that there is a possibility of reintroducing the vow for women. The opposition seems to lie mainly in the fact that an appropriate method needs to be agreed upon. Considering the length of time that women have been waiting to receive full ordination, this seems to be a small obstacle.

Preserving Endangered Ordination Traditions in the Sakya School

David Jackson

The Sakya school may be unique among Tibetan Buddhist traditions for consciously preserving two distinct monastic ordination lineages over many centuries. Both lineages were similar in that they were introduced into Tibet from India in the early thirteenth century by the same great Kashmiri abbot, Śākyaśrībhadra (ca. 1140–1225), who is well known in the history of Tibetan Buddhism for having trained a small group of Tibetan monks in Vinaya practice, thus establishing an important new monastic community. This community later divided several times, ultimately resulting in four communities (*tshogs pa bzhi*); in recent times one community was settled in central Tsang (Gtsang) and three were in southern Ü (Dbu) province. One of the greatest Vinaya abbots in the Sakya school, Ngorchen Künga Sangpo (Ngor chen Kun dga' bzang po, 1382–1456), received full ordination in a lineage passed down through the abbots of one of these four communities.

The second Sakya lineage did not pass through these four usual monastic communities. Instead, it was transmitted directly from Śākyaśrībhadra to Sakya Pandita (Sa skya Paṇḍi ta, a.k.a. Sapan, 1182–1251), creating a distinctly Sakya lineage. But by the mid-fifteenth century, Ngorchen's influence and ordination lineage dominated, and within a few more generations it held a virtual monopoly on ordinations. Sapan's tradition was threatened with extinction. It would not be until the mid-sixteenth century that Sakya Pandita's lineage was revived in Tibet.

It is worthwhile to consider the strategies those lamas used to keep the threatened tradition alive. Since ordination provides the Buddhist practitioner with an enormously increased spiritual potential, in Tibet it has been the object of careful preservation and propagation over the centuries. Several main ordination traditions were preserved, but generally only one tradition was cultivated among the monks of one monastery. However, sometimes adherents of a school prized one lineage more highly than another. The young Kongtrül Lodrö Thayé (Kong sprul Blo gros mtha' yas, 1813–99), for instance, was made to take ordination again in a new lineage, although he was not happy when forced to do so. One of the older monk ordination lineages, or "vow currents" (*sdom rgyun*), passed through the ninth-century master Gongpa Rapsal (Dgongs pa rab gsal) and at one point entailed the participation of some Chinese monks to form the necessary quorum to keep the endangered lineage alive. This lineage lived on with the abbots of Narthang (Snar thang) and was the source of the lineage of the First Panchen Lama and Fifth Dalai Lama, though some later Vinaya purists questioned the legitimacy of those foreign monks.

Ga Lama Saves Ngorchen's Lineage

A highly esteemed ordination lineage might become rare, but there still existed the possibility of revival. The great embodiment of monastic virtue Deshung Rinpoché once mentioned this fact to me, explaining that important ordination lineages had sometimes been saved by the timely efforts of far-sighted lamas. One example he shared was an episode from the life story of his uncle Ga Lama Jamyang Gyaltsen (Sga bla ma 'Jam dbyangs rgyal mtshan, 1870–1940), known as Jamgyal.

Jamgyal was a prominent Ngorpa monk from northwestern Kham (Khams) who as a young monk had been ordained in the lineage of Sakya Pandita. But by the 1920s, Jamgyal was upset to find that the lineage of their school's founder, Ngorchen Künga Sangpo, was becoming scarce. To remedy this, Jamgyal gave up his existing ordination and retook his full monk vows in Ngorchen's tradition from Drakri Dorjéchang Jamyang Chökyi Nyima (Brag ri rdo rje 'chang 'Jam dbyangs chos kyi nyi ma), who possessed the rarer lineage. One method of preserving an endangered tradition was to find a venerable monk of that lineage (or better yet, a small group of them) and to have him pass on the tradition to prominent younger monks who, as future abbots, would be likely to pass on that lineage themselves to many disciples. To arrange this, Lama Jamgyal first formally gave up his previous vows, for a person could not possess more than one set of vows (and, hence, ordination lineage) at the same time. Later, Jamgyal passed these new vows to his nephew, Ngawang Yöntan Gyatso (Ngag dbang yon tan rgya mtsho, 1902–ca. 1963, Ngor abbot 1933–36), a candidate to the Ngorpa abbacy. When his nephew, later famed as the Ngor "Bhutan Abbot," or Drukpa Khenpo ('Brug pa mkhan po), went to Ngor in 1933 and ordained many monks, he further worked to preserve the Ngorchen ordination lineage.[1]

Mangthö Ludrup Gyatso

Deshung Rinpoché immediately added, when telling me the story of Lama Jamgyal's contributions, that several such instances had occurred in the past. He said that sometimes it had been the other lineage, that of Sapan, that had required reviving.

One particular instance is found in the autobiography of Mangthö Ludrup Gyatso (Mang thos klu sgrub rgya mtsho, 1523–96), the learned and highly realized disciple of Tsarchen Losal Gyatso (Tshar chen blo gsal rgya mtsho). In his autobiography, composed in 1594, Mangthö explains the circumstances of his second ordination. What went without saying was that already in the sixteenth century, Ngorchen's lineage greatly dominated in Sakya monastic circles.

Chögyal Namkha Tsewang Dorjé (Chos rgyal Nam mkha' tshe dbang rdo rje), the lord of Latö Jang (La stod byang), approached Mangthö with the problem that his own ordination lineage in Sapan's tradition (which he had taken at Ngam ring monastery, in a lineage that he suspected might go back to Gzhon nu rgyal mchog, but could not confirm) was endangered. He implored Mangthö to re-take ordination from a small group of lamas from a different temple, who had the same Sapan lineage, which by then had completely died out within Sakya Monastery. Mangthö Ludrup eventually

1. Deshung Rinpoché, *'Jam rgyal rnam thar*, 45–46. See the sources and quotations in the appendix at the end of this volume.

did take this ordination, in the presence of a group of just four monks. The same master functioned as combined preceptor (*mkhan po*) and ritual master (*las kyi slob dpon*), which is allowed in some Tibetan Vinaya traditions. Such a slight bending of the rules called to his mind Butön's criticism that such things were practiced in Tibetan Vinaya but not found taught in the authoritative texts, whereas many things taught in the texts were not practiced. Despite such misgivings, Mangthö accepted and justified this as a special case.

Final Remarks

Following this instance, a number of similar efforts to preserve Sapan's lineage were made in the seventeenth and eighteenth centuries. So great was the success of this ordination lineage that by the mid-ninteenth century it came to predominate even among the abbots of Ngorchen's own monastic seat, leading to the need for Lama Jamgyal to revive the other lineage during the early 1930s.

The above episodes have been drawn from a context of Vinaya history and practice not directly applicable to the question of the full ordination of nuns. Here, the monks already possessed full ordination, and they were making special efforts to preserve one or another particularly valued ordination lineage. Full nun ordination, by contrast, does not yet commonly exist, and to get it one must search outside the normal places. What these sources do show, however, is the legitimacy of going to great trouble with—and even purposefully manipulating—the procedure of ordination for a good reason. A few other points that emerge from the texts:

1. One's existing full ordination must be formally given up before engaging in a second ordination ceremony.
2. Mangthö also tried to take ordination in a full quorum of five monks but the group was reduced to four out of dire necessity. (He evidently did not want to mix the lineage by adding a fifth monk from the readily available other tradition.)
3. Such circumstances entailed, for Mangthö, problems of a formal but not essential nature. He, a great scholar of Vinaya, accepted the

> imperfect situation with misgivings, in the interest of attaining a higher good.

To avoid burdening the paper body with the relevant Tibetan texts, I have gathered the relevant sources and quotations in the appendix at the end of this volume.

Presuppositions for a Valid Ordination with Respect to the Restoration of the Bhikṣuṇī Ordination in the Mūlasarvāstivāda Tradition

Petra Kieffer-Pülz[1]

THE AIM of this paper is to investigate the possibilities for reestablishing a bhikṣuṇī saṅgha in the Mūlasarvāstivāda tradition. Only three traditions of monks' ordinations have survived up to the present day (Dharmaguptaka, Mūlasarvāstivādin, and Theravādin) and only one tradition of nuns' ordination (Dharmaguptaka).

On the revival of a bhikṣuṇī ordination within the Mūlasarvāstivāda tradition, there are three options:

1. Don't revive the bhikṣuṇī saṅgha.
2. Introduce the bhikṣuṇī lineage from the Dharmaguptaka tradition into the Mūlasarvāstivāda tradition.
3. Create a new bhikṣuṇī lineage within the Mūlasarvāstivāda tradition by ordaining women through monks.

The lively interest of women in becoming fully ordained Buddhist nuns and their concerted efforts to realize that idea show the strong impact of Buddhism on women's lives. Details aside, two options exist. This paper focuses primarily on the prospects for the second option, that of enlisting

1. I thank Dr. William Pruitt for his suggestions and corrections of an earlier version of this article and David Kittelstrom for the final improvement of the English.

Dharmaguptaka bhikṣuṇīs in the reintroduction of the Mūlasarvāstivādin bhikṣuṇī lineage.

A practice of reintroducing monks' ordination from other subgroups within the same tradition is attested in the Theravāda tradition.[2] Doctrinally, and from the point of view of Vinaya, these subgroups belong to the same school. Nevertheless, subgroups often differ with respect to the ordination lineage, either because of variations in the development of Buddhism in different geographical areas, or because of differences in the interpretation of Vinaya rules connected with ordination.[3] Reintroducing an ordination lineage from a different Vinaya tradition is similar to the reintroduction of an ordination lineage from another subgroup of the same Vinaya school except the deviations are more plentiful, because distinct legal systems have developed for over two thousand years.

Were the bhikṣu ordination lineage of any of the three existing Vinaya schools to die out, men seeking ordination would be able to reintroduce a Vinaya tradition from one of the two other traditions. Since no monk of the earlier tradition would be left to oppose the reintroduction of this new Vinaya tradition, the new tradition could be accepted universally. Women do not have the same option. Bhikṣuṇīs are to be ordained by a bhikṣuṇī saṅgha first and thereafter by a bhikṣu saṅgha or, in the case of the Mūlasarvāstivāda tradition, a woman must first receive the allowance to enter the holy life (*brahmacaryopasthānasaṃvṛti*)[4] from the bhikṣuṇī

2. Bechert 1974.

3. Although the differences between various subgroups of the Theravāda tradition (i.e., Syāmanikāya, Amarapuranikāya, Rāmaññanikāya in Sri Lanka) are not as great as between different traditions (i.e., Dharmaguptaka, Theravādin, Mūlasarvāstivādin), they are often sufficient to render joint legal procedures of two subgroups impossible (for instance between the Saddhammavaṃsa and the Mūlavaṃsa, two subgroups of the Amarapuranikāya).

4. The *brahmacaryopasthānasaṃvṛti*, "the allowance (*saṃvṛti*) to enter the holy life (*brahmacarya*)," corresponds in other schools to the karma with which female candidates are ordained as nuns within the bhikṣuṇī saṅgha. Since the Mūlasarvāstivādin have changed what is for other schools an ordination within the bhikṣu saṅgha into a joint ordination performed by a monks' and a nuns' saṅgha, for them it would make no sense to perform a first ordination in the bhikṣuṇī saṅgha. The first ceremony within the bhikṣuṇī saṅgha has been kept, but instead of an ordination, the Mūlasarvāstivādin perform the legal procedure giving the candidate the allowance to enter the state of brahmacarya. This *brahmacaryopasthānasaṃvṛti* corresponds to the Theravāda tradition's *vuṭṭhānasammuti*, "agreement as to ordination." The *vuṭṭhānasammuti* marks the formal termination of a successful sikkhamānā period and

saṅgha and then the ordination in a joint legal procedure of bhikṣu and bhikṣuṇī saṅgha members. Thus monks have to agree to the introduction of full ordination of nuns. In the option under consideration, this means that the bhikṣus of the Mūlasarvāstivāda tradition would have to allow nuns of the Dharmaguptaka tradition to perform the bhikṣunī role in the joint legal procedure.

One precondition, then, would be the acceptance of the legitimacy of the Dharmaguptaka bhikṣuṇī lineage—and implicitly the Dharmaguptaka bhikṣu lineage—by the Mūlasarvāstivāda bhikṣu saṅgha. This legitimacy depends on an uninterrupted ordination lineage going back to the time of the Buddha and on the acceptance of the legal procedures used to perform these ordinations. It is difficult, if not impossible, for any of the existing traditions to authenticate both points. Within a tradition, this is generally not a problem, since a tradition normally accepts its own lineage as pure, even if it cannot produce an uninterrupted list of names. As soon as one tradition views another tradition's lineage and seeks to evaluate it, however, problems can arise.

A second concern is whether the Mūlasarvāstivāda tradition can accept the Dharmaguptaka tradition's legal procedure for performing ordination and the other legal procedures connected with it. In general, the legality of an ordination ("it is fit to stand," Sanskrit: *sthānāraha*, Pāli: *thānāraha*; and "it is undisputable," Sanskrit: *akopya*, Pāli *akuppa*) is to be known by the complete suitability of four elements:

1. The subject matter (*vastu*) of that procedure (i.e., the candidate for ordination)
2. The legal procedure (*karman*), consisting of a motion (*jñapti*) and proclamations (*anuśrāvaṇā*)
3. The monastic boundary (*sīmā*)
4. The assembly (*pariṣad*)

As for the first, the candidate for ordination, the conditions to be fulfilled are

opens the way for ordination. If one ordains a female candidate that has not received the *vuṭṭhānasammuti* from the bhikkhunī saṅgha, this is counted as a *pācittiya* offense (Vin IV: 320–24; Pāc 64, 67, 73 for nuns).

nearly identical in both traditions (i.e., one is not allowed to ordain someone who is less than twenty, has previously committed an extreme offense, belongs to one of the categories of unqualified individuals, and so forth),[5] and the woman seeking ordination must have successfully completed her time as a śikṣamāṇā. However, the Dharmaguptaka and Mūlasarvāstivādin differ in smaller details, such as the number of rules to be observed by a śikṣamāṇā (Dharmaguptaka six, Mūlasarvāstivādin twelve) and the content of those rules.[6] Whether the discrepancy is as big as it seems to be at first sight is uncertain, especially considering that śikṣamāṇās in all traditions seem to have had to comply with not only the special rules for śikṣamāṇās but also with nearly all the rules for bhikṣuṇīs.[7] This question mainly depends on whether the Mūlasarvāstivādin can accept the bhikṣuṇī ordinations of the Dharmaguptaka from the point of view of the candidate for ordination.

Regarding the second element necessary for an ordination to be legally valid, the formulas for performing the ordinations in the bhikṣuṇī saṅgha and the bhikṣu saṅgha must be correctly spoken, correct in both word order as well as pronunciation.[8] The formulas used by the Dharmaguptaka and

5. Some of these points are reflected in the ordination criteria (*antarāyika dharma*) of the Mūlasarvāstivāda tradition, i.e., the woman has to be either twelve or twenty years old depending on whether she is married or not (Schmidt 1993: 21a5), and she may not be a *nānasaṃvāsikā* or an *asaṃvāsikā* (Schmidt 1993: 20a1), etc.

6. The rules for a Dharmaguptaka śikṣamāṇā are the four *pārājika*s and the prohibition of eating after midday and drinking alcohol; Mūlasarvāstivādin, on the other hand, transmit six main rules and six secondary rules (1) she may not walk alone [SV 8]; (2) she may not go to the other side of a river [SV 9]; (3) she may not touch a man [Pār 5]; (4) she may not sleep in the same house as a man [Pāy 50]; (5) she may not act as a go-between [SV 1]; (6) she may not conceal a sin [SV 7, Pāy 35]; (7) she may not take gold and silver [NP 11]; (8) she may not remove the hair [that grows] in secret places [Pāy 74]; (9) she may not dig in the earth [Pāy 56]; (10) she may not cut fresh greenery [Pāy 11]; (11) she may not use something not formally received [Pāy 27]; and (12) she may not use something stored [Pāy 26] (Chung 2006: 8–9). In addition, according to the Dharmaguptaka one gets the allowance to become a śikṣamāṇā with a *jñapticaturthakarma* (so also the Mahāsāṅghika and Sarvāstivādin), whereas the Mūlasarvāstivādin (and also the Mahīśāsaka and the Theravādin) perform a *jñāptidvitīyakarma* (Chung 2006, 6–7).

7. However, the formula generally used by the Mūlasarvāstivāda bhikṣu saṅgha for the ordination of a nun could not be used, since there it is stated that the candidate for ordination lived as a śikṣamāṇā following the six rules and the six secondary rules.

8. See von Hinüber 1987.

the Mūlasarvāstivāda traditions differ, for the Mūlasarvāstivāda formulas are more developed historically than any other Vinaya tradition. There the age of the candidate, her having a robe and bowl, her having received the training in the rules for śikṣamāṇās, her having completed this training, her having received the allowance of brahmacaryopasthāna, her being free from the stumbling blocks, and so on, are mentioned. The Dharmaguptaka formulas also mention that the candidate is to be free from the stumbling blocks, be at least twenty years old, have her robes, and so on, but the formulas are not as detailed. Thus, from the point of view of the ordination formulas, the bhikṣuṇī ordination of the Dharmaguptaka presumably cannot be accepted by the Mūlasarvāstivāda tradition and vice versa.

With regard to the third element, a saṅgha must assemble in full number within a ceremonial boundary (*sīmā*). If this *sīmā* is defective, then all legal procedures performed within it are defective too. Among the Vinaya traditions, the Dharmaguptaka and the Mūlasarvāstivādin are most similar on this question.[9] Both differentiate between a great boundary (*mahatī sīmā*) and a small boundary (*khuḍḍalikā sīmā* or *maṇḍalaka*), which are already outlined in their Vinayas. Both hand down lists of objects allowed as marks for the great and the small boundaries.[10] Both transmit formulas for a great and a small boundary.[11] A general difference between the

9. Nevertheless, each of the schools has *sīmā* types peculiar to them; thus the Dharmaguptakas have various *sīmās* for cases of emergency (Chung and Kieffer-Pülz 1997: 21–23, 32–33), and the Mūlasarvāstivādin admit a legal procedure to determine *sīmā*s in a combined way (*mahatī sīmā* with *khuḍḍalikā sīmā*; Kieffer-Pülz 1992: sec. C, p. 6).

10. In case of the *mahatī sīmā*, the common set of objects includes a mountain (slope), a tree, a stone, a wall, and a circular wall. Listed only by the Mūlasarvāstivāda are a path, an anthill, a well, a fence, a stake, a raised stone, and a driven stake. Allowed only by the Dharmaguptaka are a forest, a pond, a trench, a village, a town, and a ridge of a field. In case of the *khuḍḍalikā sīmā*, the common set consists of a stone and a (driven) stake. The Dharmaguptaka in addition allow a ridge, the Mūlasarvāstivāda a raised stone, a wall, a tree, a circular wall, the slope of a mountain, a ploughed furrow, a fence, an anthill, and a taut rope.

11. Regarding the small *sīmā* the Dharmaguptaka explicitly state that this *sīmā* is provided for ordination (*upasaṃpadā*). For the formula for the determination of the small *sīmā*, see Chung and Kieffer-Pülz 1997: 19–20. The Mūlasarvāstivādin hand down differing formulas for the determination of the small *sīmā* in the Sanskrit and Tibetan versions of their Vinaya on the one hand and in their collection of formulas for legal proceedings (*karmavācanā*) on the other. Whereas in the Vinaya they use the terms "small *sīmā*" and "*maṇḍalaka*" (Tib. *dkyil 'khor*; see for this formula Kieffer-Pülz 1992: 407ff. and sec. C, p. 8), in their Karmavācanā collection they only speak of determining the small *sīmā* (Chung and Kieffer-Pülz 1997: 32–33).

formulas for determining boundaries is that the Mūlasarvāstivādin formula lists each object announced as a mark for the respective boundary, whereas the Dharmaguptaka formula summarily states that the marks have been announced.

Regarding the formula for the great boundary, the Mūlasarvāstivāda school alone excludes villages and their surroundings from the purview of the *mahatī sīmā*.[12] The differences in the small boundary, in contrast, are relatively small. Thus, in judging the validity of the Dharmaguptaka ordination lineage from the point of view of *sīmā*, the Mūlasarvāstivādin might object to the great boundary, since the Dharmaguptaka tradition includes villages and their surroundings, but hardly any objection should be raised regarding the small boundary. However, since it is unknown in what type of *sīmā* the ordinations of the past 2,500 years have taken place, one cannot be sure that the chosen boundaries would have been acceptable for the Mūlasarvāstivādin in every case. Further, the formulas with which the Dharmaguptaka and the Mūlasarvāstivādin determine their respective boundaries differ. Therefore, though the differences in *sīmā* are minor, it probably would be difficult nonetheless for Mūlasarvāstivādin to accept Dharmaguptaka ordinations from the point of view of *sīmā*.

The fourth element of a legally valid procedure, a suitable assembly (*pariṣad*), means that all monks and likewise nuns within the boundaries have to participate in the procedure, all who are absent have to give their consent, and there must be none who protest the procedure. As we have noted, a bhikṣuṇī is ordained by first being ordained within a bhikṣuṇī saṅgha and second in a bhikṣu saṅgha, or in the case of the Mūlasarvāstivādin, by receiving brahmacaryopasthānasaṃvṛti within the bhikṣuṇī saṅgha and subsequently joint ordination from the bhikṣu saṅgha and the bhikṣuṇī saṅgha. Regarding the second ordination in the bhikṣu saṅgha, Dharmaguptaka and Mūlasarvāstivāda traditions differ. In the Dharmaguptaka tradition, the female candidate asks the bhikṣu saṅgha for ordination, and a monk who acts as the *karmakāraka* asks the bhikṣu saṅgha to confer the ordination

12. All other schools exclude them when they determine the *ticīvarena avippavāsa*. For the Mūlasarvāstivādin formula for determining a *mahatī sīmā*, see Chung and Kieffer-Pülz 1997: 29–30, and for that of the Dharmaguptaka, see Chung and Kieffer-Pülz 1997: 19.

(*upasaṃpadā*) on the candidate.[13] In the Mūlasarvāstivāda tradition,[14] not only the candidate for ordination, but also a saṅgha of at least twelve nuns, must join a bhikṣu saṅgha of at least ten monks. The bhikṣu saṅgha and the bhikṣuṇī saṅgha are each placed within a small boundary (Skt. *maṇḍalaka*, Tib. *'khor*), thus forming two separate and independent saṅghas. The candidate for ordination sits in front of the bhikṣu saṅgha and requests ordination. The *karmakāraka* addresses the ordination formula to both saṅghas. Thus the legal procedure is performed by a double assembly within two separate boundaries, and both assemblies have to agree. From the perspective of *pariṣad*, then, the Mūlasarvāstivādin method differs considerably from that of the Dharmaguptaka.

If considered only in terms of traditional law, then, it is seemingly not possible for the Mūlasarvāstivādin to accept Dharmaguptaka ordination in a way that allows them to carry out formal procedures together. Other traditions have faced similar problems and in the course of time solved these problems by pursuing new directions. The Theravāda tradition developed the so-called *daḷhīkamma*, or strengthening procedure, which is testified in the canonical scriptures in a wholly different context and in the commentarial layer in again another context.[15] If a monk from Sri Lanka were to visit

13. See the formula in Wieger 1910: 207–9.

14. This is based on the Ridding and La Vallée Poussin 1920 fragment (re-edited by Schmidt 1993), which corresponds to the description in the *Kṣudrakavastu* of the Mūlasarvāstivāda Vinaya. Jin-il Chung prepared a comparative study in which he analyzes the contents and gives the Sanskrit and the Tibetan text as well as a German translation of the Chinese parallel. He kindly made this unpublished work accessible to me.

15. Sp 1396,6–15: *Avasesā terasa sammutiyo senāsanaggāhakamatakacīvaradānādisammutiyo cā ti etāni lahukakammāni apaloketvāpi kātuṃ vaṭṭanti, ñattikamma-ñatticatutthakammavasena pana na kātabbam eva. Ñatticatutthakammavasena kayiramānaṃ daḷhataraṃ hoti, tasmā kātabban ti ekacce vadanti. Evaṃ pana sati kammasaṅkaro hoti, tasmā na kātabban ti paṭikkhittam eva. Sace pana akkharaparihīnaṃ vā padaparihīnaṃ vā duruttapadaṃ vā hoti tassa sodhanatthaṃ punappunaṃ vattuṃ vaṭṭati. Idaṃ akuppakammassa daḷhīkammaṃ hoti, kuppakamme kammaṃ hutvā tiṭṭhati.* "The 'light' procedures [i.e.,] the remaining thirteen appointments and the appointments of the distributor of lodgings, of giving trifling things, clothes, etc., may be carried out also by approval (instead of by carrying out a *ñattidutiyakamma*; i.e., the simpler *apalokanakamma* is allowed instead of the prescribed *ñattidutiyakamma*), but [such a one] may in no case be carried out by a *ñattikamma* (procedure consisting in a motion) or a *ñatticatutthakamma* (procedure consisting in a motion and three resolutions). Some say: 'Carrying it out by a *ñatticatutthakamma* is stronger, therefore it should be carried out.' [This] is in fact refuted [in the following way]: 'If it were so, a confusion of procedures would arise; therefore it should not be carried out.' But if a loss of a syllable or a loss of words or a badly

a Buddhist community in Burma, he would again be ordained there because the host community would want to be sure that the legal procedures were not rendered invalid by his original ordination, which, according to the principles of the hosts, might have been invalid. In that way a monk could receive many ordinations by *daḷhīkamma* throughout his life.[16]

The Kīrtipur Vihāra in Nepal received a new house for the Buddhist *uposatha*, sponsored by the Mahānikāya of Thailand. When it came to determining the boundary, nobody from the Thai fraternities wanted to determine the boundary in conjunction with the Nepalese monks, since they had been ordained and educated in different nikāyas in Burma, Thailand, and Sri Lanka. Following the description of one of the subcommentaries about how to abolish an unknown boundary, they determined the boundary in just that way. They formed three saṅghas, each representing one of the three countries' traditions, and then recited the formula for the determination of the boundary according to the dictates of the respective country. By this method they made the legal procedure acceptable for each tradition.

---

pronounced word is given, it is permitted to repeat [the *kammavācā*] again and again in order to purify the [procedure]. This is a strengthening procedure (*daḷhīkamma*) of an undisturbed procedure; in the case of a disturbed procedure, [the *daḷhīkamma*] becomes the [basic] procedure (i.e., it ascends from a mere *daḷhīkamma* to the basic procedure)."

16. Described for example by the Burmese Saṅgharāja Ñeyyadhamma in his *Sīmāvivādavinicchayakathā* (Minayeff 1887). In other cases monks wanted several ordinations because of an uncertainty regarding the validity of their ordination; see for instance Somdet Phra Vanarat Buddhasiri (1806–91), who ordained seven times (Taylor 1993: 43). Vajirañāṇavarorasa (1859–1921), Saṅgharāja of Siam in the beginning of the ninteenth century, speaks of his *daḷhīkamma* ordination (Vajirañāṇavarorasa 1979: 46).

According to Saraṇajoti Tissa's *Daḷhikaraṇanicchaya*, the Burmese in the fifteenth century performed such *daḷhīkamma*s only after having made the monks return to the status of a householder, whereas the Mahāvihāra monks regularly re-ordained without first making the monks give up their monks' status ([Doḍanduva-nāma-gāme Gaṅgārāmavāsi Vinayācariya] Saddhammakitti Siri Saraṇajoti Tissa [Adhikaraṇanāyaka-tthera], *Daḷhikaraṇanicchayo* [Doḍanduva, 1933]: 44, verse 159: *patvāna dhammakirtyādi-saṅghato upasampadaṃ, pabbajjañ ca gihi hutvā alabhiṃsu yathārahaṃ*; verse 160: *mahāvihāriyā bhikkhū daḷhikammaṃ akaṃsu ce, gihibhāvaṃ na pāpenti te bhikkhu mrammaraṭṭhike*). The statement concerning the Burmese of the fifteenth century is based on the Kalyāṇi inscription of King Dhammaceti (1476 C.E.). The king thought the ordination of the Burmese monks to be defective. This might have been the reason why he made them become householders before they received new ordinations (Taw Sein Ko 1893: 210.23–26; the translation on page 43.42–47 is somewhat imprecise).

If the Mūlasarvāstivāda saṅgha decides to re-establish the bhikṣuṇī ordination lineage by introducing the Dharmaguptaka bhikṣuṇī ordination, this could only be realized by approaching it through new directions. Creating a mixed Vinaya tradition for nuns of Dharmaguptaka and Mūlasarvāstivāda would create a new subgroup of the Dharmaguptaka nuns. Against this background, the third option mentioned at the outset seems far less controversial. As was done during the Buddha's lifetime for the first order of nuns, the Mūlasarvāstivāda bhikṣuṇī lineage would be re-established by first ordaining the female candidates through the Mūlasarvāstivāda bhikṣu saṅgha and then handing over the task of ordaining within the bhikṣuṇī saṅgha to the nuns once that saṅgha fulfills the required conditions.[17]

17. The Vinayas themselves give guidelines for the situations not regulated by the canonical texts. According to these, everything that has not been allowed or rejected by the Buddha and that is consonant with what is allowable (*kappiya*) is allowed (for the Theravādin, Vin I: 250,34–251,6). These guidelines leave ample space for various decisions and practices.

Creating Nuns Out of Thin Air:

PROBLEMS AND POSSIBLE SOLUTIONS CONCERNING THE ORDINATION OF NUNS ACCORDING TO THE TIBETAN MONASTIC CODE

Shayne Clarke

THE INTRODUCTION or re-introduction of female ordination into established Buddhist institutions is a complex issue. As with most problems, it is unlikely that meaningful solutions can be found unless we fully understand the complexities involved. Here I would like to problematize a number of commonly held assumptions concerning Buddhist ordination in the hope of clarifying the complexity of the issue from the standpoint of Buddhist monastic law. I will base my remarks primarily on the legal tradition of the Mūlasarvāstivāda Vinaya, the monastic law code followed by Tibetan Buddhist saṅghas and, it seems, one group of monks in Tokugawa Japan.[1]

Unlike some other genres of Buddhist literature, the Vinayas address a large range of exceptional situations. They deal not only with ideals but with deviations from normal or standard protocol. In doing so, the authors or redactors of these monastic law codes seem to show an awareness that Buddhism in India did not always conform to the ideal. More important for our purposes, however, is that the authors or redactors of the Vinayas negotiate the limits of acceptable and unacceptable, valid and invalid monastic practices. In discussing the issue of female ordination it may prove fruitful to differentiate between ideal and acceptable practices.

1. Clarke 2006.

It is commonly asserted that a candidate for ordination must pass through the noviciate initiation (*pravrajyā*) before becoming an ordained (or as some prefer, fully ordained) monastic. In the case of a male candidate, he can become a monk (*bhikṣu*) only after having gone through the previous stage of a novice (*śrāmaṇera*).[2] A female candidate must go through a similar progression of stages, albeit with the addition of the stage of a probationer (*śikṣamāṇā*).[3]

Ideally, a woman trains under a nun for at least two years; she goes through the successive stages of novice (*śrāmaṇerikā*) and probationer in which—according to the Mūlasarvāstivādin tradition—having studied the six dharmas and six anudharmas, she finally progresses to ordination, that is, to the status of a nun (*bhikṣuṇī*). With this there can be little argument; this is how a nun postulant is supposed to train in the Mūlasarvāstivādin tradition. Moreover, despite differences in the content of the śikṣamāṇā stage, this seems to hold true for all other Vinaya traditions. It is, I suggest, a commonly accepted "fact" of Buddhist Studies.

But what happens, for instance, if a woman does not go through these stages? Can a woman be ordained without first having gone forth (*pra* √*vraj*), having studied in the training for two years? If a woman becomes a nun without first going through the previous stages of training, is she still considered to be a bhikṣuṇī? Is she officially recognized as a bhikṣuṇī? In other words, is her ordination deemed to be valid, or is her nunhood somehow jeopardized or invalidated?

A partial answer concerning the validity of such an ordination can be gleaned, I suggest, from a passage in a text called the *Nidāna* (*Gleng gzhi*), deep in the depths of the Mūlasarvāstivāda Vinaya, in what is known as the *Uttaragrantha* (*Gzhung dam pa*).[4] Admittedly, this passage does not deal

2. One of the first sūtras in Guṇaprabha's *Vinayasūtra* seems to confirm this (Bapat and Gokhale 1982: 6.4 and Vinayasūtra's Pravrajyāvastu Study Group 2003: 67.27; see also Sankrityayana 1981: 1 [*sūtra* 5]: *nānupapannasya pūrvaṃ upāsakatva-śrāmaṇeratva-bhikṣutvānām uttaram*). The Tibetan reads (*'Dul ba'i mdo*, Tengyur Q ['dul ba'i 'grel pa] *zu*: 2a5–6): *dge bsnyen nyid dge tshul nyid dang dge slong nyid dag gi snga ma bsnyen par ma rdzogs pa la phyi ma mi bya'o* //. Guṇaprabha's *Autocommentary*, however, suggests that this passage is not as straightforward as it might first appear.

3. Sankrityayana 1981: 12 (sūtra 564) (= Bapat and Gokhale 1982: 51.29–30): *śrāmaṇerikātva-bhikṣuṇītvayor antarāle varṣadvayañ caraṇasya kālaḥ*.

4. On the *Nidāna* and the structure of the *Uttaragrantha*, see Clarke 2002 and Clarke forthcoming.

specifically with nuns but neither does it preclude them. It is, I suggest, most naturally understood as a question about the ordination of monastics in general and, in the absence of any evidence to the contrary, could be interpreted to apply to both orders.[5] The passage in question starts with Upāli's question to the Buddha:

> "Reverend, if the bhikṣus ordain [one] without [first] initiating [that one], is that one deemed to have been ordained or deemed to have not been ordained?"
>
> "Upāli, though indeed ordained, those who ordained [him/her] come to commit an infraction."[6]

Tibetan:

> *btsun pa rab tu ma byung bar dge slong dag gis bsnyen par rdzogs par bgyis na / de bsnyen par rdzogs pa zhes bgyi 'am / bsnyen par ma rdzogs pa zhes bgyi /*
>
> *u pa li bsnyen par ni rdzogs mod kyi / bsnyen par rdzogs par byed pa ni 'das pa dang bcas par 'gyur ro //*

Here, then, it should be clear that not only can one receive ordination (*upasampadā*; *bsnyen par rdzogs pa*) without first being initiated (*pra√vraj*; *rab tu byung ba*), but that doing so seems to have no negative effect on the ordination of an individual. Is this ideal? No. Should a monk or nun be initiated, that is to say, properly trained, before receiving ordination? Ideally, yes. But the world of ideals is not the question before us and not what seems to have attracted the attention of the Venerable Upāli, the Blessed One himself, or the monastic authors or redactors of our texts. The answer here put into the

5. In the case of the Mūlasarvāstivādins—and in fact for most other schools for which we have extant law codes—technically, there is no such thing as a *Bhikṣuṇī Vinaya* or monastic code for nuns. The monastic codes generally contain rules for individual nuns in a *Bhikṣuṇī Vibhaṅga*, but the *Vibhaṅga* is only one section of a Vinaya. The other main section, the *Vastu* section, is a series of chapters on various themes such as ordination. The *Vastu*s deal not with the individual monastic but with the institution itself. These chapters are shared by—and therefore apply to—both the male and female monastic orders.

6. *Nidāna*, in *Uttaragrantha*, *'Dul ba gzhung dam pa*, Kangyur S ('dul ba) *na*, 101b1–3.

words of the Buddha in no way suggests that what some might be tempted to call an improper ordination was in any way invalid, impure, or even open to challenge. In fact, according to this Vinaya passage, the Buddha states that one ordained in such a manner is indeed ordained. In other words, the Buddha here effectively proclaims the validity of such an ordination. If we may apply the principle from this case to cases of female ordination, then a woman who is ordained without first receiving the initiation would be, according to Mūlasarvāstivādin monastic law, unquestionably and undeniably considered properly ordained; she is—or has become—a bhikṣuṇī.

There remains, however, the small problem of the infraction. Note, however, that the infraction is a non-specified offense; it seems not to be a serious transgression. An infraction, nevertheless, it is, but one for the ordaining monks or nuns, not—it is important to note—for the ordinand. Clearly, the "requirement" that one presenting oneself for ordination have the so-called prerequisite training was not an absolute rule but an ideal. If the ordination of such a person had presented problems for the authors or redactors of the Mūlasarvāstivāda Vinaya, it would have been a simple matter to nullify or invalidate the ordination, and this in fact is exactly what happens, for instance, in the case of one who has the qualities that are impediments to ordination (*bar chad kyi chos*).

> "Reverend, if an individual has qualities that are impediments [to ordination] and says, 'I have qualities that are impediments [to ordination],' but is ordained by the bhikṣus as a bhikṣu (or "according to bhikṣu protocol" [?]), is [he] deemed to have been ordained?"
>
> "Upāli, [he] is deemed not to have been ordained, and one who ordains him commits an infraction."[7]

Tibetan:

> *btsun pa bar chad kyi chos dang ldan pa zhig bdag bar chad kyi chos dang ldan no zhes smra ba'i gang zag de dge slong rnams kyis dge*

7. *Upālipariprcchā*, in *Uttaragrantha*, *'Dul ba gzhung dam pa*, Kangyur S ('dul ba) *da*, 324a5–7. See also *Nidāna*, 101b5–6.

> *slong gi dngos por bsnyen par rdzogs par bgyis na bsnyen par rdzogs*
> *pa zhes bgyi 'am /*
>   *u pa li bsnyen par ma rdzogs pa zhes bya ste / bsnyen par rdzogs*
> *par byed pa ni 'das pa dang bcas pa'o //*

Likewise, one who falsely claims not to have qualities that are impediments to ordination is also "deemed not to have been ordained" (*bsnyen par ma rdzogs pa zhes bya ste*).[8] The ordination of one who erroneously claims to have such impediments, however, stands.[9]

There are many other surprises in this law code: exceptions allowing for the ordination of bhikṣus under the age of twenty,[10] those who are ill,[11] those who do not have the requisite robes and bowl[12] or parental consent,[13] those who are debtors,[14] slaves,[15] possibly *paṇḍaka*s (*ma ning*)[16] but not ṣaṇḍhas

<hr/>

8.   *Upāliparipṛcchā*, 324a7–b1: *bar chad kyi chos rnams dang ldan na bdag ni bar chad kyi chos dang mi ldan no zhes smra ba'i gang zag de / dge slong rnams kyi[s] dge slong gi dngos por bsnyen par rdzogs par bgyis na bsnyen par rdzogs pa zhes bgyi 'am / u pa li bsnyen par ma rdzogs pa zhes bya ste / bsnyen par rdzogs par byed pa'i rnams kyang 'das pa dang bcas pa'o //*.

9.   *Upāliparipṛcchā*, 324b1–3 (see also *Nidāna*, 101b6–102a1): *bar chad kyi chos rnams mi ldan la bdag ni ldan no zhes smra ba'i gang zag dge slong dag gis dge slong gi dngos por bsnyen par rdzogs par bgyis na bsnyen par rdzogs pa zhes bgyi 'am / u pa li bsnyen par rdzogs pa zhes bya ste / bsnyen par rdzogs par byed pa ni 'das pa dang bcas pa'o //*.

10.   *Upāliparipṛcchā*, 324b5–6: *...lo nyi shur ma lags pa...shes par nus pa ma gtogs par lhag ma rnams ni bsnyen par rdzogs pa zhes bya'o //*.

11.   *Upāliparipṛcchā*, 328a4–5: *...nad pa...bsnyen par rdzogs pa zhes bya ste....*

12.   *Upāliparipṛcchā*, 324b6–325a1: *...lhung bzed ma mchis chos gos ma mchis bar...bsnyen par rdzogs pa zhes bya ste....*

13.   *Upāliparipṛcchā*, 325a1–2: *...pha dang mas ma gnang ba...bsnyen par rdzogs pa zhes bya ste....*

14.   *Upāliparipṛcchā*, 325a3: *...bu skal zhig na de gang la gsol ba gdab / gang gi bu yin par khas blangs pa'o //*.

15.   *Upāliparipṛcchā*, 325a3–4: *...bran...bsnyen par rdzogs pa zhes bya ste....*

16.   *Upāliparipṛcchā*, 325a7–b1: *...ma ning...bsnyen par rdzogs pa zhes bya ste....* The Sde dge edition states that *paṇḍaka*s may *not* be ordained; *Uttaragrantha*, *'Dul ba gzhung dam pa*, Kangyur D ('dul ba) *na*, 236a4. Clearly, a critical edition of this and other Vinaya texts is a desideratum.

(*za ma*),[17] and some defilers of nuns,[18] matricides, patricides, arhanticides,[19] and various other individuals whose ordination is usually interpreted as being ruled out according to the ordination formularies of this and other monastic codes.

So far we have seen that faults of the ordinand in no way automatically invalidate an ordination; some do, some do not. The same also holds for those of the ordaining committee of monks and even the officer presiding over the ordination. It is generally accepted, for instance, that an ordinand "must" have a preceptor (*upādhyāya*) at the time of ordination.[20] It seems reasonable to assume that the preceptor *must* be ordained before sponsoring the ordination of his (or her) own disciple. But while this may have been the ideal, at least according to the Mūlasarvāstivāda Vinaya, the Buddha appears not to have required this at all. Neither he nor the authors or redactors of our monastic code seem to have expected that this would always be followed. Indeed, according to the Mūlasarvāstivāda Vinaya, Upāli seems to have at least entertained the possibility that an unordained preceptor may present a novice for ordination. This much is clear from the following passage:

"Reverend, if [bhikṣus] ordain [one] with a lay preceptor, is [that one] deemed to have been ordained?"

"Upāli, [he/she] is deemed to have been ordained, but those who ordained [him/her] commit an infraction."[21]

17. *Upāliparipṛcchā*, 325a6–7: ...*za ma...bsnyen par rdzogs pa ma yin zhes bya ste....*

18. *Upāliparipṛcchā*, 325b1–3: ...*dge slong ma sun phyung ba...kha cig ni bsnyen par rdzogs pa zhes bya'o // kha cig ni bsnyen par ma rdzogs pa ste....*

19. *Upāliparipṛcchā*, 325b3–6: ...*ma bsad pa'i gang zag...kha cig ni bsnyen par rdzogs pa zhes bya'o // kha cig ni bsnyen par ma rdzogs pa ste...ji ltar ma bsad pa de bzhin du pha bsad pa dang / dgra bcom pa bsad pa la yang brjod par bya'o //.*

20. Note, however, that the *Upāliparipṛcchā* seems to call even this into question (328a5–6): *btsun pa mkhan po ma mchis par bsnyen par rdzogs par bgyis na bsnyen par rdzogs pa zhes bgyi 'am / u pa li bsnyen par rdzogs pa zhes bya ste / bsnyen par rdzogs par byed pa ni 'das pa dang bcas pa'o //.*

21. *Upāliparipṛcchā*, 332b5–6.

Tibetan:

> bstun pa mkhan po khyim pas bsnyen par rdzogs par bgyis na
> bsnyen par rdzogs pa zhes bgyi 'am /
>   u pa li bsnyen par rdzogs pa zhes bya ste / bsnyen par rdzogs par
> byed pa rnams ni 'das pa dang bcas pa'o //

While one's preceptor may be a layman (*khyim pa*), the same does not seem to hold for the officiant or *karmakāraka* (*las bgyid pa*). Ordination is not recognized if, for instance, performed by a lay officiant (*las bgyid pa khyim pa*), by one who is a *paṇḍaka* (*ma ning*), by a defiler of nuns (*dge slong ma sun phyung ba*), or by one who has committed matricide, patricide, or arhanticide (*pha dang ma dang / dgra bcom pa bsad pa*).[22] The ordination, however, is valid even if the officiant goes elsewhere ('gro ba gzhan du gnas pa)[23] or has a sex change (*mtshan 'phos*).[24] Likewise, if the officiant passes away during the ordination ceremony, the candidate is considered ordained as long as "the formal act is mostly done" (*las mang du byas par gyur na ni bsnyen par rdzogs pa zhes bya'o*).[25]

There are many other things that can "go wrong" in an ordination ceremony without affecting the validity of the ordination. Consider, for instance, the following situation:

> The Venerable Upāli asked the Buddha, the Blessed One, "Reverend, if at the time of ordination [a male candidate] changes sex, is he deemed to have been ordained or deemed to not have been ordained?"
> The Blessed One said, "Upāli, though indeed ordained, [he] must be sent (or admitted) among the bhikṣuṇī."[26]

22. *Upāliparipṛcchā*, 331b5–332a2.

23. *Upāliparipṛcchā*, 332a4–5.

24. *Upāliparipṛcchā*, 332a5–6.

25. *Upāliparipṛcchā*, 330b3–4.

26. *Nidāna*, 101a3–4.

Tibetan:

> *sangs rgyas bcom ldan 'das la / tshe dang ldan pa u pa lis zhus pa / btsun pa bsnyen par rdzogs pa'i tshe mtshan 'phos na / de bsnyen par rdzogs pa zhes bgyi 'am / bsnyen par ma rdzogs pa zhes bgyi /*
>
> *bcom ldan 'das kyis bka' stsal pa / u pa li bsnyen par ni rdzogs mod kyi / dge slong ma'i nang du ni thong zhig //*

Here we see that a male novice's change of sex in no way invalidates his ordination. His—actually now her—ordination is valid, but since technically he has become a woman, he—now she—should be sent to the bhikṣuṇīs: *he* has become a *nun*. Now, while one could conceivably use the above ruling to create individual bhikṣuṇīs, finding enough novices or monks willing—and indeed able—to change sex and become nuns may present a problem.[27]

What at first sight appears to offer a more feasible solution is to invoke a precedent that allows for the ordination of a nun by means of a formal ecclesiastical act of a monk. Yet, as we will see, what exactly this means is not at all clear.

> "Reverend, if a bhikṣuṇī is ordained with the formal act of a bhikṣu, is that one deemed to have been ordained?"

27. This, however, does not need to be an individual choice. At least according to one passage in the Mūlasarvāstivāda Vinaya, it seems possible for an entire monastic community or saṅgha to change sex. We see this in a passage that discusses the five ways to dissolve a previously established ecclesiastical boundary (*sīmā*). These include the whole saṅgha leaving and returning to lay life (*dge 'dun thams cad kyis bor te dong ba*), changing sex (*dge 'dun thams cad mtshan 'phos pa*), and passing away (*dge 'dun thams cad dus byas pa*). *Nidāna*, 107a2–3: *btsun pa rnam pa dus mtshams 'jig par 'gyur / u pa li lnga ste / dge 'dun thams cad kyis bor te dong ba dang / dge 'dun thams cad mtshan 'phos pa dang / dge 'dun thams cad slar babs pa dang / dge 'dun thams cad dus byas pa dang / gsol ba'i las dang lnga'o //*.

If a saṅgha of monks willing to change sex could be found, then a ready-made order of nuns, a bhikṣuṇī saṅgha, might be able to be created. I do not, however, see this as a particularly realistic or practical option. For one, when a saṅgha changes sex *en masse*, the ecclesiastical boundary (*sīmā*) is destroyed; in other words, the former community ceases to exist. How one would then establish the *sīmā* for a newly formed—newly transformed—community of nuns, I do not know. This requires further consultation with the legal literature. In any case, I do not think the future of female monasticism is to be found in sex changes, even if it is legally possible.

"Upāli, [she] is deemed to have been ordained, but those who ordained [her] commit an infraction."[28]

Tibetan:

btsun pa dge slong ma dge slong gi las kyis bsnyen par rdzogs par bgyis na bsnyen par rdzogs pa zhes bgyi 'am /

u pa li bsnyen par rdzogs pa zhes bya ste / bsnyen par rdzogs par byed pa rnams ni 'das pa dang bcas pa'o //

According to the highest of canonical legal authorities (i.e., the Buddha and the Vinaya), then, the ordination of a bhikṣuṇī by means of a bhikṣu *karman* (*dge slong gi las*) is considered valid. It is important to note here that we are not told by whom the ordination is performed. Is it performed solely by monks or is it performed by both saṅghas? In isolation, this passage might be taken to suggest that nuns could be ordained without the presence of other nuns, that is, through ordination by a bhikṣu saṅgha alone. The same or a very similar ruling is also found elsewhere in the Mūlasarvāstivāda Vinaya. When we place the two passages side by side, however, it becomes clear that what was missing in the first passage is given in the second.

"Reverend, if a bhikṣuṇī is ordained by bhikṣus and bhikṣuṇīs with the formal act of a bhikṣu, is that one deemed to have been ordained or deemed to not have been ordained?"

"Upāli, [she] is deemed to have been ordained, but both saṅghas come to commit an infraction."[29]

Tibetan:

btsun pa dge slong ma la dge slong dang / dge slong ma rnams kyis dge slong gi las kyis bsnyen par rdzogs par bgyis na / bsnyen par rdzogs pa zhes bgyi 'am / bsnyen par ma rdzogs pa zhes bgyi /

28. *Upālipariprcchā*, 330b2–3.

29. *Muktaka*, in *Uttaragrantha*, *'Dul ba gzhung dam pa*, Kangyur S ('dul ba) *na*, 212b6–213a1. On the *Muktaka*, see Clarke 2001.

u pa li bsnyen par rdzogs pa zhes bya ste / dge 'dun gnyis ka yang 'das pa dang bcas par 'gyur ro //

Note that the nun is ordained by monks and nuns, by, it seems, both monastic communities, and this is as we might expect: it is commonly held that nuns must be ordained by both saṅghas, whereas monks only require ordination by the bhikṣu saṅgha, although the degree to which Buddhist monastic law requires nuns to participate in the ecclesiastical affairs of the bhikṣu saṅgha may need to be reexamined.[30] But here the presence of nuns is, I suggest, of some significance.

The nun is ordained by means of a bhikṣu *karman* or a formal act for (or of) a monk. This passage does not go into any further detail, so it is difficult to know exactly what this means. The reverse situation, however, is also given. There a monk is ordained by means of a formal ecclesiastical act for (or of) a nun (*dge slong ma'i las kyis*), but the ordination is performed by other monks (*dge slong rnams kyis*) without any mention of nuns.[31] Whatever is meant by "a formal act for (or of) a nun," a bhikṣuṇī *karman* (*dge slong ma'i las*), the execution of it seems not to require the presence of nuns, although as we noted above, a bhikṣu *karman*, when performed in order to ordain a woman, seems to require the presence of nuns. In other words, at least from these passages, it seems that in these cases it is the ordination of a woman that requires the presence of nuns and not the performance of a bhikṣuṇī *karman* per se. The distinction may be subtle, but legally it seems to be of some importance.

The formal act of a monk (*dge slong gi las*) or of a nun (*dge slong ma'i las*), at least here, then, seems not to refer to ordination ceremonies to ordain monks and nuns respectively but to something else. It may refer specifically to the formula or legal pronouncement that is made during an ordination ceremony. If it referred to the ordination ceremony per se, the ordination of a monk according to a bhikṣuṇī *karman*, for instance, would presumably require the presence of nuns, but this is not the case as is clear from the passage itself.

30. See *Kṣudrakavastu*, *'Dul ba phran tshegs kyi gzhi*, Kangyur S ('dul ba) *tha*, 179b4–180a1.

31. *Muktaka*, 212b4–6.

"Reverend, if a bhikṣu is ordained by bhikṣus with the formal act of a bhikṣuṇī, is that one deemed to have been ordained or deemed to not have been ordained?"

"Upāli, [he] is deemed to have been ordained, but those who ordained him come to commit an infraction."[32]

Tibetan:

btsun pa dge slong rnams kyis dge slong la / dge slong ma'i las kyis bsnyen par rdzogs par bgyis na / bsnyen par rdzogs pa zhes bgyi 'am / bsnyen par ma rdzogs pa zhes bgyi /

u pa li bsnyen par rdzogs pa zhes ni bya ste / bsnyen par rdzogs par byed pa rnams ni 'das pa dang bcas par 'gyur ro //

The situation presented here might explain, for instance, a ceremony intended to ordain monks but during which the presiding officer accidentally started reading (or reciting) a ritual manual for nuns. This, of course, is mere conjecture, but it might account for the fact that, seemingly, a monk is ordained as a bhikṣu by means of a bhikṣuṇī *karman* despite the fact that there appear to be no nuns in attendance.

In sum, if the above passages tell us anything about ordinations in general, it is, I suggest, that we need to be careful about our language: where we previously said "must" we might now have to use "should," and this shift in language seems to allow for a whole range of new possibilities. It would seem to allow for valid ordinations with lay preceptors, which, given the technically "lay" status of many contemporary "nuns," may prove useful. Likewise, we see a precedent for direct ordination, that is, for the ordination of one who has not gone forth, one who has not been initiated as a novice. This too may prove useful, as it seems to suggest that a woman may be ordained without the so-called requisite training. This, again, is not ideal, but a reading of the Mūlasarvāstivāda Vinaya suggests it would be acceptable. More important, however, we see that any number of things can—we might before have said—go wrong during the ordination, without in any way affecting the validity of the ordination itself. And this stands in stark

32. *Muktaka*, 212b4–6.

contrast to contemporary Western scholarship—based, as it is, primarily on the Pāli Vinaya—which generally suggests that even the slightest mishap in an ordination renders it invalid.

Bhikṣuṇī Ordination:

LINEAGES AND PROCEDURES AS INSTRUMENTS OF POWER

Jan-Ulrich Sobisch

IN THE TIBETAN Mūlasarvāstivādin tradition of the *prātimokṣa*, the vows are considered to be material, and hence we may speak of "materialization of the vow." But materialization can perhaps also be understood in a quasi-metaphorical way, meaning "having successfully received the vow" (at least from the point of view of a result, as a literal and a metaphorical understanding amount to the same point of valid vow possession). In general, four aspects are often quoted as important for the materialization of the vow, namely the existence of (1) a qualified recipient, (2) a correct procedure, (3) a valid boundary or area, and (4) a valid assembly. Since the validity of an ordination is questioned and threatened when these legal aspects do not correspond to the Vinaya code, it seems only logical to assume a direct connection between these legal aspects and a successful materialization of the vow.

When we analyze the chronology of the introduction of the Vinaya's legal procedures, however, we find that it is nowhere mentioned that earlier full ordinations of monks were invalidated through the introduction of new, additional rules regarding the process of ordination by the Buddha. It is widely known that during the first years of the Buddha's forty-five-year teaching period, the method for conferring ordination was adjusted several times. In the very first period, for instance, the Buddha alone bestowed full ordination upon request by stating: "Come, bhikkhu(s)...."[1] Later the Buddha ordered Sāriputta to perform the ordination, abolishing the earlier form of ordination by a threefold repetition of the refuge formula. From that point onward, ordination was bestowed by a "formal act of the saṅgha in which the announcement (Pāli: *ñatti*) is followed by three questions."[2] Little by little, new changes and adjustments were introduced, many of which concerned the qualities of the monk who bestowed the vows.[3] But others pertained directly to the formal procedure of the ordination, such as the newly introduced rule according to which those who were to be ordained had to be asked clearly during the process whether they wanted to receive the vows (*Mahāvagga* I.29.1). Candidates for ordination had to request ordination from the assembly (I.29.2); they had to be warned about the ascetic lifestyle (I.30.4). The order of the elements of the ritual was changed (I.31.1), the number of attending bhikṣus was regulated (I.30.2), and a detailed procedure of questioning was introduced (I.76.1). When women received full ordination (after a female saṅgha was first established by the Buddha), further additional laws pertaining in general to the subordination of the nuns' order under the monks were added. After each change or adjustment of the procedure, there were many hundreds and even thousands of monks who had received the vows earlier according to procedures that were now no longer valid.[4] Yet it is not once mentioned that these monks had to retake their vows! We can safely assume that they did not have to, because—as already mentioned—there would have been hundreds, if not thousands, of cases, and the silence of our sources can in this case be taken as evidence.[5]

1. *Mahāvagga* I.6.32 and 34; I.7.15; I.9.4.

2. *Mahāvagga* I.28.3.

3. Among other things, the announcement had to be brought forth by a learned, competent monk (*Mahāvagga* I.28.4); the monk who bestowed the vows had to have *upasaṃpadā* for ten years (I.31.5); he must not be ignorant and unlearned (I.31.8); he should possess the qualities of morality, concentration, wisdom, and so forth (I.36.2–3); and must be believing, modest, of ready memory, etc. (I.36.6–7); not guilty of transgressions and so forth (I.36.8–9); capable of serving the sick new monk under his care, dispel his doubts, etc. (until I.36.17).

4. The number of monks who received the ordination simply by being called by the Buddha ("Come, monk," *ehi bhikkhu*) is stated in the commentaries as 1341 (Sp 240) or 1350 (Th-a III: 203). See further Kloppenborg 1983: 166.

5. In many other cases the invalidity of previous ordinations for reasons different from the change of the procedure of ordination is mentioned very clearly.

In other words, the new contents of the procedure are not essential for the materialization of the vow, because if that were the case, the earlier procedures could not have materialized a valid vow. In this context Ria Kloppenborg (1983: 159–60) has pointed out that as monastic life gradually became more complicated and regulated when the saṅgha grew, the rituals (that is *uposatha, pabbajā, upasampadā*), too, became more elaborate to ensure unity and stability. New and more elaborate rules became necessary because doubts about certain points arose, and, in addition to that, certain organizational, social, economic, and political considerations played a role. It is nowhere mentioned that the new elements in the ordination procedure had to be introduced to ensure the materialization of the vow itself. It is certainly also interesting in this context to take note of Ria Kloppenborg's (1983: 161–63) analysis of the "canonical attitude toward ritual and ritualism, summarized by the term *sīlabbata-upādāna*, the 'grasping after [mere] rules and rituals,'" which obstructs a person's spiritual growth and consequently needs to be overcome. In concluding this brief analysis, I think that we can ascertain that it is not the contents of the procedure that renders it correct but the mere fact that it is carried out in accordance with what has been established as the law. Or in other words: if the law is changed authoritatively, the new procedure is as correct as the previous one.

At several points in the history of Buddhism, the validity of someone's ordination was questioned or the admission of a certain group of people was denied based, for instance, on caste, as happened in Sri Lanka,[6] or gender, as is arguably the case with women seeking bhikṣuṇī ordination in several traditions today. This denial may be more or less well argued, but in most cases it is formally presented as a legal problem. In Sri Lanka, for instance, the legal argument is that the prescribed ordination procedure demands the presence of both fully ordained monks and nuns. Since no "properly" ordained Theravāda nun is available, ordination is said to be impossible.[7] This line of argumentation, however, builds largely on slanderous accusations of Chinese nuns as meat eaters, money handlers, and noncelibates, and on the fact that they follow the Mahāyāna rather than the

6. See Bechert 1970: 768 and Abeysekara 1999: passim.

7. See Hüsken 2006: 223.

Theravāda philosophy and practice,[8] and it completely overlooks the fact that the nuns' ordination was introduced in China by Sri Lankan nuns in the fifth century![9] Apart from the reference to the alleged hesitancy of the Buddha to found a nuns' order, which in its narration is full of misogynous stereotypes, the remaining arguments and sentiments reveal the actual motivation of the denial, namely to locate fitting female activities in social work (instead of asceticism or renunciation), family life, and providing of alms for the monks.[10] Instead, women dare to become an economic threat to the monks as eligible receivers of alms!

There is of course no doubt that the legal issues serve an important pur-

8. See Hüsken 2006: 221nn46–47.

9. See Hüsken 2006: n45 and Heirmann 2001. Tsai (1994), translating biographical accounts of Chinese nuns, provides further details. At about 429/431 C.E., the Kashmiri monk Guṇavarman came to China and was questioned about the validity of the status of Buddhist nuns in China, who had only received ordination from the assembly of monks but not first from the assembly of nuns. Thus they are like the Buddha's stepmother Mahāprajāpatī, who received the vows directly from the Buddha (as there were no nuns before her). Then the text seems to say that the previous Chinese procedure may have led to an offense for the monks who ordained women without the prescribed inevitable probation period (pp. 36–37)—but not to an invalidation of the nuns' vows. Another biographical account (pp. 53–54) reports the arrival of some Buddhist nuns from Sri Lanka in the capital of the Sung dynasty in 429. Again the fact that the Chinese nuns did not until then also receive the vows as required from the assembly of nuns is discussed, and the situation is once again likened to that of Mahāprajāpatī. Nevertheless, one Chinese nun had doubts about her status, and she consulted Guṇavarman about it. He agreed that receiving the vows a second time would be of benefit. When in 433 another group of eleven nuns arrived from Sri Lanka, a group of over three hundred Chinese nuns received from them the vows once again. The ritual was presided over by the Indian monk, Saṅghavarman. These stories suggest that the previous ordinations were not considered invalid (for instance, explicitly by Guṇavarman, see p. 63), but that it was still considered to be beneficial to repeat the ceremony (as an "augmenting [of] the good value of the obligation that had already been received," p. 63). The only ones who suffered an offense were the monks who had bestowed the vows earlier without the proper probation period that must precede the full ordination of nuns.

10. See Hüsken 2006: 223–24 and n60, and the alleged need for male supervision of the sensual, unintelligent, fickle, erotic, fecund, and impure women, and their praise as obedient and subservient daughters and wives in the pre-Buddhist Indian culture with the discussion in the context of "eight heavy rules" (*aṣṭau gurudharmāḥ*) for the nuns, which echoes most of these ideas. On the female stereotypes in early Buddhism and their Indian roots, see Kloppenborg 1995: passim. On the eight heavy rules for nuns, see Hüsken 1997: 346ff., Heirmann 1998, and Chung 1999. In this same context, Sponberg (1992) points out that the texts clearly state that liberation is available for all, regardless of sex, class, or caste ("soteriological inclusiveness"). Cf. also Vin II: 254 (Cv X.1.3), which clearly states that women are able to realize the fruit of entry into the stream, once-returner, nonreturner, and arhat.

pose, since without clear rules regarding the procedure and without autonomy and the ultimate authority of the saṅgha to decide these matters, the authenticity of the vow transmission would indeed be challenged. In a positive or constructive sense, restrictions have a regulatory character, and as such, they are desirable as an instrument to keep the transmission pure, trustworthy, and authentic. In particular, such a transmission is a guarantee that no one outside of already established saṅghas can establish a (Buddhist) saṅgha of his or her own; the saṅgha can only multiply from the inside, and no one can add to it from the outside. I am sure that all who aspire to become bhikṣuṇīs wish to keep it that way.

The fact that the saṅgha has autonomy and the authority to decide the matter is probably unchallenged. Andrew Huxley has introduced the modern legal term "autocthonisation of the grundnorm" into the debate, pointing out that when Mahākāssapa put the motion to a selected saṅgha of five hundred that the saṅgha should not promulgate new rules or abandon old ones and when that move was properly seconded by silence, the saṅgha had taken over the authority to decide matters as crucial as the actual vows (Vin II: 287).[11] This, Huxley points out, resembles the exercise of the governments of Canada and Australia, who passed a "new" constitution—which was identical with the old one—and thereby have "autocthonised their grundnorm from London to Canberra and Ottawa."

We also have several precedents where full ordination was reestablished, such as the reintroduction of valid full ordination to Sri Lanka from Burma under King Vijayabāhu (1055–1110), from Arkan under Vimaladharmasūrya I and II (reigning 1592–1604 and 1687–1707), and from Siam in 1753.[12] It should also be noted here that in their various crises, the saṅgha(s) of ordained monks of Sri Lanka gave up its autonomy, at least temporarily, and allowed the kings or the state to lead the reform process in the fashion of the Indian king Aśoka, the "protector of Buddhism."[13]

Another problem in this context is the important question of what constitutes "the saṅgha"—is there a global saṅgha or are saṅghas local

11. See Huxley 1996: 157.

12. See Bechert 1970: 764–65, 767.

13. For the "cleansing of the order" by the kings of Sri Lanka, see Bechert 1970: passim; 1961: n30.

phenomena? Huxley (p. 161) rightly points out that above the local level, "the sangha is merely an abstract notion. There is no Rome or Canterbury where bureaucrat monks administer the sangha of the Four Quarters."[14] When the monk Sumangala, for instance, in 1985 wanted to reintroduce the conferring of full ordination on all qualified candidates irrespective of their caste, he formed a monastic committee (*sangha sabhā*) of 170 monks from various temples of his region who reached a collective consensus on the matter.[15] As the proverb says: where there's a will, there's a way, at least when the interest of male persons is at stake. It is in fact an interesting question, whether for the bestowing of full ordination on nuns a consensus of all saṅghas is necessary. It seems that this would be an unrealistic demand, and such a general assembly of all the monks of even only one tradition has also probably never taken place. Bechert (1961: 46 and passim) has shown that the so-called councils initiated by King Aśoka were regional—if not local—affairs. They nevertheless came to far-reaching decisions for their local saṅghas. It is understandable that today's female novices wish to get the general consent from all Buddhist saṅghas for the full ordination of women. Yet when the Theravāda monks of Sri Lanka on several occasions reintroduced a valid *upasaṃpadā* from other countries, they obviously didn't need to seek such consent. It is telling that they nevertheless constitute the toughest opposition to female full ordination in Sri Lanka today.

Considering these points, it becomes obvious that the problem is not only one of legal dispute but also of authority and power. In general—almost needless to say—Buddhism, like every practiced religion, has to involve itself with numerous issues in the context of authority. In what follows, I would like to investigate briefly some Tibetan concepts of authority and of authority transmission.

In a general sense, a living spiritual tradition going back (in our case

14. Cf. in this context the clarification of the Pāli term *saṃghe samag(g)e kaṭe* in Bechert 1961: 21–24, especially p. 23 (my translation from Bechert's German text): "In this freedom [i.e., of the monk to move freely between communions/*sīmā*] lies but the only point through which, from the point of view of the Vinaya, the Order of the Four Points of the Compass, i.e., the all-embracing saṅgha, becomes a reality."

15. See Abeysekara 1999: 262.

several millennia) to a founder and to his teaching must negotiate in each generation the validity and import of each teaching received. Often this is done based on certain concepts of transmission and on the authority of the persons who transmit the teachings. There is, of course, the famous maxim according to which it is better to "rely on the teaching, not on the person," which is supposed to go back to the *Kalama-sutta* of the *Aṅguttara-nikāya*. But that would not be accepted as a maxim if it did not appeal to an ideal. In reality in Tibetan Buddhism, even though ideally one would want to rely on the teaching and not on the person, there exist probably more (and also more complex) ways of furnishing a person with authority than in any other religion. And most of these ways of furnishing a person with authority are based on what one might call "having received proper transmission," in contrast, for instance, to an ideal meritocracy. In other words, there are many examples in Tibetan Buddhism where a proper transmission of authority is believed to ensure a proper authority of the person.

Therefore, proper transmission and authority of the person in fact depend on one another: the authority of the person depends on the receiving of proper transmission, and the proper transmission depends on its being transmitted by authoritative persons. This is perhaps nowhere as evident as in the Tibetan genre of the "documents of transmission," the *gsan yig*, or *thob yig*, which are to my knowledge a uniquely Tibetan form of literature, where we find, among other things, ongoing documentation of the origins of teachings and of their transmitters. We also find documented in them the Vinaya lineages of fully ordained monks. As a rule of thumb they are quite reliable from the historian's point of view from perhaps the twelfth century onward, and they are problematic in the earlier periods, where they are perhaps more realistically perceived as reconstruction rather than documentation, especially their record of transmission in India. One of the most important collections of "documents of transmission" is that of A mes zhabs, which can be found in the second volume of his writings.[16] Here, on folios 3v–4v of Bsod nams dbang po's *gsan yig*

16. For A mes zhabs, his life, transmissions, and writings, see Sobisch 2007. I deal with his *gsan yig* collection in chapters 2 and 3 of that book. See also Sobisch 2002b and the forthcoming article by Jowita Kramer, "The gSan yigs of A mes zhabs: Observations Regarding Their Stylistic and Formal Features," in the proceedings of the 2006 IATS conference. She has carried out a detailed study of these *gsan yig*, and a publication is forthcoming.

(1559–1621), the document presents the transmission lineage of the bhikṣu and novice ordinations brought to Tibet by the famous Kashmiri paṇḍita, Śākyaśrībhadra.[17] The beginning of this lineage (fol. 3v) is slightly illegible in our document, but it is clear enough that it starts with (1) Buddha Śākyamuni. The next person on the list (fol. 4r) is his close disciple (2) Śāriputra. Then follow Buddha Śākyamuni's son (3) Rāhula, the (4) Brahman Rāhula (identified in an interlinear note as Saraha), (5) Ārya Nāgārjuna, (6) Guṇamati,[18] (7) Rin chen bshes gnyen (identified as Dharmamitra), (8) Dpal ldan chos skyong (identified as Virūpa), (9) Guṇasari(?), (10) Chos kyi phreng ba (Dharmamālā?), (11) 'Byung gnas sbas pa (Ākaraguhya?), and (12) Mahāpaṇḍita Śākyaśrībhadra, who is believed to have been ordained circa 1165 and then passed the lineage on to the famous Sa skya Paṇḍi ta (Sapan) in 1208.[19] Thus if we set the date for Śāriputra's ordination roughly at 500 B.C.E., then this lineage with the nine Indian masters who follow (until ca. 1165) covers almost 1,700 years, with an average of 185 years to be covered by each person. To this we have to add the ordination age of approximately twenty—in other words, we are dealing here with supposed lifespans of over two hundred years! This lineage is even more astonishing if you consider that Sapan, the first Tibetan member of this transmission, worked under the assumption that the Buddha lived some two thousand years B.C.E., which would again double the lifespan of these masters.[20] I can hardly imagine that Sapan believed that these nine persons bridged over a period of almost three thousand years. Unless the information of the

17. *Chos kyi rje dpal ldan bla ma dam pa rnams la dam pa'i chos ji ltar thos pa'i tshul legs par bshad pa zab rgyas chos kun gsal ba'i nyin byed las rje btsun grub pa'i 'khor lo bsgyur ba dpal ldan sa skya pa chen po 'jam mgon bsod nams dbang po'i zhal snga nas kyi rjes su bzung ba'i sar ka,* from a manuscript collection (photo copy) of A mes zhabs Ngag dbang kun dga' bsod nams' collected works held at the University of Hamburg, vol. *kha*, fols. 3v ff. On the development of this lineage in Tibet, see David Jackson's article in this volume.

18. In an interlinear note he is said to have authored a commentary on the *Mūlamadhyamakakārikā*.

19. See Jackson 1987: 27. See also *Tsong kha pa'i gsan yig* (27v–28v): (1) Buddha, (2) Śāriputra, (3) Sgra gcan 'dzin, (4) Bram ze Sgra gcan 'dzin, (5) Nāgārjuna, (6) Yon tan blo gros mchog, (7) Rin chen bshes gnyen, (8) Chos kyi bzang po, (9) Yon tan rgya mtsho, (10) Chos kyi phreng ba, (11) 'Byung gnas sbas pa, (12) Paṇ chen Shākya shrī. I owe the reference to this passage in Tsong kha pa's *gsan yig* to Carola Roloff (Bhikṣuṇī Jampa Tsedroen).

20. Sapan's system of reckoning the Buddha's parinirvāṇa at 2134 B.C.E. is briefly mentioned in A mes zhabs' *Legs bshad dpyod ldan yid 'phrog*, vol. *kha*, 395v. See also Sobisch 2007: 137.

Indian part of this ordination lineage got corrupted in Tibet—which at the moment I believe to be less plausible, because it is a widespread phenomena that the Tibetan parts of records of teachings are usually well documented while the Indian parts are not—Śākyaśrībhadra seems not to have passed on the full documentation of his lineage when he ordained Sapan. It may have been that at Śākyaśrībhadra's time such meticulous documentation as required today was not necessary: the Mūlasarvāstivādin saṅgha was established as the one to which Nāgārjuna, Guṇamati, Dharmamitra, Virūpa, and so on belonged, and that was perhaps considered enough validation.[21]

From the point of view of the tradition, however, these Vinaya lineages still carry enormous prestige: they function as proof that a particular tradition of full ordination is valid, because it goes back to the Buddha in a supposedly unbroken transmission. These transmissions are, by the way, also not uncontested within the tradition itself. There is for instance sometimes noticeable a certain tension between the so-called "lower Vinaya" (*smad 'dul*) of the Rnying ma tradition, which had survived in the Khams region of Tibet, and the Vinaya going back to Śākyaśrībhadra. The nineteenth-century master 'Jam mgon Kong sprul (1813–99) first received full ordination in the lower Vinaya tradition at Zhe chen monastery, but a year later at Dpal spung monastery he was told to return those vows to receive the vows in Śākyaśrībhadra's lineage.[22] The circumstances give the impression that this was an entirely sectarian act for the purpose of unhinging a promising student from his former context and binding him to a new one. Such lineages were in fact not only contested out of concern for the purity of the ordination but also out of rivalry, contesting for prestige and power. The Vinaya lineages and their histories therefore obviously share many characteristics with other more or less similar forms of Tibetan transmission lineages, and it is therefore helpful to briefly investigate these in order to understand the peculiarities of the Tibetan ordination lineages.

21. I am not saying that Tibetan monks claim the Indian parts of their Vinaya transmissions to be complete, although many of them certainly assume that, without ever having thought about the matter. But it is a fact that many monks are demanding proof from the female devotees that certain lineages of female ordination are intact. In other words, they are demanding something that they themselves would not be able to provide in their own cases.

22. See Barron 2003: 19 and 22.

One of the most ancient forms of such transmissions of authority in Tibet is the spiritual transmission from father to son. The tradition that is perhaps best known to us is the family lineage of H. H. Sa skya 'Khri 'dzin, the family lineage of the 'Khon clan of Tibet, which they claim goes back to imperial times, i.e., well before the time of the so-called second spread of the teachings in Tibet. Here, the authority of occupying the teaching throne of Sa skya was handed down from father to son (and sometimes from brother to brother or from uncle to nephew), and it is perhaps interesting to note that in some cases the authority that came with the family was deemed more important than ordination. The twenty-eighth throneholder, A mes zhabs, for instance, abandoned his monk vows in order to produce male offspring that could carry on this particular form of transmission.[23]

There were also family traditions that kept celibacy a priority, such as the holders of the throne of 'Bri gung until the seventeenth century. They evidently held family transmission and full ordination to be equally important and solved the problem by passing on the authority of holding the abbatial chair to an ordained nephew. These lineages are known as the uncle-nephew traditions (*khu dbon*), and they survived as long as there existed at least two brothers in the family, one of whom remained celibate while the other was responsible for producing male offspring.[24]

Another Tibetan form of handing down authority is one that is both the most famous and the most intriguing, namely the so-called tulku (*sprul sku*) lineages. Here it is the very same mental continuum that embodies itself again and again and carries on the authority of the previous incarnations. It resembles to some extent the authority-qua-birth models of the father-son and uncle-nephew lineages, but here, apart from the fact that it is the same mental continuum that takes rebirth, a further factor comes into

23. See Sobisch 2007: 16–18.

24. For the history of this uncle-nephew lineage, see *Nges don bstan pa'i snying po mgon po 'bri gung pa chen po'i gdan rabs chos kyi byung tshul gser gyi phreng ba* by 'Bri gung Bstan 'dzin pad ma'i rgyal mtshan (Lhasa: *Bod ljongs yig dpe rnying dpe skrun khang*, 1989), 349. When the last members of the Skyu ra family did not produce male offspring, Rig 'dzin Chos kyi grags pa (1595–1659) recognized Dkon mchog 'phrin las bzang po (1656–1718) as the incarnation of his elder brother, (= Che tshang I) Dkon mchog rin chen (1590–1654), and 'Phrin las bzang po in turn recognized 'Phrin las don grub chos rgyal (1704–54) as the incarnation of Chos kyi grags pa, the "younger brother" (= Chung tshang I). From then on the lineage was controlled by the Che tshang and Chung tshang incarnations.

play, namely that the incarnation must be searched, discovered, and confirmed by other tulkus and/or high-ranking lamas. Thereby it is certainly one of the most esoteric means of maintaining a lineage but also the most susceptible to all sorts of political corruption.[25]

A last form of transmission of authority that I would like to mention briefly is the equally esoteric method of "discovering treasures" (*gter ma*). Here the originator of the authority is in almost all cases the Indian guru Padmasambhava, who visited Tibet sometime during the eighth century. His authority was handed down through the various kinds of "treasures" (*gter*) that consisted both of material things and texts that were buried in the ground, in other places, or in the mental continuum of people, to be "rediscovered" centuries later. The one who rediscovered a treasure became known as a "treasure discoverer," or tertön (*gter ston*), and thereby enjoyed great reverence among the Rnying ma pa and to some extent also among Bka' rgyud pa and other circles, but his authority was also highly contested in Tibet and many tertons were accused of fraud. Here, too, the discoverer of the treasure obtained his status partly by birth-lineage, for he had to have a connection to Padmasambhava, the originator of the treasure, in a previous life, but also by spiritual maturity and by confirmation through other masters of high status.[26]

These are some of the principal Tibetan methods of handing down authority—or of keeping authority centralized. The number of uncle-nephew, father-son, tulku, and tertön lineages in Tibet increased greatly over the course of several centuries, and in recent centuries we even find a few masters who combined in themselves two or more of these concepts. One of them was the above-mentioned Sa skya pa master, A mes zhabs, who was a member of a father-son lineage, but also a tulku, and he even counted among his previous births a direct disciple of Padmasambhava—who, like Padmasambhava, hid treasures for future disciples—as well as an eminent Rnying ma pa scholar whose teaching career is closely connected with several terma traditions (namely Klong chen Rab 'byams pa, 1308–

25. For testimonies of, or Western academic writings on, tulkus, see Hummel 1974, Wylie 1978, Dhondup and Tsering 1979, Bärlocher 1982, Michael 1982, Ray 1986, and Henderson 1997.

26. Excellent introductions to the phenomena of *gter* and *gter ston* are provided in Gyatso 1993 and 1996. For a critical case study, see Aris 1988.

64).[27] Similarly, the famous above-mentioned 'Jam mgon Kong sprul was a tulku and a tertön, and his previous embodiments included other discoverers of treasures,[28] and as I mentioned he was a member of two different bhikṣu ordination lineages.

Now, all these types of lineages have elements that separate them and elements in common. Among those they have in common is that whoever becomes a member or a link in such a lineage becomes endowed with authority, namely the authority that is handed down through that particular lineage. Another aspect these lineages have in common is that they are almost exclusively populated by men. This is naturally so in the cases of father-son and uncle-nephew lineages—and I am not aware of the existence of any spiritual mother-daughter or aunt-niece lineages in Tibet—but it is also the case with the tulku and tertön lineages. Before this background of lineages that endow their members with great power and great authority, the lineages of full ordination stand out in at least two ways. First of all, there certainly existed at an earlier time female lineages of full ordination in Tibet, although at present I am not aware of any traditional documentation of them, such as documentation in a *gsan yig*. If such a lineage existed today, there would be no reason why it should not be documented in the same way as its male counterpart, and I can see no reason why it should not carry the same authority for the tradition.

Secondly, unlike the father-son, uncle-nephew, tulku, and tertön lineages, the original purpose of the ordination lineages, or at least of their documentation, seems not to have been to invest the person with power and rank, at least not in the same way. It is true that by becoming a member of such a lineage, namely by receiving full ordination, a particular rank is obtained; yet this is a widespread phenomenon, and the fully ordained monk shares this position with countless other monks, while in all our other examples the one who is empowered by a transmission of authority obtains a special and truly exalted position. And, at least in theory, the only characteristic distinguishing fully ordained monks from one another is seniority. Furthermore, being born in one of the father-son, uncle-nephew, tulku, and tertön lineages is associated with enormous amounts of previously

27. For the previous births of A mes zhabs, see Sobisch 2007: 529ff.

28. See for instance Barron 2003: 98, 160, 445–49.

accumulated merit—accumulations that are believed to be equal to that of great bodhisattvas. The state of ordination, on the other hand, is a step undertaken out of one's own choice. It presupposes renunciation, the development of which also presupposes merit, but that merit is certainly not comparable with the bodhisattva's accumulations.

Regarding the custom of documenting ordination lineages, it therefore seems plausible that it has been introduced primarily in order to make an authentication of the vow transmission possible. Yet it is true that refusing access to a lineage of full ordination is an exercising of power. And it is also true that the female novices and lay devotees of today have to face in many Buddhist countries communities of bhikṣus—fully ordained male persons—who act rather hostilely to the idea of admitting women to their rank.

By now, however, more and more monks could be persuaded to take part in a bhikṣuṇī ordination, and bhikṣuṇī ordination in Sri Lanka is a fait accompli, "although these women are by no means accepted as nuns by all Sri Lankan monks" and among the monks "objections...far outweigh positive voices."[29] This seems more or less to be also the case in the Tibetan tradition, where a small number of female novices have received full ordination from the Chinese tradition. In the course of time, the problem of being accepted by the monks will in all likelihood be solved through their very presence, although the nuns will probably have to attune themselves to being accused of causing the Dharma to degenerate, much as it is claimed that the Buddha had predicted the premature end of the period of Dharma in this world because he was persuaded to allow ordination of women.

To summarize, I have argued that (1) it is not the contents of the ordination procedure that materializes the vow, (2) procedures are valid due to the mere fact that they are carried out in accordance with what has been established as the law, (3) the saṅgha has the autonomy and authority to establish these procedures, and (4) the demand to document unbroken ordination lineages and to reach a consensus of a global saṅgha is, historically speaking, problematic for the monks as well. I wonder therefore, in my final conclusion, if all this doesn't call for a shift in emphasis when we are discussing the validity of vows and ordination procedures. Wouldn't it be better and

29. See Hüsken 2006: 220–23.

more honest—instead of demanding documentation of lineages and unanimous consensus of a global saṅgha—to base the validity of ordinations on a procedure that is established autonomously and authoritatively by any one of the established saṅghas?

Human Rights and the Status of Women in Buddhism

His Holiness the Fourteenth Dalai Lama[1]

Opening Comments

In ancient cultures, gender differences were perhaps not so important. However, as civilization developed, physical strength became more vital as societies sought to protect themselves against enemies, and consequently males dominated. Later, education and intelligence came to play a more central role, and in this sphere men and women have equal capacity. Nowadays, the most crucial factor in resolving conflicts and other societal problems is affection and warm-heartedness. These two qualities can prevent the use of education and intelligence for destructive ends. Perhaps because they carry children in their wombs and have been the primary caretakers of newborn infants, women develop affection and warm-heartedness more easily than men. For this reason women must take a more central role in society. Of course men and women have equal potential for both affection and aggression, but there seems to be differences between men and women in how readily these arise.

Historically religion has often emphasized male importance. In Buddhism, however, the highest vows, namely the bhikṣu and bhikṣuṇī ones,

1. This chapter is a distillation of the Dalai Lama's comments during the congress in Hamburg and of the panel he participated in on the final afternoon. In synthesizing this chapter, the editors owe a debt to the efforts of Dr. Alexander Berzin, whose summaries of these proceedings can be found at www.berzinarchives.com. Any errors or misrepresentation of views herein are entirely the responsibility of the editors.

are equal and entail the same rights. This is the case despite the fact that in some ritual areas, due to social custom, bhikṣus go first; Buddha gave the basic rights equally to both saṅgha groups. Thus, there is no point in discussing *whether* to revive the bhikṣuṇī ordination; the Buddha clearly intended for there to be bhikṣuṇīs. The question is merely how to do so properly within the context of the Vinaya.

Śāntarakṣita introduced the Mūlasarvāstivāda bhikṣu ordination into Tibet. All the Indians in his party were men, however, and since bhikṣuṇī ordination requires a dual saṅgha of both bhikṣus and bhikṣuṇīs, he was unable to introduce the bhikṣuṇī line. In later times, some Tibetan lamas ordained their mothers as bhikṣuṇīs, but from the point of view of Vinaya, these were not considered authentic ordinations.

After 1959, I determined that the educational options for nuns needed to be raised to the level available to monks. We have since enacted those opportunities, and today we already have scholars among the nuns. But when it comes to re-establishing the bhikṣuṇī ordination, I cannot act alone. As an individual, I do not have the power to decide this issue. This question must be decided according to the Vinaya.

Today we have the opportunity to discuss this question with Buddhists from the traditions of China, Korea, and Vietnam, which still have bhikṣuṇī ordination. Already about two dozen Tibetan women have taken bhikṣuṇī ordination according to the Dharmaguptaka tradition. No one rejects that they are now bhikṣuṇīs.

For the last thirty years, we Tibetans have been conducting research on the Mūlasarvāstivāda and Dharmaguptaka Vinaya texts. Since the Vinaya is found in both these two Sanskrit-based traditions as well as in the Pāli tradition, it is useful that saṅgha elders from all three living Vinaya traditions come together to discuss the matter and share their knowledge and experiences. Bhikṣuṇī ordination has already been re-established in Sri Lanka, and there is interest to do the same in Thailand. Further research is useful so that one day we will be able to establish it in Tibetan Buddhism as well.

Summarizing the Conference

Dr. Thea Mohr, moderator

Your Holiness, for the last two days, we have heard from sixty-five learned scholars from both monastic and non-monastic backgrounds, addressing an audience of nearly four hundred people from nineteen countries. Based on these diverse presentations, the consensus seems to be that a dual ordination involving both a bhikṣu and a bhikṣuṇī saṅgha is a the most satisfactory method for reinstating the lineage, both practically and in terms of scripture. The dual-saṅgha method also has several historical precedents. However, the Tibetan nuns present at the congress expressed a strong interest in seeing the Mūlasarvāstivāda bhikṣuṇī ordination re-established in a single-saṅgha ceremony conducted by Tibetan Mūlasarvāstivāda bhikṣus in the Tibetan language. Support was unanimous, however, for recognizing whichever method for re-establishing the Mūlasarvāstivāda bhikṣuṇī ordination that Your Holiness and the Tibetan Vinaya masters decide.

We will first hear from the bhikṣu saṅgha and then from the bhikṣuṇīs.

Bhikṣu Samdhong Rinpoche, Kalon Tripa of the Tibetan Government-in-Exile. Ordained 1960

Although some Tibetans have received bhikṣuṇī ordination in the Dharmaguptaka lineage and are well accepted by us as Dharmaguptaka bhikṣuṇīs, they wish to become bhikṣuṇīs in the Mūlasarvāstivāda tradition. Many objections arise, however, when examining the legality of any procedure.

Concerning the Mūlasarvāstivāda Vinaya, we Tibetans strictly follow the Indian commentaries on it by Guṇaprabha and Dharmamitra. There is no mention in their texts of single-saṅgha bhikṣuṇī ordination being permissible. On the contrary, they state that earlier methods of ordination were invalidated when Buddha instituted new methods.[2]

Some Tibetan commentators assert that the bhikṣu saṅgha can confer

2. This invalidation is unknown in the Theravāda and Dharmaguptaka traditions and it seems to stem exclusively from the later commentarial tradition. The Tibetans researching the issue have provided no source within the thirteen volumes of Vinaya in the Kangyur that supports this invalidation.

brahmacarya ordination and even leave the summer retreat to do so. The brahmacarya ordination is just a preparatory phase preceding the full ordination, which is performed by the bhikṣuṇī saṅgha, and these passages do not state that the bhikṣu saṅgha alone can confer full bhikṣuṇī ordination. Thus, these sources do not sanction single-saṅgha bhikṣuṇī ordination.

A Vinaya passage, however, states that, if requested, bhikṣus may if necessary leave their summer retreat to confer śikṣamāṇā ordination, which is normally given by bhikṣuṇīs alone. This allowance implies that bhikṣuṇīs are not available to give such ordination themselves. Inferring from this one source, these scholars say that in a circumstance where no bhikṣuṇīs are available, the brahmacarya and bhikṣuṇī ordination ceremonies may also be performed by the bhikṣu saṅgha alone. This is one possibility, therefore. But many other Tibetan commentators say the allowance in this one passage cannot be generalized to include bhikṣuṇī ordination.

There is also opposition to the dual-saṅgha method of bhikṣuṇī ordination in which Mūlasarvāstivāda bhikṣus and Dharmaguptaka bhikṣuṇīs together confer ordination according to the Mūlasarvāstivāda ritual. The objection is that two different nikāya traditions of Vinaya cannot administer an ordination together.

These are the alternatives that the Department of Religion and Culture is investigating in accord with His Holiness's wish to restore the complete fourfold assembly of disciples—bhikṣus, bhikṣuṇīs, laymen, and laywomen—and establish Tibet as a central land. Our efforts toward re-establishing the Mūlasarvāstivāda bhikṣuṇī ordination are not driven by Western influence or feminist concerns about the equality of the sexes—this issue cannot be determined by social or political considerations. The solution must be found within the context of the Vinaya codes.

Bhikkhu Bodhi, former president of the Buddhist Publication Society, Kandy. Ordained 1973

The Vinaya rules about methods of ordination exhibit a great deal of flexibility depending on circumstances and conditions. We should not regard the Vinaya as a system inscribed in stone, fixed and unchangeable for all time. The Vinaya has certain clear guidelines that reveal the Buddha's intention, and we must not allow these guidelines to become a means to block his intentions.

One of Buddha's intentions was to establish a bhikṣuṇī saṅgha. He made it an autonomous body supported by the bhikṣu saṅgha in certain ways, but he gave it a great deal of independence, and he repeatedly extolled and praised the bhikṣuṇīs on many occasions. To accord with the Buddha's intention, the bhikṣuṇī saṅgha should be restored to all the schools of Buddhism in which it has disappeared and should be established in any school of Buddhism that has never had it.

I see two possible methods of conferring bhikṣuṇī ordination within the Mūlasarvāstivāda tradition. Both will meet with objections from Vinaya legalists, but I have to explain them anyway. One way that I prefer is through a dual-saṅgha ordination. There are now many Tibetan Buddhist practitioners who have taken bhikṣuṇī vows in the Dharmaguptaka tradition. This does not mean they are practicing Chinese or Korean Buddhism; they are practicing Tibetan Buddhism. Some of them have been practicing it for twenty or thirty years—they wear Tibetan Buddhist robes, know the Tibetan language, practice at Tibetan Buddhist centers, and live in Tibetan monasteries. I therefore suggest that a saṅgha of Mūlasarvāstivāda bhikṣus perform an act of the saṅgha either formally or informally to accept the Tibetan Dharmaguptaka bhikṣuṇīs as Mūlasarvāstivāda bhikṣuṇīs. Theravāda has this type of procedure with the *daḷhīkamma* custom, where a monk of one nikāya can transfer to another. This act would change the lineage of those bhikṣuṇīs to Mūlasarvāstivāda and allow them to then fulfill the role of Mūlasarvāstivāda bhikṣuṇīs in a dual-ordination ceremony.

If that is not acceptable, the second manner of bhikṣuṇī ordination would be by means of a single saṅgha. According to the Pāli sources, at least, before there were any bhikṣuṇīs, Buddha said that bhikṣus alone may ordain bhikṣuṇīs. The present circumstances are similar to those at that time; and if one insists that the Mūlasarvāstivāda bhikṣu saṅgha may not interact with a bhikṣuṇī saṅgha from another lineage, then a single-saṅgha ordination is the only possible method. After ten years,[3] the dual-saṅgha method of

3. According to the Pāli and Dharmaguptaka Vinayas, both women and men need to be fully ordained for ten years before acting as one of the main ordination masters. According to the Mūlasarvāstivāda tradition, however, while a man needs to be fully ordained for ten years, a woman needs to be fully ordained for twelve.

bhikṣuṇī ordination could then be restarted. Thus, in order to fulfill the Buddha's intention in the present circumstances, either the *daḷhīkamma* or the single-saṅgha method would be acceptable.

Bhikṣu Thich Quang Ba, founding abbot of Van Hanh Monastery, Canberra. Ordained 1974

If Your Holiness, with the support of the Tibetan saṅgha, re-establishes the bhikṣuṇī ordination, the benefits would extend well beyond the Tibetan community. I believe that Buddhists in Thailand, Burma, and Sri Lanka and other countries lacking bhikṣuṇī ordination would follow suit. We request you to establish Mūlasarvāstivāda bhikṣuṇī ordination for women no matter what country they come from, just as Tibetan women are free to receive bhikṣuṇī ordination in another tradition. If you require the participation of senior bhikṣuṇīs from other nikāya traditions or bhikṣuṇīs ordained in other traditions but following the Tibetan tradition, I believe there are many who are more than happy to assist.

This international approach would make the bhikṣuṇī ordination most accessible to women worldwide and be most conducive to harmony and friendship among the saṅghas. Single-saṅgha ordination performed by Mūlasarvāstivāda bhikṣus is also acceptable, however, if it is required to preserve the purity of the tradition. Either way, we need and hope that the Tibetan Buddhists will take the lead in re-establishing this ordination as soon as possible.

Prajna Bangsha Bhikshu Mahathero, Secretary General of the Supreme Saṅgha Council of Bangladesh. Ordained 1973

I fully support Bhikkhu Bodhi's recommendation—a decision must be made in accordance with the times and situation. According to the Pāli tradition, Buddha said that if the saṅgha feels that something needs to be changed, then if the whole saṅgha agrees, it may be changed, but the decision must not be based on the opinion of just a partial saṅgha. Also, in the *Mahāparinirvāṇa-sūtra*, the Buddha at the end of his life told Ānanda that the minor precepts may be changed to better suit the time and place.

Thus, the door is always open for the saṅgha to make such decisions, and it is best to begin this process of re-establishing the bhikṣuṇī saṅgha now for the benefit and propagation of the Buddha sāsana.

Bhikkhu Dhammavihari Thero (Prof. Jotiya Dhirasekera), former Director of the Postgraduate Institute of Pali and Buddhist Studies, University of Kelaniya. Ordained 1990

I am nearly in agreement with everything expressed by my senior brother monk Bhikkhu Bodhi from the point of view of Theravāda Buddhism. That enables Your Holiness in whatever manner you wish to bring harmony among monks and nuns within your Tibetan Buddhist community. Dual-saṅgha ordination was meant for the purpose of promoting harmonious coexistence between the bhikṣu and bhikṣuṇī communities.

In Theravāda, we have a novice ordination for young men but we do not at present have a tradition of sāmaṇerī novice nuns; our novitiates are referred to as renunciates, *pabbajita*. I think young men and women around the world, if they aspire to be full-fledged members of the Buddhist saṅgha, should have the opportunity to take novice vows. The question is, for what? As they mature in the Dhamma, it is vital that they be able to take greater responsibility and status through the upasampadā ceremony in order to fulfill the destination of spiritual life, the goal of nibbāna. It is for this that we must have bhikkhunī ordination.

Your Holiness, I wish you success in getting your own communities of monks and nuns in harmonious relation where the females are not subordinates but cooperative partners in the spiritual community, fully responsible for their own order. May we all succeed in bringing back to the world a Buddhism where all four branches of the community—bhikkhus and bhikkhunīs, laymen and laywomen—can flourish.

Bhikṣu Huimin Shih, Professor at Taipei National University of the Arts and Principal of the Chung Hwa Institute of Buddhist Studies (CHIBC). Ordained 1979

I have been personally involved with this issue since 1997 when Geshe Tashi Tsering came to Taipei, and I also attended the 1998 conference at the Norbulingka Institute in Dharamasala. Using whatever method is most appropriate to revive bhikṣuṇī ordination will solve the twin concerns of making the Tibetan Buddhist saṅgha a complete saṅgha and bringing it in line with the universal value of gender equality, so important in the modern world. Whichever decision the Tibetan saṅgha makes concerning the re-establishment of the Mūlasarvāstivāda bhikṣuṇī ordination will receive international saṅgha recognition and approval. May it happen here and now.

Venerable Khammai Dhammasami, Oxford Centre for Buddhist Studies, UK, and Professor, International Theravada Buddhist Missionary University, Myanmar

Nyanissara Sayadaw from Myanmar had to cancel at the last minute, so I am here to represent the Burmese tradition. I am originally from Burma, where I received my sāmaṇera ordination as a young man in 1982, but I have been living abroad for two decades.

Although both options for re-establishing the Mūlasarvāstivāda bhikṣuṇī ordination mentioned by Bhikkhu Bodhi would be possible and valid, I would recommend the single-saṅgha method. When, at the time of the Buddha, the dual-saṅgha ordination was introduced, the single-saṅgha method was still a valid option. I say this because the Pāli suggests that a nun who has completed only one half of a dual ordination is still considered a bhikkhunī, for her transgressions of Vinaya rules are considered the transgressions of a bhikkhunī.

Another reason I prefer single ordination is the social convenience of post-ordination supervision and instruction. It will be more convenient for a Tibetan bhikkhunī to receive such training from a Tibetan master. These are my personal observations.

Geshe Rinchen Ngödrup, Sera Jé Monastery. Ordained 1990

My deep respects to my abbot, His Holiness the Dalai Lama. Buddha said that if an action is not permitted, one needs to refrain from it. However, those actions that Buddha did not specifically disallow during his lifetime, but which accord with Buddha's intentions, are to be allowed.[4] Although the Vinaya texts state that the brahmacarya ordination is to be given by a bhikṣuṇī saṅgha, other passages state that a bhikṣu may give full ordination to a śikṣamāṇā if requested and that a bhikṣu may give brahmacarya ordination. The implication is that if a bhikṣuṇī saṅgha is not available, bhikṣus may give brahmacarya ordination as a single saṅgha. Since brahmacarya ordination must be followed in the same day by bhikṣuṇī ordination, the further implication is that bhikṣuṇī ordination by a single bhikṣu saṅgha is also allowed. There is no mention, however, of śikṣamāṇā ordination by a bhikṣu saṅgha.

Bhikkhu Sujato, Abbot, Santi Forest Monastery, Australia. Ordained 1994

Any decision regarding the method for bhikṣuṇī ordination must be guided primarily by the broad principles of the Vinaya. Traditional commentaries, customary practices, and personal preferences should be respected but should not be the deciding factors. The Vinaya never mentioned Mūlasarvāstivāda, Dharmaguptaka, Theravāda, Tibet, China, or Sri Lanka, and therefore we need not give such importance to these distinctions.

4. Geshe Rinchen Ngodup is referring here to a well-known passage in the Vinaya, where it says:

> "Bhikkhus, whatever I have not objected to, saying, 'This is not allowable,' if it conforms with what is not allowable, if it goes against what is allowable, that is not allowable for you.
>
> "Whatever I have not objected to, saying, 'This is not allowable,' if it conforms with what is allowable, if it goes against what is not allowable, that is allowable for you.
>
> "And whatever I have not permitted, saying, 'This is allowable,' if it conforms with what is not allowable, if it goes against what is allowable, that is not allowable for you.
>
> "And whatever I have not permitted, saying, 'This is allowable,' if it conforms with what is allowable, if it goes against what is not allowable, that is allowable for you." (Mv VI.40.1)

According to Dr. Petra Kieffer-Pültz (personal communication), in the Theravāda tradition this passage is given in Vin I: 250–51. In the Tibetan tradition they are found in the *mātṛkā* embedded in the *Uttaragrantha*, Kangyur D ('dul ba) *pa*, 252b3–253b4 (courtesy of Shayne Clarke).

Rather, the Vinaya establishes procedures for enabling a candidate to go forth in the Buddha's dispensation to seek the end of suffering.

The general consensus of the congress has been that either of the two options outlined by Bhikkhu Bodhi would be acceptable. The main criterion for making the choice should be the spiritual welfare of the newly ordained bhikṣuṇīs, not legal technicalities. Buddha's intention was to protect the saṅgha from unsuitable candidates and to ensure that suitable applicants be guaranteed material and spiritual support, primarily through the mentor-disciple relationship that is established between preceptor and ordinand.

The single-saṅgha method of ordination would offer bhikṣuṇīs the great benefit of receiving formal education from the living Tibetan bhikṣu saṅgha, but the absence of a bhikṣuṇī preceptor would severely limit the possibilities for personal mentorship. On the other hand, the dual ordination by Mūlasarvāstivāda bhikṣus and Dharmaguptaka bhikṣuṇīs also enjoys the full benefit and support of the bhikṣu saṅgha but adds to it a number of benefits that flow from the close and special understanding that grows between nuns who live together in community—looking on each other, as the Vinaya says, like mother and daughter. It also allows the bhikṣuṇīs to assess the readiness of the candidates, and this should happen in close coordination with senior Tibetan ten-precept nuns. The ceremony should be performed according to the Mūlasarvāstivāda Vinaya and include senior bhikṣuṇīs who have ordained in the Dharmaguptaka tradition but who have been adopted within the Mūlasarvāstivāda lineage by an act of the saṅgha. Such a dual ordination has all the benefits of single ordination and none of the drawbacks.

The only restriction on dual ordination found in the Pāli Vinaya is when two saṅghas are in a relation of *nānāsaṁvāsa*, or "different communion." However, this status only arises in two ways: either one declares oneself *nānāsaṁvāsa*, or one is expelled by formal punishment by the saṅgha. Since the three Buddhist nikāyas presently extant did not arise on the basis of a schism in the saṅgha, there can be no objection to bhikṣuṇī ordination by a dual saṅgha with members from more than one of these nikāyas.

Therefore, it is my sincere wish that His Holiness the Dalai Lama together with the Tibetan saṅgha, out of compassion for the whole world, institute the bhikṣuṇī saṅgha now through the dual-saṅgha method. We can never assure that any ordination lineage, including that of the bhikṣus, is 100 percent valid. It is unreasonable to expect the spiritual aspirations of nuns to be indefinitely postponed in order to satisfy impossible demands. Let us do the ordination as best we can. If this is not yet perfect, we can do better next time.

Bhikṣuṇī Myongsong Sunim, President of the National Asscociation of Korean Bhikṣuṇīs. Ordained 1957

On behalf of the Korean bhikṣuṇī order, I unconditionally support the re-establishment of the Mūlasarvāstivāda bhikṣuṇī ordination and recommend the dual-saṅgha method. In Korea, we first revived our Dharmaguptaka bhikṣuṇī lineage after World War II through single-saṅgha ordination, but then we switched to the dual-saṅgha method in 1982, for we believe that dual ordination is preferable. The saṅgha needs both wings to fly—the bhikṣus and the bhikṣuṇīs. Please do not postpone the decision.

Bhikṣuṇī Wu Yin, Founder and Abbess of the Luminary National Buddhist Society, Taiwan. Ordained 1959

I feel very grateful to have this opportunity to be here and express the sincere support of the bhikṣus and bhikṣuṇīs saṅgha in Taiwan to the Tibetan Buddhist community. When I see so many saṅgha members and scholars from all over the world expressing their concern about the well-being of the Tibetan saṅgha, I rejoice for the Buddhadharma. The harmony among the worldwide saṅgha gives us great hope about the establishment of the lineage in the Tibetan Buddhism. I also support Bhikkhu Bodhi's proposals, as long as the Tibetan Buddhist community can improve itself, as long as the Tibetan nuns' training can be enhanced, and as long as the seven groups of the Buddha's disciples can be present in the Tibetan saṅgha. I will respect and support whatever decision the Tibetan Buddhist community makes—provided it is not that we need further research.

Bhikkhunī Thich Nu Hue Huong, Deputy in the Central Vietnamese Buddhist Association

If we wish to penetrate deeply the meaning of Buddhadharma, we must throw away our preconceived notions and apply a merciful mind. The first thing we should recall is why the Buddha came into the world. The Buddha was born to teach living beings to become enlightened, emancipated. He used to declare: "I became Buddha so that you may become Buddha." In offering his path, he did not discriminate among beings, and he proclaimed the spiritual capacity of women. Buddhism is the most egalitarian religion, and monks and nuns in Vietnam are governed by one charter and one set of regulations. We are proud of such success in sex equality in Vietnam. The Vietnamese saṅgha supports the re-establishment of the Mūlasarvāstivāda bhikṣuṇī ordination, and we are willing to help in any way that we can.

Bhikṣuṇī Heng-ching Shih, Professor Emeritus at Taiwan National University and Co-founder of the Chinese Buddhist Electronic Text Association. Ordained 1976

For the past twenty-seven years, it has been my honor to be involved in the movement to establish a Tibetan bhikṣuṇī saṅgha, and I have experienced a close sisterhood with my bhikṣuṇī friends in the Tibetan Buddhist saṅgha. We have had enthusiastic expectations but also many disappointments along the way. May a Tibetan bhikṣuṇī saṅgha be born soon!

I agree with the two options clearly explained by Bhikkhu Bodhi. The dual-saṅgha method is preferable, but if you decide on following the single-saṅgha method, I will support that. According to the Vinaya, the bhikṣus have the responsibility to give bhikṣuṇī ordination when requested. On behalf of Buddhist women in general and Tibetan nuns in particular, Your Holiness, we request you to make history today.

Bhikṣuṇī Karma Lekshe Tsomo, University of San Diego. Ordained 1982

I think all of us were very heartened to hear a strong statement from Your Holiness in support of women's rights and for the full ordination of women in the Tibetan tradition. The advantages of a single ordination for the Tibetan nuns are that it will be convenient in terms of language, location, and custom, and will be more easily acceptable to the Tibetan community. Since bhikṣuṇīs do exist, it is not the ideal method, but the infraction involved for the ordaining bhikṣus is minor. The ordination might be criticized as partial, however, and there is no assurance that such a method would continue in the future.

Dual-saṅgha ordination would be more acceptable to the other nikāya traditions since it is found in all the Vinaya lineages; it would garner the recognition of bhikṣuṇī saṅghas worldwide. By involving Mūlasarvāstivāda bhikṣus, it would also gain the support of learned Tibetan scholars. Later, the ordination procedure could be switched to a dual saṅgha comprising both Mūlasarvāstivāda bhikṣus and bhikṣuṇīs.

In various places in Asia there has already been the precedent of single-saṅgha bhikṣuṇī ordination, as well as dual-saṅgha ordination involving two nikāyas. Both methods have been found to be valid and acceptable. After thirty years of research, we have all the information we need to decide which method is best at this time. For the welfare of the world, we hope that you will make a decision soon.

Bhikṣuṇī Jampa Tsedroen, University of Hamburg.
Ordained 1985

Thank you, Your Holiness. I do not have prepared comments, so I speak from my heart. It was exactly twenty-five years ago in 1982, when I was a one-year novice, that you gave your first public talk in Germany, in this very hall. At that time I first asked you about bhikṣuṇī ordination; you asked me whether I was in a hurry. After asking several more times over the next three years, you told me in 1985 that the time was right, and I went to Taiwan.

My ordination was by the bhikṣu saṅgha alone; bhikṣuṇīs were present but were not part of the saṅghakarma. I have sometimes feared that if single-saṅgha ordination were judged to be invalid, then my own ordination and that of many other bhikṣuṇīs would become nullified. My teacher, the late Ven. Geshe Thubten Ngawang, always told me I should not worry; if the bhikṣus acted incorrectly, it is they who get the infraction, not the bhikṣuṇīs. And we have many historical precedents for the single ordination, so I think this is not a significant concern.

The dual ordination is acceptable, too. As for those of us who have already ordained as Dharmaguptaka bhikṣuṇīs but wear the red robes of the Mūlasarvāstivāda, I think we all would be happy to become Mūlasarvāstivādins, if the possibility mentioned by Bhikkhu Bodhi of adopting us through an act of the saṅgha is accepted. If that is not acceptable, then recognize us as Dharmaguptaka bhikṣuṇīs and perform the dual ordination that way.

In either case, at the time of the bhikṣuṇī ordination of Mahāprajāpatī, there were no nikāyas, and when Buddhism came to Sri Lanka, it was not called "Theravāda." Therefore, let us not make the nikāya issue the major obstacle. There has already been the precedent of ordination by a mixed saṅgha of two nikāyas with the establishment of the Dharmaguptaka bhikṣuṇī ordination in China in 433 and the re-establishment of the Mūlasarvāstivāda bhikṣu ordination in Tibet with Gongpa Rapsal in the tenth century.

The research has been done, and so, in the Tibetan custom, I beg you, please make a decision now.

Bhikkhunī Kusuma Devendra, Founder of Ayya Khema International Buddhist Temple in Sri Lanka. Ordained 1996

My dear friends in the Dhamma, I have nothing more to add save that it is best to expedite this process. There is only one Vinaya. The one in Sri Lanka came from India in the third century B.C.E. and later traveled to China in the fifth century, from where it spread to the rest of East Asia. The procedure is essentially the same. Though I and other Sri Lankan nuns received our bhikkhunī vows from the Korean Dharmaguptakas, we practice according to the Pāli Vinaya. That is all we know, though we are ever grateful for the supportive relationships with our Korean and Taiwanese sisters. Such sharing promotes unity in the saṅgha; it has made me very comfortable with the nuns of all the Buddhist traditions.

Bhikkhunī Dhammānanda (Prof. Chatsumarn Kabilsingh). Ordained 2001

Before becoming a nun, I considered taking ordination in the Tibetan tradition, but there I could only become a sāmaṇerī, a novice nun. In my country, Thailand, novice vows are for those under twenty; if you are older than twenty and not fully ordained, then it is like you are not capable. The Tibetan tradition has sāmaṇerīs who are capable spiritually, physically, and mentally, so why should they stay sāmaṇerīs? That is why I contacted the Sri Lankan lineage and took ordination there.

The Aśokan pillars discovered over the last century across India date from the third century B.C.E. Of all the Aśokan pillars, the only pillar to have remained standing in its original location is the one in Vesālī, the place where the bhikkhunī saṅgha was first established. I believe this is an auspicious sign. We are missing the second column in our fourfold Buddhist saṅgha, and we must now replace it. Newly establishing bhikkhunī saṅgha where it has been discontinued will strengthen and uplift Buddhism.

All the beautiful teachings in Buddhism are a source of so much peace. Why should we deny our spiritual sisters the same access to these beautiful teachings afforded the bhikkhus? We cannot wait any longer; it is urgent that our practice match the teachings.

Venerable Lobsang Dechen, Co-Director of the Tibetan Nuns Project

The main thing I want to say is thank you to Your Holiness for supporting the goal of bhikṣuṇī ordination from the very beginning. Re-establishing the Mūlasarvāstivāda bhikṣuṇī ordination is important not just to the Tibetan women here but for Tibetans worldwide, both inside and outside Tibet, and for those of future generations. I hear that in the West, people have no time even to eat or drink, so I am especially grateful to all the Vinaya holders and scholars who have come so far to spend three days discussing this issue and demonstrating their support.

As Professor Samdhong Rinpoche outlined, many years of research have narrowed down the options to single ordination and double ordination, neither of which is a perfect solution in terms of the Vinaya code. Having heard all these discussions and the objections, we Tibetan nuns feel that since neither solution is a perfect one, we would prefer to have single ordination through our own Mūlasarvāstivāda tradition. Please, Your Holiness and the Tibetan saṅgha, it is in your hands to decide.

Response by His Holiness the Dalai Lama

Spiritual brothers and sisters, I am extremely happy to hear from bhikṣus and bhikṣuṇīs of different Buddhist traditions from around the world all in favor of introducing and establishing bhikṣuṇī ordination. It is really a great encouragement. As I mentioned this morning, this has been a serious concern of mine since the 1960s, and such a meeting as this I have dreamed of and encouraged for a long time, but it has not materialized until today. Thank you for organizing this event.

First off, I just want to make clear that we all accept and recognize as bhikṣuṇīs those Tibetans and Westerners who have received Dharmaguptaka bhikṣuṇī ordination. This is not the issue. The issue is to find the way to ordain bhikṣuṇīs that is in accordance with the Mūlasarvāstivāda Vinaya texts. There needs to be a Buddha alive and here and now to ask. If I were a Buddha, I could decide; but that is not the case. I am not a Buddha. I can act as a dictator regarding some issues, but not regarding matters of Vinaya.

For instance, I can institute that the Tibetan bhikṣuṇīs ordained in the Dharmaguptaka tradition meet in groups to perform the three saṅgha rituals.[5] Recently, a Korean who ordained as a bhikṣuṇī asked me whether she could join the bimonthly *sojong* confession ritual with the bhikṣus, but we need to have separate ceremonies for bhikṣus and bhikṣuṇīs, according to the Vinaya. This is something we can organize now. But as for re-establishing the ordination ceremony, this is a different matter. Although I may wish for this to happen, it requires the consensus of the senior monks. Some of them have offered strong resistance. There is not unanimous agreement and that is the problem. However, I can have the appropriate texts for the Dharmaguptaka versions of these three saṅgha rituals translated from Chinese into

5. These three are the bimonthly *sojong* purification of transgressions (*gso sbyong*, Skt. *poṣadha*, Pāli: *uposatha*), the installation of the summer retreat (*dbyar sbyor*, Skt. *varṣopanāyikā*, Pāli: *vassūpanāyikā*), and the parting from the restrictions of the summer retreat (*dgag dbye*, Skt. *pravāraṇā*, Pāli: *pavāraṇā*).

Tibetan immediately and encourage the Tibetan bhikṣuṇīs to begin doing these practices as a community. With the support of the other bhikṣus here, I can say that much; no one will oppose that.

As for other aspects, we need more discussion. The support from the saṅgha of other Buddhist traditions is important, and so this meeting is a helpful stage in the process. The recognition of Tibetan bhikṣuṇīs is already there, and there have traditionally been female Tibetan teachers and tulkus. And as I often respond when questioned, it is even entirely possible for the next Dalai Lama to be a woman, if in that form the Dalai Lama will be more effective, more attractive! That is not a problem.

The Buddhadharma in general is very flexible, and the Buddhadharma as a whole has to respond to reality. Based on the common-sense viewpoint, I am 100 percent certain that were the Buddha here today, he would give permission for bhikṣuṇī ordination. That would make things much easier. Unfortunately there is no Buddha here, and I cannot act as the Buddha.

Ven. Dhammānanda: Your Holiness, in the Mahāparinirvāṇa-sūtra, *the Buddha on his deathbed tells his followers that minor rules can be emended by the the saṅgha; they don't need to wait for the future Buddha.*

His Holiness: That's true, and that's why I have to ask the saṅgha. I wish the participants here could come to India and discuss the matter with those Tibetans who are a bit narrow-minded and who along with their supporters oppose re-establishment of the Mūlasarvāstivāda bhikṣuṇī ordination.

Ven. Thich Quang Ba: Your Holiness, you yourself made it clear that you have worked so hard to support this idea over the past forty or more years; the time to make a milestone decision is now. Which method is used is of secondary importance—this can be left to the council of elders—but as the leader of the saṅgha, you can accept this request and declare that bhikṣuṇī ordination will start today or at some specific time in the future. The question of method can even be left open-ended; in Vietnam, where we have had bhikkhunī ordination for two thousand years, we still make use of single-saṅgha ordination from time to time. Both methods are valid.

His Holiness: Although monasticism has been in Tibet since the eighth century, there have never been bhikṣuṇīs among us doing the three saṅgha rituals, so now this will happen. But it is too soon to decide about the ordination.

It may be difficult to start these three bhikṣuṇī saṅgha rituals for this year's retreat season, but by next year we should be able to begin. The Dharmaguptaka *Bhikṣuṇī Prātimokṣa* and *Bhikṣuṇī Ordination Rite* are already available in Tibetan translation. The Tibetan Dharmaguptaka bhikṣuṇīs will need to learn the *Bhikṣuṇī Prātimokṣa* by heart. But the actual ritual texts for the three saṅgha rituals still need to be translated.[6]

Ven. Karma Lekshe Tsomo: We are very happy to hear Your Holiness saying that these three rituals should be instituted and we can practice them if we are willing to learn the Bhikṣuṇī Prātimokṣa *by heart. Many of us are over sixty and were raised by television and comics, but if you think this will bring ordination into the Tibetan tradition, we will certainly do our best. The Dharmaguptaka version is a bit shorter—in the book in English translation that I sent you, you can see that the Dharmaguptaka prātimokṣa has only 348 precepts whereas the Mūlasarvāstivāda prātimokṣa has 364, so it would be a little shorter for us to memorize the Dharmaguptaka prātimokṣa. But which would really be best for bringing this into Tibetan? Will you prefer that we bring the Mūlasarvāstivāda in?*

His Holiness: We do recognize the validity of the bhikṣuṇī ordination taken in the Dharmaguptaka lineage, but I am suggesting that these rituals be conducted separately according to the Dharmaguptaka tradition. Once the Dharmaguptaka bhikṣuṇī rituals are conducted in Tibetan, then it will become a living Tibetan tradition. Although they need to conduct their rituals according to Dharmaguptaka, those Dharmaguptaka bhikṣuṇīs are welcome to read and study the Mūlasarvāstivāda bhikṣuṇī vows. However, the issue of non-bhikṣuṇīs not being able to study these vows remains.

6. According to the Tibetan Department of Religion and Culture (personal communication May 15, 2009, and June 1, 2009) with regard to conducting the three basic rituals by bhikṣuṇīs in line with the Dharmaguptaka tradition, the DRC has consulted and met with the president of the Tibetan Nuns Project, Rinchen Khando Choegyal. Eight nuns from Tilokpur Nunnery in Dharamsala have taken full ordination in the Dharmaguptaka tradition, but of these, two have passed away and one is in the United States, and thus only five could be traced. So far no gathering of these nuns has taken place, and the necessary translations have not been undertaken due to the lack of competent translators trained in Vinaya, Buddhist Chinese, and Tibetan.

Ven. Bodhi: The point in having the Tibetan bhikṣus recognize those who are ordained according to Dharmaguptaka Vinaya is to accept them as Mūlasarvāstivāda bhikṣuṇīs so that they can constitute a bhikṣuṇī saṅgha to perform the dual-saṅgha ordination. If the Tibetan bhikṣus recognize the bhikṣuṇīs as Dharmaguptaka bhikṣuṇīs but say they cannot perform a dual-saṅgha ordination, then there is no point in recognizing their Dharmaguptaka ordination; you are not creating the conditions for holding the bhikṣuṇī ordination. If I may use a secular analogy, it is like saying at the university: oh yes, women can work at the university, but they cannot serve as professors.

His Holiness: Although the Tibetan nuns may wish for ordination as Mūlasarvāstivāda bhikṣuṇīs, the Dharmaguptaka bhikṣuṇī ordination cannot be accepted as a Mūlasarvāstivāda one. If the two were interchangeable, then there would have been no reason for Atiśa to have been asked not to confer Mahāsāṅghika bhikṣu ordination in Tibet.[7] Further, if a Dharmaguptaka ordination were a Mūlasarvāstivāda ordination, then a Theravāda ordination would also be a Mūlasarvāstivāda ordination and this would be absurd. All Tibetan Buddhists respect the bhikṣus from the Theravāda tradition as Buddhist bhikṣus, no problem. Similarly we wholeheartedly recognize the Dharmaguptaka bhikṣuṇīs as bhikṣuṇīs. The question is whether a monk ordained according to a particular tradition's vows can confer that ordination; this is the problem. We need to re-establish the Mūlasarvāstivāda bhikṣuṇī ordination purely according to the Mūlasarvāstivāda Vinaya.

Ven. Jampa Tsedroen: Allowing the recitation of the Dharmaguptaka version of the three rituals does not solve the bigger problem. It is a big step forward, but it leaves many practical obstacles intact. Say, for instance, we developed a large bhikṣuṇī saṅgha of Western and Tibetan nuns near Dharamsala. On our own we could ordain śikṣamāṇās and śrāmaṇerikās, but if we accept śikṣamāṇās, then after two years, we would be obliged to offer bhikṣuṇī ordination as well. The Tibetan bhikṣus who live nearby would not be able to help us—we would have to bring in bhikṣus from the Dharmaguptaka tradition. Then, we would

7. When the Indian master Atiśa was invited to Tibet by King Jangchup Ö in the early eleventh century, the king's grandfather, King Yeshé Ö, had already sponsored the revival of the Mūlasarvāstivāda bhikṣu ordination in his kingdom with the invitation and subsequent visit there by the East Indian master Dharmapāla. Atiśa was requested not to confer Mahāsāṅghika bhikṣu ordination, since that would have introduced two Vinaya lineages to Tibet.

have to figure out what language to perform the ceremony in, and it would get very complicated. It would really be better to do it with the Tibetan bhikṣus.
Samdhong Rinpoche: Whatever step we take next, there are going to be complications and training issues that will need to be resolved gradually. From the administrative side, we are determined to work toward the restoration of the bhikṣuṇī order. Therefore, this announcement by His Holiness is an important milestone and a step toward fulfilling the larger intention; we don't have to work out all the implications today. Let us work a little more, and at an appropriate stage, all things may become clear.

Comments by His Holiness at an Audience for Congress Delegates the Following Day

It is really wonderful that this panel of international Buddhist saṅgha was able to convene on the topic of bhikṣuṇī ordination. It really moves the issue forward. Actually, the Buddha himself already decided this issue. It is just up to us in those Buddhist countries without bhikṣuṇī ordination to find a way to introduce it.

I have two suggestions. As far as I know, the saṅghas in Thailand and also Sri Lanka, Burma, and Cambodia have some kind of leader, a *saṅgharāja*. My first suggestion would be to get a letter of endorsement from the saṅgharāja of each of these countries in favor of reinstating bhikṣuṇī ordination. If not the highest monk, then at least someone prominent. If they support bhikṣuṇī ordination in their own countries, this becomes an important kind of moral support for the Tibetan cause.

My second suggestion is that this winter, we hold a conference similar to this one, but in India—either in Bodhgaya or Sarnath, or in Delhi or somewhere like that. In addition to the international saṅgha elders, we will invite all the top Tibetan saṅgha leaders and all the abbots of the major monasteries of all four Tibetan traditions. Maybe we even include the Bönpos. Since the Bönpos still have bhikṣuṇīs, it might be easier to introduce the bhikṣuṇī vow from the Bön tradition! Of course, that is not actually feasible, but when I went to their center recently I told them how easy they have it! Anyway, we should invite the senior, most respected bhikṣu scholars, perhaps a hundred altogether. Then I would request the international elders to state before them, in person, their reasonable arguments in favor of re-establishing bhikṣuṇī ordination. This would be very, very useful. We Tibetans can finance such a conference; you should decide who would be best to organize it.[8]

I'd like to give a little background on our fifty years of experience with this issue. As you know, the Buddhist scriptures have three sections: Vinaya, Sūtra, and Abhidharma. Abhidharma is in general more open to interpretation, and over many centuries, differences developed between the Pāli and Sanskrit versions of Abhidharma. Nāgārjuna, for instance, collected and emphasized certain points, and likewise we can also investigate Abhidharma teachings in light of scientific observation. So although Vasubandhu in his *Abhidharmakośa* mentions Mount Meru, says that the earth is flat, and says that the sun and moon are nearly the same size and same distance from the earth, we know today that these are unacceptable. When I was still in Lhasa, I would look at the moon with the telescope that belonged to the Thirteenth Dalai Lama. Traditionally, we were taught that the moon produced its own light, but even my own tutors in Lhasa saw, through my telescope, shadows from the mountains on the moon and had to agree that the moon did not give off its own light. Like Nāgārjuna, we have the liberty to accept such revisions on the basis of our own investigation. Since it is an individual prerogative, we don't need an act of the saṅgha.

The sūtras are such that questions of revision do not really come into play, but it is a little different when it comes to the Vinaya. Whereas in the Abhidharma texts, the opening salutation is made to Mañjuśrī, the bodhisattva of wisdom, all translations of the Vinaya texts begin "I prostrate to the Omniscient One." This salutaion to the Omniscient One, the Buddha, means that only an omniscient Buddha knows what actions are to be practiced and what actions are to be abandoned according to the Vinaya rules. No one else has the power to make that decision. That salutation therefore serves a very specific purpose in relation to the Vinaya. Still we know

8. Later the same day, the organizers of the conference, members of the Committee of the Western Bhikṣuṇīs, and the director and co-director of the Tibetan Nuns Project agreed that it would be impossible to organize such a conference as soon as that winter. Everybody had agreed that it would be good to have the conference one year later, in winter 2008–2009, perhaps at the Central Insititute of Higher Tibetan Studies in Sarnath, India. On December 25, 2009, in response to an inquiry, the Department of Religion and Culture informed Bhikṣuṇī Jampa Tsedroen that discussions about holding a hundred Vinaya scholars conference were held with representatives of the Tibetan Nuns Project, but no plans had yet been confirmed.

that, historically, after the Buddha's passing, saṅgha councils were held that made some alterations to the Vinaya. When the Buddha was approaching his last days, he gave permission for this to be done, and this allowance can be extended to other points as situations arise.

For example, we Tibetans practice the Vinaya within both Mahāyāna and Vajrayāna contexts, and each vehicle has its sets of vows. These points and precepts could theoretically contradict each other, in which case the higher vow would take precedence over the lower. This is the background.

As I mentioned yesterday, I think men and women in prehistoric societies were probably more equal in status. Then, as societies became more complex with armies and wars, the physical power of the men came to be more central. As societies progressed further still, education and the brain became more important, and in this sphere, sex differences are a much smaller factor; in modernity, intellectual brilliance has been prized. In this same period, from the seventeenth through the twentieth centuries, the concept of war and therefore hero worship was still there, some emphasis on physical power remained. But now, in the twenty-first century, war is obsolete. We need conflict resolution, and the capacity to respect different perspectives, take others' rights seriously, and find ways to promote the spirit of dialogue. The root of these vital skills is compassion, warm-heartedness. Whether due to biological or cultural factors, women seem to have more sensitivity to the feelings and suffering of others. Intelligence is good, but without compassion, it can create enormous problems. It must be bound with warm-heartedness to foster a more peaceful society, and for this, women's involvement I think will be crucial. I'm not saying this to flatter you.

In the area of religion, yes, sometimes women are sidelined, though I think Buddhism is better on this score, since the Buddha gave equal rights for full ordination to both sexes. The fourfold community of Buddha's disciples—bhikṣus, bhikṣuṇīs, upāsakas, and upāsikās—is so precious. But, at present among the Tibetans, the fourfold community is incomplete. With one part missing, it is only an approximation. Tibetan lamas have been noting this for centuries.

Among the eighteen qualities of a precious human rebirth, one is being born in a central land. This can be defined in two ways. Geographically, Tibet is not the central land, since that just means India. Defined in terms of Buddhadharma, however, a land is central if and only if the fourfold community of disciples is complete; thus Tibet is not a central land and birth there is not a precious human rebirth. In effect, Tibetans have been saying that if bhikṣus are present, that suffices to make it a central land, because bhikṣus are the most important of the four groups. Clearly it is a central place for the Dharma, they say. But that is just a similitude of a central land and doesn't qualify fully. The early masters should have taken this more seriously and made greater effort to ensure the bhikṣuṇī vow was introduced in Tibet.

Now, for my personal experience. When we first arrived in India, we took a serious look at the conditions for nuns. To improve educational opportunities for nuns does not rely on the consent of a saṅgha group. So, at that time, we began a program for training nuns in Buddhist philosophy, and that has now reached a high level. At one gathering at the monasteries at Mundgod in South India, I announced that since we had started the study program for nuns, we needed to make preparations for a geshema examination. A senior monk, the leader of one of the traditions, was skeptical, but I insisted that since Buddha offered men and women the equal right to become bhikṣus and bhikṣuṇīs, why not the equal right to become geshes and geshemas? He just remained silent. I don't think this senior monk was being particularly negative; he was just not accustomed to this line of thinking.

Here's another story. In the sixties, I told the nuns they could join in the bimonthly *sojong* (*poṣadha*) ceremony along with the novice monks in Dharamsala. In those years, there were no bhikṣuṇīs, and the śrāmaṇerikās didn't have anything to do during the confession ceremony. So, I consulted with my two tutors, and we decided to start doing that.[9] There were some sarcastic remarks from the big monasteries in South India about how monks

9. No one who is not fully ordained is allowed to stay during the actual sojong, which is the recitation of the *Prātimokṣa-sūtra*. His Holiness is refering here to the confession and remedy ritual of the novices, for which they are called in following the bhikṣus' remedy rite. They have to leave before the recitation of the *Prātimokṣa-sūtra*. In Dharamsala novice nuns have been allowed to join that part together with the novice monks since the 1980s. According to the Vinaya, they are to perform this rite in front of bhikṣuṇīs, but these do not exist in the Tibetan tradition.

and nuns now did sojong together in Dharamsala. But no monk or nun has ever disrobed because of that!

Now regarding the movement to restore the bhikṣuṇī vow, I think the first Tibetan took bhikṣuṇī ordination from the Chinese tradition in the 1960s, and it has been steadily growing since then. One of the main reasons for my visit to Taiwan was to see for myself the bhikṣuṇī lineage there and check on its situation, and I had discussions with Taiwanese bhikṣus and bhikṣuṇīs on several occasions. Among Tibetans ourselves, we also had quite a few discussions, and we appointed Tashi Tsering to do research about the bhikṣuṇī vow, which he has done now for more than twenty years. We have made the maximum effort.[10]

I requested the main Taiwanese bhikṣus who give bhikṣuṇī ordination regularly to organize an international saṅgha meeting, but that never materialized. Some time back, I myself suggested we convene such a meeting in Switzerland, but we could not invite Buddhist leaders from Sri Lanka, Burma, or Thailand, because as soon as the Dalai Lama's name is there, difficulties arise. They always come! It is better if another organization convenes such a meeting, and now Jampa Tsedroen and her organization have done that. That is wonderful, wonderful! All that an individual monk can do we have done. Now we need broad monastic consensus from the Tibetan bhikṣu elders. Unfortunately, that is not in my power.

As I said, I think a meeting this winter could be very helpful. One thing the organizers should keep in mind is that it is not sufficient to just introduce the bhikṣuṇī vow; one has to consider subsequent issues as well. One example is identifying the proper objects of reverence. In the novice monk ordination rite, it says that one should know which objects are objects of reverence and service. It is said that although bhikṣuṇīs are superior in terms of the vow itself, they are not objects of reverence for novice monks. We have to look at this in the wider perspective of the bodhisattva and tantric vows, especially the tantric vows, wherein it is considered a downfall if you don't show respect and proper deference to women. From that point of view, women clearly are objects of reverence and service. So, the

10. According to the Tibetan Department of Religion and Culture, Geshe Tashi Tsering retired and ended his contract term as researcher in August 2009 and no new researcher for bhikṣuṇī ordination has been confirmed.

prātimokṣa commitment, when it says that holders of the bhikṣuṇī vow are not objects of reverence, is in tension with the higher tantric vow. Thus, in maintaining the three sets of vows, some minor points may also need to be modified. I hope there can be some open discussion of these issues, recognizing that we are practitioners of all three vehicles.

As I mentioned yesterday, were the Buddha here, he would certainly make the modification. But I cannot do that. If you don't understand that, then all the blame comes to me, and it looks like I am blocking this effort. That is not the case. If you look at the last thirty to forty years, I have always taken the female side. Since I have the name Dalai Lama, there are some issues I can decide, without regard for what people might say, even if they threaten me. If I feel it is in line with Buddhist principles, I can decide based on reason and scripture. But Vinaya is different. It doesn't have to be 100 percent consensus, but it has to be a good majority of those senior respected monks in support. We could probably find the ten bhikṣus necessary to perform a bhikṣuṇī ordination today, but when it comes to re-establishing the Mūlasarvāstivāda bhikṣuṇī ordination, it is extremely important that we avoid a split in the saṅgha. We need a broad consensus within the Tibetan saṅgha as a whole, and we need to address not only bhikṣuṇī ordination but subsequent issues as well.

Now it's time to go. I thank you all for your efforts. See you again!

Statement of His Holiness the Dalai Lama on Bhikṣuṇī Ordination in the Tibetan Tradition

Hamburg University, Germany
July 18–20, 2007

- The Buddha taught a path to enlightenment and liberation from suffering for all sentient beings and people of all walks of life, to women as well as men, without discrimination as to class, race, nationality, or social background.
- For those who wished to fully dedicate themselves to the practice of his teachings, he established a monastic order that included both a bhikṣu saṅgha, an order of monks, and a bhikṣuṇī saṅgha, an order of nuns.

- For centuries, the Buddhist monastic order has thrived throughout Asia and has been essential to the development of Buddhism in all its diverse dimensions—as a system of philosophy, meditation, ethics, religious ritual, education, culture, and social transformation.
- While the bhikṣu ordination lineage still exists in almost all Buddhist countries today, the bhikṣuṇī ordination lineage exists only in some countries. For this reason, the fourfold Buddhist community (of bhikṣus, bhikṣuṇīs, upāsakas, and upāsikās) is incomplete in the Tibetan tradition. If we can introduce bhikṣuṇī ordination within the Tibetan tradition, that would be excellent in order to have the fourfold Buddhist community complete.
- In today's world, women play major roles in all aspects of secular life, including government, science, medicine, law, arts, humanities, education, and business. Women are also keenly interested in participating fully in religious life, receiving religious education and training, acting as role models, and contributing fully to the development of human society. In the same way, nuns and followers of Tibetan Buddhism around the world are keenly interested in full ordination for nuns within the Tibetan tradition.
- Given that women are fully capable of achieving the ultimate goal of the Buddha's teachings, in harmony with the spirit of the modern age, the means and opportunity to achieve this goal should be completely accessible to them.
- The most effective means and opportunity for achieving this goal is full ordination (*upasaṃpadā*) as a bhikṣuṇī and full participation in the life of a community of bhikṣuṇīs, that is, a bhikṣuṇī saṅgha in their practice tradition.
- Full ordination for women will enable women to pursue wholeheartedly their own spiritual development through learning, contemplating, and meditating, and also enhance their capacities to benefit society through research, teaching, counseling, and other activities to help extend the life of the Buddhadharma.

On the basis of the above considerations, and after extensive research and consultation with leading Vinaya scholars and saṅgha members of the Tibetan tradition and Buddhist traditions internationally, and with the backing of the Tibetan Buddhist community, since the 1960s, I express my full support for the establishment of the bhikṣuṇī saṅgha in the Tibetan tradition.

Within the Tibetan community, we have been striving to raise the standards of nuns in terms of education. We have introduced Buddhist philosophical studies and also worked to introduce the bestowal of a geshe degree (highest academic degree of monastic studies) for nuns as well. I am pleased that we have been successful in accomplishing these aims to a great extent.

I also believe that, since a bhikṣuṇī saṅgha has long been established in the East Asian Buddhist traditions (of China, Taiwan, Vietnam, and Korea) and is presently being revived in the Theravāda tradition of South Asia (especially Sri Lanka), the introduction of the bhikṣuṇī saṅgha within the Tibetan Buddhist tradition should be considered seriously and favorably.

But in terms of the modality of introducing bhikṣuṇī vows within the tradition, we have to remain within the boundaries set by the Vinaya—otherwise, we would have introduced the bhikṣuṇī vow in the Tibetan Buddhist tradition a long time ago.

There are already nuns within the Tibetan tradition who have received the full bhikṣuṇī vow according to the Dharmaguptaka lineage and who we recognize as fully ordained. One thing we can do now is to translate the three primary monastic activities (*poṣadha*, *varṣa*, and *pravāraṇā*) from the Dharmagupta lineage into Tibetan and encourage the Tibetan bhikṣuṇīs to do these practices as a bhikṣuṇī saṅgha.

I hope that these combined efforts of all Buddhist traditions bear fruit.

The Buddhist bhikṣu Tenzin Gyatso,
the Dalai Lama

From left to right: Bhikkhunī Kusuma Devendra, Geshe Rinchen Ngodrup, Bhikkhu Dhammavihari Thero, Ven. Khammai Dhammasami, Bhikkhu Bodhi, Bhikṣu Huimin Shih, Bhikṣu Thich Quang Ba, Bhikkhu Sujato (obscured), Prajna Bangsha Bhikshu Mahathero, Bhikṣu Samdhong Rinpoche, H.H. the Dalai Lama, Bhikṣuṇī Myongsong Sunim, Bhikṣuṇī Wu Yin, Bhikkhunī Dhammānanda, Bhikṣuṇī Heng-ching Shih, Bhikṣuṇī Jendy Shih, Bhikkhunī Thich Nu Hue Huong, Bhikṣuṇī Karma Lekshe Tsomo, Ven. Lobsang Dechen, Bhikṣuṇī Jampa Tsedroen (photo by Holger Gross)

Gender Equity and Human Rights

Karma Lekshe Tsomo

IN THE PAST fifty years, efforts to bring women into the mainstream of human society have greatly accelerated. Advances have been made in many areas due to the courage and conscientious efforts of women and men. Yet, unfortunately, the idea of equal rights remains a dream for women in most societies. Outdated attitudes about women's nature and potential continue to keep women at a disadvantage politically, economically, educationally, and in religion. Gender equality is a key principle of the United Nations Declaration of Human Rights and U.N. Resolution 1325. Despite this, gender discrimination continues in all human societies. The failure to adequately educate one half of the world's population reflects this discrimination, leading to enormous human suffering the world over, especially for women and children.

The religious traditions that help shape society's attitudes toward women and also women's attitudes toward themselves often send mixed messages. The world's major religions—Buddhism, Hinduism, Christianity, Judaism, and Islam—assert that women and men have equal potential, whether for liberation or in the sight of a higher being, but social realities reveal a stark contradiction between rhetoric and reality. Women continue to lack equal representation in social, political, and religious institutions. For many, the failure of the world's religions to live up to their professed ideals not only exposes their lack of social responsiveness to the needs of human society but is also hypocritical.

Contemporary human rights debates raise two important issues. The first issue is political: Is the language of human rights applicable to all human beings across cultures and societies or does it grow out of a specific context or dynamic, such that it may not be applicable to all? For example, the People's Republic of China maintains that the concept of human rights was framed in a European context and is a Western imposition on non-European cultures, whereas many others, including His Holiness the Dalai Lama, feel that human rights are universal and follow naturally from concepts of compassion and interrelatedness. The second issue raised in the human rights debate is philosophical: What is the nature of human rights and to whom do they apply?

Three major critiques of contemporary human rights philosophy can be leveled. The first is that the human rights doctrine is simply an abstract concept, divorced from real human needs. Yet the doctrine *does* speak to human needs and inequities. The United Nations has documented that 60 percent of the work in the world is done by women, but only 20 percent of the wealth in the world belongs to women and only one percent of the land. It is clear that woman are not only concerned about abstract concepts such as the right to "life, liberty, freedom of expression, and equality before the law; and social, cultural, and economic rights," but also about such very real needs as food and education.

The second critique is that contemporary human rights doctrine is a Western theory and therefore its application is a Western imposition rooted in Western hegemony. While it can legitimately be argued that human rights theory is of Western origin, rooted in European enlightenment thinking and secular humanist ideals, that does not render it a cultural imposition. No matter what their origins, human rights are equally applicable to human beings of all descriptions and capabilities. No one in any culture or society wishes to be deprived of adequate food, shelter, health, or education. All thinking people value the freedom to think as they wish, believe as they wish, and associate with whom they wish. As a bhikṣuṇī from Hong Kong once told me, "Even birds and dogs want to be free. Why shouldn't human beings also want to be free?"

The third major critique is that contemporary human rights doctrine is an unattainable dream. Because human beings are selfish, this argument goes, there will always be those who take more than they need; human beings naturally grab power and wealth and some may even leave others without. Statistically, there *is* enough food for the world's population; it simply is not distributed equitably. The sufferings of the world are largely due to inequalities in the distribution of resources. The disproportionate poverty of women and children is a glaring instance. As a whole, women are the poorest, hungriest, least educated, least enfranchised, and most vulnerable human beings on Earth. To address gender inequalities is therefore of crucial importance in implementing human rights theory in actual practice.

Buddhists around the world contend that Buddhism is an equal opportunity religion and proudly declare that enlightenment is equally available to everyone, whether female or male. But barriers to women's education and ordination reveal that women are not institutionally equal, either in theory or practice. Even if women are assumed to have equal potential to achieve liberation or enlightenment, do they truly have equal opportunities to realize that potential?

Philosophically, Buddhists claim that all sentient beings have the potential to achieve liberation or enlightenment. The logic of this affirmation is straightforward. Liberation or enlightenment is achieved by purifying one's mind of all mental afflictions. All beings who possess consciousness, whether they are female or male, are capable of these goals. Yet, the process of purifying one's consciousness requires knowledge and conducive conditions for practice. The process of mental cultivation or spiritual development is traditionally framed as hearing, contemplating, and meditating on the Buddha's teachings. Although all sentient beings (beings with consciousness) theoretically have the potential to achieve liberation or enlightenment, it is obvious that beings in unfortunate states of existence face so many obstacles that it is virtually impossible for them to attain these goals while in those states. Beings in unfortunate states of existence are said to achieve the fruits of the path *eventually*, but it is only as a human being endowed with sufficient intelligence, leisure, and opportunity that one is able to realize that potential.

Does this mean that some sentient beings have a greater chance than others of attaining enlightenment? The answer would have to be yes. Because the circumstances for achieving enlightenment differ markedly for beings in different circumstances, some have a better chance than others to realize their potential. For example, although all sentient beings are said to have the potential to purify their minds and achieve awakening, the probability of a frog realizing that potential is vastly different from the probability of a human being born into a devoutly religious family in a Buddhist society where all the knowledge and facilities for achieving awakening are available.

Similar reasoning can be applied when questioning the potentials of women and men. Since all sentient beings can achieve enlightenment and women are sentient beings, it follows that women have the potential to achieve enlightenment. The question is whether women have equal opportunities to realize that potential. Of course, the probability of women realizing that potential depends on their individual circumstances. Women may possess a precious human rebirth but be constrained by social and cultural factors, such as early childhood conditioning (for example, to bear and care for children), preconceptions of incapability (internalized oppression), and special religious restrictions (the eight gurudharmas, or special rules for Buddhist nuns). These social, cultural, and religious constraints, which often do not apply to men, may impede women's ability to realize the goals of the path. Although women are assured of their equal potential for awakening, in actuality, women's probability of achieving this goal may differ markedly from men's due to myriad constraints. Chief among the constraints facing women in Buddhist societies are fewer opportunities to receive systematic Buddhist education and fewer opportunities to receive ordination, especially full ordination.

A question remains about whether these constraints derive from the words of the Buddha or from social expectations and religious bureaucracies. In essence, the central concern for Buddhists is the purification of consciousness and consciousness has no gender. The aim is to eliminate suffering, and there is no question that women suffer equally and perhaps significantly more than men. The sufferings of women are not only due to factors of women's physical nature, which traditionally is portrayed as weaker; women's sufferings are also due to gender-biased restrictions and gender-based violence. Even when women develop a strong determination to purify their consciousness of all defilements, as instructed, they are often denied access to the required knowledge and conditions for practice that would enable them to do so.

Women are often counseled to accept the reality of gender discrimination and deal with it humbly, as a form of practice. However, men are rarely taught to reflect on the mental afflictions associated with gender discrimination and antiquated attitudes toward women as a form of practice. Nuns are often told that the precepts of full ordination are very difficult to keep and that keeping eight or ten precepts is enough for them, yet monks are never advised to forgo full ordination and remain novices for life. In the Tibetan tradition, nuns are not allowed to study the Bhikṣuṇī Vinaya, the monastic codes for nuns, because they are not fully ordained, even though this knowledge is necessary to qualify for the *geshé* degree in philosophical studies. This restriction hinders women from achieving intellectual leadership in the tradition. Discrimination against women in monastic education and ordination deprives women of equal opportunities to hear, contemplate, and meditate on the Buddha's teachings. For these reasons, the lack of full inclusion for women in the monastic system is wrong both from a Buddhist perspective and from a human rights perspective.

The Buddha is said to have enjoined his followers to "see things as they really are." In this light, it is useful to recall that Buddhism developed in a Brahmanical cultural setting in ancient India in which women were thoroughly subordinate to men. In the traditional accounts, the Buddha initially hesitated to admit women to the saṅgha. One likely reason was concern for societal perceptions, to ensure that his teachings would not be discounted or rejected in a patriarchal culture. To allow women to leave their families and take up the saṅgha's mendicant lifestyle would have been so unusual, uncomfortable, and counter-cultural that it might have jeopardized social acceptance of the Buddha's teachings.

Today, we live in a vastly different society, one in which women are accepted as being fully human, entitled to all the rights and freedoms that other human beings enjoy. To assert women's inferiority or to limit women's admission to monastic orders on the basis of gender not only contravenes Buddhist ethics, it is sadly out of step with the times. If Buddhists today discriminate against women on the basis of gender, thinking people are likely to reject Buddhism as outdated, inconsistent, and invalid. To "see things as they really are" is to see that gender discrimination is both contradictory to Buddhist principles and contrary to the norms of enlightened societies. If women are excluded from religious institutions, then their access to religious knowledge is restricted. If women are restricted in their opportunities to hear, contemplate, and practice the Buddha's teachings—the keys to achieving spiritual realizations and awakening—then their potential for awakening is severely curtailed. To exclude women from full membership in the saṅgha—regarded as the best channel for realizing the fruits of the Buddhist path—is to deprive women of the optimum circumstances for becoming free from suffering. Loving kindness, a core Buddhist value, entails recognizing the immensity of human suffering caused by gender discrimination, both to individuals and to society. To exclude half the human population from the benefits of Buddhist practice contradicts both Buddhist wisdom and the spirit of compassion.

Twenty years ago, Sakyadhita ("Daughters of the Buddha") began a movement to give voice to women's concerns and deepest aspirations. Since then, the movement has become a catalyst for change in the lives of millions of women (and men) around the world. As women network and exchange ideas, they discover their diversity and the similar challenges they face as Buddhist practitioners. Being a Buddhist in Laos or Mongolia is very different from being a Buddhist in London or New York, but the experience of being a women unites Buddhists from vastly different cultures and backgrounds.

Since 1987, Buddhist women from around the world have begun to unite globally and to assume new roles in working for the welfare of human society. Representing an estimated 300 million women worldwide, the Buddhist women's movement has emerged from the shadows into the international spotlight as a highly dynamic force for social change. Given equal opportunities, Buddhist women have enormous potential to effect global transformation.

Working toward gender equity in Buddhism has not been easy. Denial and resistance persist. Advocates of gender equity have been denigrated, slandered, and intimidated, yet many have continued to move forward steadily and courageously—working to eradicate ignorance and discrimination. Yet even today, when the value of women's rights is taken for granted in most of the world, Buddhist women's efforts to achieve gender equity are often seen as threatening. Advocates are warned not to raise the topic of women's rights, because it might offend the monks. Since it is perfectly acceptable, even admirable, to champion human rights, why should championing women's rights be perceived as threatening?

Perhaps the liberation of Buddhist women is viewed as threatening because of their great numbers. But as His Holiness the Dalai Lama has said, "Peace can only last where human rights are respected, where people are fed, and where individuals and nations are free." Unfortunately, until Buddhist women's religious rights are respected by guaranteeing their right to receive full ordination, it cannot be said that Buddhism gives equal opportunities to women. Denying full ordination to women is not just a matter of monastic law and cannot be explained away simply as the influence of sexism in society. Buddhist institutions must recognize equal rights for women in order to be consistent with Buddhism's socially liberating message. Convinced by the logic of this reasoning, women have worked patiently to assume their full responsibilities as members of the Buddhist community, refusing to be silenced, and the results thus far have been very encouraging. The reinstitution of the bhikṣuṇī saṅgha in Sri Lanka in 1998, after a lapse of nearly a thousand years, was a landmark. The freedom to receive full ordination is not only in the best interests of women, it is in the best interests of society at large, since it helps optimize the potential of all human beings. The animated discussions on the ordination issue among scholars, practitioners, and human rights advocates in Hamburg was testimony to the gathering support for the social liberation of Buddhist women.

In traditional Buddhist parlence, human beings are composed of five aggregates or components: bodies, feelings, recognitions, karmic dispositions, and constantly changing streams of consciousness. Consciousness is the most significant aggregate, because it is central to perception and decision-making. Consciousness ("knowing and awareness") is affected by many factors, including education and socialization. The nature of consciousness itself is not characterized by gender, however. Over time, in the course of many lifetimes, sentient beings take male and female rebirths intermittently. Human beings have the capacity to transform their individual states of consciousness, regardless of whether they are female or male. Hence, from the perspective of consciousness, human development is not dependent on gender nor is gender intrinsic in human nature.

In today's troubled world, humanity's greatest hope is that a critical mass of the world's population will wake up and reject the images that make them willing slaves to power, money, violence, and greed. Global corporations, governments, and religious institutions will only change when people wake up and demand that they do so. Compassionate individuals have a responsibility to wake up and speak out in order to help correct social injustices.

Rights entail duties for women and men alike. In Asian societies where monks accept donations from laywomen, it follows that they then have an obligation toward their benefactors—a responsibility to respect the rights of women and to refrain from violating those rights—but also, I believe, a duty to speak out against injustices against women. What does it say if monks are willing to go to the streets to protest government taxation of monastic land holdings but remain silent about the trafficking of women and children? In societies where Buddhist notions of liberation from suffering are championed, the sufferings caused by the exclusion of women and the damage caused by perpetuating, over generations, the myth that women are a lower form of rebirth must be exposed and addressed.

What remedies do Buddhists have for resolving these issues? Similar to other religions, the Buddhist path offers the hope of a better future life and the possibility of liberation from suffering for those who practice virtue. Great emphasis is placed on engaging in wholesome actions and avoiding unwholesome actions, no matter how small. It may be argued that women are disadvantaged in the pursuit of virtue, however, since expectations for women are generally limited to domesticity or glamour, neither of which guarantees well-being in the afterlife or progress on the path to liberation. Yet if women should reject these expectations and dedicate their lives to religious pursuits instead, they often find their options limited. It is here that Buddhism may fail to deliver for women. The promised rewards of religious practice are the same for women as for men, but the means of obtaining those rewards are seriously circumscribed for women and often off-limits altogether. In denying opportunities to women, Buddhist institutions come into direct conflict with the human rights, such as the right to religious freedom, that women have been promised. This contradiction is not only an enormous disappointment to women who have come to expect better of Buddhist institutions; it is also an international embarrassment if Buddhist institutions perpetuate these inequalities.

In general, the term *human rights* denotes that human beings possess certain fundamental rights and freedoms. Religious rights and freedoms are typically regarded as among the most basic of all human rights. To practice the Dharma freely, all human beings, both female and male, need access to equal opportunities to learn and practice their religious beliefs and to pursue their religious goals. Just as countries who refuse women the right to vote are considered backward today, Buddhists will certainly go down on the wrong side of history if they deny fundamental rights and freedoms to women. Concurrently, it is evident that access to full ordination for women must go hand in hand with Buddhist education and community support for women in monastic life. Given equal opportunities for education and ordination, women promise to become pillars of the tradition, bringing many benefits to Buddhist societies and to human society as a whole. Recognizing full ordination for women is not only a matter of social justice, it is also simply a matter of common sense.

Appendix

Below find the supporting texts for David Jackson's article in this volume, "Preserving Endangered Ordination Traditions in the Sakya School."

Introduction

The Fifth Dalai Lama gives this lineage in his record of teachings received: Dalai bla ma V, Ngag dbang blo bzang rgya mtsho, *Zab pa dang rgya che ba'i dam pa'i chos kyi thob yig gang ga'i chu rgyun.* 4 vols. Delhi: N. Sonam Kazi, 1971. Vol. *ka*:

[9b] yongs rdzogs bstan pa'i mnga' bdag blo bzang chos kyi rgyal mtshan gyis mkhan po dang gsang ste ston pa'i slob dpon sbrags/ 'jam dbyangs bla ma dkon cog chos 'phel gyis las kyi slob dpon/ byes pa zhal snga nas byams pa smon lam gyis grib tshod pa/ chos sde chen po dpal ldan 'bras spungs kyi grva tshang bdun dang se ra theg chen gling gi grva tshang gsum gyi slob dpon lung sde snod gsum la rab tu sbyangs shing mngon rtogs bslab pa gsum gyis thugs rgyud yongs su gtams pa'i gnas brtan 'dul ba 'dzin pa bcu phrag gcig gis las kyi kha skong mdzad de bstan pa la zhugs la yongs su rdzogs pa dge slong gi dngos po legs par thob pa'i brgyud pa ni/ yang dag par rdzogs [10a] pa'i sangs rgyas shākya seng ga/ 'phags mchog sh'a ri'i bu/ sras sgra gcan 'dzin/ bram ze sgra gcan 'dzin/ dpal mgon 'phags pa klu sgrub/ slob dpon legs ldan 'byed/ dpal sbas/ ye shes snying po/ mkhan po zhi ba 'tsho/ sba ratna/ dmar shākya mu ni/ g.yor dge 'byung/ bla chen dgongs pa rab gsal/ spa gong ye shes g.yung drung/ grub

pa ye shes rgyal mtshan/ klu mes tshul khrims shes rab/ gzus rdo rje rgyal mtshan/ sne po grags pa rgyal mtshan/ 'bre shes rab 'bar/ bya brtson 'grus 'bar/ mkhan po gzhon nu seng ge/ gro bdud rtsi grags/ mchims nam mkha' grags/ mkhan po grags pa shes rab/ mchims blo bzang grags pa/ gro ston kun dga' rgyal mtshan/ dpang ston grub pa shes rab/ thams cad mkhyen pa dge 'dun grub/ gnas rnying chos rje kun dga' bde legs/ thams cad mkhyen pa dge 'dun rgya mtsho/ dga' ldan khri rin po che bde ba can pa dge legs dpal bzang/ thams cad mkhyen pa bsod nams rgya mtsho/ paṇ chen dam chos yar 'phel/ mkhan rin po che blo bzang chos kyi rgyal mtshan/ des bdag ngag dbang blo bzang rgya mtsho la bka' drin du stsal to// bla chen brgyud dang paṇ chen brgyud gnyis kar sras sgra gcan 'dzin dang bram ze sgra gcan 'dzin gyi bar du bla ma gzhan mi 'dug pa/ de bzhin gshegs pa mya ngan las 'das nas lo brgya dang bcu na mi rung ba'i gzhi bcu sun dbyung ba'i bka' bsdu bar pa'i tshe thams cad 'dod dang nor can sogs kun dka' [10b] bo'i slob ma sha stag gi dgra bcom pa bdun brgya 'dus pa las sras sgra gcan 'dzin sogs dngos su bzhugs par ma bshad/ bka' bsdu bar pa nas lo nyis brgya skor na rab tu byung ba'i mtshan bram ze sgra gcan 'dzin spyod pa la gshegs nas sa ra har grags pa byon par chos 'byung mang po las bshad pas dus mi mtshungs pa'i dbang gis bar der mkhan po gcig gnyis shig chad pa 'dra/ theg pa chen po'i skabs sprul pa bstan pa dang 'ja' lus rnyed nas rjes su bzung ba sogs bshad kyang 'dul ba'i lugs la lus tha mal du gnas pa sogs nges par dgos pas dag snang dang le shes kyi sku mjal bskad du byas na so thar gyi rang skad la chu bun gyis tshos rgyag par 'dug pas mkhyen ldan rnams kyis dpyod cig/karma pa rang byung rdo rje'i do ha'i lo rgyus su sras sgra gcan 'dzin la theg chen dpal gyi grags pas bsnyen par rdzogs/ de la sa ra has bsnyen par rdzogs par gsung ba rang byung zhabs mkhas grub chen po yin pas khungs dang 'brel ba zhig yin nam snyam gang ltar dpyad par bya'o// paṇ chen dam chos yar 'phel gyis thog mar shangs ston blo gros legs bzang la bsnyen par rdzogs/ des spos khang tshogs su bsnyen par rdzogs pa paṇ chen brgyud yin zhing slar thams cad mkhyen pa bsod nams rgya mtsho sog yul du thegs khar bskyar nas bsgrubs par brten so so'i blo dang mthun pa'i brgyud pa gnyis ka 'dren pa snang yang bskyar sgrub kyi dus sdom gsum rim gyis nos na dge bsnyen gyi sdom pa thob pa dang lhan du sngon ma [11a] gtong bas paṇ chen brgyud kyi dogs pa'ang med/ la la skal ba bzang bzang yin zer bsnyen rdzogs khe rkyang las mi sgrub pa'i rigs yong gi 'dug pa sdom pa sngon ma ma btang bar phyi ma mi skye bas bla chen brgyud 'ong don med cing/ 'di skor gyi mdzad tshul lo rgyus zhib pa mi 'dug pas brgyud pa gang yin the tshom gyi gzhir snang yang 'dir phyi ma btsan pa'i dbang du byas nas bgrangs kyi gang ltar byang sems dang sngags sdom ltar brgyud pa mang po chu bo gnyis 'dres su byed pa dpe 'dir bkab na so thar gzugs can gyi sdem pa yin pas 'dul ba'i chos skad 'jig pa'i skyon du 'gyur ro//

Ga bla ma 'Jam dbyangs rgyal mtshan

Sde gzhung sprul sku kun dga' bstan pa'i nyi ma. *Rje btsun bla ma 'jam dbyangs rgyal mtshan gyi rnam thar mdor bsdus bskal bzang rna rgyan.* New Delhi: T. G. Dhongthog Rinpoche, 1983:

[45] lcags lug lor ga gur rje nyid kyi sku dbon khang gsar mkhan po ngag dbang yon tan rgya mtsho dang/ mkhyen sprul chos kyi [46?] dbang phyug sogs la lam 'bras slob bshad thog ma gnang/ dus phyis zhig la brag ri rdo rje 'chang 'jam dbyangs chos kyi nyi ma'i zhal snga nas ngor chen sdom rgyun gyi bsnyen rdzogs sdom pa bskyar du zhus gnang/ de dus mkhan po bsam gtan blo gros kyi sku tsha ngag dbang lhun grub dang/ dar rtse mdo pa ngag dbang chos dar gnyis nas kyang sdom pa bskyar sgrub zhus par/ bla ma'i zhal nas/ ngas bstan 'dzin dbang grub las bsnyen rdzogs zhus nas bzung nyes ltung dri mas ma gos pas sdom pa 'bul mi bra yang 'du shes bsten lugs shig yod/ khyed gnyis kyi de 'dra shes mi 'ong bas sdom pa phul dang nyes med phun tshogs kyi yan lag tu legs gsungs/ 'di ni theg chen dge slong gi sdom pa bzhes pa gor ma chags shing/ dgongs gzhi ni/ bar lam zhig nas dpal e wang chos ldan na'ang kha che paṇ chen nas sa pan la brgyud pa'i dpal sa skya lha khang chen po'i sdom rgyun las/ ngor chen rdo rje 'chang kun dga' bzang po'i sdom rgyun chad la khad du gyur pas/ ngor chen sdom rgyun spel ba'i chad yin pa ste/ rje nyid kyi sku dbon khang gsar mkhan po ngag dbang yon tan rgya mtsho mkhan khrir phebs khar bsnyen rdzogs sdom pa gnang ste de phyin ngor pa'i sdom rgyun slar yang 'phel ba yin no/

The reception by Sapan of his full ordination is briefly mentioned in his biography by his senior disciple Lhopa Künkhyen Rinchen Pal (Lho pa kun mkhyen rin chen dpal) and probably in some later Sakya records of teachings received. Lho pa kun mkhyen rin chen dpal. *Dpal ldan sa skya paṇḍi ta'i rnam thar kun mkhyen rin chen dpal gyis mdzad pa* (*Biography of Sakya Pandita*). Contained in the *Lam 'bras slob bshad* (Dergé ed.), vol. *ka*, 38b–57a. As the biography states:

[98] de nas mkhas pa chen po de la gser dang dngul la sogs pa'i rin po che dang/ gos chen dang dar la sogs pa na bza'i rigs mang po dang/ gzhan zhabs 'bring pa la sogs pa rnam grangs du mas mnyes par mdzad nas/ slar yang sngar smos pa'i sdom brtson dam pa de'i thad du byon nas bdag nyid thog ma nas tshang par spyod pa dri ma med pa'i rgyan gyis kun nas spras shing/ bslab par bya ba ji snyed pa la rtsa ba dang yan lag

gi nyes pa phra zhing phra bas ma reg pa yin du zin kyang/ shākya'i rgyal po de'i bka' drin mi 'dor bar dgongs nas sdom brtson dam pa de la gsol ba btab ste/ lo ston rdo rje dbang phyug gis bzhengs pa dang smad rgyan gong zhes bya ba'i gtsug lag khang du/ rgya mtsho lta bu'i dge 'dun gyi dbus su bsnyen par rdzogs par mdzad nas/ de nyid kyi thad du yun ring du bzhugs shing rjes su 'brangs te/

Ngor chen kun dga' bzang po. *Thob yig rgya mtsho.* Sa skya pa'i bka' 'bum, vol. 9, pp. 44.4.1–108.2.6 (*ka* 90a–217a). Ngor chen's lineage is recorded in detail in his record of teachings received:

[45c] yang mkhan po chos kyi rje don gyi slad du mtshan nas smos te/ ye shes rgyal mtshan dpal bzang po pa dang/ las kyi slob dpon mkhan chen blo gros dpal ba dang/ gsang ste ston pa chos kyi rin po che 'phags pa gzhon nu blo gros dan/ grib tshod pa 'jam dbyangs dpal ldan gzhon nu la sogs pa/ dad pa'i dge 'dun bcu bdun gyi dbus su lcags pho 'brug rnam gnon gyi lo cho 'phrul chen po'i zla ba'i tshes brgyad kyi nyin snga dro'i cha grib tshod rkang ba gnyis dang skyes bu gcig gi dus su/ dpal ldan sa skya'i chos grwa chen por/ bstan bar rdzogs pa dang dge slong gi sdom pa rnam par dag pa thob ba'i brgyud pa ni/ yang dag par rdzogs pa'i sangs rgyas thub pa'i dbang po/ shā ri'i bu/ sras sgra gcan 'dzin/ bram ze sgra gcan 'dzin/ 'phags pa klu sgrub/ guṇa mitra/ rin chen bshes gnyen/ chos kyi bzang po/ guṇa pa ti/ chos kyi phreng ba/ 'byung gnas sbas pa/ paṇḍi ta chen po shākya shrī/ mkhas chen rdo rje dpal ba/ [45d] mkhan chen 'od zer dpal ba/ mkhan chen bsod nams dpal/ mkhan chen bkra shis tshul khrims/ chos rje ye shes rgyal mtshan dpal bzang po/ des bdag la'o/

Mang thos Klu sgrub rgya mtsho

Mangthö's *Rang gi rnam par thar pa yul sna tshogs kyi bdud rtsi myong ba'i gtam du byas pa zol rdzun gyis ma bslad pa sgeg mo'i me long, Lam 'bras slob bshad*, vol. 3 in Dergé edition, describes his first full ordination:

[432] glang lo dgun chos steng du mkhan chen bzang po bkra shis kyis mkhan po dang/ 'jam dbyangs bla ma phyogs las rnam rgyal gyis las slob mdzad/ mdo rtsa bar skal ba dang ldan pa'i rang bzhin can la bar chad ma dris par yang ngo zhes gsungs pa ltar de dus gsang ston med/ gri ba tshod kha skong dang bcas pa'i dbus su ngam ring chos gling bla brang du tshigs phyi ma bsnyen rdzogs kyi sdom pa thob/ sdom rgyun de ni mkhan slob gnyis kyi lcags thang chos rje las bsnyen par rdzogs/ lcags zang chos

rjes yag chos sdings su sgye chub byams pa dkon cog dpal las bsnyen par rdzogs/ des ngam ring mkhan chen rin [433] cen rdo rje la bsnyen par rdzogs/ de yan gyi brgyud pa ma rnyed/ phyis lhas sdings slob dpon shes rab me lce ba'i gsung gis khyed kyi thugs la mkhan chen rin rdor bas sems dpa' chen po gzhon nu rgyal mchog la bsnyen par rdzogs sam dgongs pa zhig 'dug ste/ de min pa'i mkhan brgyud kyi yi ge zhig kho bo la yod de gzigs 'bul gsung ba byung kyang phyis lag tu ma byung/ de nas kho bos chos gling du glang stag yos gsum phar tshad la 'chad nyan yang 'phel po byung/

In a later passage he describes the circumstances of his second ordination:

[441] yang dgon pa lu phu de na sa paṇ gyi sngo ma rgyun bzhugs pa'i bla ma rim par byung ba la/ skabs shig bla ma gcig la sa paṇ gyi sdom rgyun de mi bzhugs pas/ chos rgyal nam mkha' tshe dbang rdo rjes khyed kyi sdom rgyun de sa paṇ gyi sdom rgyun yin pas de chad na 'phongs/ sdom rgyun bzhugs pa'i sgrub chen mkhyen pa yangs pa zhig la sdom rgyun de long zhig ces bstan pa la gces sbras su che ba'i bka' stsal phebs/ de ltar byas pas dgon pa de na sa paṇ gyi sdom rgyun rgyun ma chad par yod pa de thos nas/ bdag gis 'jam mgon bla ma la bdag sa paṇ gyi sdom rgyun cig zhu 'dong pas ji ltar legs zhus pas/ sa skya'i gra dgan gzhan gang na yang de 'dra yong par mi 'dug/ lu phun yod pa'i nges pa brtan po yod na rang re dpon slob gnyis car de ltar byas pas chog gsung/ bka'i gnang ba thob nas lu phu'i mkhan po sangs rgyas 'od zer la/ mkhan slob dge slong 'dra dang/ yag chos sdings kyi dge slong gtsang ma 'dra bsags blon po chu tshan khar dkar gur yangs po'i nang du dpon slob gnyis kyis bsnyen rdzogs mdzad/ sngar [442] gyi sdom ro rnyi pa la 'bul chog ma byas na sdom pa blangs kyang mi chags pa 'dul ba'i lugs yin te/ mdo rtsa ba las blangs pa la slar blang ba med pa'i phyir ro// zhes gsungs pas shes/ des na kho bos dge slong gi bslab pa phul/ dge tshul dge bsnyen gyi bslab pa gnyis ni kun mkhyen lcags thang pa las thob pa yin pas ma phul/ de'i tshe slob dpon dang gsang ston gyi 'os su gyur pa gzhan ma rnyed pas/ mkhan chen sangs rgyas 'od zer bas mkhan po dang las slob gnyis car mdzad/ gzhan dge slong gtsang ma gsum dang bcas te dge slong bzhi'i dbus su bsnyen par rdzogs so// mkhan slob gcig gis byed pa ni bu rin po ches/ mkhan slog gcig gis byed pa 'di bod kyi 'dul ba 'dzin pa rnams la ni snang/ gzhung nas bshad pa ni ma mthong gsungs te thugs mad/ dam chos 'dul ba'i lugs la bshad tshod yod kyang lag len med pa dang/ lag len yod kyang bshad tshod med pa'i dmigs bsal mang po yod pa de'i dmigs rnam phyed dgos so// yang 'dul 'dzin kha cig dge slong bzhi las bsnyen par rdzogs su mi rung gsung ste/ 'dul ba tshig le las/ gal te bzhi ni las brjod mkhas// tshul khrims ldan par gyur na ni// bsnyen rdzogs ma smad gyur pa ste// lha yis kyang ni phyag

byar 'os// zhes bshad pa 'di gzigs par zad/ kha cig dge slong bzhi'i steng du las brjod mkhan bsnan pa'i lnga tshang pa la dgongs zer pa'i 'bru skyog gnang mkhan yod de/ gal te bzhi dang las brjod mkhas zer pa yod na de skad rigs na'ang/ gal te bzhi ni las brjod mkhas/ [443] zhes pa'i tshag gi nus pa ma rnyed par zad do// mdor na gsang ston yod na gsang ston bsko ba'i las dgos/ bsko ba'i las la lnga tshang dgos te/ bsko ba'i yul dge slong gcig/ bsko mkhan dge slong bzhi tshang dgos pa'i gnad kyis yin/ gsang ston med na dge slong bzhis chog pa'i gnang mgo bar bab co la ma mdzad cig/ kha che paṇ chen nas brgyud sdom rgyun la// rdor byang gnyis dang sa skya paṇ chen gsum// sa paṇ nas brgyud legs kyang dkon mthong nas// 'bad bas bsgrubs 'di kho bo'i dpal du shar// lugs gang la'ang gnad 'gag ma shes na// gtam chal chol mang pos rang gzhan bslu// chos 'dul ba skra shang 'dzings 'dra la// gnad ma zin 'chol lo 'dul 'dzin rnams// des na kho bos kyang yag chos sdings su rab byung dang bsnyen rdzogs mkhan po mang po dang/...

Zhwa lu ba Rin chen bsod nams mchog grub

The Fifth Dalai Lama in his biography of Zhwa lu ba Rin chen bsod nams mchog grub (1582–1660 or 1681?) explains the role of this master in keeping the Sakya Pandita lineage alive:

Fifth Dalai Lama Ngag dbang blo bzang rgya mtsho. *Dus gsum gyi bde bar gshegs pa ma lus pa'i ngo bo khyab bdag rin chen bsod nams mchog grub bstan pa'i rgyal mtshan dpal bzang po'i rnam par thar pa dpyod ldan yid dbang 'gugs pa'i lcags kyu, Lam 'bras slob bshad,* vol. *nga*:

[16] kun dga' zhes pa shing pho stag gi lor sa skya nas bdag chen rin po che 'jam dbyangs bsod nams dbang po zha lu ri phug tu phebs pa'i tshe byang gling brang du tshigs snga ma dge tshul gyi sdom pa bzhes pa'i dus gtsug phud 'breg pa'i skabs kyi khrus chu'ang rgya bod kyi mkhas grub mang po'i rnam rgyal bum pa'i chu rgyun 'dres pa'i [17] kun mkhyen bu ston rin po che'i bum chu nas gnang/ mtshan rin chen bsod nams mchog grub tu gsol/ sang chibs kha sgyur ba gnang rgyu'i dgos/ phyag mdud/ bdud rtsi ril bu/ bum chu chen mo nas chu bum chung gang/ zang zing gi bdog pa'i tshan grangs/ om swa sti/ 'jam dbyangs ngo bo bla ma'i mchog/bsod nams ye shes mthar phyin pa'i// chos kyi dbang po dam pa la// gsol ba 'debs so byin gyis rlobs// sarba mang ga lam zhes pa phyag bris su mdzad de stsal nas 'di ngag tu 'don pa dang/ dbya 'gyur du gsung ngag 'chad pas de dus slebs pa gyis/ khyed la sa paṇ gyi sdom rgyun zhig dogs pa 'dug pas lo nyi shu lon nas nga'i rtsar shog/ gnas gsar

rje drung dbus nas byon byung na chos zhus gsung ba sogs thugs rtsar bcar ba'i bslab ston mang du phebs 'dug pa/ bu ston rin po che'i bum chu ni rje 'di nyid kyis sa zhal gyi dbang gi rgyun thams cad dngos dang brgyud pa'i sgo nas rgya cher spel te bstan pa'i srog 'thud pa dang/ 'jam dbyangs sa skya paṇ chen gyi sdom rgyun bzhes dgos sogs ma 'ongs mngon sum du mkhyen pa'i lung bstan du 'dug pa bdag chen 'di nyid slob dpon chen po pad ma'i rnam sprul du grags pa don la gnas pa'i dpon slob gnyis ka'i che bar mngon no// ...

[28] phyir phebs nas rin lding 'du khang gi shing rtsi ldebs bris kyi khur bzhes dang sgrub mchod bskang ba gzhan don gyi 'phrin las sogs rnam dkar gyi mdzad pa gong 'phel gyi ngang nas ring por ma lon par bsnyen par rdzogs pa'i dgongs pa bstad pa de yang bstan pa snga dar gyi dus thams cad mkhyen pa zhig ba 'tshos sad mi mi bdun rab tu byung ba nas bzung so thar gyi sdom rgyun dar rgyas su gyur pa rgyal po dar mas bstan la rma phyung ba'i rjes su dmar g.yo gtsang gsum gyis mdo smad nas bstan pa'i me ro gsos te rje btsun sa paṇ yan chad kyi sdom rgyun phal cher bla chen dang pa la rnam pa gsum nas dar ba'i stod 'dul ba'i rgyun yang byung mod/ ka smir ba'i paṇ chen bsod snyoms pa chen po bod du phebs pa nas bzung tshogs sde bzhi dang 'jam mgon sa paṇ nas brgyud par paṇ chen brgyud pa zhes snyan grags che zhing bdag nyid chen po bzang po dpal ba/ kun mkhyen bu/ thams cad mkhyen pa blo bzang grags pa sogs mkhas grub phal cher sdom rgyun 'di nas bzhes pa mang zhing/ khyad par ngor phyogs su bsnyen rdzogs kyi gra bzang pa nas dpal e wam chos ldan yon ta ma lus 'byung ba'i gtsug lag khang du mkhyen brtse nus pa'i mnga' bdag tshul khrims kyi dri bsung gis phyogs kun tu khyab pas 'phags pa nye bar 'khor sa 'dir byon pa lta bu brtan mkhas kyi yon tan gnyis dang ldan pa don gyi slad du mtshan nas smos te yongs rdzogs [29] bstan pa'i mnga' bdag sgrub khang pa dpal ldan don grub kyis mkhan po/ sde snod gsum dang rgyud sde bzhi la mi 'phrogs pa'i mkhyen rab dang ldan pa'i gnas brtan 'dul ba 'dzin pa chen po brang ti pa nam mkha' sangs rgyas kyis las kyi slob dpon/ mkhas grub shar chen shes rab 'byung gnas kyis gsang ston/ dad pa'i dge 'dun grangs tshang ba'i dbus su bar ma rab byung zhu ba nas bzung bsnyen rdzogs kyi dus sgo brjod pa'i bar 'dul lung rgya bod kyi rnam bshad rnams kyi dgongs pa bzhin grangs gsum du gcod pa sogs phyag len shin tu dngos gtsang ba'i sgo nas khrag skyug gces pa shing phag chu stod phag chu stod zla ba'i gza' skar 'phrod sbyor dge ba'i tshe yongs su rdzogs pa dge slong gi dngos po rnam pa dag pa bzhes te nyon mongs pa'i g.yul las rnam par rgyal ba'i rgyal mtshan bsgreng ba ni/ sum brgya par/ nyon mongs dgra g.yul rgyal byed tshul khrims te// nges par 'byung ba'i tshul khrims sdug bsngal spong// dpal 'byor sa dang me tog mda' can 'joms// rdzogs pa'i byang chub dpal snod dbang bskur ro// zhes pa'i don thog tu babs shing mkhan slob khungs btsun de 'bad

pas 'tshol ba'ang rdo rje 'chang tshar chen gyis// deng dus 'di na kha cig gzhan dbang gis// rang yul bla ma tshul 'chal dag la nod//

Gnas gsar ba

The biography of Gnas gsar ba Ngag dbang kun dga' legs pa'i 'byung gnas (1704–60) devotes a long excursus to the history of the main monastic lineages in Tibet, specifying that this master received full ordination a second time, in the Sakya Pandita lineage, from Rmor chen Ngag dbang kun dga' lhun grub (1654–1728) and Bka' 'gyur ba (1603–59).

Khyab bdag rdo rje 'chang ngur smrig gi bla gos 'chang ba dpal gnas gsar ba chen po 'jam mgon bla ma thams cad mkhyen pa legs pa'i mtshan gyi zhal snga nas kyi rnam par thar pa ngo mtshar rab 'byams, Lam 'bras slob bshad, vol. *cha*:

[80] bod yul gling dgu'i rgyal khams 'dir bstan pa snga dar la za hor rgyal rigs mkhan chen bo ddhi sat was sad mi mi bdun sogs la bstan pa'i rtsa ba so sor thar pa'i sdom rgyun 'dzugs par mdzad pa/ log smon nye bar bdo ste glang dar ma'u dum btsan gyis bstan pa bsnubs pa'i tshe chu bo ri'i sgom grwa'i dmar g.yo gtsang gsum gyis gsan pas gsang thabs kyis dre la rgyab non pa'i 'dul dpe dang bcas mnga' ris nas byang lam brgyud mdo smad rma lung dan tig yang rdzong du bon gyi bu shes rab can sngon las sad de rab tu byung bar bskul bar 'dul 'dzin gsum gyi steng rgya'i hwa shang ke 'bag gnyis kyis kha skong par mdzad nas bsnyen par rdzogs pa'i mtshan dgongs pa rab gsal du btags pas/ spa sar gnyis/ ja cog gnyis/ bzhad srags gnyis/ 'al snub gnyis/ thong tshur gnyis sogs mang dag sdom [81] par bkod/ de skabs dbus gtsang du sdom pa 'bogs len dang 'chad nyan sogs kyi rgyun lo bdun cu tsam chad pa'i rjes dbus su mdo smad nas bstan pa cung zad tshugs pa mnga' bdag tshal nas sogs kyis gsan pas cis kyang 'bad pas bstan pa spel bzhed de/ klu mes tshul shes/ 'bring ye ston/ sga tshul blo/ rag tshul 'byung/ sum pa ye blo lngar mthun rkyen dang bcas pa'i brdzang ba/ gtsang gi btsad po rnams kyis kyang thos nas lo ston tshong btsun/ mnga' ris pa gnyis/ bo dong pa ste dbus gtsang gi mi bcus bla chen por bsnyen par rdzogs pa las mched pa ka bzhi/ gdung drug dang/ lo tsho/ tshong tsho sogs mang du dar/ 'a zhwa ye g.yung gi chab gtor ma dang/ 'bre'i der bsam gnyis kyi rgyun kyang gtsang phyogs su mang po 'phel/ klu mes kyi slob ma gzugs la bu chen bzhi byung ba'i/ phyi ma gsum dang/ rgya 'dul dbang tshul gyis rgya cher spel bar snga phyi bar tshar sogs shin tu mang ngo// bstan pa phyi dar la lo chen rin bzang sogs snga rabs pa'i 'dul 'dzin sdom

rgyun der brtan pa dang/ lha bla ma ye shes 'od kyi dus/ 'phags yul shar phyogs kyi paṇ chen dharma pā la'i slob ma pa la rnam gsum las kyang mang du 'phel ba stod 'dul bar grags/ ma pham pa'i rnam sprul khro phu lo tsā ba byams pa'i dpal gyis dka' ba brgya phrag khyad du bsad nas kha che'i bsod snyoms pa paṇ chen shākya shrī gangs can bsod nams gsog pa'i mgron spyan drangs te chu shul srog ma dgon par nyin gcig la sgrub grwa gsum dang mi gnyis bsnyen par rdzogs pa'i nang nas gro shul ba khed gad byang chub dpal dang/ gtsang pa [82] rdo rje dpal gnyis mkhan bu'i gtso bor gyur te bod mun gling du 'dul bstan nyi ma ltar shar bas khyab cing khyad par sa paṇḍi ta kun dga' rgyal mtshan/ srid gsum 'gro ba'i mgon po chos rgyal 'phags pa/ dpal ldan bla ma dam pa bsod nams rgyal mtshan shes bya kun mkhyen bu ston zhabs/ rgyal sras po thogs med bzang po dpal/ ngor chen kun dga' bzang po sogs skyes chen dam pa de dag gis 'dul bstan gyi rgyal mtshan phyogs thams cad du 'dzugs par mdzad la/ bla chen sdom rgyun bka' gdams sogs phal mo ches phyag len la 'debs par mdzad pa dag min gyi/ skur pa btab na chos spong gi sgrib par mi 'gyur ram snyam spros pa bskyungs mod/ gzhan du na bla chen pos bsnyen rdzogs mdzad dus kha skong gi rgya ban gnyis sprul pa yin min the tshom pa'i sgros rnying dang chab pas sogs kyis kyang sbags ma sbags mngon shes kyis dpyod dka' zhing/ 'dir ni de rnams kyi skyon dris ma lpags shing mchog tu gyur pa kha che'i paṇḍi ta chen po de nyid las gangs can mkhas pa'i dbang po sa skya paṇḍi ta chen pos sdom rgyun bzhes par mdzad de spel ba'i rgyun bar skabs su cung zad nyag phra bar gyur pa na/ thams cad mkhyen pa mang thos klu sgrub rgya mtshos bstan pa'i rgyun la gcig tu dgongs pa'i sdom rgyun bzhes 'dun yod skabs/ byang bdag nam mkha'i tshe dbang rdo rjes/ lu phu'i sgrub chen mkhyen yangs shig la sdom rgyun long gsungs pa'i zhal te pheb nas/ de bzhin legs min phyogs las rnam rgyal la bka' 'dri zhus pas/ rang re gnyis char byas chog gsungs nas/ mkhan po lu phub sangs rgyas 'od [83] zer gyis mdzad/ gzhan dge slong kha shas dang bcas blon po chu tshan khar gur gyi nang du bsnyen par rdzogs// mdo rtsa las/ blangs pa la slar blangs pa med pa'i phyir ro zhes gsungs pas/ sngar bzang bkras la dge slong gi sdom pa gsan pa de phul/ lcags thang pa la dge tshul dge bsnyen gyi sdom pa gsan pa de ma phul/ de'i tshe slob dpon dang gsang ston 'os 'gyur zhig ma rnyed pas/ sangs rgyas 'od zer bas mkhan slob gnyis char mdzad/ gzhan dge slong gtsang ma gsum dang bcas bzhi'i dbus su bsnyen par rdzogs/ mkhan slob cig car ba 'di la bu ston rin po ches/ mkhan slob gcig gis byed pa 'di bod kyi 'dul 'dzin rnams la ni snang/ gzhung na bshad pa ni ma mthong gsungs pa de thugs mad/ 'dul pa'i lung la bshad tshod yod kyang lag len med pa dang/ lag len yod kyang bshad tshod med pa'i dmigs bsal mang bas de'i rnam dbye phye dgos/ yang kha cig dge slong bzhis bsnyen rdzogs mi rung gsung ba ni/ tshig le las/ gal te bzhi ni las brjod mkhas// tshul khrims ldan par gyur na ni// bsnyen rdzogs ma smad gyur pa ste// lha yis kyang ni phyag byar 'os// zhes pa 'di ma gzigs par zad/ yang kha cig bzhi'i steng du las rdzod mkhan bsnan pas lnga tshang dgos zer nas 'bru skyog byed kyang// gal te bzhi dang las rjod mkhan/ zer ba yod na bden mod/ gal te bzhi ni las brjod mkhas/ zhes pas tshig nus la 'bru skyog de mi 'gro/ mdor na gsang ston yod na/ gsang ston bskor ba'i las dgos/ bskor ba'i [84] las la lnga tshang dgos te/ bsko ba'i yul dge slong gcig sko mkhan dge slong bzhi tshang dgos ba'i gnas kyis yin zhing/ mdo rtsar/ skal pa dang ldan pa'i rang bzhin can la bar chad ma dris par 'ong ngo// zhes pa ltar gsang ston med na dge slong bzhis chog pa'i gnad ma go bar bab bcol ma mdzad cig ces thams cad mkhyen pa klu sgrub rgya mtsho'i rnam thar gsung rtsom las tshig cung zad bsdus nas bkod pa yin la/ mang thos klu sgrub rgya mtsho nas brgyud pa'i sa paṇ gyi sdom rgyun khyad par can de dpal sa skya'i chos grwa chen por ji ltar byung ba'i tshul ni/ 'jam mgon a mes zhabs kyi rnam thar phun tshogs bdud rtsi'i char rgyun las/ de nas sngags 'chang bla ma thams cad mkhyen pa chen po 'di nyid dgung gi 'jal byed lnga bcu rtsa bdun du pheb pa/ rnam rgyal zhes pa chu mo sbrul gyi lo gsar du shar ba na/ mdo khams nas a li chos grwa bu slob mang po dang bcas/ 'jam dbyangs bla ma nyid dang/ gdan sa chen po mjal bar 'byor/ lha khang chen mor mang ja brgyad tsam bskol zhing/ ja dang ras la sogs pa'i gral 'gyed mang po btang/ bdag nyid chen por ja gos dar la sogs pa'i 'bul nod rgya chen po sgrub cing shin tu gus par gyur/ rje btsun dam pa 'dis kyang chos dang zang zing gi longs spyod lhug par stsal nas/ de dag gi re ba'i yol go yongs su khengs par gyur to// dgun thog der gtsang gram pa rgyang nas mkhas pa chen po mang thos blo gros rnam rgyal gyi rje dbon rin po che mang thos grags pa rnam rgyal la gdan sa chen po 'dir 'jam pa'i dbyangs sa paṇḍi ta chen po nas brgyud pa'i bsnyen rdzogs kyi sdom rgyun zhig nges par dgos rgyur snang ba spel ba'i mkhan po'i 'os rigs [85] sa khyed che bar 'dug pas/ bstan pa sogs la myur ba spyon zhig ces pa'i bka'i spring yig gser gyi shing rtas legs par drangs te/ dpal sa skya'i dbu rtse snying ma'i dri gtsang mchog tu chos kyi rje de nyid kyis mkhan po mdzad de/ dge 'dun grangs tshang bas chog rnam par dag pa'i sgo nas/ chos grwa lho byang gi dge ba'i bshes gnyen mang por/ kha che'i bsod snyoms pa chen po shā kya shrī bha dra nas/ 'dzam gling byang phyogs kyi thub pa chen po 'jam mgon sa paṇḍi ta la legs par brgyud pa'i yongs su rdzogs pa dge slong gi sdom pa yang dag par 'bogs pa'i mthun pa'i cha rkyen bzang po nye bar sbyar te/ dkar phyogs kyi lha klu sa gsum na gnas pa thams cad dga' ba'i zlos gar la ngom pa med par rtser bcug go/ zhes 'byung la/ sdom rgyun de nyid gong sa rdo rje 'chang lnga pa chen po'i bzhed tshul ni/ 'jam dbyangs bsod nams dbang phyug gi rnam thar snying gi bdud rtsi las/ chu mo glang gi lor mkhan chen kun spangs pa chen po rin chen bsod nams mchog grub dpon slob rnams rnam 'dren dam pa 'di mjal bar pheb ste zhabs brtan 'bul ba dang gong sa thams cad mkhyen pa'i gsung rtsom gong ma yab sras kyi zhabs brtan/ 'jam dbyangs gdung brgyud myur 'byon gyi smon lam dang bcas pa de 'dus tshogs su 'dzugs par mdzad cing/ zab chos mang du gsan/ lhag par thub bstan lha chen gyi mkhan po byams pa bsod nams bkra shis dge 'dun grangs tshad dang bcas pa'i dbus su/ sa skya paṇḍi tas bsnyen rdzogs kyi sdom rgyun bzhes te ma 'gyangs par rgyal dbang thams cad mkhyen pa chen po la phul ba'i rgyun de nyid deng sang rgya bod hor [86] gsum du khyab ste sa skya paṇḍi ta'i bsnyen rdzogs kyi sdom rgyun rgya cher 'phel ba yin la/ zhes bshad pa ltar/ rgyal dbang thams cad mkhyen pa chen pos bsregs bcad bdar ba'i gser bzhin du legs par dpyad pas thugs nges 'drongs te dar rgyas su mdzad pa'i rgyun rnam par dag pa 'di nyid mchog tu gyur pas blang byar dgongs te/ legs sbyar skad du shubha kri ta/ shar phyogs mha tsi nar zhin yin zhes 'bod cing/ stod 'grel bod yul gyi skad du dge byed/ dbang thang dang bstun pa'i ming chu pho stag gi lo'i mnyam med yang dag par rdzogs pa'i sangs rgyas shākya'i dbang pos chos rgyal zla ba bzang po'i sangs rgyas dus kyi 'khor lo'i rtsa rgyud gsungs pa'i dus chen/ chu shel dbang po nag pa'i dga' ma dang rtse ba'i gral tshes phun sum tshogs pa'i nyin/ bod yul gyi rdo rje gdan chen po dpal bsam yas lhun gyis grub pa'i gtsug lag khang gi nye 'dabs su/ yongs rdzogs bstan pa rin po che'i mnga' bdag rig grol gyi yon tan du ma'i rgyan gyis nye bar mdzes pa/ bdag cag gi ston pa dang rnam dbyer ma mchis pa/ don gyi slad du mtshan nas brjod na ngag dbang kun dga' lhun grub bstan pa'i rgyal mtshan dpal bzang po'i zhal snga nas kyis mkhan po/ mdo sngags rgya mtsho'i pha rol tu son zhing las kyi cho ga la mkhas pa khyab bdag bka' 'gyur ba chen po sangs rgyas rgyal mtshan gyis las kyi slob dpon/ nyes ltung dri ma'i chu 'dzin las grol ba'i sdom brtson chen po tshul khrims rgya mtshos gsang ste ston pa/ dol chos 'khor gnas kyi slob dpon 'dul ba 'dzin pa kun dga' nor bus dus bsgo ba/ gnas brtan chen po phreng sgo gzhi pa gra [87] tshang gi slob dpon phun tshogs legs ldan gyis kha skong sogs mdzad de dad pa'i dge 'dun grangs tshang ba'i dbus su/ tshigs gsum rim gyis nos te bsnyen par rdzogs pa dge slong gi dngos po mngon du mdzad/ brje ba gnyis brjes pa'i mtshan brje ba'i skabs/ sngar gyi mtshan gyi steng du ngag dbang dang theg mchog dbang gi rgyal po zhes mtshan gsol bar mdzad de/ rgyal bstan rin po che'i sgor zhugs la yongs su rdzogs pas ngur smrig 'dzin pa ku/ gyi gtsug gi rgyan bla na med par gyur te/ dus de nyid nas bzung ste/ ltung ba sde lnga gnyen po'i khrims nyis brgya lnga bcu char gtogs dang bcas pa la spyan gyi 'bras bu ltar gces spras su mdzad de nyes pa'i dri ma phra mos kyang ma gos pa lags so/

Bka' 'gyur ba Mgon po bsod nams mchog ldan

Bka' 'gyur ba (1603–59) originally took full monk ordination in the tradition of Ngorchen. Later when teaching at Gong dkar he gave up those vows and took ordination anew in the tradition of Sakya Pandita. This accorded with the previous tradition at Gong dkar monastery. Here it is specified that he gave back both novice and full monk's vows and for a short time became a layman again.

Dus gsum rgyal ba'i mkhyen brtse nus pa'i rang gzugs dkyil 'khor rgya mtsho'i gtso bo khyab bdag rdo rje sems dpa'i ngo bo mgon po bsod nams mchog ldan bstan pa'i rgyal mtshan dpal bzang po'i rnam par thar pa ngo mtshar dad pa'i rlabs phreng, Lam 'bras slob bshad, vol. *nga*:

[656] de yang sngar ngor du bsgrubs pa gnang ba de phyag len mkhan slob kha skong tshang ma khungs btsun na'ang shar chen ye shes rgyal mtshan gyis yar klungs rnam rgyal du tshag mig mkhan chen dka' bzhi tshul khrims rin cen la bsgrubs pa'i sdom rgyun yin la/ gong dkar rdo rje gdan gyi sdom rgyun la sa paṇ brgyud par bzhugs pa dang/ phyogs de'i gdul bya rjes 'dzin la dgongs te smin drug zla ba'i tshes nyi shu'i gza' lhag pa dang skar ma rgyal 'dzom pa'i nyin snga dro sdom pa 'bul ba gnang ba'i brda chad tsam du tsar mo'i steng na bza' dkar po zhig bzhes/ phyi dro gnas brtan 'dul ba 'dzin pa chen po tshul khrims bkra shis bas mkhan slob sbrags ma/ gsang ston skyid tshal 'og mkhan po ngag dbang bstan 'dzin/ dus sgo ba rab 'byams chos rje rin can rgya mtsho/ kha skong ba brag thog pa shākya mchog ldan sogs dad pa'i dge 'dun grangs tshang ba'i dbus su tshigs snga ma dge bsnyen nas bzung ste sdom gsum rim gyis mnos pa'i nyi ma ri rked la yod dus bsnyen par rdzogs pa'i sdom pa thugs rgyud la bstar/ de nas zhag lnga tsam na 'dul lung khyim pa'i spyod yul du ma 'os shing rab byung sha stag dgos pa chos sde gnyis kyi gra rigs nyi shu skor gyis [657] nyi ma gling du sku ngo sbran pas rje tshul khrims bkra shis kyis da lam bskyar bzhes gnang nas yun ring ma song yang mkhan po'i bya ba mdzad dgos par gsol ba bzhin rje nyid kyis mkhan po/ mtshungs med nyi ma gling pas las slob bstar te rtses dang chen mo byang ma pa ngag dbang bstan 'dzin gyis gnos pa'i bsnyen rdzogs pa kha shas dang rdo rje brag sprul sku rin po che dpon slob lnga dge tshul du bsgrub pa gnang ba'i chen mo byang ma ba'i mtshan la slar byams pa bsnan te 'dogs par mdzad/

Tshar chen's Ordination Lineage

The different lineages are also discussed in the biography of Tsarchen Losal Gyatso (Tshar chen blo gsal rgya mtsho, 1502–66). Here the author, the Fifth Dalai Lama, embarks on an excursus about the lineages and one founder in Tibet, Kha che Paṇ chen:

[422] chu sprel khro phu'i byams chen la rab gnas mdzad pas ngo mtshar ba'i ltas bsam gyis mi khyab pa byung/ sngon bla chen po'i sdom rgyun dang stod 'dul ba sogs byung na'ang bsod snyoms pa chen po 'di nyid kyis mkhan po mdzad nas byang rdor rnam gnyis sogs bsnyen par rdzogs pa'i paṇ chen brgyud pa zhes 'phags yul 'gran bzod pa'i bstan pa rma med pa'i bka' drin rgya cher mdzad jo bo stan gcig pa'i sde btsugs/ dpal ldan sa skyar phebs dus rje btsun chen pos rdor dril nam mkha' la 'jog pa/ cang te'u sogs kyi sgra rang sgra 'khrol ba/ rgya khab ye ltar gsol te phyir 'don pa/ dhau tai'i rgyu ba bkag pas gza' 'dzin mi 'byung ba sogs la rgya gar na'ang 'di lta bu'i grub thob dkon zhes 'khor lo sdom pa'i dbang gsan/ nyang smad rgyan gong gi gtsug lag khang du rje btsun sa paṇḍi ta bsnyen par rdzogs/ bod rnams kyis bzhugs par gsol yang ma bzhed par 'bul ba'i dngos po rnams yul so so'i dge 'dun la bkye/ lo tsā bas glo bo'i bar gdan 'dren du byon par phyag gis mi theg [423] pa'i gser gyi gnang byin mdzad/ kha cher lo bcu gnyis bzhugs nas rgyal po mu stegs par song ba nang pa'i bstan pa la bkod yul der rab byung gi sde mang du btsugs/ sngar bod du slob ma rnams kyis dus mchod 'dzin pa'i dus mi shes pa 'dug gsol bas nam 'das pa'i dus na rdza sku rnams gas 'ong gsungs/ shing mo bya'i lo dgung lo dgu bcu rtsa dgur phebs pa na ngo mtshar ba'i bltas dang bcas te dga' ldan du gshegs so//

Later Tsharchen's full ordination is mentioned:

[502] zhes srid pa 'khor ba la yid 'byung ba'i rang byung gi bslab pa la brten nas myur du byang chub rnyed par gyur pa'i gtso bo ni/ dge slong la rab tu gces pa'i mdo las/ dge slong zhes bya sdug bsngal spong ba yin// dge slong zhes bya rgyal ba'i sras po'o// zhes 'khor los sgyur ba'i rgyal po la sras stong yod kyang thu bo la rgyal srid 'byung ba bzhin 'khor rnam pa bzhi'i nang nas mchog tu gyur pa [503] dge slong pha'i sdom pa yin la/ de yang bod 'dir sdom rgyun 'ga' zhig yod pa'i nang nas kha che'i paṇ chen bsod snyoms pa chen po'i sdom rgyun shin tu gtsang ba chos khung tshogs su bzhugs par brten/ gsung las/ bdag gis tshe 'di'i ngo srung rgya tu bor// phyi ma'i don chen 'ba' zhig snying nas bsams// yongs rdzogs kha che'i paṇ chen bsod snyoms pa//

shākya shrī grang na 'bad pas zhugs// zhes pa ltar dgung lo so gcig pa dga' ba zhes pa chu pho 'brug gi lo sa ga zla ba'i tshes bco lnga thub pa'i dbang pos bdud btul byang chub brnyes shing mya ngan las 'das pa'i dus chen sum 'dzom gyi nyes ltung gi cha phra mo'i 'dam gyis ma gos shing/ tshul khrims kyi 'dab brgya yongs su bzhad pa las mya ngan las 'das pa'i ze'u 'bru'i bcud kyis skal bzang ra yig gnyis pa'i dga' ston ches cher spel ba sa'i steng na 'gran pa'i zla thams cad dang bral ba'i don gyi slad du mtshan nas smos te yongs rdzogs bstan pa'i mnga' bdag grags pa rgyal mtshan dpal bzang pos mkhan po/ chos kyi rje bkra shis rnam rgyal gyis las slob/ rje ngag dbang bstan pa'i rgyal mtshan gyis gsang ston/ g.yag sde lcang ra ba blo gros phun tshogs kyis dus bsgo ba/ spos khang pa 'jam dbyangs rgyal mtshan sogs nyi shus las kyi kha bskang ste jo bo stan gcig pa'i bsti gnas nyang stod spos khang gi kun dga' ra bar bsnyen par rdzogs pa'i tshe sngar dge tshul gnang ba'i mtshan gyi steng du mkhan po'i mtshan sgra grags pa rgyal [504] mtshan dpal bzang po zhes bsnan zhing bag yod pa kho na mdzad de tshul khrims rnams par dag pa ni/

Other sources on the lineages remain to be carefully examined.

Glossary

Sanskrit	Pāli	Phonetic Tibetan	Tibetan	Meaning
—	—	ani	a ni	nun (colloq.)
anuśrāvaṇā	anussāvanā	—	—	proclamation
bhikṣu	bhikkhu	gelong	dge slong	(fully ordained) monk
bhikṣuṇī	bhikkhunī	gelongma	dge slong ma	(fully ordained) nun
brahmacarya	brahmacariya	tsangpar chöpa	tshangs par spyod pa	pure conduct
Dharmaguptaka	—	chösungpa/ chöbepa	chos srungs pa / chos sbas pa	Indian school whose Vinaya lineage is dominant in East Asia
—	—	domgyün	sdom rgyun	ordination lineage
*dṛḍhakarman	daḷhīkamma	—	—	formal act of "reinforcement" to permit movement between nikāyas
duṣkṛta	dukkaṭa	nyeja	nyes byas	minor infraction

Sanskrit	Pāli	Phonetic Tibetan	Tibetan	Meaning
—	—	geshé	dge shes	Tibetan monastic scholarly degree
—	—	geshema	dge shes ma	geshé degree for nuns
gurudharma	garudhamma	chiwai chö / lamai chö	lci ba'i chos / bla ma'i chos	the "heavy" rules for nuns
karman	kamma	lé	las	legal acts of a monastic community
karmācārya	—	lekyi lopön	las kyi slob dpon	ritual master
karmakāraka	kammakāraka	lé jepa / lé gyipa	las byed pa / las bgyid pa	ritual master
karmavidhi	kammavidhi	lekyi choga	las kyi cho ga	cermonial rite
kriyākāra	katikāvata	chayik	bca' yig	local monastic ordinances
madhyamopadeśa	majjhima-padesa	yülü	yul dbus	central land
Mahāprajāpatī Gautamī	Mahāpajāpatī Gotamī	kyegu dakmo chenmo gautami	skye dgu bdag mo chen mo ga'u ta mī	Buddha's aunt and foster mother and leader of bhikṣuṇī saṅgha
Mahāsāṅghika	—	gendün palchenpa	dge 'dun phal chen pa	Indian school whose Vinaya lineage has not survived
Mahīśāsaka	—	sasungpa/ satönpa	sa srungs pa / sa ston pa	Indian school whose Vinaya lineage has not survived
mānatva/ mānāpya	mānatta	guwar jawa	mgu bar bya ba	probation period for certain offenses
Mūlasarvāstivāda	—	shi tamché yöpar mawa	gzhi thams cad yod par smra ba	Indian school whose Vinaya lineage is dominant in Tibet

Sanskrit	Pāli	Phonetic Tibetan	Tibetan	Meaning
nikāya	nikāya	depa	sde pa	here: school or subschool of the modern Theravādins
pārājika	pārājika	pampa	pham pa	most serious of Vinaya infractions
pariṣad	parisā	khor	’khor	assembly
pāyattika	pācittiya	tungjé	ltung byed	class of offenses that can be expiated merely by confession
poṣadha	uposatha	sojong	gso sbyong	recitation of the prātimokṣa/ pāṭimokkha twice a month
prātimokṣa	pāṭimokkha	sosor tarpa	so sor thar pa	code of rules for monks and nuns
pravāraṇā	pavāraṇā	gakjé	dgag dbye	ritual marking end of rains’ retreat
pravrajyā	pabbajjā	raptu jungwa	rab tu byung ba	“going forth” pre-novice initiation
saṅghakarma	saṅghakamma	gendün gyi lé	dge ’dun gyi las	legal act of the saṅgha
saṅghāvaśeṣa	saṅghādisesa	gendün lhakma	dge ’dun lhag ma	offense entailing formal meeting of the saṅgha
Sarvāstivāda	—	tamché yöpar mawa	thams cad yod par smra ba	Indian school whose Vinaya lineage has not survived
śāsana	sāsana	tenpa	bstan pa	teaching
śikṣā	sikkhā	lappa	bslab pa	training
śikṣamāṇā	sikkhamānā	gelopma	dge slob ma	female trainee (for full ordination)

Sanskrit	Pāli	Phonetic Tibetan	Tibetan	Meaning
sīmā	sīmā	tsam	mtshams	monastic enclosure
śrāmaṇera	sāmaṇera	getsül	dge tshul	novice monk
śrāmaṇerikā	sāmaṇerī	getsülma	dge tshul ma	novice nun
Sthavira	Theriya	—	—	here: ancient Indian school from which the Dharmaguptaka, Mūlasarvāstivāda, and Theravāda descended
	Theravāda	neten gyi depa	gnas brtan gyi sde pa	Buddhist school in Sri Lanka and Southeast Asia
upādhyāya	upajjhāya	khenpo	mkhan po	male preceptor
upādhyāyikā	upajjhāyā	khenmo	mkhan mo	female preceptor
upāsaka	upāsaka	genyen	dge bsnyen	male lay follower
upasaṃpadā	upasampadā	nyenpar dzokpa	bsnyen par rdzogs pa	full ordination
upāsikā	upāsikā	genyenma	dge bsnyen ma	female lay follower
upasthāna	uppaṭṭhāna	rimdro	rim gro	ceremony
varṣā	vassa	jarné	dbyar gnas	rainy season
varṣopanāyikā	vassūpanāyikā	jarjor	dbyar sbyor	entering the rains
Vinaya	Vinaya	dülwa	'dul ba	monastic code

Bibliography

Abeysekara, Ananda. 1999. "Politics of Higher Ordination, Buddhist Monastic Identity, and Leadership in Sri Lanka." *Journal of the International Association of Buddhist Studies* 22.2: 255–80.

Abeysekara, Ananda. 2002. *Colors of the Robe: Religion, Identity and Difference.* Columbia: University of South Carolina Press.

Anālayo. 2008. "Theories on the Foundation of the Nuns' Order—A Critical Evaluation." *Journal of the Centre for Buddhist Studies, Sri Lanka* 6: 105–42. Available for download at http://www.buddhismuskunde.uni-hamburg.de/fileadmin/pdf/analayo/TheoriesFoundation.pdf.

Aris, Michael. 1988. *Hidden Treasures and Secret Lives: A Study of Pemalingpa (1450–1521) and the Sixth Dalai Lama (1683–1706).* Delhi: Motilal Banarsidass.

Bagchi, Prabodh Chandra. 1945. "A Note on the Avadanaśataka and Its Chinese Translations." *Visva-Bharati Annals* 1: 56–61.

Bagchi, S. 1967. *Mūlasarvāstivāda Vinayavastu.* Darbhanga: Mithila Institute of Post-graduate Studies and Research in Sanskrit Learning.

Bancroft, Anne. 1987. "Women in Buddhism." In *Women in the World's Religions, Past and Present,* edited by U. King, 81–104. New York: Paragon House.

Bapat, P. V., and V. V. Gokhale. 1982. *Vinaya-sūtra and Auto-Commentary on the Same by Guṇaprabha.* Tibetan Sanskrit Works Series 22. Patna: K. P. Jayaswal Research Institute.

Barber, A. N., ed. 1991. *The Tibetan Tripiṭaka.* Taiwan: SMC Publishing.

Bärlocher, Daniel. 1982. *Testimonies of Tibetan Tulkus.* 2 vols. Opuscula Tibetana. Rikon: Tibet-Institut.

Barnes, Nancy J. 1996. "Buddhist Women and the Nuns' Order in Asia." In *Engaged Buddhism: Buddhist Liberation Movements in Asia,* edited by Chris S. Queen and Sallie B. King, 259–94. New York: State University of New York Press.

Barnes, Nancy J. 2000. "The Nuns at the Stūpa, Inscriptional Evidence for the Lives and Activities of Early Buddhist Nuns in India." In *Women's Buddhism, Buddhism's Women: Tradition, Revision, Renewal,* edited by Ellison. B. Findly, 17–36. Boston: Wisdom Publications.

Barron, Richard (Chökyi Nyima), trans. 2003. *The Autobiography of Jamgön Kongtrul: A Gem of Many Colors.* Ithaca: Snow Lion.

Bartholomeuz, Tessa. 1994. *Women under the Bo Tree: Buddhist Nuns in Sri Lanka.* Cambridge: Cambridge University Press.

Barua, Subhra. 1997. *Monastic Life of the Early Buddhist Nuns.* Calcutta: Atisha Memorial Publishing Society.

Basham, A. L. 1980. "The Background to the Rise of Buddhism." In *Studies in the History of Buddhism,* edited by A. K. Narain, 13–21. Delhi: B. R. Publishing.

Bechert, Heinz. 1961. "Aśokas 'Schismenedikt' und der Begriff Sanghabheda." *Wiener Zeitschrift für die Kunde Süd- und Ostasiens und Archiv für indische Philosophie* 5: 18–52.

———. 1970. "Theravāda Buddhist Sangha: Some General Observations on Historical and Political Factors in its Development." *Journal of Asian Studies* 29.4: 761–78.

———. 1974. "Sāsana-Reform im Theravāda-Buddhismus." *50 Jahre Buddhistisches Haus,* 19–34. Berlin.

Bechert, Heinz et al. 1989. *Sanskrithandschriften aus den Turfanfunden, Teil 6.* Stuttgart: Franz Steiner.

Bechert, Heinz, and Jens-Uwe Hartmann. 1988. "Observations on the Reform of Buddhism in Nepal." *Journal of the Nepal Research Centre* 8: 1–30 [Reprinted in: Heinz Bechert, *Buddhismus, Staat und Gesellschaft in den Ländern des Theravāda-Buddhismus,* vol. II, 383–412. (Neuausgabe mit Supplementen sowie Personen- und Sachregister.) Göttingen: Seminar für Indologie und Buddhismuskunde, 2000.]

Bendall, Cecil. 1903. "Fragment of a Buddhist Ordination-Ritual." In *Album Kern: Opstellen geschreven te zijner eere,* 373–76. Leiden: E. J. Brill.

Blackstone, Kathryn R. 2000. *Women in the Footsteps of the Buddha: Struggle for Liberation in the Therīgāthā.* 1st Indian ed. Delhi: Motilal Banarsidass.

Bodhi, Bhikkhu, trans. 2000. *The Connected Discourses of the Buddha: A New Translation of the Saṃyutta Nikāya.* Boston: Wisdom Publications.

Bowker, John, ed. 2003. *Das Oxford-Lexikon der Weltreligionen.* Trans. by Karl-Heinz Golzio. Frankfurt: Fischer Taschenbuch Verlag.

Brown, Sid. 2001. *The Journey of One Buddhist Nun: Even Against the Wind.* Albany: State University of New York Press.

Cabezón, José Ignacio. 1997. "The Regulations of a Monastery." In *Religions of Tibet in Practice,* edited by Donald S. Lopez, 335–51. Princeton: Princeton University Press.

Cheng, Wei-Yi. 2007. *Buddhist Nuns in Taiwan and Sri Lanka: A Critique of the Feminist Perspective.* London: Routledge.

Chodron, Thubten. 2001. "A Contemporary Cultural Perspective on Monastic Life." In *Choosing Simplicity, Commentary on the Bhikṣhuni Pratimoksha*, by Bhikṣuṇī Wu Yin. Ithaca, NY: Snow Lion.

Christ, Carol. 1987. *Laughter of Aphrodite: Reflections on a Journey to the Goddess.* San Francisco: Harper and Row.

Chung, Jin-il. 1998. "'Bhikṣuṇī-Karmavācanā' of the Mūlasarvāstivādins." In *Facets of Indian Culture, Gustav Roth Felicitation Volume, Published on the Occasion of His 82nd Birthday*, edited by C. P. Sinha, 420–23. Patna, India: Bihar Puravid Parishad.

———. 1999. "Gurudharma und aṣṭau gurudharmāh." *Indo-Iranian Journal* 42: 227–34.

———. 2006. "Ursprung und Wandel der Aufnahme von Frauen in den buddhistischen Orden nach der kanonischen Überlieferung—eine Randbemerkung." *Sanko Bunka Kenkyusho Nenpo [Annual of the Sanko Research Institute for the Studies of Buddhism]* 28: 1–15.

Chung, Jin-il, and Petra Kieffer-Pülz. 1997. "The *karmavācanās* for the Determination of *sīmā* and *ticīvareṇa avippavāsa.*" In *Dharmadūta Mélanges offerts au Vénérable Thích Huyên-Vi à l'occasion de son soixante-dixième anniversaire*, edited by Bhikkhu T. Dhammaratana and Bhikkhu Pāsādika, 13–56. Paris: Librairie You-Feng.

Church, Cornelia Dimmitt. 1975. "Temptress, Housewife, Nun: Women's Role in Early Buddhism." *Anima* 2: 53–58.

Clarke, Shayne. 2001. "The Mūlasarvāstivāda Vinaya Muktaka 根本説一切有部目得迦." *Bukkyō kenkyū* 仏教研究 30: 81–107.

———. 2002. "The Mūlasarvāstivādin Vinaya: A Brief Reconnaissance Report." In *Sakurabe Hajime hakushi kiju kinen ronshū: shoki Bukkyō kara abidaruma e* 櫻部建博士喜寿記念論集・初期仏教からアビダルマへ, edited by Sakurabe Hajime Hakushi Kiju Kinen Ronshū Kankōkai 櫻部建博士喜寿記念論集刊行会, 45–63. Kyoto: Heirakuji shoten 平樂寺書店.

———. 2006. "Miscellaneous Musings on Mūlasarvāstivāda Monks: The Mūlasarvāstivāda Vinaya Revival in Tokugawa Japan." *Japanese Journal of Religious Studies* 33.1: 1–49.

———. Forthcoming. "Towards a Comparative Study of the *Sarvāstivāda-* and *Mūlasarvāstivāda-vinaya*s: Studies in the Structure of the *Uttaragrantha* (1): *Kathāvastu*—A Preliminary Survey."

Collins, Steven, and Justin McDaniel. n.d. "Buddhist Nuns (*Maechi*) and the Teaching of Pāli in Thailand." Unpublished manuscript.

Committee of Western Bhikṣuṇīs. n.d. "Research Regarding the Lineage of Bhikṣuṇī Ordination: A Response to Necessary Research Regarding the Lineage of Bhikṣuṇī Vinaya." Unpublished manuscript.

Cowell, E. B., and R. A. Neil, eds. 1886. *The Divyāvadāna: A Collection of Early Buddhist Legends.* Cambridge: The University Press.

de Jong, J. W. 1974. "Notes on the Bhikṣuṇī-Vinaya of the Mahāsāṃghikas." In

Buddhist Studies in Honour of I. B. Horner, edited by L. S. Cousins et al., 63–70. Dordrecht: D. Reidel.

de Silva, Ranjani. 2004. "Reclaiming the Robe: Reviving the Bhikkhunī Order in Sri Lanka." In *Buddhist Women and Social Justice: Ideals, Challenges, and Achievements*, edited by Karma Lekshe Tsomo, 119–35. Albany: State University of New York Press.

Deeg, Max. 2005. *Das Gaoseng-Faxian-Zhuan als religionsgeschichtliche Quelle.* Studies in Oriental Religions 52. Wiesbaden: Otto Harrassowitz.

Dhirasekara, Jotiya. 1967. "Women and the Religious Order of the Buddha." *The Maha Bodhi*, 75.5–6: 154–61.

Dhondup, K., and Tashi Tsering. 1979. "Samdhing Dorjee Phagmo: Tibet's Only Female Incarnation." *Tibetan Review* (New Delhi), 14.8: 11–17.

Dhongthog Rinpoche, T. G. 1968. *Important Events in Tibetan History*. Delhi: Dhongthog.

Diemberger, Hildegard. 2007. *When a Woman Becomes a Religious Dynasty: The Samding Dorje Phagmo of Tibet.* New York, Columbia University Press.

Durt, Hubert. 2005. "Kajaṅgalā, Who Could Have Been the Last Mother of the Buddha." *Journal of the International College of Postgraduate Buddhist Studies* 9: 65–90.

Dutt, Nalinaksha. 1984. *Gilgit Manuscripts, vol. III (four parts)*. 2nd ed. Delhi: Sri Satguru Publications.

Edgerton, Franklin. 1953. *Buddhist Hybrid Sanskrit Grammar and Dictionary.* New Haven, CT: Yale University Press. (Repr. Delhi: Motilal Banarsidass, 1993.)

Ellington, Ter. 1990. "Tibetan Monastic Constitutions: The Bca' Yig." In *Reflections on Tibetan Culture: Essays in Memory of Turrell V. Wylie*, edited by L. Epstein and R. F. Sherburne, 205–29. Lewiston, NY: Edwin Mellen Press.

Enomoto, Fumio. 1984. "The Formation and Development of the Sarvāstivāda Scriptures." In *Proceedings of the Thirty-First International Congress of Human Sciences in Asia and North Africa*, edited by Yamamoto Tatsuro, 197–98. Tokyo: Tōhō Gakkai.

Falk, Nancy. 1974. "An Image of Woman in Old Buddhist Literature: The Daughters of Māra." In *Women and Religion*, edited by J. Plaskow et al., 105–12. Missoula, MT: Scholars Press.

———. 1989. "The Case of the Vanishing Nuns: The Fruits of Ambivalence in Ancient Indian Buddhism." In *Unspoken Words, Women and Religious Lives*, edited by N. A. Falk et al., 155–65. Belmont, CA: Wadsworth.

Faure, Bernard. 2003. *The Power of Denial: Buddhism, Purity, and Gender.* Princeton: Princeton University Press.

Fazun 法尊 (Bhikṣu). 1979. "Xizang houhongqi fojiao" 西藏後弘期佛教 (The Second Propagation of Buddhism in Tibet). In *Xizang fojiao (II)-Lishi* 西藏佛教 (二)-歷史 *The Tibetan Buddhism (II)- History*, edited by Man-tao Chang, 329–52. Xiandai fojiao xueshu congkan 76. Taipei: Dacheng wenhua chubanshe.

Feer, Léon, trans. 1891. *Avadāna-çataka, cent légendes (bouddhiques). Annales du Musée Guimet 18.* Paris: Leroux.

———. 1901. "Le Karma-śataka." *Journal Asiatique* (Mars–Avril): 262–63.

Findly, Ellison Banks. 2000. "Women Teachers of Women: Early Nuns 'Worthy of My Confidence.'" In *Women's Buddhism, Buddhism's Women: Tradition, Revision, Renewal*, edited by E. B. Findly, 133–55. Boston: Wisdom Publications.

Finnegan, Damchö Diana. 2009. "For the Sake of Women, Too: Ethics and Narrative in the Mūlasarvāstivāda Vinaya." Ph.D. dissertation, University of Wisconsin–Madison.

Foulk, T. Griffith. 1995. "Daily Life in the Assembly." In *Buddhism in Practice*, edited by Donald S. Lopez, 455–72. Princeton, NJ: Princeton University Press.

Frauwallner, E. 1956. *The Earliest Vinaya and the Beginnings of Buddhist Literature.* Rome: Istituto Italiano per il Medio ed Estremo Oriente.

Freiberger, Oliver. 2006. *Asceticism and Its Critics: Historical Accounts and Comparative Perspectives*. Oxford: Oxford University Press.

Gabain, Annemarie von. 1954. *Türkische Turfan-Texte VIII.* Abhandlungen der deutschen Akademie der Wissenschaft zu Berlin, Klasse für Sprachen, Literatur und Kunst, Jahrgang 1952 Nr. 7. Berlin: Akademie Verlag.

Geiger, Magdalene and Wilhelm. 1920. *Pāli Dhamma: vornehmlich in der kanonischen Literatur*. München: Verlag der Bayerischen Akademie der Wissenschaften.

Geiger, Wilhelm, trans. 1912. *The Mahāvaṃsa or The Great Chronicle of Ceylon.* London: Pali Text Society.

Geng, Shimin et al. 1988. *Das Zusammentreffen mit Maitreya: Die ersten fünf Kapitel der Hami-Version der Maitrisimit.* Asiatische Forschungen, Monographienreihe zur Geschichte, Kultur und Sprache der Völker Ost- und Zentralasiens 103. Wiesbaden: Otto Harrassowitz.

Gnoli, Raniero. 1977 and 1978a. *The Gilgit Manuscript of the Saṅghabhedavastu, Being the 17th and Last Section of the Vinaya of the Mūlasarvāstivādin.* 2 vols. Serie Orientale Roma 49,1. Rome: Istituto Italiano per il Medio ed Estremo Oriente.

———., ed. 1978b. *The Gilgit Manuscript of the Śāyanāsanavastu and the Adhikaraṇavastu.* Rome: Istituto Italiano per il Medio ed Estremo Oriente.

Grant, Beata. 1996. "Female Holder of the Lineage: Linji Chan Master Zhiyuan Xinggang (1597–1654)." *Late Imperial China* 17.2: 51–76.

———. 2003. *Daughters of Emptiness: Poems of Chinese Buddhist Nuns.* Boston: Wisdom Publications.

Gross, Rita M. 1993. *Buddhism after Patriarchy: A Feminist History, Analysis, and Reconstruction of Buddhism*. Albany: State University of New York Press.

Gunawardhana, R. A. L. H. 1979. *Robe and Plough: Monasticism and Economic Interest in Early Medieval Sri Lanka.* Tucson: University of Arizona Press.

———. 1990. "Subtile Silk of Ferreous Firmness: Buddhist Nuns in Ancient and Early Medieval Sri Lanka and their Role in the Propagation of Buddhism." *Sri Lanka Journal of the Humanities* 14.1–2: 1–59.

Gyatso, Janet. 1993. "The Logic of Legitimation in the Tibetan Treasure Tradition." *History of Religions* 33.2: 97–134.

———. 1996. "Drawn from the Tibetan Treasury: The gTer ma Literature." In

Tibetan Literature: Studies in Genre: Essays in Honor of Geshe Lhundup Sopa, edited by José Cabezón and Roger Jackson, 147–69. Ithaca, NY: Snow Lion.

———. 2003. "One Plus One Makes Three: Buddhist Gender Conception and the Law of the Non-Excluded Middle." *History of Religions* 43.2: 89–115.

Harris, Elizabeth J. 1999. "The Female in Buddhism." In *Buddhist Women across Cultures: Realizations*, edited by Karma Lekshe Tsomo, 49–65. Albany: State University of New York Press.

Harvey, Peter. 2000. *An Introduction to Buddhist Ethics.* Cambridge: Cambridge University Press.

Heirman, Ann. 1997. "Some Remarks on the Rise of the Bhikṣuṇīsaṃgha and on the Ordination Ceremony for Bhikṣuṇīs according to the Dharmaguptaka Vinaya." *Journal of the International Association of Buddhist Studies* 20.2: 33–85.

———. 1998. "Gurudharma: An Important Vinaya Rule." *Indian Journal of Buddhist Studies* 10: 18–26.

———. 2001. "Chinese Nuns and Their Ordination in Fifth-Century China." *Journal of the International Association of Buddhist Studies* 24: 275–304.

———. 2002a. "Can We Trace the Early Dharmaguptakas?" *T'oung Pao* 88: 396–429.

———. 2002b. *"The Discipline in Four Parts": Rules for Nuns according to the Dharmaguptakavinaya*. 3 vols. Buddhist Tradition Series 47. Delhi: Motilal Banarsidass.

Henderson, Julie. 1997. "Tulku." In *Being Bodies: Buddhist Women on the Paradox of Embodiment*, edited by Lenore Friedman and Susan Moon, 216–22. Boston: Shambhala.

Heng-Ching Shih. 2000. "Lineage and Transmission: Integrating the Chinese and Tibetan Orders of Buddhist Nuns." *Chung-Hwa Buddhist Journal* 13.2 (May): 503–48.

Hinüber, Oskar von. 1987. "Das buddhistische Recht und die Phonetik des Pāli. Ein Abschnitt aus der Samantapāsādikā über die Vermeidung von Aussprachefehlern in Kammavācās." *Studien zur Indologie und Iranistik* 13.14: 101–27.

———. 2007. "The Foundation of the Bhikkhunī Saṃgha: A Contribution to the Earliest History of Buddhism." Paper delivered at Ryukoku University, November 5th.

———. 2008. "The Foundation of the Bhikṣuṇīsaṃgha: A Contribution to the Earliest History of Buddhism." In *Annual Report of the International Research Institute for Advanced Buddhology at Soka University for the Academic Year 2007*, 11: 3–19.

Hirakawa, Akira. 1982. *Monastic Discipline for the Buddhist Nuns: An English Translation of the Chinese Text of the Mahāsāṃghika-Bhikṣuṇī-Vinaya*. Patna, India: Jayaswal Research Institute.

———. 1998. *Bikuni ritsu no kenkyu. Hirakawa Akira chosaku-shu* 13. Tokyo: Shunjusha.

Horner, I. B. 1930. *Women under Primitive Buddhism: Laywomen and Almswomen.* London: G. Routlege and Sons.

———. 1979. "The Buddha's Co-Natals." In *Studies in Pāli and Buddhism: A Memorial Volume in Honor of Bhikkhu Jagdish Kashyap*, edited by A. K. Narain, 115–20. Delhi: B. R. Publishing.

———. 1990. Reprint of Horner 1930. Delhi: Motilal Banarsidass.

———., trans. 1952. *The Book of the Discipline.* Oxford: The Pali Text Society.

Hummel, Siegbert. 1974. "Transmigrations- und Inkarnationsreihen in Tibet unter besonderer Berücksichtigung der Bon-Religion." *Acta Orientalia* 36: 181–90.

Hüsken, Ute. 1993. "Die Legende von der Einrichtung des buddhistischen Nonnenordens im Vinaya-Piṭaka der Theravādin." In *Studien zur Indologie und Buddhismuskunde: Festgabe des Seminars für Indologie und Buddhismuskunde für Professor Dr. Heinz Bechert*, edited by R. Grünendahl, J.-U. Hartmann, and P. Kieffer-Pülz, 151–70. Indica et Tibetica 22. Bonn: Indica et Tibetica.

———. 1997. *Die Vorschriften für die buddhistische Nonnengemeinde im Vinaya-Piṭaka der Theravādin* [The Rules for the Order of Buddhist Nuns in the Vinaya-Piṭaka of the Theravādin]. Monographien zur indischen Archäologie, Kunst und Philologie 11. Berlin: Dietrich Reimer.

———. "The Legend of the Establishment of the Buddhist Order of Nuns in the Theravāda Vinaya-Piṭaka." *Journal of the Pali Text Society* 26: 43–69 [translation of Hüsken 1993].

———. 2006. "'Gotamī, Do Not Wish to Go from Home to Homelessness!': Patterns of Objections to Female Asceticism in Theravāda Buddhism." In *Asceticism and Its Critics: Historical Accounts and Comparative Perspectives*, edited by Oliver Freiberger, 211–33. New York: Oxford University Press.

Huxley, Andrew. 1996. "The Vinaya: Legal System or Performance-Enhancing Drug?" In *The Buddhist Forum*, vol. 4, edited by Tadeusz Skorupski. London: School of Oriental and African Studies.

Jackson, David P. 1987. *The Entrance Gate for the Wise (Section III): Sa-skya Paṇḍita on Indian and Tibetan Traditions of Pramāṇa and Philosophical Debate.* Wiener Studien zur Tibetologie und Buddhismuskund 17.1. Vienna: Arbeitskreis für Tibetische und Buddhistische Studien, Universität Wien.

Jacobi, Hermann. 1879. *The Kalpasūtra of Bhadrabāhu.* Leipzig: Brockhaus.

Jaini, Padmanabh S. 1991. *Gender and Salvation: Jaina Debates on the Spiritual Liberation of Women.* Berkeley: University of California Press.

Jing Yin. 2006. "The Transformation of the Saṅgha and the Emergence of Three Dimensions of the Vinaya." *Journal of the Centre for Buddhist Studies, Sri Lanka* 4: 270–311.

Jordt, Ingrid. 1988. "Bhikkhuni, Tilashin, Mae-chii: Women Who Renounce the World in Burma, Thailand and the Classical Pali Buddhist Texts." *Crossroads* 4.1: 31–39.

Juo-Hsüeh Shih, Bhikkhunī. 2000. *Controversies over Buddhist Nuns.* Oxford: Pali Text Society.

Kabilsingh, Chatsumarn. 1984. *A Comparative Study of Bhikkhunī Pāṭimokkha*. Chaukhambha Oriental Research Studies 28. Varanasi: Chaukhambha Orientalia.

———. 1991. *Thai Women in Buddhism*. Berkeley: Parallax Press.

Kajiyama, Yuichi. 1982. "Women in Buddhism." *The Eastern Buddhist* 25.2: 53–70.

———. 1989. "Women in Buddhism." In Yuichi Kajiyama, *Studies in Buddhist Philosophy (Selected Papers)*, edited by Katsumi Mimaki et al. Kyoto: Rinsen.

Kawanami, Hiroko. 2007. "The Bhikkhunī Ordination Debate: Global Aspirations, Local Concerns, with special emphasis on the views of the monastic community in Burma." *Buddhist Studies Review* 24.2: 226–44.

Keyes, Charles F. 1984. "Mother or Mistress but Never a Monk: Buddhist Notions of Female Gender in Rural Thailand." *American Ethnologist* 11.2 (May): 223–41.

Khan, J. A. 1990. "Position of Women as Reflected in Sāñcī Stūpa Inscriptions." *Journal of the Oriental Institute (Baroda)* 39.3–4: 231–37.

Khandelwal, Meena. 2004. *Women in Ochre Robes: Gendering Hindu Renunciation*. Albany: State University of New York Press.

Kieffer-Pülz, Petra. 1992. *Die Sīmā: Vorschriften zur Regelung der buddhistischen Gemeindegrenze in älteren buddhistischen Texten*. Monographien zur indischen Archäologie, Kunst und Philologie 8. Berlin: Franz Steiner.

———. 2000. "Die buddhistische Germeinde." In *Der Buddhismus I: Der indische Buddhismus und seine Verzweigungen*, edited by H. Bechert, 281–402. Die Religionen der Menschheit 24,1. Stuttgart: Kohlhammer.

Kloppenborg, Ria. 1983. "The Earliest Buddhist Ritual of Ordination." In *Selected Studies on Ritual in the Indian Religions: Essays to D. J. Hoens*, edited by R. Kloppenborg, 155–68. Leiden: Brill.

———. 1995. "Female Stereotypes in Early Buddhism: The Women of the Therīgāthā." In *Female Stereotypes in Religious Traditions*, edited by R. Kloppenborg and W. J. Hanegraaff, 151–69. Studies in the History of Religions, Numen Book Series 66. Leiden: Brill.

Kongtrul Lodro Taye, Jamgon. 1998. *Buddhist Ethics*. Translated by the International Translation Committee founded by the V. V. Kalu Rinpoche. Ithaca, NY: Snow Lion.

Kusuma, Bhikkhunī. 2000. "Inaccuracies in Buddhist Women's History." In *Innovative Buddhist Women: Swimming Against the Stream*, edited by Karma Lekshe Tsomo, 5–12. London: Curzon.

Lamotte, Étienne. 1958. *Histoire du Bouddhisme Indien: Des Origines à L'Ère Śaka*. Louvain-la-Neuve: Institut Orientaliste.

———. 1981. *Le Traité de la Grande Vertu de Sagesse de Nāgārjuna (Mahāprajñāpāramitāśāstra)*. Publication de l'Institut Orientaliste de Louvain 25, vol. 1. Louvain-la-Neuve: Institut Orientaliste. (Orig. pub. 1944.)

Laut, Jens Peter. 1991. "Die Gründung des buddhistischen Nonnenordens in der alttürkischen Überlieferung." In *Türkische Sprachen und Literaturen: Materi-*

alien der ersten deutschen Turkologen-Konferenz, edited by I. Baldauf, 257–74. Wiesbaden: Otto Harrassowitz.

Law, Bimala Churn. 1927. *Women in Buddhist Literature*. Ceylon: W. E. Bastian.

———. 1940. "Bhikṣuṇīs in Indian Inscriptions." *Epigraphia Indica* 25: 31–34.

Lefmann, S. 1902. *Lalita Vistara, Leben und Lehre des Çâkya-Buddha*. Halle: Verlag der Buchhandlung des Waisenhauses.

Lü, Cheng. "Āgama." 1963. In *Encyclopaedia of Buddhism*, edited by G. P. Malalasekera, vol. 1.2: 241–44. Sri Lanka: Department of Buddhist Affairs.

Lüders, Heinrich. 1973. *A List of Brāhmī Inscriptions, From the Earliest Times to about A.D. 400, With the Exception of those of Asoka*. Varanasi: Indological Book House.

Makley, Charlene. 2005. "The Body of a Nun: Nunhood and Gender in Contemporary Amdo." In *Women in Tibet*, edited by Janet Gyatso and Hanna Havnevik, 259–84. New York: Columbia University Press.

Malalasekera, G. P. 1938. *Dictionary of Pāli Proper Names*. 2 vols. London: Pali Text Society. (PTS repr. 1983; and Delhi: Munshiram Manoharlal, 1995.)

Martin, Dan. 1998. "The Highland Vinaya Lineage: A Study of a 12th-Century Monastic Historical Source, the 'Transmission Document' by Zhing-mo-che-ba." Forthcoming in the proceedings of the 8th International Association for Tibetan Studies conference, held in Bloomington, Indiana in 1998.

———. 2005. "The Woman Illusion? Research into the Lives of Spiritually Accomplished Women Leaders of the 11th and 12th Centuries." In *Women in Tibet*, edited by Janet Gyatso and Hanna Havnevik, 49–82. New York: Columbia University Press.

Mayeda [= Maeda], Egaku. 1985. "Japanese Studies on the Schools of the Chinese Āgamas." In *Zur Schulzugehörigkeit von Werken der Hīnayāna-Literatur*, vol. 1, edited by H. Bechert, 94–103. Symposien zur Buddhismusforschung, III,1, Abhandlungen der Akademie der Wissenschaften in Göttingen, Philologisch-Historische Klasse, Dritte Folge Nr. 149. Göttingen: Vandenhoeck & Ruprecht.

Michael, Franz H. 1982. *Rule by Incarnation: Tibetan Buddhism and Its Role in Society and State*. Boulder, CO: Westview Press.

Mill, John Stuart. 1869. *The Subjection of Women*. London. Online version: http://ebooks.adelaide.edu.au/m/mill/john_stuart/m645s/.

Minayeff, J. P., ed. 1887. "Sīmāvivādavinicchayakathā." *Journal of the Pali Text Society* 2.3: 17–34.

Mingun Jetavan Sayadaw. 1949. ["Can an Extinct Bhikkhunī Sangha Be Revived?"] In *Milindapañha Aṭṭhakathā*, pp. 228–38. Rangoon: Haṃsāvatī Piṭaka Press. Translated from the Pāli in the present volume by Bhikkhu Bodhi.

Minh Chau, Thich. 1991. *The Chinese Madhyama Āgama and the Pāli Majjhima Nikāya*. Buddhist Tradition Series 15. Delhi: Motilal Banarsidass.

Mochizuki, Shinko. 1940. "The Places of Varṣāvasāna during Forty-five Years of the Buddha's Career after His Enlightenment." *Studies on Buddhism in Japan* 2: 29–44. Tokyo: International Buddhist Society.

Murcott, Susan. 1991. *The First Buddhist Women: Translations and Commentaries on the Therigatha*. Berkeley: Parallax Press.

Ñāṇamoli, Bhikkhu. 1992. *The Life of the Buddha, According to the Pāli Canon.* Kandy, Sri Lanka: Buddhist Publication Society.

Ñāṇamoli, Bhikkhu, and Bhikkhu Bodhi, trans. 1995. *The Middle Length Discourses of the Buddha: A New Translation of the Majjhima Nikāya*. Boston: Wisdom Publications. (Rev. ed. 2001.)

Nattier, Jan. 1991. *Once Upon a Future Time: Studies in a Buddhist Prophecy of Decline.* Nanzan Studies in Asian Religions. Berkeley: Asian Humanities Press.

———. 2004. "Decline of the Dharma." In *Encyclopedia of Buddhism*, vol. 1, edited by R. E. Buswell, 210–13. New York: Macmillan.

Neumann, Karl Eugen. 1995. *Die Reden des Buddha, Mittlere Sammlung, Aus dem Pāli-Kanon Übersetzt*. Herrnschrot: Beyerlein & Steinschulte. (Orig. pub. 1896–1902.)

Ngari Panchen, Pema Wangyi Gyalpo. 1996. *Perfect Conduct*. Commentary by Dudjom Rinpoche. Translated by Khenpo Gyurme Samdrub and Sangye Khandro. Boston: Wisdom Publications.

Norman, Kenneth R. 1983. *Pāli Literature: Including the Canonical Literature in Prakrit and Sanskrit of All the Hīnayāna Schools of Buddhism*. Wiesbaden: Otto Harrassowitz.

Nyanaponika Thera and Hellmuth Hecker. 1997. *Great Disciples of the Buddha: Their Lives, Their Works, Their Legacy*, with an introduction by Bhikkhu Bodhi. Boston: Wisdom Publications.

Obermiller, E. 1932. *History of Buddhism by Bu-ston*. Part II. Materialien zur Kunde des Buddhismus 18. Heidelberg: Harrassowitz.

———., trans. 1986. *The History of Buddhism in India and Tibet by Bu-ston.* Bibliotheca Indo-Buddhica 26. Delhi: Sri Satguru.

Ohnuma, Reiko. 2006. "Debt to the Mother: A Neglected Aspect of the Founding of the Buddhist Nun's Order." *Journal of the American Academy of Religion* 74.4: 861–901.

Oldenberg, Hermann. 1879. *The Dīpavaṃsa: An Ancient Buddhist Historical Record.* London: Williams and Norgate.

Pachow, W. 1953. "Further Studies on the Avadānaśataka." *University of Allahabad Studies*: 1–12.

———. 1955. *A Comparative Study of the Prātimokṣa*. Santiniketan: The Sino-Indian Cultural Society.

Panglung, Jampa Losang. 1981. *Die Erzählstoffe des Mūlasarvāstivāda-Vinaya Analysiert auf Grund der Tibetischen Übersetzung*. Studia Philogical Buddhisca Monograph Series 3. Tokyo: The Reiyukai Library.

Pao-ch'ang. 1994. *Lives of the Nuns: Biographies of Chinese Buddhist Nuns from the Fourth to Sixth Centuries.* Translated by Kathryn Tsai. Honolulu: University of Hawaii Press.

Pāsādika, Bhikkhu. 1989. *Nāgārjuna's Sūtrasamuccaya: A Critical Edition of the mDo kun las btus pa*. Fontes Tibetici Havnienses 2. Copenhagen: Akademisk Forlag.

Paul, Diana Y. 1979. *Women in Buddhism: Images of the Feminine in Mahāyāna Tradition*. Berkeley: University of California Press. (Rev. ed. 1985.)

Plaskow, Judith. 2005. *The Coming of Lilith: Essays on Feminism, Judaism and Sexual Ethics, 1972–2003*. Boston: Beacon.

Pruitt, William, trans. 1998. *The Commentary on the Verses of the Therīs (Therīgāthā-Aṭṭhakathā Paramatthadīpanī VI) by Ācarya Dhammapāla*. Oxford: Pali Text Society.

Ray, Reginald A. 1986. "Some Aspects of the Tulku Tradition in Tibet." *Tibet Journal* (Dharamsala, India) 11.4: 35–69.

Rhoton, Jared, trans. 2002. *A Clear Differentiation of the Three Codes*. Albany: State University of New York Press.

Ridding, C. M., and L. de la Vallée Poussin. 1920. "A Fragment of the Sanskrit Vinaya Bhikṣuṇīkarmavacāna." *Bulletin of the School of Oriental Studies* 1.3: 123–43.

Roerich, George, trans. 1979. *The Blue Annals* [of Gö Lotsāwa]. Delhi: Motilal Barnasidass. (Orig. pub. Calcutta, 1949–53.)

Rosen, Valentina. 1959. *Der Vinayavibhaṅga zum Bhikṣuprātimokṣa der Sarvāstivādins*. Berlin: Akademie-Verlag.

Roth, Gustav, ed. 1970. *Bhikṣuṇī-Vinaya: Including Bhikṣuṇī-Prakīrṇaka and a Summary of the Bhikṣu-Prakīrṇaka of the Ārya-Mahāsāṃghika-Lokottaravādin*. Tibetan Sanskrit Works Series 12. Patna: K. P. Jayaswal Research Institute.

Ruether, Rosemary. 1979. "A Religion for Women." *Christianity and Crisis* (December 10): 307–11.

Ruether, Rosemary Radford. 1985. *Women-Church: Theology and Practice of Feminist Liturgical Communities*. San Francisco: Harper and Row.

Sankrityayana, Rahul. 1981. *Vinayasūtra of Bhadanta Gunaprabha*. Singhi Jain Śāstra Śiksāpītha Singhi Jain Series 74. Bombay: Bharatiya Vidya Bhavan.

Sasson, Vanessa R. 2007. "Politics of Higher Ordination for Women in Sri Lanka: Discussions with Silmātās." *Journal for the Study of Religion* 20.1: 57–71.

Schmidt, Michael. 1993. "Bhikṣuṇī-Karmavācanā, Die Handschrift Sansk. c.25(R) der Bodleian Library Oxford." In *Studien zur Indologie und Buddhismuskunde: Festgabe des Seminars für Indologie und Buddhismuskunde für Professor Dr. Heinz Bechert*, edited by Reinhold Grünendahl, Jens-Uwe Hartmann, and Petra Kieffer-Pülz, 239–88. Monographien zu den Sprachen und Literaturen des indotibetischen Kulturraumes 22. Bonn: Indica et Tibetica Verlag.

———. 1994. "Zur Schulzugehörigkeit einer nepalesischen Handschrift der Bhikṣuṇī-Karmavācanā." In *Untersuchungen zur Buddhistischen Literatur* (Sanskrit Wörterbuch der buddhistischen Texte aus den Turfanfunden, Beiheft 5), 155–64. Göttingen: Vandenhoeck & Ruprecht.

———. 1997. "Zum Titel des Saṅgīti Sūtra." In *Untersuchungen zu Buddhistischen Literatur II* (Sanskrit Wörterbuch der buddhistischen Texte aus den Turfan-

Funden, Beiheft 8), edited by H. Bechert, 303–5. Göttingen: Vandenhoeck & Ruprecht.

Schopen, Gregory. 1994. "Ritual Rites and the Bones of Contention: More on the Monastic Funerals and Relics in the Mūlasarvāstivāda-Vinaya." *Journal of Indian Philosophy* 22: 31–80.

———. 1997. "On Monks, Nuns and 'Vulgar' Practices: The Introduction of the Image Cult into Indian Buddhism." In *Bones, Stones, and Buddhist Monks: Collected Papers on the Archaeology, Epigraphy, and Texts of Monastic Buddhism in India*, 238–57. Honolulu: University of Hawaii Press. (Orig. pub. 1988–89.)

———. 2004. *Buddhist Monks and Business Matters.* Honolulu: University of Hawaii Press.

Senart, Émile. 1897. *Le Mahāvastu.* Société Asiatique, Collection d'Ouvrages Orientaux, Seconde Série, vol. 3. Paris: Imprimerie Nationale.

Shakabpa, W. D. 1976. *Tibet: A Political History.* New Haven, CT: Yale University Press.

Sharma, Arvind. 1977. "How and Why Did the Women in Ancient India Become Buddhist Nuns?" *Sociological Analysis* 38: 239–51.

Situ Chos kyi 'byung gnas, ed. 1976–79. *The Sde-dge Mtshal-par Bka'-'gyur: A facsimile edition of the 18th century redaction of Si-tu Chos-kyi-'byuṅ-gnas prepared under the direction of H. H. the 16th Rgyal-dbaṅ Karma-pa.* Delhi: Delhi Karmapae Chodhey Gyalwae Sungrab Partun Khang.

Skilling, Peter. 1993/94. "A Note on the History of the Bhikkhunī-saṅgha (II): The Order of Nuns after the Parinirvāṇa." *World Fellowship of Buddhists Review* 30.4–31.1: 29–49.

———. 1994. "A Note on the History of the Bhikkhunī-saṅgha (I): Nuns at the Time of the Buddha." *World Fellowship of Buddhists Review* 31. 2–3: 47–55.

———. 2000. "Nonnen, Laienanhängerinnen, Spenderinnen, Göttinnen: Weibliche Rollen im Frühen Indischen Buddhismus." In *Aspekte des Weiblichen in der Indischen Kultur*, edited by Ulrike Roesler, 47–102. Indica et Tibetica 39, Arbeitsmaterialien zur Religionsgeschichte 15. Swisstal-Odendorf: Indica et Tibetica Verlag.

———. 2001. "Eṣā agrā: Images of Nuns in (Mūla-)Sarvastivādin Literature." *Journal of the International Association of Buddhist Studies* 24.2: 135–56.

Snellgrove, David. 1987. *Indo-Tibetan Buddhism.* Boston: Shambhala.

Sobisch, Jan-Ulrich. 2002. *Three-Vow Theories in Tibetan Buddhism: A Comparative Study of Major Traditions from the Twelfth Through Nineteenth Centuries.* Contributions to Tibetan Studies 1. Wiesbaden: Dr. Ludwig Reichert Verlag.

———. 2002b. "The 'Records of Teachings Received' in the Collected Works of A-mes-zhabs: An Untapped Source for the Study of Sa skya pa Biographies." In *Tibet, Past and Present*, edited by Henk Blezer and Abel Zadoks, 161–81. Proceedings of the Ninth Seminar of the IATS, Leiden 2000. Leiden: Brill.

———. 2007. *Life, Transmissions, and Works of A-mes-zhabs Ngag-dbang-kun-dga'-bsod-nams, the Great 17th Century Sa-skya-pa Bibliophile*, edited by Hartmut-

Ortwin Feistel. Verzeichnis der orientalischen Handschriften in Deutschland, VOHD, Supplementband 38. Stuttgart: Franz Steiner Verlag.

Speyer, J. S., ed. 1970. *Avadānaçataka: A Century of Edifying Tales Belonging to the Hīnayāna*. Bibliotheca Buddhica III, vol. 2. Osnabrück: Biblio Verlag. (Orig. pub. 1909; Repr. The Hague: Mouton, 1958.)

Sponberg, Alan. 1992. "Attitudes toward Women and the Feminine in Early Buddhism." In *Buddhism, Sexuality, and Gender*, edited by José Cabezon, 3–36. Albany: State University of New York Press.

Stache-Rosen, Valentina. 1968. *Dogmatische Begriffsreihen im Älteren Buddhismus II: Das Saṅgītisūtra und sein Kommentar Saṅgītiparyāya*. Sanskrittexte aus den Turfanfunden 9, Institut für Orientforschung, Veröffentlichung 65. Berlin: Akademie Verlag.

Sumala. 1991. "Women in Buddhism." *Monastic Studies: Buddhist and Christian Monasticism* (Benedictine Priory of Montreal) 19: 114–18.

Suvimalee, Samaneri. 2005. "The Female in Early Buddhism: Sex Equality and Social Gender." In *Dhamma-Vinaya, Essays in Honour of Venerable Professor Dhammavihari*, edited by A. Tilakaratne et al., 203–27. Colombo: Sri Lanka Association for Buddhist Studies.

Suzuki, Daisetz T., ed. 1961. *The Tibetan Tripiṭaka: Peking Edition, Kept in the Library of Otani University, Kyoto*. Tokyo/Kyoto: Tibetan Tripiṭaka Research Institute.

Szerb, Janos. 1990. *Bu ston's History of Buddhism in Tibet*. Vienna: Osterreichischen Akademie der Wissenschaften.

Takakusu, Junjirō, and Kaigyoku Watanabe, comps. 1924–34. *Taishō Shinshū Daizōkyō*. 85 vols. (texts), 12 vols. (illustrations), and 3 vols. (catalogs). Tokyo: Taisho Issai-Kyō Kanko Kwai.

Taw Sein Ko. 1893. "A Preliminary Study of the Kalyāṇi Inscriptions of Dhammacheti 1476 A.D." *Indian Antiquary* 22: passim.

Taylor, J. L. 1993. *Forest Monks and the Nation-State: An Anthropological and Historical Study in Northeastern Thailand*. Singapore: Institute of Southeast Asian Studies.

Thomas, Edward J. 1927. *The Life of Buddha as Legend and History*. London: K. Paul, Trench, Trubner.

Thub bstan byang chub, ed. 2000. *Gzhi smra'i lugs kyi dge slong ma'i las chog gcig tu btus pa thub dbang zhal lung*. Dharamsala: Bod gzhung chos rig las khungs (Department of Religion and Culture).

Tibetan-Chinese Dictionary, Bod-rgya tshig-mdzod chen-mo. 1993. Min tsu chu pan she; Ti 1 pan edition.

Tilakaratne, Asaṅga. 2005. "Personality Differences of Arahants and the Origins of Theravāda, A Study of Two Great Elders of the Theravāda Tradition: Mahā Kassapa and Ānanda." In *Dhamma-Vinaya, Essays in Honour of Venerable Professor Dhammavihari*, edited by A. Tilakaratne et al., 229–57. Colombo: Sri Lanka Association for Buddhist Studies.

Tsai, Kathryn Ann. 1994. *Lives of the Nuns: Biographies of Chinese Buddhist Nuns from the Fourth to Sixth Centuries: A Translation of the Pi-ch'iu-ni chuan, compiled by Shih Pao-ch'ang*. Honolulu: University of Hawaii Press.

Tsedroen, Jampa. 1992. *A Brief Survey of the Vinaya: Its Origin, Transmission and Arrangement from the Tibetan Point of View with Comparisons to the Theravāda and Dharmagutpa Traditions.* Vinaya Research 1. Hamburg: Dharma Editions.

———. 2006. "Bhikṣuṇī Ordination." In *Out of the Shadows: Socially Engaged Women*, edited by Karma Lekshe Tsomo, pp. 305–9. Delhi: Sri Satguru Publications.

———. 2008. "Generation to Generation: Transmitting the Bhikṣuṇī Lineage in the Tibetan Tradition." In *Buddhist Women in a Global Multicultural Community: 9th Sakyadhita International Conference*, edited by Karma Lekshe Tsomo, 205–15. Kuala Lumpur: Sukhi Hotu Publications. Also in *Buddhism, World Culture and Human Values (Selections from the Proceedings of the International Conferences on Buddhism in Asia: Challenges and Prospects; Human Values and Buddhism and World Culture, held at CIHTS, Sarnath, Varanasi)*, edited by Pabitrakumar Roy, pp. 20–33. Sarnath, India: Central Institute for Higher Tibetan Studies, 2009.

Tsering, Tashi. 2000. *Advice of the Supreme Victor.* Dharamsala: Department of Religion and Culture. A translation of Thub bstan byang chub 2000.

Tsering, Tashi, and Philippa Russell. 2002. "An Account of the Buddhist Ordination of Women." In *Concerning the Lineage of Bhikṣhuni Ordination: Proceedings of Mūlasarvāstivāda, Theravāda and Dharmagupta Vinaya Holders.* Dharamsala: Department of Religion and Culture.

Tsomo, Karma Lekshe. 1996. *Sisters in Solitude: Two Traditions of Buddhist Monastic Ethics for Women; A Comparative Analysis of the Chinese Dharmagupta and the Tibetan Mūlasarvāstivāda Bhikṣuṇī Prātimokṣa Sūtras.* Albany: State University of New York Press.

Uebach, Helga. 1987. *Nel-Pa Pandita's Chronik Me-Tog Phren-Ba: Handschrift der Library of Tibetan Works and Archives.* Studia Tibetica, Quellen und Studien zur tibetischen Lexikographie, Band I. München: Kommission fur Zentralasiatische Studien, Bayerische Akademie der Wissenschaften.

Vaidya, P. L., ed. 1959. *Avadānaśataka.* Darbhanga: Mithila Institute of Post-graduate Studies and Research in Sanskrit Learning.

Vajirañāṇavarorasa. 1979. *Autobiography: The Life of the Prince-Patriarch Vajirañāṇa of Siam, 1860–1921.* Translated, edited, and introduced by Craig J. Reynolds. Athens: Ohio University Press.

Vinayasūtra's Pravrajyāvastu Study Group. 2003. "The *Pravrajyāvastu* of the *Vinayasūtra* and its *Vṛtti* (1)." *Annual of the Institute for Comprehensive Studies of Buddhism Taisho University* 25: 44–93.

Vogel, Claus, and Klaus Wille. 1984. "Some Hitherto Unidentified Fragments of the Pravrajyāvastu Portion of the Vinayavastu Manuscript Found in Gilgit." In

Nachrichten der Akademie der Wissenschaften Göttingen, Philologisch-Historische Klasse, 299–337. Göttingen: Vandenhoeck & Ruprecht.

Waldschmidt, Ernst. 1950 and 1951. *Das Mahāparinirvāṇasūtra: Text in Sanskrit und Tibetisch, Verglichen mit dem Pāli nebst einer Übersetzung der chinesischen Entsprechung im Vinaya der Mūlasarvāstivādins.* Abhandlungen der Akademie der Wissenschaften in Göttingen, Philologisch-Historische Klasse, Jahrgang 1949 Nr. 1, Nr. 2. Berlin: Akademie Verlag.

———. 1952 and 1957. *Das Catuṣpariṣatsūtra: Eine kanonische Lehrschrift über die Begründung der buddhistischen Gemeinde.* 2 vols. Abhandlungen der Deutschen Akademie der Wissenschaften zu Berlin, Klasse für Sprachen, Literatur und Kunst, 1952 Nr. 2, 1956 Nr. 1. Berlin: Akademie Verlag.

———. 1955. "Die Einleitung des Saṅgītisūtra." *Zeitschrift der Deutschen Morgenländischen Gesellschaft* 105: 298–318.

———. 1980. "Central Asian Sūtra Fragments and their Relation to the Chinese Āgamas." In *The Language of the Earliest Buddhist Tradition*, edited by H. Bechert, 136–74. Symposien zur Buddhismusforschung, II, Abhandlungen der Akademie der Wissenschaften in Göttingen, Philologisch-Historische Klasse, Dritte Folge, Nr. 117. Göttingen: Vandenhoeck & Ruprecht.

Waldschmidt, Ernst et al. 1971. *Sanskrithandschriften aus den Turfanfunden,* vol. 3. Wiesbaden: Franz Steiner.

Waldschmidt, Ernst, and Heinz Bechert, eds. 1973–present. *Sanskrit-Wörterbuch der buddhistischen Texte aus den Turfan-Funden.* Göttingen: Vandenhoeck & Ruprecht.

Walshe, Maurice, trans. 1996. *The Long Discourses of the Buddha: A Translation of the Dīgha Nikāya.* Boston: Wisdom Publications. (Orig. pub. 1987 as *Thus Have I Heard.*)

Walters, Jonathan S. 1994. "A Voice from the Silence: The Buddha's Mother's Story." *History of Religions* 33: 358–79.

Wang Seng. 1997. *Xizang fojiao fazhan shilue* 西藏佛教发展史略 [*A Brief History of the Development of Tibetan Buddhism*]. Beijing: Chungguo shehuikexue chubanshe.

Watson, Craig. 1978. "The Second Propagation of Buddhism from Eastern Tibet according to the 'Short Biography of dGongs-pa Rab-gsal' by the Third Thukvan bLo-bzang Chos-kyi Nyi-ma (1737–1802)." *Central Asiatic Journal* 22.3–4: 263–85.

———. 1980. "The Introduction of the Second Propagation of Buddhism in Tibet according to R. A. Stein's Edition of the sBa-bZhed." *Tibet Journal* 5.4 (Winter): 20–27.

Weeraratne, D. Amarasiri. 1998. "Revival of the Bhikkhunī Order in Sri Lanka," *The Island* Newspaper (Colombo), April 4.

Wieger, Léon. 1910. *Bouddhisme Chinois, vol. 1: Vinaya: Monachisme et Discipline. Hinayana: Véhicule Inférieur*. Paris: Guilmoto, 1910.

Wijayaratna, Môhan. 1991. *Les moniales bouddhistes, naissance et développement du monachisme féminin* (*Patrimoines bouddhisme*). Paris: Les Éditions du Cerf.

Wijetunge, Ratna. 2005. "Pali Canon on Women's Liberation." In *Dhamma-Vinaya, Essays in Honour of Venerable Professor Dhammavihari*, edited by A. Tilakaratne et al., 273–90. Colombo: Sri Lanka Association for Buddhist Studies.

Willemen, Charles. 1994. *The Storehouse of Sundry Valuables.* Tokyo: Numata Center for Buddhist Translation and Research.

Williams, Liz. 2000. "*A Whisper in the Silence: Nuns before Mahāpajāpatī.*" *Buddhist Studies Review* 17.2: 167–73.

———. 2002. "Red Rust, Robbers and Rice Fields: Women's Part in the Precipitation of the Decline of the Dhamma." *Buddhist Studies Review* 19.1: 41–48.

———. 2005. W*omen's Ordination in Theravāda Buddhism: Ancient Evidence and Modern Debates*. Ph.D. diss., University of Sunderland, U.K.

Willis, Janice D. 1985. "Nuns and Benefactresses: The Role of Women in the Development of Buddhism." In *Women, Religion, and Social Change*, edited by I. Y. Haddad et al., 59–85. Albany: State University of New York Press.

Wilson, Liz. 1995. "Seeing through the Gendered 'I.'" *Journal of Feminist Studies in Religion* 11.1: 41–80.

———. 1996. *Charming Cadavers: Horrific Figurations of the Feminine in Indian Buddhist Hagiographic Literature.* Chicago: University of Chicago Press.

Witanachchi, C. 1965. "Ānanda." In *Encyclopaedia of Buddhism*, edited by G. P. Malalasekera, vol. 1.4: 529–36. Sri Lanka: Department of Buddhist Affairs.

Wu Yin, Bhikṣuṇī. 2001. *Choosing Simplicity: Commentary on the Bhikṣhuni Pratimoksha.* Edited by Thubten Chodron. Ithaca, NY: Snow Lion.

Wylie, Turrel V. 1978. "Reincarnation: A Political Innovation in Tibetan Buddhism." *Proceedings of the Csoma de Körös Memorial Symposium*, edited by Louis Ligeti, 579–86. Budapest: Akadémiai Kiadó.

Yifa. 2002. *The Origins of Buddhist Monastic Codes in China: An Annotated Translation and Study of the Chanyuan Qinggui.* Honolulu: University of Hawaii Press.

Yinshun [印順]. 1983. 原始佛教聖典之集成 [*The Compilation of the Early Buddhist Canon*]. Taipei: 正聞出版社.

Yonezawa, Y., et al. 2001. *Introduction to the Facsimile Edition of a Collection of Sanskrit Palm-Leaf Manuscripts in the Tibetan dBu-med script.* Tokyo: Taishō University Institute for Comprehensive Studies of Buddhism.

Yuan Liang 源諒 (Bhikṣu). 1987 [1765]. *Luzong dengpu* 律宗燈譜 [*The Genealogy of Vinaya School*]. Taipei: Xinwenfeng Publishing Company.

Yuyama, Akira. 1992. "Pañcāśatī, '500' or '50'? With special reference to the Lotus Sūtra." In *The Dating of the Historical Buddha*, vol. 2, edited by Heinz Bechert, 208–33. Symposien zur Buddhismusforschung, IV,2; Abhandlungen der Akademie der Wissenschaften in Göttigen, Philologisch-Historische Klasse, Dritte Folge, Nr. 194. Göttingen: Vandenhoeck & Ruprecht.

About the Contributors

Anālayo

Bhikkhu Anālayo was born in Germany in 1962 and ordained in Sri Lanka in 1995. In the year 2000 he completed a Ph.D. thesis on the *Satipaṭṭhāna-sutta* at the University of Peradeniya (published by Windhorse in the UK). In the year 2007 he completed a habilitation research at the University of Marburg, in which he compared the *Majjhima-nikāya* discourses with their Chinese, Sanskrit, and Tibetan counterparts. At present, he is a member of the Center for Buddhist Studies, University of Hamburg, as a Privatdozent (the German equivalent to an associate professorship), and works at Dharma Drum Buddhist College, Taiwan, as a researcher. Besides his academic activities, he regularly teaches meditation in Sri Lanka.

Bhikkhu Bodhi

Bhikkhu Bodhi is an American Buddhist monk from New York City, born in 1944. He obtained a B.A. in philosophy from Brooklyn College (1966) and a Ph.D. in philosophy from Claremont Graduate University (1972). After completing his university studies he traveled to Sri Lanka, where he received novice ordination in 1972 and full ordination in 1973, both under the late Ven. Ananda Maitreya (1896–1998), the leading scholar-monk in Sri Lanka of recent times. From 1984 to 2002 he was the editor for the Buddhist Publication Society in Kandy, Sri Lanka, and lived for ten years with the elder German monk, Ven. Nyanaponika Thera (1901–94), at the Forest

Hermitage in Kandy. He returned to the U.S. in 2002. He currently resides at Chuang Yen Monastery in upstate New York and teaches there and at Bodhi Monastery in northwest New Jersey. Bodhi has many important publications to his credit, either as author, translator, or editor, including *A Comprehensive Manual of Abhidhamma* (1993), *The Middle Length Discourses of the Buddha* (Majjhima Nikāya, 1995), *The Connected Discourses of the Buddha* (Saṃyutta Nikāya, 2000), and *In the Buddha's Words* (2005). He is presently working on a complete translation of the Aṅguttara Nikāya, *The Incremental Discourses of the Buddha.*

Shayne Clarke

Shayne Clarke (Ph.D., UCLA) studied Buddhism and Asian languages in New Zealand, Japan, and the United States. He is currently an assistant professor at McMaster University, Canada. His research centers on Indian Buddhist monasticism, with particular reference to Buddhist monastic law codes (*vinaya*) preserved in Sanskrit, Tibetan, and Chinese. His recent publications include "The Case of the Nun Mettiyā Reexamined: On the Expulsion of a Pregnant *Bhikṣuṇī* in the *Vinaya* of the Mahāsāṅghikas and other Indian Buddhist Monastic Law Codes," *Indo-Iranian Journal* (2008); "Monks Who Have Sex: *Pārājika* Penance in Indian Buddhist Monasticisms," *Journal of Indian Philosophy* (2009); and "Locating Humour in Indian Buddhist Monastic Law Codes: A Comparative Approach," *Journal of Indian Philosophy* (2009).

Thubten Chodron

Thubten Chodron was ordained as a Buddhist nun in the Tibetan tradition in 1977 and received bhikṣuṇī ordination in Taiwan in 1986. She studied and practiced Tibetan Buddhism under the guidance of His Holiness the Dalai Lama, Tsenshap Serkong Rinpoche, Zopa Rinpoche, and other Tibetan masters for many years in India and Nepal. She was resident teacher at Amitabha Buddhist Centre in Singapore and at Dharma Friendship Foundation in Seattle and was co-organizer of "Life as a Western Buddhist Nun," an educational program in Bodhgaya in 1996. She is founder and abbess of Sravasti Abbey in Newport, Washington, one of the few Buddhist monasteries in the United States. Active in interfaith dialogue and prison work, she is also an author and teaches Buddhist philosophy, psychology, and meditation worldwide. Her books include *Open Heart, Clear Mind*; *Buddhism for Beginners*; *Working with Anger*; *Taming the Mind*; *Cultivating a Compassionate Heart*; and *How to Free Your Mind*. More information at www.thubtenchodron.org and www.sravastiabbey.org.

Lobsang Dechen

Lobsang Dechen is a Tibetan nun who was born in India in 1960 just after her parents escaped from Tibet due to the communist Chinese invasion there. She became a nun at the age of thirteen, while she was in school; because there was no education available within the one nunnery in the Dharamsala area at that time, she stayed in the Tibetan Children's Village, Upper Dharamsala, until class X, and then went to the Central School for Tibetans, Mussoorie, until class XII. She then attended St. Bede's College in Shimla and earned a B.A., followed by a B.Ed. she received at Chandigarh. With her teaching credentials, she returned to the Tibetan Children's Village school, Lower Dharamsala, where she taught English and geography from 1984 to 1991. In 1992, she left teaching to work full-time for the Tibetan Nuns Project in order to advance its efforts to make educational opportunities available for nuns throughout the Tibetan Buddhist tradition. While working for the Tibetan Nuns Project, of which she is a co-director, she was elected central executive member of the Tibetan Women's Association for three years.

Dhammananda (Professor Emeritus Dr. Chatsumarn Kabilsingh)

Chatsumarn Kabilsingh spent thirty years teaching at Thammasat University, Thailand. She was among 1,000 women who were nominated for the Nobel Prize in 2005; she was recognized as an Outstanding Buddhist Woman in 2004; and she was a member of the committee for the Niwano Peace Prize from 2002 to 2006. In 1987, she co-founded Sakyadhita: The International Association of Buddhist Women, and served as its president from 1991–2005. Since 1987, she has been the editor of *Yasodhara: Newsletter on International Buddhist Women's Activities*. In 2001 she received ordination in Sri Lanka and now is the abbess of Songdhammakalyani Monastery, the only monastery for bhikkhunīs in Thailand. Chatsumarn Kabilsingh is also the first Theravāda bhikkhunī in Thailand.

Damchö Diana Finnegan

Damchö Diana Finnegan (a.k.a. Ven. Lhundup Damchö) received her Ph.D. in the fall 2009 from the University of Wisconsin–Madison, on Buddhist narratives in Sanskrit and Tibetan. As a Fulbright scholar in India, her doctoral research focused on ethics and gender in the narratives of the Mūlasarvāstivāda Vinaya. Born in New York, she was ordained as a *śrāmaṇerikā* in 1999 and now lives in Dharmadattā Nuns' Community in northern India. Her next project is a book on the nuns' stories found in the Mūlasarvāstivāda Vinaya.

Janet Gyatso

Janet Gyatso, Hershey Professor of Buddhist Studies, Harvard University's Divinity School, has her B.A., M.A., and Ph.D. from the University of California at Berkeley. She is a specialist in Buddhist studies with concentration on Tibetan and South Asian religious culture. Her books include *Apparitions of the Self: The Secret Autobiographies of a Tibetan Visionary*; *In the Mirror of Memory: Reflections on Mindfulness and Remembrance in Indian and Tibetan Buddhism*; and *Women in Tibet*. She is currently completing a book on the intellectual history of traditional medicine in early modern Tibet. She has also been writing on conceptions of sex and gender in Buddhist monasticism and in Tibetan medicine. Previous topics have included visionary revelation in Buddhism; issues concerning lineage, memory, and authorship; philosophical questions on the status of experience; and autobiographical writing in Tibet. She was president of the International Association of Tibetan Studies from 2000–2006, and is currently co-chair of the Buddhism Section of the American Academy of Religion.

Tenzin Gyatso (His Holiness the Dalai Lama)

Tenzin Gyatso, the Fourteenth Dalai Lama of Tibet, was born in 1935 in northeastern Tibet and was recognized as the incarnation of his predecessor at age four. He was ordained as a monk and completed the traditional monastic scholarly curriculum as a young man before going into exile along with tens of thousands of his countrymen following the failed uprising against the Chinese occupation of his homeland in 1959. He is today renowned throughout the world for his efforts to bridge the divide between science and spirituality and to advance the causes of religious pluralism and nonviolence. He was awarded the Nobel Peace Prize in 1989 and the Congressional Gold Medal of Honor in 2007. He lives in Dharamsala, India.

Jens-Uwe Hartmann

Jens-Uwe Hartmann, born in 1953 in Munich, studied at the university of Munich in the fields of Indology, Indian art, Tibetology, sinology, and ethnology; he received his M.A. in 1977. From 1978–79 he worked for the Nepal-German Manuscript Preservation Project in Kathmandu; from 1981–95 he held various positions at the Academy of Sciences and the University of Göttingen. In 1984 he received his Dr. phil. at the University of Munich. In 1992 he held a habilitation at the University of Göttingen. From 1995–99 he served as Professor for Tibetology at the Humboldt State University in Berlin. Since 1999 he has been Professor of Indian and Iranian Studies at the University of Munich, and since 2001 he has been a member of the Bavarian Academy of Sciences.

Ute Hüsken

Ute Hüsken was trained in Indian and Tibetan studies in Göttingen, Germany. In her dissertation she analyzed the Vinaya for Theravāda Buddhist nuns. For her habilitation on prenatal life-cycle rituals in South India she went to Heidelberg University, where she also joined the Collaborative Research Centre "Ritual Dynamics," and started the project "Initiation, priestly ordination, temple festivals—ritual traditions in the south Indian temple city of Kancipuram." Since 2007 she has been a professor of Sanskrit at the University of Oslo in Norway.

David P. Jackson

Until March 2007, David Jackson was a professor of Tibetan in the Asien-Afrika-Institut of Hamburg University. He is now a curator with the Rubin Museum of Art, New York. He received his doctorate in 1985 from the University of Washington. His books include *A Saint in Seattle* (2003); *A History of Tibetan Painting: The Great Painters and Their Traditions* (1996); and *Enlightenment by a Single Means* (1994). His current research interests include the representation of religious lineages in Tibetan paintings and the life of the late Chopgyé Trichen Rinpoché (1919–2007).

Petra Kieffer-Pülz

Petra Kieffer-Pülz, Ph.D., is at present lecturer at Martin Luther University in Halle, Germany. Trained at the universities in Berlin, Basel, Bern, and Göttingen, she was research assistant at the Sanskrit-Wörterbuch der Turfan-Funde (Academy of Sciences in Göttingen) from 1984–96 and at the Martin Luther University in Halle from 2001–2007. She has published on the Buddhist traditions of India and Sri Lanka, especially on Buddhist law.

Gisela Krey

Gisela Krey worked as a high school teacher of classical languages and social sciences in Germany until 2000. Subsequently, she has been studying Sanskrit and Pāli literature. She began her studies at the Ruhr-University in Bochum. There she also gave instructions in Sanskrit at the Department of Religious Sciences. Currently she is continuing her studies at the Department of Indology at the Rheinische Friedrich-Wilhelm University in Bonn. Gisela Krey has published work in *Iudicium Verlag* and *Hsi Lai Journal of Humanistic Buddhism*.

Thea Mohr (editor)

Thea Mohr studied economics from 1974 to 1981 and was delegated to various Asian countries. From 1984 to 1988 she studied Indology, theology, and comparative religion at Frankfurt University. She completed her degree in Sanskrit studies at Lucknow University in India. From 1992–2001 she was author and director of numerous documentaries dealing with religious subjects, primarily Buddhism. Since 1994 she has been a lecturer for religious studies at Goethe University in Frankfurt. Her Ph.D. (2000) is a survey of Sakyadhita's international conferences.

Jan-Ulrich Sobisch

Jan-Ulrich Sobisch has studied Tibetology, Indology, and philosophy at Hamburg University, where he received a Dr. phil. in 1999. In the following years he worked at Hamburg, Munich, and finally Copenhagen University, where he has been associate professor for Tibetan studies since 2006. He has researched and published on Tibetan theories of harmonizing prātimokṣa, bodhisattva, and mantra vows (*sdom pa gsum*), documents of transmission (*gsan yig*), Tibetan manuscripts, and the literature on Hevajra and the Path with Its Fruit (*lam 'bras*) teaching. He presently works on Tibetan indigenous tantric theories and the reception of Indian Buddhism in Tibet between the eleventh and thirteenth centuries.

Bhikkhu Sujato

Bhikkhu Sujato is an Australian monk who received full ordination in Thailand in 1994. He trained and practiced in the Thai forest tradition and spent three years with Ajahn Brahm in Bodhinyana, Perth. He is the abbot of Santi Forest Monastery near Sydney, which supports the fourfold assembly of bhikkhus, bhikkhunīs, laywomen, and laymen. In October 2009 he took part in the first bhikkhunī ordination in the forest tradition. Sujato is the author of a number of books, including *A History of Mindfulness*, *Sects & Sectarianism*, and *Bhikkhuni Vinaya Studies*. These and other writings can be accessed through santipada.org.

Karma Lekshe Tsomo

Karma Lekshe Tsomo is an associate professor in the Department of Theology and Religious Studies at the University of San Diego, where she teaches Buddhism, world religions, and comparative religious ethics. She studied Buddhism in Dharamsala, India, for fifteen years and received a doctorate in philosophy from the University of Hawaii, with research on death and identity in China and Tibet. She was president of Sakyadhita until 2009 and director of Jamyang Foundation, an initiative to provide educational opportunities for women in developing countries. Her research interests include death and dying, Buddhism and bioethics, Buddhist feminist ethics, peace studies, and Western adaptations of Buddhism. Her publications include *Sisters in Solitude: Two Traditions of Buddhist Monastic Ethics for Women*; *Buddhist Women and Social Justice*; *Innovative Buddhist Women: Swimming Against the Stream*; and *Into the Jaws of Yama, Lord of Death: Buddhism, Bioethics, and Death*.

Jampa Tsedroen (editor)

Bhikṣuṇī Jampa Tsedroen (Carola Roloff), born in 1959, is a teacher of Buddhist philosophy at Tibetisches Zentrum in Hamburg and a lecturer and research fellow at Hamburg University, specializing in nuns' ordination and women in Buddhism. She became a novice nun in 1981 and obtained full ordination in Taiwan in 1985. She studied Tibetan Buddhist theory and practice as well as Vinaya with the late Geshe Thubten Ngawang (1932–2003) from 1981 to 1996, and then classical Indology and Tibetology at the University of Hamburg, where she received her M.A. in 2003 and her Ph.D. in 2009. In January 2010 she began a three-year research project at the University of Hamburg (DFG project) on the ordination of nuns in the Tibetan Buddhist canon and its presentation in the Tibetan commentaries. For more information, visit www.jampatsedroen.de.

Tashi Tsering

Ācārya Geshe Tashi Tsering was born in Tibet and took the *upāsaka* vow from the great mystic Phashok Lama in 1943; in 1947, he joined the village's monastery and began his education. In 1956, he was transferred to Ganden Monastery and there pursued further studies in logic and other Buddhist philosophical studies. In 1958, he received *śrāmaṇera* ordination from His Eminence Ling Rinpoche. In exile he stayed in a monastery in Dalhaousie and pursued traditional monastic studies. In 1968 he received *bhikṣu* ordination from His Holiness the Fourteenth Dalai Lama. In 1969 he completed ācārya graduation. In the year 1987, he received the *geshé* degree from Ganden Monastery. The Department of Religion and Culture of the Tibetan government in exile entrusted him to do a study on "Comparative Analysis of Theravāda and Mūlasarvāstivāda Vinaya Traditions." Though still pursuing the research today, he has been able to produce four theses related to the issue of the bhikṣuṇī lineage and its ordination in the Tibetan language, all of which were published in 2000 by the Department of Religion and Culture.

About Wisdom Publications

WISDOM PUBLICATIONS is dedicated to making available authentic Buddhist works for the benefit of all. We publish translations of the sutras and tantras, commentaries and teachings of past and contemporary Buddhist masters, and original works by the world's leading Buddhist scholars. We publish our titles with the appreciation of Buddhism as a living philosophy and with the special commitment to preserve and transmit important works from all the major Buddhist traditions.

Wisdom Publications
199 Elm Street
Somerville, Massachusetts 02144 USA
Telephone: 617-776-7416
Fax: 617-776-7841
Email: info@wisdompubs.org
www.wisdompubs.org

THE WISDOM TRUST

As a nonprofit publisher, Wisdom is dedicated to the publication of Dharma books for the benefit of all sentient beings and dependent upon the kindness and generosity of sponsors in order to do so. If you would like to make a donation to Wisdom, you may do so through our website or our Somerville office. If you would like to help sponsor the publication of a book, please write or email us at the address above.

Thank you.

Wisdom is a nonprofit, charitable 501(c)(3) organization affiliated with the Foundation for the Preservation of the Mahayana Tradition (FPMT).